Civil War Canon

CIVIL WAR AMERICA

*Peter S. Carmichael, Caroline E. Janney, and
Aaron Sheehan-Dean, editors*

THIS LANDMARK SERIES interprets broadly
the history and culture of the Civil War era
through the long nineteenth century and
beyond. Drawing on diverse approaches and
methods, the series publishes historical works
that explore all aspects of the war, biographies
of leading commanders, and tactical and
campaign studies, along with select editions
of primary sources. Together, these books shed
new light on an era that remains central to our
understanding of American and world history.

Civil War Canon

SITES OF CONFEDERATE MEMORY
IN SOUTH CAROLINA

Thomas J. Brown

THE UNIVERSITY OF NORTH CAROLINA PRESS
Chapel Hill

Designed and composed by Tseng Information Systems, Inc.
Set in Miller and Clarendon Bold types.
Manufactured in the United States of America

The paper in this book meets the guidelines for permanence and durability
of the Committee on Production Guidelines for Book Longevity of the
Council on Library Resources.

The University of North Carolina Press has been a member of the
Green Press Initiative since 2003.

Jacket illustrations: Front: vintage postcards showing Fort Sumter (top), the
Confederate Monument in Magnolia Cemetery (bottom left), and ruins at Millwood
(bottom right). Back: the Calhoun Monument in Marion Square. Author's collection.

Complete cataloging information for this title is available from the Library of Congress.
ISBN 978-1-4696-2095-4 (cloth: alk. paper)
ISBN 978-1-4696-2096-1 (ebook)

A previous version of chapter 2 was published as "The Monumental Legacy of Calhoun,"
in *The Memory of the Civil War in American Culture*, ed. Alice Fahs and Joan Waugh
(Chapel Hill: University of North Carolina Press, 2004), 130–56; a previous version
of chapter 3 was published as "The Confederate Retreat to Mars and Venus," in *Battle
Scars: Gender and Sexuality in the American Civil War*, ed. Catherine Clinton and Nina
Silber (New York: Oxford University Press, 2006), 189–213, © 2006 Oxford University
Press, reprinted by permission of Oxford University Press, USA; and a previous version
of chapter 6 was published as "The Confederate Battle Flag and the Desertion of the
Lost Cause Tradition," in *Remixing the Civil War: Meditations on the Sesquicentennial*,
ed. Thomas J. Brown (Baltimore: Johns Hopkins University Press, 2011), 37–72,
reprinted by permission of Johns Hopkins University Press.

For Carol,
who showed me the direction home

Contents

Illustrations

Civil War Canon

Map

JASPER JOHNS DESCRIBED his *Map* series of the early
1960s as the reconstruction of an everyday form "seen
and not looked at, not examined." This book revisits
a set of public monuments, historic buildings, and
other memorials that attract little scrutiny for some
of the same reasons as the map of the United States.
These familiar places define the didactic landscape of
a would-be nation, the Confederate States of America.[1]
As Johns's collage-paintings exposed the arbitrariness
and contingency of the map that his home state of
South Carolina had led the effort to alter one hundred
years earlier, *Civil War Canon* excavates the foundations of Confederate landmarks to reveal a shifting,
contested collective memory. Beneath a continuity in
racial politics, white southerners negotiated disruptive
modernity by revising presentations of the past. My
topography draws on Johns's view of the relationship
between a study and its topic. His *Map* paintings are
maps. This book charts a commemorative genealogy
and also extends that lineage of local reflection.

The book focuses on South Carolina for three sets of
reasons grounded in political, social, and intellectual
history. First, the state was the core of the Confederacy.

The movement for a separate proslavery republic thrived there for a generation before achieving traction elsewhere. Commemoration was an important feature of this radical culture, which opens comparisons between secessionist memory and the postwar formation known as the Lost Cause. Wartime devotion to the Confederacy was unsurpassed. State enlistments in the southern army were approximately equal to the entire white male population of military age in 1860; one-third of those men died in gray. The local theater of the war produced dramatic encounters from the bombardment of Fort Sumter through Sherman's March. The state was also a vital center of Reconstruction and "redemption" from the fall of Port Royal in 1861 through the disputed elections of 1876. Remembrance of the sectional conflict understandably came to occupy an especially prominent position in attempts to define a collective South Carolina identity. The wider significance of that effort is not necessarily measured by the extent to which remembrance in the state resembled patterns found elsewhere. White southern memory encompassed many local variations, and South Carolina was peculiar in some ways and less peculiar in others. A central aspect of its exceptionalism was that the state looked back on a singularly long and intense engagement with southern nationalism. In that sense, the Civil War canon of South Carolina is uniquely typical of Confederate memory.[2]

Collective memory does not originate directly in experience, even for an experience as profound as the Civil War. The first four chapters of this book emphasize that Confederate commemoration began with antebellum models such as the rural cemetery, the nationalist hero, the gender ideology of evangelical domesticity, and the historical romance. White southerners struggled over the implementation of those frameworks and the development of replacements. The resulting commemorative structures linked the legacy of the Civil War to wide-ranging social and economic transformations of the region and the country. The final four chapters focus on Confederate memory since the 1920s, when the scarcity of surviving Civil War veterans symbolized the end of a living memory. These chapters take up commemoration in mid-twentieth-century mass culture and the subsequent fragmentation of that market.

The construction of modernity across South Carolina history consequently provides a second reason to focus on the state. My analytic narrative begins chronologically in the second chapter with Charleston secessionists' campaign to honor John C. Calhoun in one of the liveliest cities of the slaveholding South. The next two chapters highlight the growth of industrial manufacturing and collapse of plantation agriculture as context

MAP 3

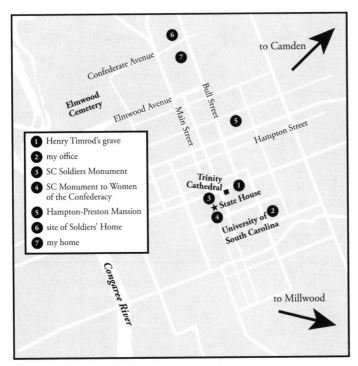

Map of Columbia, South Carolina

for monuments to the Confederacy and novels about Reconstruction as a crisis in "home rule." The fifth chapter describes the renovation of Fort Sumter within the recentering of the Charleston economy on tourism. The market in leisure and recreation is also the setting for the chapter on controversies over state display of the Confederate battle flag. The chapter on the *Hunley* submarine revolves around technological change, including the prominence of nuclear weapons facilities in South Carolina. The state canon of Civil War memory illuminates encounters with urban life, factory labor, rural stagnation, consumer society, and the military-industrial technological complex that are fundamental to the history of modernity in America.

This organization of the book underscores my effort to tell highly localized stories of national importance. The canonical commemorations are sometimes inseparable from other South Carolina places of Confederate remembrance. The founding of the Confederate Home in Charleston was pivotal in the saga of the Calhoun Monument. The Soldiers' Home in Columbia provided an outlet for ambivalence toward the state monument to Confederate women. I carefully trace such ties, and I also examine con-

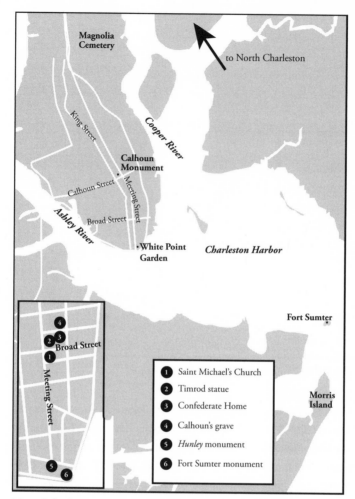

Map of Charleston, South Carolina

nections within my chosen set of sites. But the book does not pretend to
encompass every instance of Confederate remembrance in South Carolina.
The scene moves beyond Charleston and Columbia only for parts of one
chapter. I do not mention the annual Confederate memorial services at
Rivers Bridge, a statewide political forum for more than a century. I sketch
but cannot treat fully such supralocal topics as the development of the generic soldier monument and the rise and fall of the United Daughters of the
Confederacy. Instead, I investigate an ensemble of specific places.

People gave shape to those places, and the density of the state intellectual tradition is a third reason to focus on South Carolina. The book's first
and last chapters frame the overarching narrative around two South Caro-

MAP   5

linians imaginatively interested in Confederate graves at Charleston's Magnolia Cemetery. Poet Henry Timrod is one of several standard fixtures of southern intellectual history to play a prominent role in the book. Others include William Gilmore Simms, Louisa McCord, William Henry Trescot, Mary Boykin Chesnut, and DuBose Heyward. In reexamining this tradition, I have tried to help repopulate the cultural community from which the famous names emerged.[3] The chapter on home as a site of remembrance, for example, situates Chesnut alongside a dozen little-known South Carolina authors whose novels paralleled her Civil War chronicle. I devote particular attention to leaders of commemorative institutions and to antiquarians like Yates Snowden, known at the University of South Carolina in the early twentieth century as the "professor of Confederocracy."[4] At the beginning and end of this procession, joining Timrod in the first and last chapters, is Ted Phillips. The most knowledgeable and entertaining guide to Magnolia Cemetery around the turn of the millennium, he structures my book-length probe into history and memory both because he aspired to criticize as well as celebrate the local past and because my assessment of his significance merges scholarship and autobiography. The publication of his *City of the Silent: The Charlestonians of Magnolia Cemetery* in 2010 marks the resolution of an arc opened by the death of Calhoun and dedication of Magnolia in 1850.

The chronologically overlapping segments of the book tell a unified story even though the particular terms of commemorative contestation shifted as successive generations of South Carolinians negotiated different forms of modernity. The Calhoun Monument contributed to the triumph of secession but proved to be a false start for elaboration of the Lost Cause epitomized by Memorial Day. The statehouse monuments to Confederate soldiers and Confederate women better expressed the dynamic dialectic of the Lost Cause in the late nineteenth and early twentieth centuries. That synthesis of public memory and private life was not unlimited, and novelists exhausted their interest in fictions of redemption long before politicians did. But recast as a narrative of preservation rather than resurgence, the Lost Cause remained a powerful social myth until the civil rights movement toppled its candid white supremacism. Confederate commemoration then shifted to an antitraditionalist enterprise expressed almost exclusively by the battle flag until conservation of the *Hunley* elaborated postmodern Confederate memory. *City of the Silent* renewed the legacy of contestation by offering an ideologically alternative tribute to the Confederate dead.

My local focus reenvisions the commemorative landscape charted by many recent historians. This survey both draws on and departs from the depiction of Civil War memory as a struggle to realize the full emancipatory potential in the American epic of slavery and abolition.[5] Although the well-studied politics of white supremacism have inflected all phases of Confederate memory, the continuities mask important variations. White South Carolinians often disagreed strenuously about how to remember the Civil War. Racial politics are a necessary but not a sufficient explanation for the changing contours of Confederate commemoration.

This study complicates the familiar narrative of white oppression and black resistance by foregrounding the instability of remembered racial identity. Steadfast loyalty to the slaveholders' republic often tracked an uneasy awareness that the color line was permeable. In the early postemancipation period, commemorative activists repeatedly expressed anxiety about the blackening of white southerners. As the Lost Cause consolidated, its upper-class champions began to question the racial integrity of white industrial laborers and later to celebrate their own Confederate lineage through solemn mimicry of black culture. After the civil rights movement jarred public racial arrogance, the campaign for state display of the battle flag claimed kinship with African Americans as a minority heritage group. This understanding of Confederate sites of memory as intersections between the fluidity of race and the fixity of place leads *Civil War Canon* to a concluding reconsideration of the blackface Confederate anthem that gave the South its nickname, "Dixie."

South Carolina is similarly a fertile field for revisiting the popular discourse of sectional reunion, best analyzed so far in scholarship on northern memory of the Civil War. For the most part, I consider it fruitless to speculate about exactly how much former Confederates and their descendants inwardly felt reconciled with the United States after Appomattox. Sometimes sponsors of Confederate commemoration embraced the motif of sectional reconciliation in making a bid for local and national leadership; sometimes they adopted more belligerent postures. My emphasis is on a shift within reconciliationist strategies. During the late nineteenth century, reconciliationist initiatives in Charleston were largely oblivious to the professional, educational, and other institutional networks that increasingly unified the United States. This shortsightedness helped to prevent the promoters of the Calhoun Monument from achieving their larger objectives. Between the two world wars, local reconciliationist initiatives shrewdly exploited national networks, winning status and material benefits but also connecting Charleston commemorative institutions like Fort

MAP   7

Sumter to unforeseen changes in American memory of the Civil War. In neither case, however, did the logic of sectional reunion rely heavily on an argument that Confederate and Union soldiers had both fought valiantly in a war that required no ideological explanation. As David Blight has noted, "Many Lost Cause writers and activists during the reconciliationist era were not at all shy of arguing about the *causes* of the war." Whatever the trajectory of northern discourse, the decisive turn of South Carolina commemoration toward a sectionally neutral "valorization of the veteran" took place after the civil rights movement and the Vietnam War.[6]

My approach also parallels and challenges outstanding scholarship that has described the Lost Cause as a transitional phase in which white southerners rejected early postwar intransigence and developed commemorative institutions that softened the psychological shocks and obscured the power relations involved in adjustments to industrialization and urbanization during the late nineteenth and early twentieth centuries.[7] Although I find much to admire in that interpretation, I treat Confederate memory not as a single burst of regional creativity but as a variety of initiatives, some of which exercised strong appeal before or after the peak of industrialization and some of which suffered setbacks in the midst of that period. I explore the relationship of Confederate memory to modernity in settings that range from the cityscape of the antebellum era to the virtual reality of the digital age. I show how commemoration repeatedly facilitated white southerners' embrace of new ideas as well as new social structures. Although I agree that an appeal to white solidarity was central to the Lost Cause, I give more attention to the ways it justified class stratification than the ways it mitigated hierarchy.

My study particularly highlights the redefinition of gender norms as the sign of each new social order. That emphasis contrasts with research that has sought primarily to document women's participation in commemoration.[8] I carry forward scholarship that has seen a shifting balance between patriarchal and feminist strands of the Lost Cause, though I stress the long-term productive tensions within that rivalry rather than isolating temporary episodes of division. Gender was one of the principal domains in which Confederate commemoration served as a venue for contestation and negotiation within white southern culture from the antebellum period to the Civil War centennial. The chapters that focus on the half century since the 1960s provide the first account of the collapse of this gender dynamic. Women's abandonment of Confederate remembrance has been crucial in the shift of an organic social myth to the realm of fantasy.

This book shares some interpretive coordinates with recent writing about Civil War attitudes toward death. That literature explores challenges to religion from the rising prestige of the nation-state and science, as illustrated by the founding of military cemeteries and the expansion of human dissection. Although my analysis draws on the metaphorical and institutional imbrication of the Lost Cause in church life, I recognize that secularization has been an aspect of modernity and examine Confederate memory as a medium for addressing the threat that Darwinism posed to Christianity. The disruption of chronological order in the placement of the first chapter, which establishes the Confederate grave as the intellectual and emotional point of entry into the book, also follows the scholarship on death in treating mortality as the foundational problem of social remembrance.[9] Subsequent chapters analyze markings of death from the legendary Calhoun funeral through the spectacular final *Hunley* burial and the posthumous publication of *City of the Silent*. South Carolina is rich in Confederate obsequies.

South Carolina is also where I have lived and taught Civil War history since 1996, which is the most important reason that this book focuses on the state. *Civil War Canon* is a record of my effort to make a home here. The places of memory examined in the following chapters are landmarks of my everyday environment. My wife and I live one block from the former site of the Soldiers' Home on Confederate Avenue in Columbia; our favorite neighborhood walk brings us to a derelict cemetery with a brick enclosure for the humble headstones of veterans, widows, daughters, and nieces who ended their old age at the home. My children graduated from a high school located on land that was once part of the Hampton family's Millwood plantation. The school seal features the bereft columns that testify to the burning of the mansion by Sherman's army. My route to work takes me past a cottage in which Mary Boykin Chesnut lived during the war. My office is six blocks from Henry Timrod's grave, where this book properly begins.

1

At Timrod's Grave

WE WERE NOT TOO intoxicated to clamber over the
waist-high iron fence and invade the darkened churchyard. I was in Columbia because I worked for a federal judge who had come to the city for a week to hear
cases. My former college roommate Ted Phillips was
finishing law school at the University of South Carolina. I had visited his home state four years earlier,
when we both should have been college seniors. Then
he had introduced me to his beloved Charleston. Now
he was eager to expand my sense of local orientation.

The trip to Charleston took place a few months
into Ted's rustication, the consequence of his overzeal-
ousness in the ritual feud between the campus newspaper and the humor magazine. As he packed his be-
longings, he presented me with his fine copy of David
Donald's *Charles Sumner and the Coming of the Civil
War* (1960). My mentor's masterpiece, the brilliant but
problematic book was the stuff of which academic ambition is made. The gift also served as an inside joke.
During our first year of college, Ted and I had shared
with two other roommates the suite in which Sumner
had lived during his senior year at Harvard. Ted was
from South Carolina and I was from Massachusetts,

but he had never beaten me over the head with a cane. Perhaps the Civil War was finally over.

Shortly after the Charleston visit I gave Ted a copy of C. Vann Woodward's new *Mary Chesnut's Civil War* (1981). We had loved reading an earlier edition of the text in our undergraduate course on the Civil War and Reconstruction. Woodward's vastly expanded, superbly annotated version was an epic feast for someone with Ted's appetite for anecdotes. While living in Columbia during law school, he immersed himself in the setting for much of the chronicle. Chesnut fled the city only days before one-third of its buildings burned in February 1865 as General William T. Sherman took control of the state capital. The family mansion of Chesnut's symbolic young southern belle, Sally Buchanan "Buck" Preston, had survived to become a house museum that Ted and I toured during my visit to Columbia. We speculated on exactly what Napoleon III might have had in mind when he chose to present Buck with the gift of a riding crop while the Prestons lived in Europe during the late 1850s.

Our errand in the cemetery of Trinity Episcopal Cathedral at this late point in the night was to visit sites associated with Chesnut's book. Buck Preston was now in Magnolia Cemetery in Charleston with her husband, but most of her family was at Trinity. Chesnut had attended many funerals here during the war. After one of those occasions, she sat with a friend on the front steps of the South Carolina statehouse, across the street from the church, and mourned "our world, the only world we cared for, literally kicked to pieces." Ted and I began at the monument to Buck's cousin Preston Hampton, a Confederate cavalry officer killed on the front lines before the eyes of his father and commanding general, Wade Hampton III. Trinity warden and state military surgeon general Robert W. Gibbes decreed that space considerations would not permit fulfillment of the father's wish to bury his son alongside the boy's mother. Gibbes ordered another grave dug nearby, only to be overruled after the work was completed. During the funeral, the unused grave yawned in anticipation of the next Confederate casualty. Chesnut sighed that the "evil augury" compounded the gloom of the occasion. Her young friend Isabella Martin fumed that the pit should be used to bury alive the socially ambitious Gibbes, who "would be so proud to be in the Hampton graveyard." Ted observed with glee that the Gibbes family plot was fifteen paces further toward the back of the cemetery than the prime corner location occupied by the Hamptons and Prestons.[1]

We drifted among the headstones, matching the monuments to other poignant stories from Chesnut's saga. A melodramatic broken column, decorated at the top by a stone garland and at the bottom by a relief of a palmetto tree, marked the grave of States Rights Gist. Chesnut had felt obliged to clarify that Gist was "a real person—and not an odd name merely." Destined from his christening to become a Confederate general, he was killed leading a charge at the Battle of Franklin. An imposing obelisk projected from the lot of Daniel Heyward Trezevant, the Chesnuts' local doctor. Louisa McCord, who organized a Confederate hospital on the college grounds across the street from her Columbia house, told Chesnut that Trezevant believed wholeheartedly in spirit rappings even before the physician unexpectedly found his son's name on a bulletin-board list of Columbia soldiers killed in the Seven Days Battles. A relief of an urn and a weeping willow marked the final resting place of Robert Woodward Barnwell's family. The chaplain and history professor at South Carolina College had volunteered to work in Confederate hospitals in Virginia, where he contracted typhoid fever and lost his mind. Within twenty-four hours of his death in a Staunton mental hospital, his wife and baby died in childbirth in Columbia. All three were buried together in a single funeral, leaving behind three orphans.[2]

Near the high brick wall at the rear of the churchyard, we came to an iron fence surrounding the small family lot of Henry Timrod, known since the war as the poet laureate of the Confederacy. These rough-hewn headstones were the most rustic monuments in the cemetery. A three-foot-tall piece of granite marked the grave of Timrod and his infant son. Two smaller stones remembered the poet's mother and sister. Ted loved contemporary poetry more than anyone else I knew. His grief at the sudden death of Robert Lowell had startled me during our festive freshman week of college. His proudest achievement at the University of South Carolina was to have staked out a position on the periphery of the circle that surrounded writer-in-residence James Dickey. One member of this group regularly brought poets visiting Columbia to see Timrod's grave, located only a few blocks from the campus. Years ago, Lowell had theatrically fallen to his knees before the landmark. Warming up with the established tour script, Ted explained to me that the 1829 birthdate inscribed on the stone was wrong. The poet had at some point shaved a year from his age because he was disappointed that he had not accomplished more.[3] The glimpse of Timrod's ambition and frustration was typical of cemeteries, Ted continued. He firmly believed that a visit to a grave provided indispensable insights into history. This monument was particularly revealing.

Henry Timrod's grave. Photograph by Carol E. Harrison.

Long unmarked but never neglected, Timrod's grave was an important symbolic site in the struggle over the postwar direction of the white South. The initial lack of monumentation testified to Timrod's poverty at his death in October 1867. Before the war, he had supported himself as a rural school-teacher and a private tutor on South Carolina plantations. Disqualified by tuberculosis from wartime military service, he became a journalist in his hometown of Charleston. An opportunity to work as editor of the *Daily South Carolinian* brought him to Columbia and provided him the where-withal to marry. The newspaper office burned during Sherman's invasion; one of the poet's admirers would later claim that it "had the honor of being the first building to be destroyed by the Northern troops."[4] Timrod never regained his footing. Newspaper work failed. He tried without success to open a school in a competitive market. Two of his three sisters died in October 1865, followed within days by his infant son. He briefly held a political appointment as a temporary clerk for Governor James L. Orr but lost an election for a full-time position as messenger of the state House of Representatives. The sale of furniture and silver became the main support of a household that also included Timrod's wife, his mother, his widowed sister, and her four children. His precarious health collapsed in September 1867, when he suffered a hemorrhage that spattered blood on the proof sheets for a collection of Timrod's poetry prepared for publication during the Civil War but not issued. Three weeks later, he was dead. Wade Hampton headed the pallbearers at the Trinity funeral, a tribute to Timrod's stature as a Confederate casualty.

Timrod's literary friends eulogized him in different ways. William Gilmore Simms, whose warm generosity had not prevented him from privately attributing his friend's tribulations to laziness and intemperance, published a strident, frustrated appreciation. Offering a humoral postmortem that surviving relatives of the consumptive deemed insensitive, Simms sighed that the pessimistic Timrod "had none of the sanguine in his system. His blood worked languidly and gave no proper support, stimulus, or succour to his brain." Nevertheless, he had produced "verse far superior to anything that could or can be done in Boston, by any or all of the sweet-singing swans of that American Olympus." Simms's anthology *War Poetry of the South* (1867) had recently presented his younger colleague to the restored Union as the star of a Confederate literature "essentially as much the property of the whole as the captured cannon" of the war. He now urged fellow southerners "to see that a graceful tablet shall indicate to posterity the sleeping place of the bard." William J. Rivers, one of Timrod's schoolteachers in Charleston before taking the faculty position in classics at South Carolina College coveted by his former student, delivered a tribute before a "crowded and select audience" at the college chapel. Physician and litterateur J. Dickson Bruns, a friend of Timrod's since childhood, presented an elaborate lecture in his new home city of New Orleans that he later reprised on a visit back to Charleston.[5]

Paul Hamilton Hayne, Timrod's closest friend since the two young men shared a desk at Christopher Cotes's school in Charleston, took charge of preparing a verse collection for posthumous publication. Like Simms, he understood his editorial project to be in part a literary phase of Reconstruction politics. Hayne, however, cast himself as a sectional diplomat rather than a defiant champion of Confederate achievement. Building on friendships formed on a trip to Boston during the 1850s, he saw that his role as Timrod's representative provided an opportunity to cultivate the goodwill of the New England literati, not least because his late friend was a better poet than he was. Hayne focused his efforts on the politically conservative Oliver Wendell Holmes Sr., to whom he sent his threnody, "Under the Pines," for publication in Boston, along with a letter describing the sad fate of Timrod and the continued destitution of the white South. His preface to the collection published in 1873 lamented that Timrod had not managed to travel after the war to the North, where "such high-hearted men as Bryant, Whipple, Holmes, and Whittier, would have recognized the genius of the man" and helped him survive. But if the foster son of Robert Hayne proposed to unite in a postwar republic of letters with the intellectual heirs of Daniel Webster, he expected sympathy in exchange for his loyalty. The unmarked grave in the Trinity churchyard was a silent reproach, he declared, "in the ruined capital of his native State, whence scholarship, culture, and social purity have been banished to give place to the orgies of semi-barbarians and the political trickery of adventurers and traitors." That outburst served as a prelude to Hayne's "South Carolina to the States of the North" (1876), a plea for acquiescence in the violent overthrow of Republican government in the state that he dedicated to "redeemer" gubernatorial candidate Wade Hampton. Holmes told Hayne that the poem filled him with "a thrill of sympathy and an aching of regret that my fellow countrymen of your proud record and sensitive race should be doomed to such suffering."[6]

Vitriolic as its depiction of Reconstruction was, Hayne's view from Timrod's grave touched off a conservative protest in Columbia. Northern newspapers noted Hayne's emphasis on Timrod's "grim encounters with starvation" and suggested that the poet's death reflected an inadequate southern appreciation for art. The *Boston Globe* observed that "in Massachusetts we contrive to honor equally such a citizen as Charles Sumner and such a citizen as Henry W. Longfellow" and speculated that "had [Timrod] lived in the North he would have been valued, respected and read, as Whittier is valued, respected and read." South Carolina newspapers retorted that "if the Boston critics could have looked upon the destitution and desolation then prevailing in Columbia, they could better understand how he parted with his silver plate to procure the means of living. He was more fortunate than many others, in having saved the plate, to be thus used, from Sherman's bummers." Young schoolteacher Isabella Martin reported that Wade Hampton had asked her father, a Methodist minister, to attend to Timrod as a special case for alms in December 1866. Though the poet had initially refused to accept the charity, Martin alleged, he had eventually recognized the necessity and remained under the protection of the community leadership until disease killed him. Hayne rose to defend the accuracy of his account and its implications. Although complimentary to "the General's cordial and sympathetic spirit" and disavowing any blame of "individuals or communities," he insisted on the economic as well as medical harshness of Timrod's fate. Hayne was an unimpeachable patrician, but he strongly believed that his region undervalued the arts. As editor of *Russell's Magazine* in the late 1850s, he had published one of the most forceful statements of that position, Timrod's essay on "Literature in the South."[7]

Hayne composed another religious meditation in 1874, "By the Grave of Henry Timrod," but Carlyle McKinley's "At Timrod's Grave" (1877) became a classic in the political verse of redemption. A cheerleader for the Red Shirt campaign as Columbia correspondent for the *Charleston News and Courier*, McKinley looked back across Reconstruction from Timrod's "last sad home / Of all memorial bare / Save for a little heap of leaves / The winds have gathered there!" He argued that South Carolina had shown its resistance to postwar restructuring by declining to produce a successor to the poet laureate of the Confederacy: "Our one sweet singer breaks no more / The silence sad and long / The land is hushed from shore to shore, / It brooks no feebler song!" With the restoration of Democratic control in sight, even Timrod's grave joined in a hopeful regeneration as "one tender, tearful bloom / Wins upward through the grass, / As some sweet thought he left unsung / Were blossoming at last!" McKinley's closing exhortation applied equally to the fallen soldiers of the Confederacy and their bard: "'Hold up the glories of thy dead!'/ To thine own self be true, / Land that he loved! / Come, honor now / This grave that honors you!"[8]

The first monument for Timrod followed a few years later. His friend Hugh S. Thompson, state superintendent of education since the Democratic victory of 1876, coordinated the project. Donors received a printed copy of William J. Rivers's lecture on his former student, to which Rivers appended his 1870 poem "Eldred," about a former Confederate soldier vowing to remain at home and "help foul wrong descend into her pit" rather than emigrate from occupied South Carolina to seek fortune and freedom. The gravestone was a six-foot-high marble obelisk inscribed with quotations from Timrod's "Vision of Poesy." A newspaper commentary described the belated shaft as indicative of the post-Reconstruction "change from barbarism to civilization."[9]

The memorial boulder now in the Trinity churchyard resulted from a separate initiative. Felix G. de Fontaine, chief editor of the *Daily South Carolinian* during Timrod's tenure on the staff, helped to plan the undertaking shortly before his death in 1896, but the dominant force was William Ashmead Courtenay. Mayor of Charleston during the 1880s, Courtenay was a leading figure in many South Carolina historical enterprises. He had begun his career as a bookstore owner in the 1850s and worked briefly for the *Charleston Mercury* before enlisting in the Confederate army. Through these literary experiences he came to know Hayne, who despised him. Evidently the antipathy was mutual, and Courtenay did not hesitate to circulate the report that Hayne, who died in 1886, had failed to turn over to Timrod's widow the profits from the 1873 collection. Courtenay had told

Timrod in January 1865 that he would gladly seek to arrange publication of the volume set in proof sheets during the war. He tried to broker such a deal after Timrod's death and was miffed when the poet's sister turned the project over to Hayne. Apart from these animosities, Courtenay personified the so-called New South of Henry Grady, which Hayne regarded with deep skepticism. President of the Charleston Chamber of Commerce before his election as mayor, Courtenay had later opened a cotton-textile mill. He brought a self-consciously modern commercial orientation and middle-class constituency into the turn-of-the-century cultural campaign that he branded the Timrod Revival.[10]

In contrast to Hayne's literary diplomacy, the Timrod Revival was a mass-marketing operation. Courtenay's initial plan was to arrange for publication of a new edition of Timrod's poetry and use the profits to "provide a handsome tomb at his grave." By the time South Carolina chartered the Timrod Memorial Association in November 1898, with Courtenay as president, its mandate was instead to use the book proceeds for an artistic memorial to Timrod in Charleston. The volume released in the spring of 1899 added a few minor poems to the out-of-print 1873 collection, re-arranged the entire set, and replaced Hayne's memoir with a new introduction. Responsible for the financial risk of the venture, the association ordered a substantial run of four thousand copies, which Courtenay and his collaborators worked feverishly to sell. Courtenay later recorded that he had sent twenty-five hundred letters around the country in connection with the campaign, "not counting thousands of various issues of printed matter." The print run sold out by October 1901, when Courtenay dissolved the corporation. Five months earlier, the association had dedicated the Timrod Memorial in Washington Square, a park that was one of the prominent civic improvement projects of Courtenay's mayoral administration. The new work of public art featured a bronze portrait bust by Edward Valentine atop a ten-foot-high granite pedestal decorated with large bronze panels. The key inscription declared that "this memorial has been erected with the proceeds of the recent sale of very large editions of the author's poems by the Timrod Memorial Association." Timrod was not merely distinguished; he was also marketable. Even after paying for the Charleston monument, the association was able to undertake an upgrade to Timrod's grave at Trinity Church.[11]

The Timrod Revival took place after southern tentativeness had faded from sectional cultural politics. Northern interest in the writings of Mark Twain, Thomas Nelson Page, Joel Chandler Harris, George Washington

Cable, and other southern authors had established the region as an important source of American literature. Confederate veterans took less interest in blue-gray reunions than during the previous decade and insisted more stridently on northern appreciation for southern valor as the celebration of sectional reconciliation intensified during the Spanish-American War. Courtenay launched the Timrod Revival by planting an illustrated article in the flagship journal for regional literature and postwar reconciliation, *Century* magazine, and he gladly recounted the northern encomiums. But the Timrod Revival maintained not only that the Old South had produced a fine poet but that the New South appreciated him. The region had caught up to the North and was a distinctive contributor to a common national literature. In one turn-of-the-century South Carolina novel that echoed many academic essays, the Charlestonian heroine teased her Bostonian suitor for failing to know the work of Timrod as well as that of Lowell, Longfellow, and Holmes. Presented by Timrod's widow with the manuscript for an unpublished wartime lecture on "A Theory of Poetry," Courtenay arranged for the essay to appear in the *Atlantic*. Like the selection of Houghton Mifflin as publisher for the new edition of Timrod's poetry, the claim to a presence in the preeminent New England literary forum asserted parity between the sections.[12]

The tombstone Courtenay chose for the Trinity churchyard encapsulated the themes of the Timrod Revival. Boulder monuments were now fashionable. Shortly before Courtenay ordered the new grave marker, the trade magazine of the cemetery industry featured an article praising consumers in Brookline, Massachusetts, for the "rare taste" demonstrated by the use of a strong, dignified boulder, "the antithesis of the ornate and gaudy memorials that so often mar the beauty of a well-kept cemetery." New South appreciation for the commercial production of bourgeois order converged with Courtenay's desire to evoke one particular boulder tombstone, the piece of New England granite that Emerson had chosen to mark his grave in Concord. The memorial to the guiding soul of New England was equally appropriate for the poet laureate of the Confederacy. Courtenay certainly did not regard his rustic design as mere imitation. A final report described Timrod's tombstone as "a boulder of the good gray granite of his native State, as true in grain and firm in texture as the warlike Carolina he celebrated."[13]

But the solidity of Timrod's gravestone was an illusion. The three men who most effectively promoted his fame—Simms, Hayne, and Courtenay—advanced conflicting views of the relationship between the former Confederacy and the restored Union. These interpretations were not merely phases of a chronological progression. Simms's argument that southern poetry was like captured cannon, alien and superior to New England literature, remained an alternative to Hayne's emphasis on the intersectional affinities of intellectual elites and Courtenay's vision of a New South developing in concerted parallel with the rest of the country. Isabella Martin's remembrance of Timrod as a beneficiary of aristocratic patronage similarly clashed with the narratives that stressed his resemblance to his father, a bookbinder who epitomized artisan democracy. Enthusiasm for Timrod was sufficiently universal to symbolize and facilitate a variety of attempts to forge consensus among white South Carolinians, including the straight-out Democratic assault on Reconstruction for which Carlyle McKinley spoke. But a little inquisitive pressure on the Lost Cause exposed the fissures in that ostensible unity. Timrod's admirers had acted wisely, if inadvertently so, in choosing an unfinished stone to represent the poet in the Trinity churchyard. And Ted was right, too. The cemetery did offer illuminations available nowhere else.

When I next returned to Columbia eleven years later, I came to stay permanently. Ted and I had both left the legal profession. Perhaps we were, as one of Timrod's friends called him, unfit "to keep company long with so relentless, rugged, and exacting a mistress as the law."[14] I had slipped into a doctoral program in American history and taken a faculty position at the University of South Carolina. Ted's retirement from the practice of law was more abrupt. He had collapsed in December 1993 and nearly died. He spent a month in a Charleston hospital, where he learned that he had contracted AIDS. By the time I settled in South Carolina almost three years later, he had accepted his true vocation as a collector of art, books, friends, and stories.

That adjustment was not easy. He was understandably depressed by his diagnosis and fatigued by disease and medication. He worried about his wife and their two young daughters. His mother, a prominent Charleston matron, shrewdly rallied Ted's spirits by focusing his limited energies on a project he had long contemplated, the writing of a book about people buried in Magnolia Cemetery. He had been obsessed by Magnolia ever since he scored a summer job cutting the grass in the beautiful rural cemetery at the age of sixteen. He claimed that by the end of that first season, he had read the inscription on every tombstone at least ten times. Thirty years later, now a member of the Magnolia board of trustees and a lot-owner thinking seriously about taking up permanent residency, he resolved to become the historian of what William Gilmore Simms had called in a dedicatory poem "the city of the silent."

Ted plunged into his task without time or taste for the academic training I had pursued. He began by building a list of about two hundred noteworthy figures from the tombstone inscriptions and burial registers. He then started to research that gallery, working mostly at the Charleston Library Society. He drew on decades of reading about South Carolina history, which he supplemented with a variety of reference works, newspaper obituaries, city directories, and census records. He drafted the biographical sketches in longhand on yellow legal pads at an office he rented in the Confederate Home, originally an institution for widows and orphans of the Civil War. Each day he carried his latest essay to his parents' house, three blocks from his own. His mother's secretarial skills were rusty, but she acquainted herself with the art of word processing to help her technophobic son. The pages gradually piled up as Ted and LaVonne resolved a series of family debates over grammar and punctuation.

Ted handed me a partial draft of the book when I interviewed at South Carolina, and we talked about his project frequently after I moved to Columbia in the summer of 1996. The Civil War era, my academic field, was his greatest vexation. Confederate commemoration was an unavoidable topic in a book about Magnolia Cemetery, home to the graves of fourteen signers of the Ordinance of Secession, seven generals, a thousand Rebel soldiers, and many other heroes and heroines of the Lost Cause. This feature had given Magnolia a prestige within Charleston comparable to the status of the downtown churchyards. But the politics of Confederate remembrance were repulsive to Ted, who had come of age after the civil rights movement and Vietnam War protests of the 1960s. We wondered if the longtime center of white southern identity offered any prospect for fresh incorporation into a respectable fabric of community memory.

We also discussed models for historical writing. His undertaking in some ways resembled guidebooks like Judi Culbertson and Tom Randall's *Permanent Parisians* (1986). Ted's project was an attempt to provide an enduring counterpart to his personal tours of the cemetery, which were a minor legend in Charleston. He knew that it would be difficult for his text to match his enchanting and amusing performances as a raconteur, which he typically enhanced by sharing a bottle of port. But he hoped to help a broad audience see Magnolia as the historical playground that he loved.

Despite this eagerness to entertain, his ambitions were fundamentally less popular than antiquarian. Apart from a handful of well-known figures like William Gilmore Simms and Buck Preston, his subjects were far more obscure than the luminaries profiled by Culbertson and Randall. Or to be more exact, interest in the permanent Charlestonians was more exclusively local. Not even many scholarly experts in late-nineteenth-century southern history could provide an adequate offhand summary of William Ashmead Courtenay's life; only someone specifically interested in Charleston was sure to know him. With few exceptions, the reputations of the artists, politicians, ministers, entrepreneurs, and other citizens profiled by Ted were equally bounded, and in many cases much more narrowly.

Ted's passion for genealogy, the marrow of antiquarianism, epitomized his highly localized approach to history. His friend Allan Gurganus aptly remarked that walking the streets of Charleston with Ted "felt like beach-combing the Galápagos strand alongside Darwin himself," an exercise highlighted by brief lectures about the ancestors of passing neighbors. Like the great biologist, Ted was attentive to the intricacies of the fossil record. He deemed Robert Bentham Simons's *Thomas Grange Simons III, His Forebears and Relations* (1954) "fascinating" and enthused that it "comes as close as any book probably ever will to cutting the Gordian knot of Charleston bloodlines."[15] And like the great biologist, Ted recognized that useful observation converges with interpretive speculation. Although fascinated by continuity, he was not a simple determinist. He understood genealogy, like evolution, as a cumulative record of opportunities and obstacles that individuals negotiated in specific settings. Place was the fundamental conceptual frame.

Henry Timrod offers a good example of the lessons I learned from Ted about the abuses and potential of genealogy. Launched in the heyday of social Darwinism, the Timrod Revival was saturated with evolutionary rhetoric. George Armstrong Wauchope, longtime professor of literature at the University of South Carolina and a state antiquarian of the first water, declared that "the student of the mysterious law of heredity need not go farther back than two generations to account for the personality of the poet." That imputed inheritance took two forms. Timrod's father wrote verses, several of which Simms collected in *The Charleston Book* (1845). Commentators dutifully fancied that Timrod inherited his poetic gift, despite the evidence offered by William Henry Timrod's compositions. Commentators also rhapsodized about Timrod's "eugenically promising combination" of grandparents, which included the German-born Heinrich Dimroth (who took the name Henry Timrod in America), the immigrant's Scotch-Irish third wife, the poet's English-born maternal grandfather, and a half-Swiss maternal grandmother.[16] In the hands of antiquarians as knowledgeable as Wauchope and his research collaborator Yates Snowden, this pseudotheory of ethnic inclination was more useful for what it disguised than for what it explained, as Wauchope hinted in declining to look back more than two generations. For as some of Timrod's contemporaries knew, though subsequent scholars refused to acknowledge, an aspect of Timrod's genealogy crucial in his time and place was that the poet laureate of the Confederacy was descended from African American slaves.

Timrod's ancestry was particularly difficult to hide because the head of the family line was a famous slave. Doctor Caesar, as he called himself, was in 1749 a sixty-seven-year-old bondsman of John Norman in Colleton County, South Carolina, well known in his community for his remedies for snake bites, pleurisy, yaws, and other maladies. When a set of nearby whites—including the immensely wealthy Henry Middleton and his overseer—felt that they had been poisoned by slaves, Caesar administered an effective antidote. After investigation, the South Carolina legislature voted in 1750 to buy Caesar's freedom from Norman and award the ex-slave an annuity of one hundred pounds in exchange for disclosure of his formulas. Such a spectacular story did not fade quickly from local memory. As late as 1855, it appeared in a widely circulated southern agricultural magazine.[17]

Nor was the emancipation of the next generation calculated to escape lasting notice in low-country South Carolina. At some point before his death in 1754, Doctor Caesar made a will that allocated almost all of his estate to purchasing the freedom of his daughter Hannah from John Norman. But when Norman made out his own will in 1756, his estate still included that "one Mestizo Girl called Hannah." Norman divided his personal property equally among his four children, bequeathing to each child one specifically named slave. Hannah went to his daughter, Sarah, who was also Hannah's daughter. When Norman died shortly thereafter, twelve-year-old Sarah Norman became Sarah Caesar. Mother and daughter moved to Charleston, where Hannah worked as a nurse, cultivating referrals through the administrator of the municipal poorhouse. Sarah Norman Caesar married recent Swiss immigrant John Faesch around 1768 and eventually had four daughters.[18]

The Caesars' passage into white society met with a public setback in 1786 when burglars broke into Hannah's house on King Street and robbed her. Charleston newspapers reported in detail the proceedings of the ensuing trial. The perpetrators' attorney was Charles Cotesworth Pinckney, who in the following year would represent slaveholding interests at the Constitutional Convention in Philadelphia. As Henry Middleton's son-in-law, Pinckney had particular reason to know who Doctor Caesar had been and who Hannah Caesar was. He moved to disqualify her as a witness on the grounds that she was a mulatto and therefore incompetent to testify against whites. The prosecutor shrugged and secured the conviction of the defendants solely on the testimony of an accomplice. When the trial ended, Hannah Caesar raised a protest on behalf of her "descendants that might be injured by her being considered to be of mixed blood." The prosecutor read into the record two affidavits from purported former neighbors attesting that "they knew her as Hannah Brown, afterwards Hannah Caesar, and always understood her mother to have been a white woman." No one in the courtroom had any cause to explore or contest these claims. But the measure of local skepticism was the 1790 federal census, which recorded "Free Sarah Fash," or Sarah Norman Caesar Faesch, as a woman of color living on King Street with another free person of color as well as one white man and two slaves. The other free woman of color was probably Hannah Caesar, who died in 1791, or one of Sarah's daughters, Sarah Faesch, who soon married neighboring tinner Charles Prince.[19]

The tombstone of Timrod's mother in the Trinity Cathedral churchyard in Columbia provides startling genealogical context for the poet's adjacent boulder. Thyza Prince Timrod had been married to William Henry Timrod for four years when Sarah Norman Caesar Faesch died in 1816. Thyza and William's residence was then directly across King Street from her parents' home. Sarah Faesch Prince lived until 1862, and the poet shared a residence with her for substantial periods of time.[20] Thyza Timrod outlived her son. The persistence of the African strain in her family history is underscored by the experience of Timrod's last surviving sibling, Emily Timrod Goodwin, who outlived her brother by five years. In May 1870, one month after the lingering death of her mother, Goodwin sent her first letter in almost two years to Paul Hamilton Hayne, with whom she had corresponded frequently in the immediate aftermath of Henry's death in 1867. She reported sadly that she had been ostracized in Columbia after poverty drove her to open a boardinghouse for "several of the Federal officers" living in the city during Reconstruction. She was about to lose her lease at the beginning of June and did not know what she would do, though she counted on the kindness of the northerners, "far truer in their friendship than most of my southern friends." The federal census taken in June 1870, shortly after she relocated, indicates that she had opened a new boardinghouse in which her tenants were African Americans who worked as domestic servants in Columbia. The census also reported that Emily Timrod Goodwin was black. Like her great-great-grandmother, Hannah Caesar, and her great-grandmother, Sarah Norman Caesar Faesch, the poet's sister had crossed the color line, though in the opposite direction.[21]

Mixed racial ancestry, however remote, attracted attention in Timrod's society. Thomas J. Mackey, a low-country contemporary long active in public life, remarked in 1884 that the admired poet "was well known to be an octoroon." Ludwig Lewisohn, who grew up in Charleston a few years later, recalled that it "was whispered to me in a kind of murderous secrecy" that Timrod "had 'a touch of the tar-brush.'" The eulogies by Timrod's literary friends offer tantalizing hints that they were well aware of his family background. Simms was especially likely to be informed, not merely because he was a full generation older than his protégé and acquainted with William Henry Timrod's social circle but also because Simms knew more about South Carolina history than anyone else of his time. It is tempting to speculate that his strange emphasis on the inadequacy of Timrod's blood was a winking racial allusion in the immediate aftermath of the younger poet's death. Hayne may have had all manner of schoolboy memories in mind when he reported that "more than once I have known [the young Timrod] to engage in a desperate *affaire d'honneur*, the issue of which was decided by a primitive species of science that would have disgusted the orthodox 'ring.'" It is more difficult to understand what else J. Dickson Bruns might have meant when he praised Timrod in 1870 for overcoming a "hereditary taint."[22]

By the time Bruns made that remark, he had moved to New Orleans and become friendly with George Washington Cable, whose wife the physician treated. Bruns also emerged as one of Cable's literary advisers, in part because the aspiring novelist was impressed that the South Carolinian "had been the friend of Pinckney, Timrod, and William Gilmore Simms."[23] In this capacity, Bruns contributed significantly to Cable's popularization of the "tragic mulatto" as a representative character in American literature in *The Grandissimes* (1880). Many of the giveaway traits that Bruns proposed for the fictional prototype closely matched his recollection of his longtime friend. Timrod, too, demonstrated "a morbid sensitiveness, an invincible incapacity for any of the robuster avocations of life, an ineradicable defect of will (the offspring of a diseased temperament)." The poet's most distinctive physical features were "the shallow chest, the slender waist, the thin

Henry Timrod, 1856. Tinted sixth-plate daguerreotype by Tyler & Co., Charleston.
Courtesy of the South Caroliniana Library, University of South Carolina, Columbia.

transparent hands and habitually lax attitude." His characteristic languor
mirrored the moral weakness that led him to drink. He was an unnatural
being whose transgression of gender lines implied a transgression of racial
lines. Bruns swerved toward the homoerotic in recalling Timrod's exqui-
sitely sensitive lips and deep-set eyes "full of melancholy and pleading tenderness" before concluding more conventionally that his "almost feminine
gentleness" was "the key to his social character." For the doctor, the most
revealing sign of hybridity was a constitution doomed by medically elusive
defects. As Cable's quadroon suffered from a weak heart, Timrod's "physician said that he was dying of consumption—and so he was, but it was
want and wretchedness and moral agony that were consuming him."[24] The
tragic mulatto, adapted from Cable by Twain and Faulkner, may have been
a literary ghost of the Confederate poet laureate.

Black memory of Timrod's mixed ancestry was more forthright. Charleston barber Thomas Carr testified after the death of his frequent customer
that "the gossip around was quite general to the effect that Timrod was an

octoroon." Whitefield McKinlay, an associate of Booker T. Washington and businessman in Washington, D.C., but born in Charleston in 1857, similarly reported that his aunt "knew Timrod's mother, and that she was a quadroon."[25] These calculations of the poet's lineage match up with the federal census classification of Sarah Norman Caesar Faesch as a free person of color in 1790, regardless of the exact ethnic strains that came together in her planter father and enslaved mother.

Because scholars have failed to examine Timrod's genealogy, they have not asked how his sense of racial identity may have influenced his writing. The texts do not necessarily beg the question. "Ethnogenesis" (1861), with which Timrod decisively advanced from the ranks of Victorian mediocrity in a celebration of the new Confederacy, is a dramatic ode to white supremacism even if the poet could not have foreseen the twentieth-century cinematic connotations of his neologism for "birth of a nation." Its oft-quoted final stanza envisions a proslavery millennium in which "to give labor to the poor, / The whole sad planet o'er, / And save from want and crime the humblest door, / Is one among the many ends for which God makes us great and rich!"[26]

Timrod's wartime editorials for the *Daily South Carolinian* suggest that this imperial idyll was not merely a momentary burst of enthusiasm. He scorned suggestions that the South might offer emancipation to slaves who enlisted in Confederate service. "The hour for even consideration of the question of emancipation has not yet arrived, and probably never will," he declared in January 1865. Criticizing Jefferson Davis's mobilization proposal, Timrod wrote that "for many years past, the Southern people have been spending a great deal of logic and erudition in the not altogether unsuccessful attempt to convince the world that slavery is the condition most fitted to the negro; that in that condition alone he attains his physical, social, moral, and intellectual height; that in a state of freedom he becomes, through his sensual and indolent nature, degraded rather than elevated, and that, consequently, freedom to him is anything but a boon." He believed that enslaved and free African Americans "have learned that their best friends are on Southern soil" and would happily volunteer to fight under the discipline of white men who had known them since childhood. The editorialist was apoplectic on the subject of miscegenation, a word that entered the political lexicon in 1864. Informed that Boston abolitionist Wendell Phillips had argued that America owed its power and vitality not to the purity of Saxon blood but to the admixture of ethnicities, which might be further invigorated by an African American fusion, Timrod replied that such an idea surpassed "the worst sensational novel ever issued from the Parisian press."[27]

Timrod's writings also support a contrary inference that his racial views differed significantly from the dominant ideology of his society. "Ethnogenesis" and his anonymous work for the *Daily South Carolinian* constitute most of his substantial references to race or slavery. The *Boston Globe* conjectured in 1873 that Timrod's refusal to indulge white supremacism more fully may have limited the community support he received: "He gives voice to some of the strongest aspirations of human sentiments and passions; but how is he on the one great question that should alone occupy the Southern intelligence, the question of 'niggers'? Well, we reluctantly admit, that he is very little on this point. Any bawler at the hustings would exceed him at that matter." Louis Rubin has made Timrod's reticence on these topics central to an argument for the poet's achievement. According to Rubin, the war-related poetry was much better than anything else Timrod wrote before, during, or after the war because it drew strength from the reservations that informed his stance as a Confederate poet. Prior to the war, his distaste for the politics of slavery prevented him from becoming a civic poet at all. Amid the war, he found more congenial Confederate themes in civilian anxiety and mourning. When he did engage the driving purpose of secession, as in the apostrophe of "Ethnogenesis," his verse benefited from his frank recognition of slaveholders' materialism and his adoption of a correspondingly direct, commercial diction even as he calculated that on balance, the flawed southern republic offered promise to the world. "One assumes that privately Timrod must have been of two minds about the whole business," Rubin concluded.[28] The poet's awareness of his genealogy may have prompted him to see the Civil War with what W. E. B. Du Bois would later describe as a double consciousness.

Rubin's portrait of a conflicted Timrod did not insinuate any mixed racial ancestry. His emphasis on the Confederate poet's doubts instead reflected the admiration for literary modernism that inspired the critic to devote much of his career to the twentieth-century Southern Renascence. The heart of that modernism was inner tension. "It is precisely the ambivalence of Timrod's best work that accounts for its superiority as literature," Rubin posited. Literary professionalism, he added, was the primary social foundation for the expression of self-division. Timrod's attack on William J. Grayson, the author of "The Hireling and the Slave," combined the younger poet's diffidence toward proslavery polemics and his disgust with "amateur critics, poets and philosophers, the regular business of whom is to demonstrate truisms, settle questions which nobody else would think of discussing, to confirm themselves in opinions which have been picked up from the rubbish of seventy years ago." The establishment of a full-time authorial class enjoying some insulation from the broader community was the surest route to a modern, penetrating literature. Rubin's study of Timrod underscored that partial separation need not lead to alienation and might produce eloquent patriotism.[29]

I shared Rubin's self-interested sympathy with this ideal of intellectual professionalism. My conversations with Ted, however, suggested that the potential of amateur antiquarianism deserved fuller examination. Basic genealogical research offered a perspective on Timrod that scholars had ignored. The hallmark of Ted's approach to genealogy and most other first-rate antiquarianism was a grounding in specific places, almost always near the antiquarian's home. Ted had chosen Magnolia Cemetery as the little postage stamp of native soil that he would cultivate. Unlike academic historians who adopt localized research frameworks, he did not claim that his subject was indicative of regional or national trends. He had enjoyed many midnight rambles at Mount Auburn Cemetery, but he was not much interested in Magnolia as a southern adaptation of the rural cemetery movement launched in Massachusetts. He cared little about the landscape principles, the monument designs, or the economic organization that characterized rural cemeteries.[30] His attachment was to the community of the dead, a collection of individuals who shared a variety of institutional connections to his living neighbors. Common burial was the last of these ties.

This particularity did not necessarily diminish the cemetery as a field for imaginative generalization. The society that defined itself at Magnolia used the site to address problems of wide importance. The person who best realized the expansive potential of the place was Henry Timrod, in his "Ode Sung on the Occasion of Decorating the Graves of the Confederate Dead, at Magnolia Cemetery, Charleston, S.C., 1866." The most significant literary text associated with southern observance of Memorial Day, the "Ode" made every Confederate grave into Timrod's grave.

The "Ode" is Timrod's permanent literary monument. During the Timrod Revival, his most admired poems included martial anthems like "Carolina," which the South Carolina legislature named the official state song in 1911. Later generations dismissed those effusions as mere bombast, and today even proud South Carolinians do not know the words to "Carolina." The scholars interested in Timrod since the early 1940s have shifted their attention to his anguished wartime meditations like "The Unknown Dead" and "I Know Not Why." Throughout these fluctuations, critical and popular appreciation for the "Ode" has remained considerable. Emerson was reading the text at public performances by 1872 and included it in his anthology *Parnassus* (1875). Louis Rubin developed a lasting attachment to it during the 1930s as one of countless Charleston schoolchildren required to learn Timrod's poem by heart. A voice-over recites it in the closing scene of the 1999 television movie *The Hunley*. Praise for the work has varied. Wauchope exclaimed in 1915 "how fitting it was that the poet who had proudly sung the prologue to the Confederacy in 'Ethnogenesis' should have lived long enough to write sadly but with no less pride its epilogue and apotheosis in his 'Magnolia Cemetery.'" Edd Winfield Parks retorted fifty years later that "it is appropriate that [Timrod's] finest single poem should be a mournful celebration not of a dead nation but of the men who died for it. There is a significant difference." For all this attention, few readers have followed the lead of Timrod's long title by firmly placing the "Ode" at the decoration of the graves of the Confederate dead at Magnolia Cemetery in June 1866. Closer attention to local context reveals Timrod's disagreements with other poets of the Lost Cause and exposes connections to modernist and postmodern poets who have taken up his themes.[31]

Timrod's "Ode" gently presents a vigorous argument. The dead Confederates buried at Magnolia should "Sleep sweetly in your humble graves, / Sleep martyrs of a fallen cause, / Though yet no marble column craves / The pilgrim here to pause." A tangible military tribute is forthcoming: "In seeds of laurel in the earth, / The blossom of your fame is blown; / And, somewhere, waiting for its birth, / The shaft is in the stone!" But those martial honors will not replace the "memorial blooms" strewn on the graves today by the tearful "sisters" of the dead. The shades "will smile / More proudly on those wreaths to-day, / Than when some cannon-moulded pile / Shall overlook this bay." Tension between warfare and culture propels Timrod's blissful conclusion that "There is no holier spot of ground, / Than where defeated valor lies / By mourning beauty crowned." The deceptively quiet poem includes only three words of more than two syllables. The most arresting of these highlighted words is "defeated," the root meaning of which is "undone" or "unmade." Like the vanquished Confederacy, the soldiers' bodies are decomposing into nothingness. Sacred reconstitution of their disintegrated valor, or value, cannot take the shape of "some cannon-moulded pile," a provocatively ugly image. True redemption comes with "mourning beauty" in the generative forms of the flowers, the ceremony, and the poem.[32]

This argument differed starkly from the themes highlighted in other phases of the June 1866 observance organized by the Ladies' Memorial Association of Charleston. The choir that sang Timrod's "Ode" stood along-side a wreath that framed a resilient palmetto tree and that was inscribed, "Bent, but not broken." The Ladies' Memorial Association chose June 16 for the ceremony because that date was the anniversary of the Battle of Se-cessionville, the most noteworthy Confederate victory in the army engage-ments near Charleston. Except for Timrod, every participant in the com-memoration fervently defended ideological rationalizations for so many deaths. Caroline Augusta Ball's ode claimed that "No orphans mourn, no mothers weep; / No sister's tears are shed" because "Dear was the cause for which they bled." A third ode, by Baptist minister Edwin Winkler, stressed that Charleston "chants their fame / Because they fought and fell for her, for home / And liberty." Presbyterian minister John L. Girardeau, the ora-tor of the day, delivered a comprehensive statement of this position. "We can never, never forget that they were sacrificial victims on an altar which we helped to rear," he insisted, and that they died "struggling to uphold the great principles of civil and religious liberty for which their fathers before them had bled." Like Christianity, the Confederacy forged holy meaning in violent death that resurrection would vindicate. "Truth struck to the earth shall rise again," quoted Girardeau, a motto that would evolve into "the South shall rise again," although the phrase came from a Civil War poem by northerner William Cullen Bryant. The sacralization of war and death stood diametrically opposed to Timrod's veneration of culture and life.[33]

Place was fundamental to this contrast. The "Ode" locates itself much more specifically than Girardeau's oration or similar Confederate remem-brances. Timrod's poem literally takes place at Magnolia Cemetery. He situ-ates the June 1866 ceremony in the rural cemetery movement, an essen-tial prelude to the zeal of both northerners and southerners for Memorial Day exercises centered on floral decoration of soldiers' graves. Timrod had shared in the antebellum enthusiasm for the shift from bleak, crowded urban churchyards to sylvan sites of regeneration. The hymn he composed at the age of twenty-two for the November 1850 dedication of Magno-lia Cemetery was one of the earliest publications he included in wartime plans for a collection of his work. The poem rued that humanity had previ-ously painted death "in the false aspect of a ruthless foe" and welcomed a Charleston cemetery defined by harmony with nature: "we have fixed / And beautified, O Death! Thy mansion here, / . . . / Make it a place to love, and not to fear." His professional interest in Magnolia linked the rural cemetery to what Timrod considered "to us of the present day the most important of all literary revolutions." After Wordsworth, poetry emphasized that "behind the sights, sounds and hues of external Nature, there is 'something more than meets the senses, something undefined and unutterable which must be felt and perceived by the soul' in its moments of rapt contemplation." Refusal to acknowledge this "super-sensuous" romanticism was the hallmark of "old fogyism." For Timrod, the floral decoration of Confederate graves in Magnolia Cemetery was a beautiful modern rite consistent with the spirit of the rural cemetery and contemporary poetry.[34]

Though confident in the imaginative power of the sensibility he championed, Timrod also understood its vulnerability. In June 1866, the soldiers' ground at Magnolia Cemetery contained between six hundred and seven hundred graves laid out in a series of long rows. The arrangement reinforced the separation of the military grid from the winding lanes and picturesque vistas that characterized the rest of the rural cemetery. Temporary decoration of the soldiers' graves symbolically incorporated them into the original institution, but the Confederate dead portended a new order. The "Ode" foresaw that sooner or later "some cannon-moulded pile / Shall overlook this bay" and that Girardeau's regime of martial sacrifice would supplant Timrod's ideal. Modernity, he recognized, was malleable and contested.

Timrod's sense of Confederate commemoration as a crisis of modernity made his work a valuable touchstone for later poets. Allen Tate's "Ode to the Confederate Dead," which the author first drafted in 1926 but revised for ten years, similarly takes place in a Confederate cemetery that is significantly martial in its rank-and-file organization ("Row after row with strict impunity / The headstones yield their names to the element"). Tate, too, identifies ritual remembrance with seasonality, though he shifts from Timrod's vernal meditation on Memorial Day to the autumnal imagery of falling leaves, "of nature the casual sacrament / To the seasonal eternity of death." Where Timrod's rites of spring epitomize a besieged romanticism, Tate depicts the gated Confederate cemetery as an Eden that dramatizes "the cut-off-ness of the modern 'intellectual man' from the world." Tate's dense mulch of classical and literary allusion deepens this impression of loss. As in Timrod's "Ode," the poet is endangered by the fragility of tradition. The inability of Tate's protagonist to associate the falling leaves with dying soldiers consigns to emptiness a metaphor presented in Homer, Virgil, Dante, and Milton as well as in Tate's ode.[35]

Moss Oaks Lake and Confederate Monument, Magnolia Cemetery, 1883. Published by Witteman Brothers. Courtesy of the Margaretta Childs Archives at the Historic Charleston Foundation, Charleston, S.C.

Timrod's "Ode" also occupies a neglected position in the literary gene-alogy of Robert Lowell's "For the Union Dead" (1960), a pendant to his former teacher Tate's "Ode for the Confederate Dead" and the climax of a long line of New England poems about Robert Gould Shaw. Timrod's and Lowell's projects intersect at many points. The dead mourned by the first presentation of the "Ode" included Confederates killed at Battery Wagner on the night of July 18, 1863. Other soldiers honored at Magnolia Ceme-tery in June 1866 may well have participated in the relegation of Shaw and his black comrades to the unmarked ditch that became one of the most fa-mous graves dug by the Confederacy. Timrod volunteered again for mili-tary service immediately after the heroic charge of the 54th Massachusetts, only to be dismissed again within twenty-four hours for medical inca-pacity.[36] Lowell echoed Timrod's contrast between "mourning beauty" and a "cannon-moulded pile" in comparing the Shaw Memorial to "the stone statues of the abstract Union soldier" that steadily diminish in meaning as the generic productions "grow slimmer and younger each year." The decline from Augustus Saint-Gaudens's artistic achievement paralleled the threat to Timrod's rural cemetery. In the aftermath of Hiroshima and Nagasaki, the conscientious objector to World War II was tarter than his Civil War prede-cessor in assessing the relationship between war and culture. Nuclear weap-onry was the direst dimension of a new crisis of modernity that Lowell also associated with obeisance to television. "There are no statues for the last war here," he observed, recasting Timrod's correlative for pure sympathy into a manifestation of human depravity. "The ditch is nearer," Lowell warned.[37]

Tate's and Lowell's modernist classics have inspired postmodern re-mixes by African American poets Kevin Young and Natasha Trethewey that affirm Timrod's position in the Civil War palimpsest. Young's "For the Con-federate Dead" (2000) is a variation on the line of criticism that empha-sizes the racial hierarchy and New England chauvinism of the Shaw Memo-rial. The epigraph of the poem is Whitman's heartier identification with a jaunty and expert black teamster in "Song of Myself." Young's conflation of Lowell's and Tate's titles denies meaningful distinction between Union and Confederate perspectives. He brings the two modernists together in the central image of his poem, a description of the speaker sitting in a low-country café at a dilapidated hotel. Near him is a little-noticed mural, a parody of Saint-Gaudens's relief sculpture. The speaker also links the decorative artwork to the Confederate monument toward which his table looks, and the paint chips peeling from the mural evoke the falling leaves in Tate's cemetery. The painted scene is an antebellum cotton plantation: "in its fields Negroes bend / To pick the endless white."[38]

The clever mashup shares artistic anxieties with Timrod's work. The de-terioration of the mural reflects not only its dated subject but also the ob-solescence of entire genres. The hipster poet tries to achieve permanence astride a rapidly changing popular culture. Pitching an alternative to the Shaw Memorial, he proposes that "In my movie there are no / horses, no heroes." Ridiculing Lowell's intimidated response to early television, Young particularly laughs at weather reports. He was born in 1970, five years after Bob Dylan announced that "You don't need a weatherman / To know which way the wind blows." Movies, television, and music feed the poet's riffs, but his entanglement in the twenty-first-century global entertainment mar-ket complicates his view of emancipation in the nineteenth-century global cotton market.

Trethewey, born to a black mother and a white father in Mississippi in 1966, embraces the mixed racial heritage that Timrod hid. A couplet set re-counts her life alongside the story of Faulkner's tragic mulatto Joe Christ-mas. In another poem she dreams about posing for a photograph alongside the Fugitive Poets. "*Say 'race,'* the photographer croons" as he snaps the pic-ture, and the camera freezes Trethewey in blackface. Trying on a blond wig as a child, she notes that "with my skin color, / like a good tan—an even mix of my parents'— / I could have passed for white."[39] Her "Elegy for the Native Guards" (2002) centers on a unit of black Union soldiers less celebrated than the regiment Lowell recalled. After the Battle of Port Hudson, fallen soldiers of the Louisiana Native Guards remained unburied because commanding general Nathaniel Banks of Massachusetts denied that any of his troops were in the area. In freedom as in slavery, African Americans must attend to their own remembrance. Trethewey reports that cotton fields are "hallowed ground— / as slave legend goes—each boll / holding the ghosts of generations."[40]

Young's and Trethewey's attention to the commercial and racial foundations of the Cotton Kingdom evoke its bard Timrod, who predicted in "Ethnogenesis" that "THE SNOW OF SOUTHERN SUMMERS" would provide the Confederacy an invincible defense. "The Cotton Boll" (1861) likewise envisioned contented black labor as the frame for a gleaming vision of white independence. International demand for the vital raw commodity of the industrial economy would enable the South to dictate surrender terms at New York, "where some rotting ships and crumbling quays / Shall one day mark the Port which ruled the Western seas." Timrod ruefully acknowledged the ruins of that confidence in the "Ode," which assured the Confederate dead that "the blossom of your fame is blown," like the flower that precedes the emergence of the mature cotton boll.[41] The specificity of place reinforced the irony. The poet probably knew that before Magnolia became a cemetery, the land had most recently been used for cotton cultivation.[42]

In its transformation from a spectral rural cemetery for blacks to a verdant rural cemetery for whites, the setting for Timrod's "Ode" mirrored the racial layering of his family history. The local institution of Memorial Day recorded by the poem was a further amalgamation. The exercises in the June 1866 observance inevitably stirred memories of the similar rites conducted in May 1865 to honor the graves of more than 250 Union soldiers who had died in a Confederate prison on the site of the Charleston horse-racing track, less than two miles from Magnolia Cemetery. Featuring a crowd estimated at ten thousand people, mostly newly liberated slaves, the solemn event capped a series of celebrations of emancipation that began shortly after the Confederate evacuation of the city. Participants included black schoolchildren, black ministers, a patriotic association of black women, a benevolent society of black men, and members of the 54th Massachusetts Regiment and two units of the U.S. Colored Troops as well as white missionaries and army officers. The ceremony drew no mention thirteen months later at Magnolia.[43] But Timrod's interest in the sentimental dislocations embedded in places of memory invited reconsideration of other ostensibly fixed coordinates of his society, including the color line.

Like Timrod's grave in the Trinity churchyard, his elegy for the decoration of the soldiers' ground at Magnolia Cemetery shows that the Lost Cause was not monolithic. Although the poet was a Confederate patriot, he differed sharply from his fellow Memorial Day eulogists. His "Ode" was no less of a Lost Cause standard than Catholic priest Abram Joseph Ryan's popular "March of the Deathless Dead," also written for a Ladies' Memorial Association in 1866 ("Gather the sacred dust / Of the warriors tried and true. / Who bore the flag of a Nation's trust / And fell in a cause, though lost, still just, / And died for me and you.").[44] But a closer look at the Charleston text—and especially the precise location at which the poem takes place—shows that Confederate commemoration could achieve a resonance that differed dramatically from Ryan's deplorable formulation. Timrod foreshadowed Tate, Lowell, Young, and Trethewey in his nervous determination to comprehend and criticize his unfolding era as he looked backward. Confederate memory provided him with a field on which to engage modernity. This enduring achievement offered inspiration for thoughtful hopes to find a usable past at Magnolia Cemetery.

Ted Phillips died on January 17, 2005. I inherited responsibility for completing his book about Magnolia Cemetery. As my remembrance of him took the form of an editorial ghostwriting project, I developed a broader historical perspective on my friend's struggle to define his relationship to the Confederate legacy. Ted wanted to bring local antiquarianism into line with the values of contemporary America, just as Courtenay aimed for the Timrod Revival to express the spirit of the New South. Ted rejected the viewpoints of some neighbors who shared his passion for Magnolia, just as Timrod and Girardeau disagreed on the significance of Memorial Day, but Ted's irreverent tours nevertheless shared features with Confederate reenactors' solemn ceremonies at the cemetery. When I came to understand conflict as the norm rather than the exception in Confederate tributes and to regard that commemoration not merely as a retrograde political instrument but as a flexible vehicle for addressing modernity, I reconsidered some of what I had previously written about the Lost Cause and began to appreciate more fully the significance of recent phases of white southern Civil War memory. The preparation of Ted's manuscript for publication eventually led into the writing of my own book.[45]

Although now an academic cliché, Pierre Nora's observation that "memory attaches itself to sites, whereas history attaches itself to events," offers a

valuable approach to affections for a local past that are strained by "the acceleration of history." Timrod's grave and his "Magnolia Ode" illustrate the
interplay between a "will to remember" and a "capacity for metamorphosis"
that Nora described as characteristic of "*lieux de mémoire.*" He expected
that detailed examination of such places of memory would prove "at once
banal and extraordinary." Worrisome as the first half of that prediction may
have been, Nora thought the study might offer "a kind of reawakening" to
historical scholarship if "practiced in the fragile happiness derived from re-
lating to rehabilitated objects and from the involvement of the historian in
his or her subject." He had in mind a scholar like Louis Rubin, returning
with enlightened but ineradicable attachment to the Lost Cause orthodoxy
drilled into him during youth.[46]

The relationship of a Boston native to the subject of Confederate memory is more problematic, even after making much of my life in South Carolina. As the following pages indicate, however, many northerners have
participated imaginatively in Confederate remembrance. The lineage of
abolitionist and neoabolitionist homage to Timrod that begins with Emerson extends through Bob Dylan. Long before the state hired me to teach
Civil War history, South Carolinians routinely invited distant aid for the
local commemorative project. Some northern artists commissioned to design Confederate monuments made thoughtful and welcome contributions
to the landscape of civic memory. Tourism is another venue that has modeled the possibility of semidetached initiation. Uncompromising travelers
have found ways to expand creatively on aspects of the Lost Cause encountered during South Carolina sojourns. Henry James best traced a path into
the state of mind prescribed by Nora. After a visit to Magnolia Cemetery,
the novelist reported that "something that I scarce know how to express
but as the proud humility of the whole idle, easy loveliness, made even the
restless analyst, for the hour, among the pious inscriptions that scarce ever
belie the magniloquent clime or the inimitable tradition, feel himself really
capable of the highest Carolinian pitch."[47]

Friendship with Ted Phillips familiarized me with a restless analyst
capable of the highest Carolinian pitch. As Allan Gurganus has noted, "Ted
resembled those Quentin Compson lawyer-collector-raconteur-historian-
archivist-tibbler-liberal-wits" found mostly in fiction.[48] To me fell the challenging role of Shreve McCannon. This book continues countless conversations in our college dormitory sitting room about the history of the South.
If Ted had lived a little longer, I trust he would have assured me that he
didn't hate it.

Secessionist Commemoration and Its Aftermath

IN JOSEPHINE HUMPHREYS'S novel *Rich in Love* (1987), the figure of John C. Calhoun epitomizes the incompletely hidden past that shapes the present. Seventeen-year-old narrator Lucille Odom dismisses a schoolbook explanation of Calhoun's nullification doctrine as "a red herring" except insofar as it demonstrates "how men can dress greed as philosophy." But she takes a "consuming interest" in the adulatory Calhoun Monument in Charleston. The statue atop the immense shaft brings the statesman alive for Lucille in an immediate and even intimate way. She cranes her neck to stare at "the deep brow, the wild mane." "I loved Calhoun's looks," she recalls. The virile figure inclines her to believe the Carolina legend that Calhoun was the true father of Abraham Lincoln. Unlike "the otherwise dry heart of politics," the fanciful blood tie between Calhoun and Lincoln is to Lucille a viable interpretation of the Civil War—animated by the irony, the generational tensions, and the "behind-the-scenes passion" that mark her discovery of her own past and her sexual awakening in a relationship with the historian married to her older sister. Wary of academic evasions, she finds meaning in the memorial landmark of her hometown.[1]

John Massey Rhind, Calhoun Monument, Charleston. Detroit Photographic Company, ca. 1907. Courtesy of the Library of Congress, Washington, D.C.

The sponsors of the monument installed in 1896 would have been scandalized by Lucille's reflections on Calhoun, but they shared her conviction that "history was a category comprising not only famous men of bygone eras, but *me, yesterday*." During the 1850s, the Ladies' Calhoun Monument Association (LCMA) was one of the first southern women's groups to assume a leading role in civic memory. The group's enactment of citizenship developed deeper significance after the Civil War as the LCMA became the nucleus for several Confederate commemorative organizations. The women's monument expressed their pride in themselves as well as their veneration for Calhoun. The design program adopted in 1866 and finalized over the next thirty years envisioned the tribute to the antebellum statesman in terms that referred specifically to wartime trauma shared by the members of the LCMA.

The Calhoun Monument presents a partial view of its sponsors as well as its bronze hero. The granite column does not acknowledge that the

LCMA shouldered aside rival efforts to commemorate Calhoun. The imposing structure also belies the women's diminished postwar interest in the project. They found Calhoun less fascinating in the late nineteenth century than Lucille Odom did in the late twentieth century. They had felt very differently when they placed a lock of Calhoun's hair in the hollow cornerstone in 1858. Excavation of the history embedded in the monument reveals continuities and discontinuities between the culture of secession and the culture of the Lost Cause.

The foremost radical exercise in white southern memory during the decade before Fort Sumter, the Calhoun Monument demonstrates the factional maneuvers and ideological appeals that led to disunion. Calhoun's death during the debates over the Compromise of 1850 made remembrance of the South Carolina political leader a useful vehicle for arguments about the state's response to the sectional crisis. For much of the decade, proponents of unilateral secession lost ground to advocates of cooperative secession with other slaveholding states, but the competing groups eventually united to defeat the strategy of defending slavery through the Democratic Party. The Calhoun Monument contributed to this process not only because the Nullifier personified distrust for party politics but also because the LCMA's campaign promoted a cross-class solidarity essential to the success of secession. Students of disunion have understandably centered on slaveholders' fears, but the antebellum emphasis on the Calhoun Monument as a setting for urban sociability illustrates Charlestonians' hopes for a modern proslavery republic.[2]

As a secessionist project that survived the death of the Confederacy, the Calhoun Monument illustrates the postwar adjustments of white southern commemoration. Waning enthusiasm for the Nullifier fostered a proposal to channel the LCMA's funds to the Home for Mothers, Widows, and Daughters of Confederate Soldiers, an institution established by LCMA leaders. Only when frustrated in this attempt to implement a more expansive view of women's commemorative citizenship did the LCMA commission a statue of Calhoun. The sponsors' program abandoned the romantic nationalism of the antebellum era, but the northern sculptor hired by the LCMA nevertheless tried to recall that vision. When his work prompted African Americans to enjoy their freedom with satirical remarks that white Charlestonians adapted into a blackface parody, the women destroyed the monument they had ceremoniously dedicated. The LCMA ordered a replacement that highlighted the victimization of the Confederate home front during the war, the preservation of embattled honor by virtuous women, and the restoration of elite South Carolinians to their customary position of leadership in the reunited nation and the local community.

The LCMA's intersectional ambitions achieved an unforeseen fulfillment in musings that Calhoun may have fathered Lincoln. The monument promoters addressed their assertions of southern dignity largely to influential northerners like the geologist Clarence King, who visited Charleston three months after the June 1896 installation of the second statue. He was startled by its resemblance to Lincoln and became fascinated with the paternity legend he encountered in South Carolina. He urged his close friend John Hay, one of Lincoln's personal secretaries during the war and coauthor of a reverential ten-volume biography, to "trace up the threads" despite the implausibility of the rumors. King knew a few things about hidden histories: he led a double life as both a white intellectual celebrity and a black Pullman porter with an ex-slave common-law wife and five mixed-race children. Like the fictional Lucille Odom, he saw in the Calhoun Monument a resonant myth of intertwined private and public conflict "nearer the Greek than anything I ever came across in modern life."[3] That imaginative engagement, more vivid than any recorded response along the lines envisioned by the LCMA, illustrated the work's inescapable moorings in the origins of the Civil War. An artifact of secession as well as a tribute to the Lost Cause, the Calhoun Monument encouraged ruminations on the fluidity of personal identity and the self-destructiveness of racial slavery that Confederate commemoration ordinarily aimed to suppress.

Rollin Osterweis may have exaggerated in arguing that the apotheosis of Calhoun was to the emergence of romantic nationalism in South Carolina what the cult of Beethoven was to the development of romantic music in Europe, but the Nullifier was clearly one of the most potent symbols in the state during the 1850s. His dominance had long irked rivals, and his successors would abandon some of his key strategies, but competing secessionist factions fervently sought to get right with Calhoun. They treated his legacy of leadership as a touchstone of South Carolina identity. When a spiritualist reported in 1853 that he had made contact with Calhoun in the afterworld, one wag shrugged that nothing could be less of a revelation than the received message, "I'm with you still." More surprising was the discovery that Calhoun had become an expert guitar player since his death.[4] The magical momentum of mortality shaped but also frustrated efforts to fashion a hero for southern nationalism.

The circumstances of Calhoun's demise did as much to propel his post-humous appeal as his long career. His lingering fade from center stage at the most dramatic congressional debates since the adoption of the Constitution captured the collective imagination of his constituents. Charleston banker Franklin Elmore, who succeeded temporarily to the vacated Senate seat, declared that Calhoun had "given us a lesson of patriotism and of exalted courage, far more heroic than a thousand deaths in the field of battle, in calmly and resolutely surrendering his life . . . rather than abandon the post where the call of duty stationed him." Clergymen agreed that the removal of such a leader amid such a crisis could only reflect the mysterious workings of Providence. Leading theologians James Henley Thornwell and James Warley Miles took the occasion to reflect on the religious dimensions of nationhood as white South Carolinians contemplated suggestions that the state should leave the Union if Congress did not protect the institution of slavery in territories acquired from Mexico. Quoting Byron in the funeral sermon at St. Philip's Church in Charleston on April 26, 1850, Miles predicted that the Nullifier's philosophical genius and moral character would secure him a position among "The dead but sceptered sovereigns, who still rule / Our spirits from their urns."[5]

The elaborate funeral ceremonies constituted a powerful expression of collective remembrance. Although Calhoun's daughter correctly observed that "almost all the great men of the country are buried on their own places," civic leaders in Charleston and Columbia pressed for interment in a location more accessible to the public. Floride Calhoun surrendered initial plans to bury her husband at their upcountry Fort Hill plantation and agreed to deposit his remains temporarily in the St. Philip's churchyard, pending final action by the state legislature. A cortège of six U.S. senators escorted the body from Washington to Charleston, accompanied by a committee of twenty-five South Carolinians. Governor Whitemarsh Seabrook signaled the state's unity by appointing men who had taken prominent positions on both sides of the bitter dispute between Nullifiers and Unionists in the early 1830s. Another committee of forty leading Charlestonians arranged the grandest civic procession in the city's history. The Washington delegation transferred custody of the iron coffin at the longtime city limits, on the green across Boundary Street, to an assembly that reportedly included "every white man in the city." The procession brought together officeholders, clergymen, militia units, fire companies, teachers and schoolchildren, members of at least thirty voluntary associations, sailors currently in port, and miscellaneous citizens. The line extended for a mile as it passed houses with windows respectfully closed and public buildings draped in mourning. The official report on the rite indicated that "no one was seen to gaze upon the spectacle." Calhoun became the first person to lay in state at Charleston City Hall. After the public paid its respects, two hundred members of an honor guard kept an overnight vigil. Business in town remained suspended the next day for the services at St. Philip's Church. Following Miles's sermon, pallbearers carried the coffin across the street to the newer section of the church cemetery. The proceedings closed with the interment beneath an unadorned stone inscribed simply "Calhoun."[6]

The performance of community was so stirring that participants sought to relive and share their vivid memories of the event. Boundary Street was promptly renamed Calhoun Street. Two Charleston residents painted a panoramic reproduction of the procession on twelve hundred feet of canvas, which they exhibited nightly to the accompaniment of a composition entitled "Calhoun's Funeral March." The city council commissioned G. P. A. Healy, who had previously painted Calhoun's portrait, to make a full-length canvas to hang in City Hall. The council asked Healy to depict the dying statesman "pronouncing his last discourse in the United States Senate." The council had already resolved to raise a monument to Calhoun in the center of the small park fronted by City Hall.[7]

The shadow of death colored reception of the first prospect for a permanent memorial, Hiram Powers's portrait statue of Calhoun. Several of the politician's supporters in Charleston banking circles had commissioned the work when Calhoun was preparing a bid for the 1844 Democratic presidential nomination. Powers put the project aside for several years, but in early April 1850, he announced his readiness to ship the statue from Italy. When this letter crossed the transatlantic tidings of Calhoun's death, Powers's portrait became to an exceptional degree emblematic of art as a form of afterlife. The funereal associations of the statue deepened when its cargo vessel foundered near Fire Island in July, resulting in the drowning of Margaret Fuller and her family. Divers soon salvaged the well-packaged marble, though one of its arms was broken off in the process.[8]

The effigy finally arrived in Charleston in mid-November, amid a new flurry of commemorative events. Calhoun's immediate institutional legacy, the Nashville Convention of southern states disturbed by the congressional debate over slavery in the federal territories, was holding its second session. The gathering would clearly achieve little, and a contest had already developed in South Carolina over the best response to the federal compromise legislation adopted in September. One faction argued that the Nashville Convention had proven cooperative strategies fruitless and that South Carolina should unilaterally secede from the Union; an opposing group advocated eventual secession but called for more time to rally the other slaveholding states. The stoutly cooperationist Charleston City Council had invited James Henry Hammond to deliver a Calhoun eulogy on November 21 to advance his bid for Calhoun's seat in the Senate. Governor Seabrook, a leading separatist, had invited fire-eater Robert Barnwell Rhett to deliver a competing address to the state legislature one week later, before it chose the emissary to Washington.

The delivery of Powers's portrait statue in this context dramatized the rebirth of Calhoun as an icon. One poet looked ahead hopefully to "Marble more quick than flesh—and Death more quick than life." South Carolinians outraged by the Compromise of 1850 found significance in the fracturing of the scroll inscribed, pursuant to Calhoun's instructions and in simulation of his handwriting, "Truth, Justice, and the Constitution." "The fate of this statue seems prophetic of the destiny of our country, more especially of the South," wrote financier Henry Gourdin, leader of the syndicate that had commissioned the statue. "Truth and Justice have been trodden in the dust by the late acts of Congress, and the Southern states will have very soon to make their choice of legislative annihilation & utter degradation, or a secession from the Union." The city council bought the statue from its sponsors and placed it on display in City Hall while making preliminary arrangements to install it permanently outdoors in a gaslit domed octagonal temple decorated by an interior frieze of the epic funeral procession.[9]

As the state divided sharply between cooperationists and separatists, Calhoun's body became the preeminent symbol of the sovereign unity of South Carolina. At the dedication of Magnolia Cemetery on November 19, cooperationist William Gilmore Simms presented a long poem, "The City of the Silent," that imagined the future of the rural cemetery as the successor to the mortuary achievements of Egyptian, Greek, and Roman civilizations. The climax to this vision was

> . . . the spire,
> White-shafted, 'neath the sun that glows like fire,
> Our city rear'd in sadness, but in pride,
> To one who, battling, in his harness died,
> Late for *his* glory,—for *our* peace too soon,
> The wondrous man of statesmen, our Calhoun!

The following week, Seabrook called on the legislature to purchase a four-acre lot in front of the statehouse and design a park around a suitable monument for Calhoun's remains. Sharing in the eagerness to manifest the dignity of South Carolina, the legislature authorized the construction of an entirely new capitol building. Remembrance of Calhoun figured prominently in the project from the beginning of construction in December 1851, when his valedictory speech in the U.S. Senate was the only document placed beneath the cornerstone. At Seabrook's request, the legislature also initiated state publication of Calhoun's long-awaited treatises on government, which promised extraordinary communications from the tomb.[10]

Fascination with the Nullifier's two bodies, his mortal remains and his sovereign state, undercut efforts to make Powers's statue the primary civic memorial. The sculptor emphasized Calhoun's representation of South Carolina by placing a marble palmetto tree alongside the statesman. But the composition eschewed any narrative of death and rebirth. Powers aimed to translate into stone Harriet Martineau's famous description of Calhoun as "the cast-iron man, who looks as if he had never been born, and could never be extinguished." He chose not to depict the flowing locks that animated Matthew Brady's widely reproduced photograph of Calhoun because "where all is angular and masculine, long hair is effeminate and soft; it does not accord with the 'cast-iron man.'"[11] Most important, Powers chose to present Calhoun in a toga. Like Antonio Canova's portrait of Washington in classical dress for the North Carolina capitol (1821) and Horatio Greenough's depiction of Washington as Zeus for the U.S. Capitol (1840), the strategy envisioned the cast-iron man as a timeless force exempt from history.

Although Powers's approach anticipated eulogists' praise for Calhoun as a model of Roman civic virtue, neoclassicism failed to satisfy local desires to situate the fallen hero and his secessionist polity squarely in the passage of time and particularly in the emergence of a fresh modernity. Frederick A. Porcher, professor of history and belles lettres at the College of Charleston, examined this failure in an essay for the *Southern Quarterly Review*, a journal edited by Simms. Powers may have rendered an accurate likeness of Calhoun's face and physique, Porcher acknowledged, but the sculptor had failed in the higher challenges of art. Those demands were to a considerable extent political. Arguing that "art can flourish as a living principle, only so far as it is popular," Porcher criticized the portrait for ignoring the time and place of the subject and the intended audience. "Our only hope of living in the future, is to live for our age, and in sympathy with it," the history professor observed. Calhoun had done so, but Powers had tried to set him in antiquity. Although aspiring to universality, the imitative strategy was pathetically provincial. Closer attention to locality would have informed a

Hiram Powers, Calhoun Statue, stereograph ca. 1860. Courtesy of the New York Public Library, New York.

broader interpretation, for Calhoun's "greatness was the reflection of the moral and intellectual excellence with which he was surrounded." A portrait of a hero "should strive to inweave his national character into his conception, and not assign to him a mere conventional greatness." Because Powers had worked in the visual equivalent of a dead language rather than the regenerative narrative of nature, his attempt to free Calhoun from mortality lacked vitality. "The first glance of curiosity satisfied, the statue stands unheeded, in the City Hall," Porcher reported, "and there it will stand, a monument of the public spirit of the citizens and of their disappointment. We have asked for our statesman, and have received a Roman Senator. . . . We have asked for our Calhoun, the Carolina planter, and have received an elaborately carved stone."[12]

Despite the momentum infused by the timing of its delivery, Powers's work slid toward fulfillment of Porcher's prediction. Critics scoffed at "the incongruous blending of the Roman toga with the palmetto" and ridiculed the statue as a depiction of Calhoun after emerging from his bath, wrapped in a sheet. The city government delayed for seven years before providing Powers with the casts necessary to repair the damage from the underwater salvage of the statue. A newspaper reporter described the work in 1857 as "broken and neglected." Plans for an elaborate outdoor setting quickly faded. Admiration for Calhoun helped to generate engravings of the statue and its reproduction in Parian ware on a small scale suitable for display at home.[13] But the marble effigy in City Hall was clearly unable to fill the void left by the body that had rested in state at the same site.

Early responses to Powers's statue coincided with an intensified political mobilization of Calhoun's luster. In addition to sending Rhett to the U.S. Senate, the state legislature provided for February 1851 elections to a state convention with authority to declare secession; it would meet after an anticipated January 1852 southern congress in Montgomery, Alabama, for which South Carolina would choose delegates in October 1851. Separatists swept the February 1851 elections, drawing organizational strength from the formation of Southern Rights Associations in many parishes and districts. They strenuously maintained that Calhoun would now support immediate secession if he were still alive. Rhett's organ, the *Charleston Mercury*, declared shortly after a statewide convention of Southern Rights Associations in May that "in the warfare which is impending . . . the name of Calhoun is destined to be a talisman." Cooperationists angrily replied that the godfather of the Nashville Convention had consistently favored southern coordination.[14] They prevailed in the October 1851 elections, which served as a referendum on the issue even though the Montgomery congress would never meet. The state convention in April 1852 ratified the defeat of the separatists. The Southern Rights Associations disbanded, and Rhett resigned from the Senate. In the wake of this failure, separatists sought to rehabilitate their movement by promoting a monument to Calhoun. They did not manage to replace their organizational infrastructure, but they formed alliances that opened a path in Charleston toward sponsorship of a Calhoun monument as a secessionist project.

The fire-eaters' campaign began only six weeks after the state convention with the formation of a Calhoun Monument Association in the separatist stronghold of St. John's Colleton Parish in June 1852. Most prominent among the founders was Whitemarsh Seabrook, who had left the governor's office at the expiration of his term in December 1850 and served as a separatist delegate to the April 1852 convention. The organization supported by his kinsmen and political allies built on his earlier proposal for a state monument to Calhoun. Sea Island planters encouraged the establishment of similar local groups that would meet in a central state association. The *Charleston Mercury* quickly hailed the effort as "the only feasible plan" to ensure "adornment of the grave of Calhoun." Copying a successful technique of the Southern Rights Associations, the newspaper pointed out that upcoming July 4 gatherings offered an ideal opportunity for communities to set up local Calhoun Monument Associations.[15]

The invitation mostly attracted other tarnished separatists. Calhoun Monument Associations sprang up in several more low-country parishes and a few inland districts that had supported separate action. Some moderates welcomed the conciliatory gesture. "Here is a matter upon which there surely cannot arise divisions among us," predicted the *Edgefield Advertiser*. "All will agree to honor our immortal Calhoun, and in honoring him, hands that have been estranged may clasp each other again, and hearts that have been severed, may mingle with the warmth and friendship of other and better days." But separatist dominance of the Southern Rights Associations too plainly portended similar manipulation of the Calhoun Monument Associations. After the call for a statewide meeting failed to muster interest, the planters of St. John's Colleton resolved in January 1853 to "regard with much regret the apathy and indifference which prevails in many parts of the State" and suspend operations.[16]

The Rhett faction shifted to a tactical variation focused on cooperationist Charleston. The urban alternative began in mid-February 1853 with a committee of militia and firefighting companies of the city rather than the grandees who organized the rural groups. The resulting Calhoun Monument Association of the Military and Fire Departments of Charleston (CMAC), formally established on the third anniversary of Calhoun's funeral, featured some of the most conspicuous separatists in town. The first corresponding secretary was twenty-five-year-old William R. Taber Jr., co-owner of the *Mercury* and nephew of Robert Barnwell Rhett as well as captain of the Charleston Riflemen. Warmly endorsed by the *Mercury*, the CMAC aimed to energize the formation of monument associations across the state. Unlike previous plans to rely on a statewide convention to choose the site of the monument, however, the CMAC constitution committed the group to a memorial in or near Charleston.[17] This policy put more pressure on local cooperationists and Unionists to support the tribute. The maneuver promised momentum but risked the possibility that the intervening Charlestonians would redefine the meaning of the project.

Organization of the CMAC around militia and fire companies envisioned affirmation of long-standing South Carolina leadership by the most dynamic demographic forces in the city. German-born John A. Wagener and Irish-born Edward F. Sweegan, active members of the CMAC who figured prominently in municipal politics after the Civil War, personified the antebellum tide of immigration into Charleston partly mirrored in its military and fire units. The population of foreign-born workers increased 25 percent during the 1850s, while the agricultural boom in the South Carolina hinterland and even more in the cotton-growing states further west pulled almost half of the city slaves out of the urban economy. Charleston was becoming a wage-labor island in an intensively enslaved state. German artisans and Irish workers often competed with the peculiar institution rather than re-inforcing it. Immigrants also offered a solid base for politicians interested in aligning with the national Democratic Party. Led by upcountryman James Orr, this movement gained traction after the secessionist-cooperationist debates of 1850–52. The emphasis on protecting slavery through the Demo-cratic Party implied much more patience with Unionism than did the co-operationism of southern nationalists like Simms, who merely sought time to build popular support for independence. The chief representative of immigrant political strength in Charleston in the 1850s would be Charles Macbeth, who was elected mayor one year after he joined the South Caro-lina delegation to the Democratic presidential nominating convention of 1856. In encouraging immigrants to honor Calhoun, the champion of non-affiliation with national parties, secessionists sought to counter social and political trends that threatened to make cooperationist Charleston even warier of radicalism. The commemorative initiative was in this respect a celebratory parallel to Leonidas Spratt's provocative campaign to reopen the African slave trade, also launched in Charleston in 1853.[18]

Even more important, the formation of the CMAC linked the separatist initiative to a set of overwhelmingly cooperationist merchants and profes-sionals interested in the development of Charleston. Several CMAC leaders had close ties to the South Carolina Institute for the Promotion of Art, Me-chanical Ingenuity, and Industry. Both the second and third CMAC presi-dents, attorney Wilmot Gibbes DeSaussure and cotton factor Francis James Porcher, were founding directors of the institute. Organized in 1849 with pioneer southern industrialist William Gregg as president, the institute aspired to serve as a hothouse for the economic modernization of the state and especially the city. That goal was related to the demographic transfor-mation of Charleston, as entrepreneurs expected the diversified economy to provide work for the increasingly white population. The institute's chief activity was a large annual fair for the display of industrial and artisanal products. Shortly after the sensational Crystal Palace exposition in Lon-don in 1851, the institute began to build an up-to-date exhibition facility featuring extensive use of cast iron, glass, and gas lighting. The designer of the spacious showcase was the institute secretary, Edward C. Jones, the dominant Charleston architect of Victorian modernity. He had already supervised the construction of such urban harbingers as the South Carolina Railroad Depot (1849), the grounds of Magnolia Cemetery (1850), the Browning and Leman department store (1852), and Roper Hospital (1850–53). Public monuments similarly defined the mid-nineteenth-century metropolis, and Jones not surprisingly had put forward a plan for a Calhoun memorial.[19]

The commitment to build the monument in Charleston broadened ideological support for the project. Richard Yeadon, co-proprietor and Whiggish former editor of the *Charleston Courier,* had not joined the *Mercury* in touting the formation of Calhoun Memorial Associations around the state. With the establishment of the CMAC, however, the energetic city promoter entered the campaign. At a meeting of the Fellowship Society, an artisans' benevolent club for which he served as president, Yeadon urged a donation to the memorial fund while noting that he and Calhoun had disagreed on almost all political issues. The project was of "vast importance," the *Courier* explained shortly afterward, because it would "fix and mark the public taste" with a timely demonstration of mature civic self-perception. "We are fast advancing towards the monumental age of civilization," observed the newspaper, "towards that stage of progress at which monuments become necessary to any free, intelligent people, who have had a past worth commemorating, or whose condition offers guarantees for a future."[20]

The proposed Calhoun Monument assumed a central place among efforts during the 1850s to construct South Carolinian identity through history and culture. It shared in the impulse behind the founding of Magnolia Cemetery, the building of the new statehouse and its embellishment with a memorial to the casualties of the Palmetto Regiment in the Mexican War, the 1855 cornerstone-laying ceremony for a monument at the Kings Mountain battlefield of the Revolutionary War, the dedication of a monument to the Washington Light Infantry at Cowpens a year later, the creation of the South Carolina Historical Society in 1855, and the organization of the Carolina Art Association in 1857. These initiatives supplied institutional leverage for South Carolina nationalism but did not appeal exclusively to radicals. The founding members of the South Carolina Historical Society included Unionist attorney James Louis Petigru as well as ardent secessionists Simms and Frederick Porcher.[21]

After the failure of a proposal for legislative funding of the monument in December 1853, the CMAC expanded its publicity efforts while northern outrage over the Kansas-Nebraska legislation returned sectional tensions to fever pitch.[22] The association adopted Calhoun's birthday as an anniversary meeting date and organized a large rally on March 18, 1854, that began with a parade designed to shift memory of Calhoun's funeral procession into a more festive register. Charleston state senator William D. Porter, a cooperationist who had not entirely forsworn support for the national Democratic Party, delivered the inaugural address. The CMAC also continued to look statewide for financial support. The group issued "An Appeal to the Planters of Carolina in Behalf of the Calhoun Monument" that urged "the wealth of the state" to match the efforts under way in Massachusetts and Kentucky to honor Webster and Clay. Drafted by twenty-nine-year-old John W. R. Pope, the son of a planter in St. Helena Parish, the circular noted that the CMAC consisted "mostly of young men whose means are therefore limited." Pope echoed the argument that recognition as an advanced civilization depended on the construction of memorials, but he emphasized that this test challenged the entire state. Calhoun was "not the particular representative of Charleston," Pope pointed out. He maintained that "we would not, if we could, have the Monument built by Charleston means and men alone."[23]

The CMAC also called attention to the project by making pivotal decisions about its location and design. Although the city council had previously planned to place a Calhoun monument in the small square next to City Hall, in July 1854 the council approved the CMAC's request to install its monument in White Point Garden. Laid out in the late 1830s, the elegant park on the waterfront Battery was the favorite promenade ground of Charleston elites. Children strolling with their parents would learn to look up to Calhoun. The landmark toward which ships headed in approaching Charleston from the sea, White Point Garden offered symbolic as well as aesthetic potential. Pope told the planters that "the great scene of commercial labor and wealth is thus kept perpetually under the eye of him, who for many long years was the acknowledged master-spirit of the free trade policy."[24] At the same time, the selected site at the foot of Meeting Street promised to punctuate a vista along a primary avenue, in keeping with principles of urban planning emanating from Paris.

The CMAC conducted a design competition when it arranged the site of the monument. The seven entries included three proposals that clearly understood the commission to include a crypt for Calhoun; the other proposals were vague on that possibility. Almost half of the designs were settings for Powers's statue or a copy of it. Classical architectural vocabulary was pervasive, but no more so than what the firm of Barbot and Seyle called "*bold, if not outré*" incorporation of the South Carolina palmetto. The winning design came from Edward C. Jones and his junior partner, Francis D.

Edward C. Jones and Francis D. Lee, design for monument to Calhoun.
Harper's New Monthly Magazine, June 1857, 21. Courtesy of the South
Caroliniana Library, University of South Carolina, Columbia.

Lee. They proposed a Doric column with a suggested height of 150 feet,
topped by a 20-foot-tall statue of Calhoun delivering a speech. Decorating
the base were emblematic statues of Wisdom, Justice, Truth, and Firmness.
The plan struck a balance between the priorities of the Rhett and institute
factions of the CMAC. The waterfront allusion to northern tariff oppression
echoed fire-eaters' rhetoric. The interpretation of "simple dignity" reflected
a contemporary sensibility. In contrast with Powers's rigidly allegorical re-
publicanism, Jones and Lee sought a more eclectic historicism featuring
"new combinations of long established classical forms and proportions."
The ancient association of columns with military victory notwithstanding, the Charleston architects sought to unify CMAC secessionists behind a
political symbol that Pope described as "the finger of might and strength,

pointing to high and holy efforts, to Heaven for the issue, the great issue, with which our destiny seems involved."[25]

With an estimated cost of between eighty thousand dollars and one hundred thousand dollars, the proposed Calhoun Monument was a highly ambitious undertaking for a state that had not raised any significant outdoor public monuments since the colonial legislature commissioned a statue of William Pitt after the Stamp Act controversy. In addition to his faith in planters' gratitude for the Nullifier's representation, Pope pinned his confidence in the enterprise on the CMAC's latest partner. The organized assistance of Charleston women had "given a new impulse to the work," he reported.[26] He did not yet foresee that this ally would take over and recast the commemorative project.

The LCMA enjoyed strong ties to the sponsors of Powers's statue and shared the modernizing tendencies of the South Carolina Institute for the Promotion of Art, Mechanical Ingenuity, and Industry. The LCMA took a fresh approach, however, to the primary challenge of the Calhoun Monument, the construction of a Confederate public. Powers's portrait attempted to model that public by presenting Calhoun as an exemplar of republican virtue. The monument proposed by Jones and Lee identified the plantation economy as the foundation and fortress of community identity. The LCMA advanced secessionist nationalism less through education in personal character or protection of material interests than through facilitation of social relations. Recognizing that the process of making a monument partly defines its meaning, the women adopted a fund-raising strategy that not only generated resources but also fostered a local culture of sociability and entertainment accessible without private invitation. They placed their monument in a new zone of cross-class urban interaction and stimulation that promised to become the heart of the expanding city. Their site also underscored the ideal of paternalism that they expected would maintain private and public order in the slaveholders' confederacy. They struggled to find a satisfying form for their monument, in part because they never reconciled their plans for a dynamic public space with the hypnotic aura of death that remained integral to Calhoun's symbolic significance. Although they had not yet commissioned a design, they took pride in December 1860 that they had helped to make the most fitting and important monument to Calhoun, an independent southern nation.

The formation of the LCMA in January 1854 did not merely reflect the emergence of the CMAC. None of the LCMA's antebellum leaders was married to or immediately related to an officer of the CMAC. The LCMA's organizational roots could more accurately be traced to the Ladies Benevolent Society, the traditional charitable vehicle of elite local women; eminent historians of antebellum Charleston report that the organization "resembled a modern-day Junior League."[27] Fifty years old in 1854, Juliana Conner was one of the senior Ladies Benevolent Society members active in the LCMA; her husband, Henry Workman Conner, was president of the Bank of Charleston during the 1840s and president of the South Carolina Railroad during the early 1850s. Other links between the women's organizations included LCMA president Mary Robertson, whose husband was a wealthy cotton broker and commission merchant; Emmeline Porter, sister-in-law of state senator William D. Porter; and Mary Yeadon, wife of Richard Yeadon. The most active alumnae of the Ladies Benevolent Society were thirty-four-year-old Mary Amarinthia Yates, the longtime treasurer and final president of the LCMA, and her older sister, Isabel Sarah Snowden. Their brother was the long-standing chaplain of the Charleston Port Society, another prominent welfare organization. Despite its prestige, the Ladies Benevolent Society was waning in energy by the early 1850s as its program of family visiting gave way to increased municipal responsibility for indigent white residents, a rising proportion of whom were Irish immigrants. The shift from charity to commemoration offered the women an opportunity to remain collaboratively engaged in civic voluntarism and regulation of social norms.[28]

The selection of collective memory as a new outlet had specific origins in a highly publicized women's initiative. It was no coincidence that Yates first assembled the founders of the LCMA in her Church Street drawing room a few weeks after Ann Pamela Cunningham, writing to the *Mercury* as "A Southern Matron," launched her campaign to save "the home and grave" of George Washington. Yates had attended Elias Marks's seminary at Barhamville with Cunningham, whose mother urged Yates to lead the Mount Vernon campaign in Charleston. A commission as Cunningham's lieutenant did not entice Yates, whom one Calhoun Monument worker later described as "always distracted with many projects, trying to work everything her own way . . . the very quintessence of excitement." Ideologically, Yates's countermove repudiated the Unionist symbolism of Mount Vernon, underscored in South Carolina by the close friendship between Cunningham and Benjamin F. Perry. The LCMA's initial appeal "To the Women of Carolina," written by promising young author Esther B. Cheesborough, paralleled

Cunningham's letter "To the Ladies of the South" by summoning women to remedy a failure of the legislative process, describing the undertaking as an extension of traditional female duties to preserve burial sites, and pointing to commemoration as an opportunity to instill virtue in children. "Let us not suffer Calhoun to sleep any longer beneath the lowly tomb that covers him," Cheesborough implored.[29]

The CMAC welcomed the LCMA chivalrously but assumed that the women would remain in a subordinate fund-raising role. In the March 1854 inaugural festivities, the city's fire companies, militia units, and other male voluntary associations paraded through the streets while LCMA members waited in a theater. The CMAC did not solicit the views of the LCMA or any of the rural associations in choosing the White Point Garden site for the monument or selecting the design proposed by Jones and Lee.[30]

The LCMA in turn maintained institutional separation from the CMAC, which the women utterly outpaced in fund-raising. The CMAC soon began to importune the LCMA to merge. The committee of fifteen men appointed by the women for these negotiations illuminated the differences between the organizations. The LCMA's advisers were a much older and more powerful group than the fire and militia officers. The youngest member of the LCMA committee was Charleston mayor William Porcher Miles. In addition to Conner, Porter, and Yeadon, the key figure was cotton factor Henry Gourdin, a founder and longtime director of the Bank of Charleston and currently president of the ambitious Blue Ridge Railroad, which renewed Charleston efforts to establish direct commercial connections with the Ohio River Valley. Gourdin and his brother, Robert Newman Gourdin, confirmed bachelors who lived and worked together, were active in the French Protestant (Huguenot) Church that Amarinthia Yates also attended. Several influential members of the gentlemen's committee maintained commitments to the Charleston Orphan House that paralleled the LCMA's ties to the Ladies Benevolent Society. Henry Alexander DeSaussure, solicitor of the State Bank, served as chair of the orphanage board of commissioners for twenty-seven years. Rice-milling magnate W. Jefferson Bennett was equally active in the institution. His adoptive brother, attorney Christopher Memminger, was the most celebrated example of a promising child brought from the Orphan House into an elite Charleston family.[31] Politically, the predominantly cooperationist group was staunchly opposed to the Rhett faction. James Conner, the son of Juliana and Henry W. Conner, served as second for Edward Magrath when the federal judge's brother killed William R. Taber Jr. in a September 1856 duel over *Mercury* attacks on Andrew Magrath for his willingness to work with the national Democratic Party. Fire-eating separatist John Cunningham, an officer of the CMAC, served as second for Taber.[32]

The LCMA's fund-raising success reflected not merely its wealthy patrons but also the women's efforts to draw the monument from a rewarding urban culture. Unlike the CMAC, the LCMA made no special appeal to the planters whose economic interests Calhoun had defended in Washington. The LCMA established a statewide board of directresses and welcomed contributions from every part of South Carolina, but the organization sought primarily to mobilize local residents rather than concentrate the resources of a broader area in the city. All of the officers lived in Charleston, and city residents provided well over half of all contributions received by the LCMA from 1854 to 1861. The women announced even small donations with a flourish in the *Courier* and *Mercury*, using the local print realm to invite imaginative participation in common experiences and sentiments. A typical acknowledgment in July 1857 reported that "a small, but patriotic party which celebrated the glorious Fourth amid the cool breezes of Morris' Island, alike honored the day and themselves by subscribing eleven dollars toward the Calhoun monument." The recognition of informal, temporary gatherings envisioned a more fluid urban life than the CMAC's strategy of building on firmly established civic organizations. The LCMA created collective identity among local youth by encouraging all schoolchildren to contribute fifty cents to the monument. Eager to keep pace with their peers, even James Petigru's grandchildren begged a few coins from the anti-Nullifier for the campaign.[33]

Donations from all sources comprised a smaller share of the LCMA's revenues than the money the women generated by organizing fund-raising events. Benefit performances presented the city as a site of evanescent but elevating social interactions and figured the monument as the culmination of a cultural effusion. These programs brought together diverse segments of the community. Irish expatriate Thomas Francis Meagher traveled from New York to deliver a public lecture with particular appeal for immigrant Charlestonians. The great Norwegian violinist Ole Bull filled the South Carolina Institute exposition hall for one of antebellum Charleston's most memorable concerts, which included a fantasia on the theme of Calhoun. In addition to demonstrating the appeal of the monument for celebrated romantic nationalists like Meagher and Bull, the benefit performances showcased local talent, including vocalists John Sloman and his daughters, Elizabeth and Ann, who taught music and performed regularly in town. In March 1855, the Charleston Theatre staged a premiere production of *Michael Bonham*, a play about a native South Carolinian in the Texas Revolution that William Gilmore Simms had written in 1844 in support of Calhoun's efforts as secretary of state to annex the independent slaveholding republic. Simms further contributed to the evening an introductory ode to Calhoun, which opened with the observation that "Nations themselves are but the monuments / Of deathless men." The LCMA's fundraising strategy suggested that its national monument would be in part a tribute to the Charleston audiences that came together around creative work.[34]

The LCMA made more than 40 percent of its entire revenue at two "Floral Fairs" held at the South Carolina Institute Hall in May 1855 and May 1859. Ladies' fund-raising fairs had become familiar in Charleston by the 1850s after gaining popularity much earlier in the North, but the LCMA's bazaars were the most sophisticated events of their kind in the antebellum South, the closest proslavery parallels to the combination of theatricality and ideology that characterized the innovative fairs sponsored by the Massachusetts Female Anti-Slavery Society. Institute Hall pulsed with spectacular decorations and *tableaux vivants* as well as an extensive assortment of items available for purchase. An in-house post office enabled "bashful lovers to convey to their sweethearts the presents suggested by their affections." A raffle offered chances to win a set of silver. The LCMA toasted its patron saint by selling a painting of Calhoun, portrait busts of Calhoun (including one made from cast iron), an edition of Calhoun's works, and "a full variety of leaves and flowers from the grave of Calhoun, arranged like Mosaics." Even more than the LCMA's benefit performances, the festive emporium described Charleston as a kaleidoscopic urban assembly. The opening night for the 1859 bazaar attracted a crowd estimated at two thousand, maintained steadily by the cycle of arrivals and departures.[35] A Calhoun monument funded by these means would represent the permanent self-renewal of the nineteenth-century city.

Women's leadership was an important aspect of that urban modernity. A privileged bourgeoisie expanding on conventional gender roles, LCMA members stood prominently at the forefront of southern women's participation in public affairs. Cheesborough later recalled that "our grandmothers had confined their monumental efforts to the family graveyard, and some thought that their granddaughters had better do the same." LCMA leaders were quick to provide reassurance that they were "not prone to the errors and heresies and vagaries, which have in some regions seduced woman from her own and her gracefully occupied sphere" and that the monument initiative was "not simply a pretext or occasion for public display, or for an invasion of a province distinctively assigned to the sterner sex." The women referred crucial decisions to their gentlemen friends and arranged for male endorsement of the floral fairs. Commentators expressed no alarm about a transgression of gender norms despite the proven potential for political argument in Calhoun commemoration. Charleston men welcomed women to the project with blithe expectations that "their noble and lovely example should prick the sides of masculine intent, and lead to the speedy completion of a monument." The main precedent for this confidence, the Bunker Hill fund-raising campaign led by *Godey's Lady's Book* editor Sarah Josepha Hale, was a prime example of self-consciously contemporary Victorian womanhood.[36]

In addition to clarifying women's civic sphere, the LCMA's efforts encouraged reconsideration of republican reservations about public monuments. When a professor at the Arsenal Academy in Columbia edited a collection of Calhoun eulogies, he appended the well-worn observation that the indestructible, circulating book was "perhaps better than even a 'starry-pointing pyramid.'" He nevertheless donated to the LCMA all profits from *The Carolina Tribute to Calhoun* (1857).[37] More controversial was the bid launched in March 1857 by James Gadsden, a student at Yale with Calhoun and recent U.S. minister to Mexico, to "perpetuate the memory of the *Carolinian Lycurgus*" by using the LCMA's fund to endow a school of political science. Newspapers printed many similar letters over the next year. Proponents maintained that Calhoun doubtless would have preferred a school to a monument. They also attacked nonutilitarian memorials more broadly. "The subject of monuments is, perhaps of all others, the most unsettled and unsatisfactory," one debater sweepingly asserted. Advocates of a memorial school scoffed that "a merely obituary monument, rather physical than intellectual, more form than substance, is anything, nothing, was Jove yesterday, is St. Peter today." But public monuments were multiplying in Baltimore, Richmond, and Savannah as well as New York and Washington. When Simms wrote an article in a national magazine in June 1857 observing that "there are two very distinct cities in Charleston—the old and the new—representing rival communities," he concluded his introduction to the new Charleston with a report on the effort to build a Calhoun monument.[38]

The LCMA ended this debate in May 1858 by announcing its intention to dedicate the cornerstone of the monument on June 28. The event aimed to "give a new impulse to subscriptions" and demonstrate the potential of a civic monument to realize the sponsors' vision for Charleston and the projected southern nation.[39] Unlike the CMAC, the women did not rush into selecting a design for their memorial. The focal features at this point were the selected site, chosen by a committee of gentlemen, and the exercises of the day. Like the successful fund-raising strategy, these expressions of the LCMA's mission identified the city as a model for slaveholders' independent confederacy.

Rejecting White Point Garden as "a mere pleasure promenade," the LCMA resolved to build its monument at Citadel Square rather than the Battery location chosen by the CMAC. The decision recalled the funeral of April 1850, as this ground was the site at which South Carolina ceremoniously received Calhoun's body from the cortège appointed by the U.S. Senate. Citadel Square was also a showcase for civic ambitions that looked inward rather than out toward the harbor. A few months after Calhoun's funeral, the city annexed four wards north of the former Boundary Street, doubling the size of the municipality. Citadel Square became the center of town. Simms called it "the only public square in Charleston that merits the title."[40] His standard reflected the revival of large urban piazzas illustrated by the recent completion of Union Square in New York and Trafalgar Square in London. The LCMA looked to the Calhoun Monument to unify the conceptual as well as visual strands that intersected to form this public space.

Framed by King Street on its western side, Citadel Square was the pedestrian delta for the trendiest and most intellectually stimulating shopping district in the city. In April 1838, one of the worst fires in Charleston history destroyed almost all property along King Street in the half mile leading to the square as well as acres to the east. Abundant state financial assistance facilitated rapid redevelopment. By the 1850s, the five blocks on King Street running north from the Browning and Leman department store to Citadel Square represented the vanguard of urban retail culture. Leading establishments included Russell's bookstore, George S. Cook's photography gallery, the Siegling Music House, and the silversmith and jewelry firm of Hayden, Gregg, and Company as well as a variety of other boutiques and the elegant American Hotel. Radcliffeborough, located across King Street to the northwest of Citadel Square, became a fashionable residential neighborhood at the same time, although the vicinity of the square remained home to many artisans, shopkeepers, and laborers. As a venue for cross-class urban sociability, the site chosen for the Calhoun Monument was the topographic equivalent of the benefit performances and floral fairs sponsored by the LCMA.[41]

Backed on its northern edge by a state military academy, Citadel Square took its name from an institution with several levels of significance for a Calhoun memorial. South Carolina began the facility as the Arsenal in direct response to the Denmark Vesey conspiracy of 1822. In addition to dramatizing the readiness of white Charlestonians to suppress slave uprisings, the Arsenal became closely associated with Nullification doctrine after the state replaced its federal garrison with South Carolina militia at the height of the tariff crisis. The elaborate "States Rights Ball" held at the Arsenal in March 1831 and "Volunteer Ball" of March 1833 deepened this connection; the latter event drew two thousand South Carolinians. The state military academy chartered in 1842 further layered a defense of South Carolina sovereignty atop the defense of slavery. The LCMA proposed to place the monument's cornerstone fifty feet from the front gate of the school, where the women hoped the Calhoun Monument would soon "speak eloquently to the youths of the Citadel, prompting them to emulate the virtues of the great statesman." The didactic goal extended to other nearby institutions, as Citadel Square anchored an educational district that also included the College of Charleston, the male High School of Charleston, and the Girls' High School and Normal School. This clustering, which complemented administrative and financial and welfare zones elsewhere, demonstrated Charleston officials' pioneering efforts to establish coherence in the increasingly complex nineteenth-century cityscape.[42]

Overlooking the western edge of Citadel Square was the bell tower of another vital educational counterpart to the LCMA's proposed monument, the Charleston Orphan House. The rebuilding of the facility during 1853–55 was the most significant public construction project in the city during the late antebellum era. More than any other institution, it encapsulated the ideal of paternalism cherished by elite Charlestonians. Here the master class promised to care for needy white children and admit deserving youths into the privileged circle. The LCMA similarly relied on Calhoun to merge polity and the family. Despite the Nullifier's fascination with constitutional theory, the women maintained that his true importance was "not identified with the prevalence or acceptance of any political dogma or philosophical tenets." He personified the southern nationalist impulse because his domesticity defined his patriotism. According to the LCMA, he "loved his country—his whole country—but God had given him the heart which sees and feels entirely and overpoweringly the nearer and in some respects plainer and humbler duties which begin at home and radiate in widening embraces." An organization grounded in the Ladies Benevolent Society and advised by directors of the Orphan House logically sought a monument that used familial authority to organize the public.[43]

The largest donation received by the LCMA suggested the resonance of this conjunction. William J. Rivers had been placed in the Orphan House at the age of nine when his father died; his mother soon moved into the facility as a nurse and continued to live there after Rivers attracted a patron who provided for his education. He joined in founding the South Carolina Historical Society shortly before assuming the professorship in Greek literature at South Carolina College, where he liked to compare his native polity to the slaveholding city-state of Athens. After the LCMA announced the site of its monument, Rivers pledged a contribution of one thousand dollars to the project but asked to remain anonymous. The women reported that their benefactor was not rich but "the recipient of a salary," encouraging other members of the middle class to support the celebration of the Charleston social structure.[44]

Calhoun particularly personified application of the paternalist ideal to defend slavery as not merely a problematic inheritance but what he labeled "a positive good." He stressed that the bondage of blacks fostered cordial class relations among whites. From slaves' standpoint as well, he told the U.S. Senate, "every plantation is a little community, with the master at its head, who concentrates in himself the united interests of capital and labor, of which he is the common representative." To ratify this illusion, the managers of the April 1850 funeral invited local African Americans to participate in the proceedings. Swedish traveler Fredrika Bremer, who attended the procession, reported that some black Charlestonians rejoiced openly at the event because "Calhoun was indeed a wicked man, for he wished that we might remain slaves." The *Mercury*, in contrast, claimed that African Americans "embraced . . . with considerable numbers" the privilege of visiting the coffin. The LCMA's planned monument would similarly stand for tacit black acquiescence in the racial order. This implication was especially vivid because the area around Citadel Square recently annexed by the city was disproportionately populated by free people of color deemed threatening to the slave regime. One goal of the annexation was to consolidate local regulation of white supremacism.[45]

The LCMA's site also symbolized the slaveholder vigilance that balanced paternalism. Apart from the Citadel complex that stirred memories of Denmark Vesey, the new commercial development on King Street re-

minded white Charlestonians of widespread suspicions that black arson-
ists had started the devastating 1838 fire. In this respect, the bell tower of
the Orphan House was again an architectural pendant to the shaft that
LCMA supporters envisioned. The central addition of the mid-1850s renovation stood ready to sound the alarm against the twin dangers of rebellion
and fire. The cupola echoed the bell tower of St. Michael's Church, located
a mile away, which tolled the evening curfew for African Americans and
housed the overnight watch. The figure of Calhoun, alert during his career
to any antislavery threat, promised to complement an infrastructure of sur-
veillance threaded artistically but insistently through the expanding city.

The LCMA planned the cornerstone-laying ceremony as carefully as it
chose the site for the monument. The women did not hold the event on
Calhoun's birthday in March, which had achieved so much currency that
South Carolina College students rioted in 1858 when the school failed to
honor the occasion with a holiday. Nor did the LCMA observe the anniversary of Calhoun's funeral in April. The organization instead chose Palmetto Day, a commemoration of the successful patriot resistance on June
28, 1776, to British naval bombardment of a makeshift Sullivan's Island
fortress faced with spongy palmetto logs that absorbed cannonballs. An
event with no direct connection to Calhoun's life, Palmetto Day nonetheless perfectly suited the LCMA's purposes. Slipping into desuetude until the
sectional conflicts of the 1820s, the anniversary became a durable organ
for political historicism in Charleston during the Nullification controversy.
The festival's secessionist implications intensified sharply after state militia officer William E. Martin delivered a confrontational June 1850 address
that prompted the local U.S. Army commander to ban future observances
of Palmetto Day at the federal post on Sullivan's Island. The LCMA's plans
for a spectacular celebration in June 1858 tapped into a vehicle of South
Carolina identity that southern nationalists largely dominated. Moreover,
the identification of Calhoun with the Revolutionary festival effectively
conflated the Nullifier's legalistic doctrines with the popular legacy of the
Declaration of Independence, renewed annually in the week after Palmetto
Day. The timing of the cornerstone-laying suggested that secession might
advance simultaneously as a constitutional procedure and a revolutionary
right of self-determination.[46]

The ceremonies implementing this plan combined solemnity and festivity. Henry Gourdin's committee on arrangements named Martin chief
marshal of the parade. The line reversed the steps of Calhoun's funeral
march by moving from the Battery to Citadel Square. Diarist Jacob

Schirmer called it "one of the grandest processions we have ever had." Looking back at the occasion a quarter century later, Cheesborough recalled that "Charleston saw what it had never seen before and what it has never seen since—a woman's procession, all the ladies forming it being in carriages." The LCMA continued its program of urban sociability by sponsoring a Calhoun Promenade Concert. The organization placed in the hollow cornerstone a cannonball recovered from the palmetto fort on Sullivan's Island, a lock of Calhoun's hair, and a banner carried by Port Society mariners during the funeral procession. Supporters exulted afterward that memories of Calhoun and Revolutionary heroes "are henceforth indissolubly united."[47]

Like the decision to hold the ceremony on Palmetto Day, the selection of Lawrence Keitt as principal orator signaled rapprochement between the LCMA and key separatists of the early 1850s. Keitt was one of the most fervent fire-eaters. He shared ground with the cooperationist program of public education, however, in advocating disunion as a cultural imperative rather than a mere remedy for violation of the federal compact. Congratulating Charleston on its "spirit of useful embellishment," he suggested that erection of a monument showed readiness to make a permanent public commitment. The Union was rapidly becoming an instrument for destruction of slaveholders' rights. The South was "wandering to the goal of her destiny, and she should look only to the eternal landmarks which beckon her onward."

The Calhoun Monument was the ideal landmark for this purpose. "One of those witnesses to whom God sometimes calls out from the crowd to testify to truth," the Nullifier was a romantic personification of antimajoritarianism. He was a sublime genius, blessed with such originality that "the glorious 'substance of things,' hoped for and unseen by others, hourly passed athwart the disc of his mighty intellect, like high-soaring eagles across the surface of a noon-day sun." He courageously championed his moral discoveries despite the petty envy of rivals, and he disdained the political opportunism that permitted his inferiors to advance. The public monument suited his greatness, for it was through the "instructive wrecks" of such artifacts that glorious ancient civilizations revealed themselves to posterity. Like the classical monuments revered by the educated, Calhoun would "rise above the tide of ages, incessantly swelling behind us, and ever defy that level which merges in the waters of oblivion the lower summits of the past."[48]

The LCMA's failure to settle on a monument design during the eighteen months after the cornerstone ceremony revealed an ambivalence in the

secessionist imagination. New York sculptor Henry Kirke Brown felt confident for a while that his sketch of Calhoun in modern dress would win him
the commission for a heroic portrait. He bragged to his wife that his model
was "universally known to be not only better than that made by Powers,
but the best thing which has been made in the country." Gourdin's advisory
committee did recommend in the spring of 1859 that the LCMA order "a
colossal bronze statue of Mr. Calhoun standing on a base of South Carolina
granite." But the proposal languished, and Brown instead devoted himself
to a parallel project, the design of an elaborate pedimental sculpture for the
new statehouse in Columbia intended to celebrate slave labor as the foundation of South Carolina prosperity and social order. The chief obstacle to
the plans of Brown and Gourdin was that many Charlestonians still looked
to the LCMA to replace the provisional grave in the St. Philip's churchyard.
Prominent local architect Edward Brickell White offered a new design for
a grand mausoleum in August 1859. Such a course would require legislative
approval and additional funds. A measure to appropriate fifty thousand
dollars for a monument failed in the next legislative session, its doubtful
prospects further dimmed by increased expenditures for the new statehouse and military preparations for secession. Eager to instantiate nationhood through monuments to urban modernity and heroic mortality, the
LCMA did not complete either.[49]

The triumph of secession in 1860, in which many friends of the LCMA
played leading parts, demonstrated enthusiasm for all available Calhoun
monuments. A delegate to the Democratic National Convention in Charleston, brought by local hosts to Calhoun's grave, later recalled that he was "expected to feel a due sense of his inferiority to the natives of the soil, which
the presence of that superhuman individual had made more sacred than
aught else of Mother Earth." When the state secession convention met at
South Carolina Institute Hall, the banner that hung behind the president's
chair featured a picture of Powers's portrait statue standing atop the South
Carolina keystone of a cooperationist Confederate arch formed by blocks
inscribed with the name of each slaveholding state. Observers noted that
the LCMA had achieved its ultimate objective if not its immediate aim. The
Courier asked "what nobler monument to Calhoun could any wish, however, than a Southern league or Confederacy of independent, equal states,
embodying and developing in all their bountiful beauty of significance the
great cardinal truths of government and political science which Calhoun
living taught . . . and Calhoun dying bequeathed." When the state convention adopted the Ordinance of Secession, a correspondent to the Mercury

suggested that Charleston should mark the historic day with "the sublime moral effect" of a formal civic procession to Calhoun's tomb.[50]

Identification of the Confederacy as a monument to Calhoun added to a set of related Charleston tributes that included the grave in St. Philip's churchyard, the statue by Powers in City Hall, and the LCMA fund, valued at $39,610 in March 1861.[51] The Civil War would test South Carolinians' ability to protect all of these secessionist commemorations.

Confederates honored Calhoun as a precursor surpassed only by Washington. The pairing was apt, for Calhoun's final Senate address had demanded recognition of the slaveholding Mount Vernon planter as "an illustrious Southerner" after Henry Clay appealed to Unionist sentiment by brandishing a fragment from Washington's coffin at the peroration of the speech introducing the compromise measures of 1850.[52] But Washington and Calhoun offered different prototypes for Confederate nationalism. Reverence for Washington described the rebellion as a reenactment of the American Revolution and a return to the pure intentions of the founding generation. Northerners sidestepped debate over those claims by focusing on Calhoun as the malignant spirit behind disunion. When southern military fortunes crumbled, Calhoun offered an intersectional symbol of what the Confederacy had defended and lost.

Confederate remembrance of Calhoun took many forms. One entrepreneur offered to donate land near Montgomery, Alabama, for the construction of a capital city to be called Calhoun. Half of the states in the Confederacy already had counties named in his honor, which gave rise to many military units with designations like the Calhoun Avengers and the Calhoun Rifles. South Carolina, which did not yet have a Calhoun County, fielded the Calhoun Light Infantry, Calhoun Troop, Calhoun Minute Men, Calhoun Mounted Men, Calhoun Mountaineers, Calhoun Artillery, Calhoun Flying Artillery, and a half dozen sets of Calhoun Guards. The CSS *Calhoun* served as a Confederate privateer and later as a commissioned gunboat. Copies of Matthew Brady's daguerreotype appeared on Confederate currency, Confederate bonds, and an unissued Confederate penny stamp. Engravings after Powers's portrait statue decorated bonds issued by the Confederacy and notes issued by the Bank of the State of South Carolina.[53]

The LCMA became a more oblique source of Calhoun remembrance by developing into an organizational template for Confederate womanhood.

Confederate currency with Matthew Brady portrait of Calhoun, 1862.
Courtesy of the Library of Congress, Washington, D.C.

Meeting on the eve of the first Battle of Manassas, the group formed the
Soldiers' Relief Association of Charleston. LCMA officers took positions as
president, vice president, and corresponding secretaries of the wartime society. LCMA founder Amarinthia Yates, who had married her brother-in-
law's kinsman William Snowden in 1857, played an equally prominent role
in the Soldiers' Relief Association and assumed its presidency after Mary
Robertson left Charleston.[54] Amarinthia Yates Snowden and other women
who had recently solicited contributions for a Calhoun monument now
collected clothing and medical supplies for soldiers. LCMA alumnae also
helped to raise funds for construction of a naval vessel to defend Charleston Harbor, and their experience in managing the Floral Fairs provided a
basis for organizing the Ladies' Gunboat Fair held in Charleston in May
1862. "For the present these daughters of Carolina are contributing towards
the best and most enviable monument," observed the *Courier*, by aiding "a
great movement, which is the crowning result of the teachings and utterances of Calhoun."[55]

Calhoun figured even more prominently in the northern view of southern idols. Unionists routinely referred to Confederate constitutional theory
as "the Calhoun school." *Harper's Weekly* featured a front-page picture of
Calhoun's tomb to illustrate a report on the imminent secession of South
Carolina, summarizing the northern belief that the dead hand of Calhoun
guided the South toward disunion. Anna Ella Carroll distributed ten thousand copies of a pamphlet denouncing secession as "the wicked and anar-
chical doctrine of Calhoun."[56] A Unionist from Texas moved north at the
end of the war and published a widely read novel about secession in which
Calhoun was a South Carolinian's "ideal of earthly glory. Not exactly Cal-

Calhoun's tomb. *Harper's Weekly*, November 24, 1860, 737. Courtesy of the Irvin Department of Rare Books and Special Collections, Ernest F. Hollings Special Collections Library, University of South Carolina, Columbia.

houn the cold dialectician; nor Calhoun the spotless husband and father; nor Calhoun the irreproachable gentleman only—but Calhoun the scourge of the North." The fictional Charlestonian stopped by City Hall regularly to linger in "the awful presence" of Powers's portrait statue of Calhoun, "standing there in a marble coldness which harmonizes with his character."[57]

Charlestonians recognized that northern identification of the Confederacy with Calhoun imperiled commemorative artifacts as Union troops advanced. Keenly aware that the Lincoln administration had hoped since the outset of the war to retake Fort Sumter, municipal officials removed Powers's statue from City Hall and sent it inland for safekeeping in the statehouse. When Union rear admiral Samuel F. DuPont assembled twenty-eight warships near the harbor bar in April 1863 in preparation for a naval attack, the Gourdin brothers resolved to hide Calhoun's remains lest invading Yankees violate his tomb. The merchants gathered at the western section of St. Philip's churchyard in the middle of the night with their friend Edward P. Milliken, one of the marshals for Calhoun's funeral procession. They were joined by the free black sextons of St. Philip's and the Huguenot Church, an undertaker, and several stonemasons. After the laborers opened Calhoun's tomb, which took more than an hour, they placed the metal coffin in a pine box and carried it across the street to St. Philip's. The Gourdins indicated to the workmen that the remains would be sent out of town. Calhoun's bones rested for the day at the bottom of a staircase in the church vestibule, hidden by a piece of carpeting. Late at night, the Gourdins, Milliken, the sextons, an officer of the Calhoun Guards, and two gravediggers reburied the coffin in the older section of the churchyard in the grave of Amelia Welsman, the late wife of a business associate of the Gourdins.[58]

Confederate forces repelled DuPont's attack and continued to hold Charleston for almost two more years, but Union forces eventually entered the city in February 1865. As the Gourdins had anticipated, Calhoun's grave did become a target for some vandalism and souvenir seeking. The long-awaited encounter also produced a memorable elegy for the Confederacy. Walt Whitman reported that while working in a Union hospital in Washington at the end of the war, he overheard a feverish young patient recently returned from South Carolina describe Calhoun's simple monument in St. Philip's churchyard to a more experienced soldier. Whitman's veteran replied:

> I have seen Calhoun's monument. That you saw is not the real monument. But I have seen it. It is the desolated, ruined South; nearly the whole generation of young men between seventeen and thirty destroyed or maim'd; all the old families used up—the rich impoverished, the plantations covered with weeds, the slaves unloos'd and become the masters, and the name of Southerner blackened with every shame—all that is Calhoun's real monument.[59]

Other northerners used similar imagery to summarize the war. Newspaper editor Whitelaw Reid applied Christopher Wren's famous epitaph ("If you seek his monument, look around you") to Calhoun's legacy for Charleston in ruins. An anonymous poem, "The Dark Iconoclast," meditated on the report that an emancipated slave had smashed the bust of Calhoun in the offices of the *Charleston Mercury*. William Lloyd Garrison paid a visit to Calhoun's tomb with several fellow abolitionists after watching the U.S. flag restored at Fort Sumter. "Down into a deeper grave than this slavery has gone," Garrison declared, "and for it there is no resurrection."[60]

The climactic wartime crisis of the Calhoun Monument took place in Columbia, where even Amarinthia Snowden had evacuated as a refugee when the bombardment of Charleston intensified. There, she spent the last weeks of the Confederacy helping to organize the Great Bazaar, the southern attempt to match the Sanitary Fairs held in major northern cities during the late stages of the war. The opening of the Great Bazaar on January 17, 1865, in the chambers of the South Carolina Senate and House of

Representatives generated a first-day sale of thirty-eight hundred tickets. Many features of the carnival would have been familiar to veterans of the LCMA's Floral Fairs or the Ladies' Gunboat Fair, though reports of General William T. Sherman's advance added an undercurrent of desperation to the gaiety. Fancy merchandise imported through the blockade commanded vertiginous prices. Sponsors relied on displays of captured Union trophies and a fortune-telling station to supply Confederate hope. Women reportedly donated their wedding rings for the fund-raiser. Snowden's addition of the project to her previous duties prompted her mother to complain that "between looking after Calhoun money, hospital stores and the Bazaar," she "took no time to look after her children, and her own affairs."[61]

Sherman's arrival in Columbia transformed the LCMA. Frolicking in the legislative chambers where the Great Bazaar had ended prematurely, a few dozen Union soldiers convened a mock senate. After adopting a resolution of censure against Calhoun, "whose states' rights doctrines had found their logical sequence in the existing wicked and unhappy rebellion," they unleashed a barrage of legislators' inkwells and spittoons on a portrait bust of the Nullifier. By this point, fires had already begun to break out at various locations around town. The largest conflagration, running south on Main Street toward the statehouse grounds, grew to become nine blocks long and almost four blocks wide. Flames consumed about one-third of the buildings in the capital on the night of February 17. The old statehouse, made mostly of wood, burned to its foundation, leaving only the blackened brick walls of the basement. Hiram Powers's marble statue of Calhoun "dissolved into a quicklime puddle."[62]

Snowden's preservation of the LCMA's treasury became one of the legendary incidents of this storied night. On the advice of Gourdin and Conner, the women had invested their antebellum revenues in municipal bonds and securities of the Bank of Charleston and the South Carolina Railroad. During the war, they patriotically put their accruing interest and dividends into Confederate paper. As Snowden prepared to flee into Columbia streets teeming with uncontrolled Union soldiers and chaotic terror, she sewed the certificates into her petticoat. This basic narrative would accumulate embellishments over the years. In one predictable version, a faithful slave watched unseen while the LCMA treasurer and her sister hid the securities but did not betray the secret. In a variation that stressed the American unity beneath the sectional conflict, Snowden claimed the personal protection of Sherman, whom she had supposedly met before the war at a wedding in which she was a bridesmaid and he was her groomsman.[63]

The crucial, consistent heart of the story was that Snowden "carried, concealed on her person, the sacred fund." The safeguarding of treasures within women's garments was an important trope in gendered narratives of Confederate identity, for it imagined the war as an encounter between northern military advantage and loyal southern women who appealed to the restraints of morality. The sexual drama enacted in the ruse—the risk of exposure and the implied possibility of rape—assumed a new magnitude amid the breakdown of male protection in Sherman's March. The sack of Columbia became one of the most oft-recounted episodes of violence against civilians in the entire Civil War. Southerners often remembered this "war upon women" as an outrage in which plunder subsumed rape. As Simms put it, "Cupidity, malignity and lust, sought to glut their several appetites. The cupidity generally triumphed over the lust. The greed for gold and silver swallowed up the more animal passions." Snowden's private triumph on behalf of the Calhoun Monument became a symbol of the resourcefulness, the pluck, and the inviolate virtue of Confederate womanhood.[64]

The burning of Columbia provided the LCMA with new significance. After the Confederacy sacrificed a generation of young men on the battlefield, the magic of mortality no longer attached to the distant death of a statesman near the age of seventy who had succumbed to tuberculosis after a long career of public applause. The modernity framed by reunion and emancipation would not include a slaveholding republic personified by Calhoun. Henry Gourdin told Hiram Powers that the sculptor's portrait statue had "shared the common fate" and typified what the white South had lost. The fund preserved by Snowden in turn symbolized what the white South had saved. The LCMA decided soon after the war that its monument "should consist of a base and pedestal of native granite, surmounted by a bronze statue of Calhoun, similar to that of Powers's, which formerly stood in the city-hall at this place."[65] The antebellum LCMA had developed as an alternative to Powers's interpretation of Calhoun, but the connotations of the statue had changed. Rather than a timeless republican masculinity, it now represented an obliterated society dependent on loyal women for an afterlife in memory.

Although the war turned the LCMA in a fresh direction, remembrance of Calhoun could not withstand erosion over time and displacement by competing Confederate memories. Supporters of the LCMA saw "the now sleeping enthusiasm for the Great High Priest of State Sovereignty" and recognized that Calhoun's "intellectual exploits and noble associations have been forced from the public view by years, filled with glowing deeds."[66] Amarinthia Snowden personified this diminished interest. Disillusion with the unifying promise of romantic southern nationalism inflected her observation that "the misfortunes of the war and the sufferings that have followed in its train have dulled in the minds of *the many* the admiration once universally felt for Mr. Calhoun."[67] As leader of the three most important postwar commemorative organizations in Charleston, she directed a variety of intertwined initiatives that addressed incompletely overlapping constituencies and concentrated on partially distinct themes. The LCMA developed in subordination to the commitments Snowden prioritized. The circuitous path toward completion of the Calhoun memorial began by testing the limits of women's citizenship in the shadow nation of the Lost Cause.

As the LCMA had provided the foundation for the Soldiers' Relief Association, so the latter group reconstituted at the end of the war as the Ladies' Memorial Association of Charleston (LMA). Snowden served as president of the organization from its formation in 1866 until her death in 1898. The LMA originated in parallel with similar organizations throughout the South to plan the local inauguration of Memorial Day exercises, which included the commissioning of Timrod's "Ode." Coordination of Memorial Day observance subsequently remained the LMA's central purpose, supplemented by intermittent additional projects focused on the Confederate graves at Magnolia Cemetery. For the installation of permanent headstones, the women obtained legislative funding and a donation of granite and marble unusable in the resumed construction of the new statehouse. Snowden was active in finding and consolidating improvised Confederate graves scattered along roadsides and in isolated fields. She also led the negotiations involved in repatriation of the remains of eighty-four South Carolinians from the battlefield at Gettysburg. Six thousand people attended the Memorial Day 1871 reinterment, at which minister John L. Girardeau delivered an anti-Reconstruction address as fiery as his oration at the first Magnolia observance of Memorial Day. The LMA laid the cornerstone for a monument in the center of the Confederate section on Memorial Day 1870 and dedicated the completed work in 1882, five years before the LCMA unveiled the Calhoun Monument in Marion Square.[68]

The LMA periodically consumed Snowden's attention, but her steadiest postwar commitment was the Home for Mothers, Widows, and Daughters of Confederate Soldiers, which she and her sister formed with seven other women and Huguenot Church pastor Charles Vedder in August 1867. Snowden headed the governing board until her death. The widowed Snowdens mortgaged their Church Street house to rent a facility for the institution. The core of the property was the former Carolina Hotel on Broad Street, which connected through a rear addition to a building used during the antebellum period for sessions of the federal court. It was here that Snowden's friend Robert Newman Gourdin had initiated secession in Charleston on the day after Lincoln's election by declaring as foreman of the federal grand jury that the United States no longer exercised jurisdiction in South Carolina, an assertion seconded by the immediate resignations of federal judge Andrew Magrath and federal district attorney James Conner.[69] The spacious accommodations of the Confederate Home served two different groups. The first set consisted of fallen Confederate soldiers' destitute mothers and widows, including women with daughters. The second set consisted of young South Carolina women who wished to attend school in Charleston. Two years after opening, the institution reported in November 1869 that it provided housing for seventy-two dislocated mothers and widows and their children; thirty young women—at least nominally daughters of Confederate soldiers—attended private academies at discounted tuition rates negotiated by the Home.[70]

The intersections of the LCMA, the LMA, and the Confederate Home only began with Snowden's leadership. Other women also served as officers in more than one of the organizations. They worked with the same men in multiple contexts. In addition to the redoubtable Henry Gourdin, a key carryover from the LCMA gentlemen's advisory committee to the Confederate Home gentlemen's auxiliary association was cotton factor Peter C. Gaillard, whose wife was the sister of Isabel Snowden's late husband. After losing an arm at Battery Wagner as lieutenant colonel of a Confederate regiment, Gaillard won election as the first postwar mayor of Charleston and remained in that position until dismissed by the district commander under the Military Reconstruction Acts of 1867. The LMA did not have a male counterpart, but the officers of Magnolia Cemetery became part of the commemorative network. George Walton Williams, the wealthiest businessman in postwar Charleston and longtime president of the cemetery corporation, took charge of the Confederate Home auxiliary association after the deaths of the Gourdin brothers. Henry E. Young, the attorney for the cemetery, succeeded Henry Gourdin as chair of the LCMA gentlemen's advisory committee. This pattern of interlocking administration reflected a unity of purpose. The girls of the Confederate Home performed the ritual decoration of the soldiers' graves at Magnolia Cemetery during the annual Charleston observance of Memorial Day.

The Confederate commemorative institutions also differed in signifi-cant ways. The LMA's sponsorship of Memorial Day centered on the graves of rank-and-file soldiers. The ceremony involved much of the white com-munity and featured participation by veterans, politicians, ministers, and poets with varying interests in the construction of a broad public. The Con-federate Home was in contrast a private entity dominated by a circle of old-line families who shared kinship and commercial ties. Peter Gaillard's first cousin Harriet Porcher (Gaillard) Stoney was a longtime officer of the man-aging board. Her brother-in-law, cotton factor Theodore D. Stoney, was a charter member of the auxiliary executive committee; her son, Samuel Gaillard Stoney, headed its finance committee for decades. The perpetua-tion of this local elite shaped the Confederate Home as the institution turned from housing mothers and widows of the Confederate dead to edu-cating young women, for the boarders were mostly of a much higher social status than the women interested in charity lodgings. In 1870, the Home established its own school, which competed with local academies for young women. By 1872, when the Home stopped receiving women with children, the seventy-three pupils already outnumbered the forty-six mothers and widows. An early list of students included a Gaillard, two Izards, a Porcher, a Ravenel, and a Seabrook, among other familiar South Carolina names. The older women lived in a separate section of the facility from the stu-dents and had no contact with the school. Annual reports of the Confeder-ate Home noted the deaths of permanent residents only tersely if at all but devoted warm tributes to officers, donors, and students who died. The per-manent residents were not eligible for burial in the lot at Magnolia Ceme-tery set aside for young women from the Confederate Home.[71]

Snowden's ambitions for the school prompted her to seek an even closer relationship between the Confederate Home and the Calhoun project. In the fall of 1873, she suggested that the LCMA use its funds to commemorate Calhoun through support of the Home. Her precipitating goal was to pur-chase and refit the property rented by the Home thereby reducing expenses and also providing income from the building's Broad Street storefronts. Statewide discussion of the idea expanded to a wide range of possible ar-rangements, including LCMA endowment of a school named for Calhoun.[72]

The proposal sparked a vigorous debate over the aims of postwar com-memoration. Skeptics noted that the number of widows in the Home had declined sharply since the immediate postwar adjustment and argued that the emergency facility would not offer a permanent memorial to Calhoun. Proponents of a school maintained that a monument of the sort for which the LCMA had dedicated the cornerstone in 1858 would now be a waste of resources, but they disagreed on whom a school should serve. Francis Warrington Dawson, the influential editor of the *Charleston News and Courier*, seconded Snowden's position that a school for girls would not only provide a suitable Calhoun memorial but also acknowledge women's leadership in the LCMA. Others insisted that a Calhoun Memorial College for young men would be better, particularly because the Citadel military academy had remained closed since Union troops occupied Charleston in February 1865 and the rechartered University of South Carolina had begun to enroll African American students in October 1873.[73]

Calhoun's son-in-law, Thomas Green Clemson, led the most vitriolic attack on Snowden's plan. Although Anna Calhoun Clemson responded with broad sympathy to an early request for support, her husband soon disagreed in a sweeping assessment of the state and the possible uses of Calhoun's legacy. Faced with a challenge from "a race entirely distinct from ours . . . not capable of reaching a high degree of civilization," white Carolinians needed "to make a stand against the degrading torrent . . . by cultivating to its utmost our superior intellectual faculties." Calhoun offered the best possible model for this movement, and Clemson told Snowden that "it has long been my hope and desire, to connect his name with our regeneration." The LCMA fund and its corporate charter, which afforded protection from legislative interference, offered a start toward achievement of Clemson's goal. He urged the dedication of these resources to the founding of a college that would lead the redemption of the state. The school would be located at Fort Hill, in part to escape from low-country Republican strongholds. "This same radical rule, and other reasons, have made us long desirous to remove the remains of Mr. Calhoun from Charleston," Clemson noted, and he looked forward to the final interment of Calhoun in a memorial chapel at the proposed college.[74]

Clemson dismissed the proposal to support the Confederate Home as "entirely inappropriate, and subversive of the original design, not being in any sense of the word, a monument to Mr. Calhoun." The difference between the two educational uses of the LCMA fund was that "Mr. Calhoun was peculiarly *manly*, and his example to our young men, of the greatest importance, and I must confess, frankly, that there is something inappropriate attached in my mind, to the idea of making a *female* school a memorial to his memory." Snowden assured Clemson of her support for his long-term goals if not his hopes to use the women's funds for them, but he remained adamant and publicized family disapproval of the LCMA's attempt to make commemoration of Calhoun "a secondary consideration" in organizational goals.[75]

The clash over the comparative educational needs of white men and women reflected the ways in which the transformation of the Confederate Home challenged gender conventions. The institution originally honored the Confederate dead by dramatizing the helplessness of their mothers, widows, and orphans. Critics called on the Home to retain this model of remembrance and to fade away as the soldiers' dependents died or grew to adulthood. Supporters of Snowden's proposal responded that the Home also testified to the social impact of a war that had given new priority to girls' education. Young women now needed not only training for motherhood but also "a means of self-support, influence, and usefulness." Esther Cheesborough aptly summarized the implication that white southern women had left a world defined and limited by male protection. "There was a time when the chivalry of our men prompted them to throw their velvet cloaks over the damp places of the world for the queens of home to step on," Cheesborough observed in a letter supporting Snowden's proposal. "The tender, chivalrous spirit is still there, but alas! the velvet cloaks are not; and to step over these damp places without hurt, our women must now wear the sandals of preparation."[76]

Although the attempt to merge the Calhoun Monument into the Confederate Home promised to expand women's participation in public life, the LCMA decisively recoiled from any progress aligned with the interracial democracy of Reconstruction. After voting thirty-six to seven to apply the fund to educational purposes, the directresses proposed in January 1874 to purchase the property rented by the Confederate Home and name that building the Calhoun Memorial Institute. The LCMA asked a committee of six men to ratify the lawfulness of the plan. Unable to achieve unanimity, the advisory committee recommended that the LCMA submit the question for final arbitration by the three surviving chancellors of the antebellum South Carolina bench. Through this informal procedure, the women refused to tie their initiative to the authority of the reconstructed judicial system. The ex-chancellors ruled by a two-to-one vote that the educational memorial proposed by the women was not "the sort of monument intended by the word as used in their Constitution" and that an equity court would not approve temporary investment of LCMA funds in real estate until a more favorable occasion for commissioning a monument of the sort in-

'tended. Strict construction and the LCMA's hostility to Reconstruction had thwarted the women's boldest effort to build on their commemorative citizenship.[77]

The Confederate Home and the Calhoun Memorial advanced along separate but parallel lines after the March 1874 decision of the former chancellors. The overlapping management of the Home and the LCMA regarded these projects, much more than community observance of Memorial Day, as commemorations addressed to national audiences as well as the city and state. In theory, the appeal to northerners would rebound home in a reinforcement of class privilege. Northern sympathy with southerners reduced by the war to the charity of the Home, as well as northern respect for the plantation society that produced Calhoun, offered support for the status claims of traditional elites. This strategy focused the Home and the LCMA on the theme of intersectional leadership, though both efforts overlooked emerging structures of authority in the reunited nation and overestimated local deference to old-fashioned sources of entitlement.

The Confederate Home did not let the LCMA funding setback halt the development of the institution. The officers borrowed money to purchase the building and found help in repaying the loan and establishing an endowment. Long-standing low-country families remained crucial supporters, but the largest donations came from other parts of the country. Washington banker William Wilson Corcoran, well known for his southern political sympathies and his educational philanthropy, was an obvious prospect whom the Home quickly cultivated with success. Massachusetts reference-book publisher George Merriam made substantial contributions, and the Home received many gifts from New York. The Home's annual reports expressed pride that the institution enjoyed the respect of benefactors with nationwide horizons. The most generous donor was Josephine Newcomb, whose late husband had similarly provided scholarship funding for impoverished white southerners at Washington College during Robert E. Lee's time as the school's president.

Newcomb's identification with the founding of a women's college within Tulane University offered a useful point of contrast for the aspirations of the Confederate Home. Snowden sought to update the education she had received at Ann Marson Talvande's French School for Young Ladies in Charleston and Elias Marks's South Carolina Female Collegiate Institute near Columbia. The chief teachers at the Confederate Home during the de-

cade after the LCMA controversy were George Alexander, a veteran of Ace-
lie Togno's fashionable antebellum school as well as the Calhoun Guards,
and his wife and her mother.[78] The key difference between the Confederate
Home and the antebellum academies—or the postwar schools operated by
Adèle Petigru Allston, Elizabeth Richmond Pinckney, and other Charleston matrons—was that the Home was much less expensive to attend. The
officers of the Home did not use its resources to raise its educational ambitions. Instead they helped the accepted applicants from the low country and to a lesser extent other parts of South Carolina receive a modestly
priced high school education unavailable in many rural districts, participate in Charleston society, and prepare for possible work as schoolteachers. Annual reports frequently announced with pride that alumnae had
returned to join the Home's staff but never indicated that a graduate had
advanced to college.

As an institutional expression of postwar adjustment, the Confederate
Home eschewed the new path marked by the Charleston Female Seminary,
which Henrietta Aiken Kelly founded in 1870. Pointedly located in the educational district near the College of Charleston, where Kelly had unsuccessfully sought the admission of women students, the Charleston Female
Seminary featured a college-preparatory curriculum. The four Poppenheim
sisters trained there for Vassar, future poet Beatrice Witte for Radcliffe.
Eager as the officers of the Home were to recover the prestige of South Carolina and maintain the status of their families, they disregarded the educational ladder that increasingly defined national power and class standing.

The LCMA followed a similar intersectional strategy. Obliged to commission a work of art, the women returned to the project in 1876 and affirmed the basic concept endorsed immediately after the war—a bronze
portrait statue that evoked Powers's lost marble. The gentlemen's committee appointed to finalize the program and identify an artist specified that
the sculpture would depict Calhoun "in his usual dress, draped with a cloak
and resting on a palmetto tree, and holding in his hand a scroll representing 'Truth, Justice, and the Constitution.'" Virginia poet Margaret Jun-
kin Preston suggested to Snowden that "it would make Calhoun stir in his
grave if he were sculptured by a Northern chisel," but the search process relied on northerners' judgments and led to the selection of a northern sculptor, Albert E. Harnisch. He campaigned for the lucrative commission with
the aid of author Anne Hampton Brewster, the fellow Philadelphia native
with whom he lived in Rome. The committee indicated that it attached particular weight to the opinions of Boston expatriate William Wetmore Story.

The southerner who most influenced the decision was Caroline Carson, daughter of Calhoun's staunch Unionist critic James Louis Petigru and herself so antagonistic to secession that she relocated from Charleston to New York at the outbreak of the Civil War. A friend and client of Henry Young, who chaired the LCMA selection committee, Carson was an acquaintance of Harnisch in the Rome circle of American artists.[79]

Harnisch's backers had little basis for their recommendations, for the thirty-six-year-old sculptor had never received a major commission or completed a large work. Young's committee reported that it did not hold a competition because established artists would not enter such contests, but the LCMA had sufficient funds for the attractive premiums that often drew impressive fields and that artists' societies considered essential to a well-run juried selection. The commission ultimately went to an unproven sculptor who had recently entered high-profile competitions for memorials to Lincoln and Lee.[80] Like the bid to make the Confederate Home an institution of national significance, the attempt to entrust the Calhoun Monument to an artist of national reputation ignored the postwar professionalization that was binding the restored Union with modern cords.

The great Charleston earthquake of August 1886 deepened the shared resonance of the Calhoun Monument and the Confederate Home as symbols of a community defined by crisis. LCMA contractors had begun preparations for the installation of Harnisch's statue, moving the cornerstone to the opposite side of Citadel Square. The square became the epicenter for the social upheaval caused by the natural disaster, as hundreds of black and white Charlestonians spent the following month living there in segregated outdoor camps that frequently collided in racial conflict. When the contractors found their work still intact and resumed the construction of the massive granite base amid the turmoil of the encampments, newspapers optimistically reported that the LCMA had planted the civic monument on solid ground. The Confederate Home, severely damaged by the earthquake, deftly incorporated a recovery narrative into its institutional identity. An emergency appeal yielded generous contributions from both North and South. President Grover Cleveland chose the Confederate Home and an African American church as the recipients of his personal donations to the shaken city. Henry Young selected the Home as the logical beneficiary of the relief contribution he received from John Brown Jr. The Home quickly repaired and dramatically improved its facility. A marble tablet placed above the front entrance announced that the building had been "Ruined by the Earthquake 1886, Restored by the people of the Union 1887."[81]

Confederate Home and College, Charleston, 1907. Courtesy of the South Caroliniana Library, University of South Carolina, Columbia.

   Plans for the dedication of Harnisch's monument in spring 1887 reflected the dwindling public interest in the Nullifier and the LCMA's intensified emphasis on sectional reconciliation. Charleston merchants demanded a "monster excursion" of state residents taking advantage of special rail fares to visit the city, but the LCMA made "no elaborate plan" for a spectacle and refrained from "any systematic working up of the feelings of the people" in preparation for the dedication. "Great Scott!," roared one businessman interviewed in Dawson's boosterish *News and Courier*. "A half a dozen live, go-ahead, progressive men could take this thing in hand and make it the biggest thing of the century in Charleston, except, perhaps the Calhoun funeral and the earthquake." The nub of contention was funding to involve Confederate veterans in the festivities, for observers acknowledged that enthusiasm for Calhoun would not produce a crowd. "Soldiers are stars of the first magnitude for occasions of this kind," exclaimed a merchant. "The presence of a regiment or two of volunteers from the State at large will necessarily bring thousands of visitors." Under heavy public pressure, Young's committee invited military units to march at the head of the procession and made an appropriation to help the Fourth Brigade entertain visiting soldiers. The satisfied *News and Courier* pronounced the extravaganza the "gayest, largest and most variegated throng of people that has been seen here for many years."[82]

LCMA allies like Young, who had served on Lee's staff until Appomattox, certainly did not lack appreciation for Confederate veterans, but they wanted the event to center on the theme of national leadership. Scheduling the dedication for the April 26 anniversary of Calhoun's funeral, they avoided connecting the monument to the May 10 observance of Memorial Day. The anniversary of the funeral instead marked a legendary moment of civic unity in Charleston and recalled the outpouring of respect highlighted by the tributes that Clay and Webster delivered in the Senate. The dignitaries invited to the dedication included a few Confederate heroes, such as Jefferson Davis and P. G. T. Beauregard, but also Grover Cleveland, the members of his cabinet, the governors of all states, and Union heroine Clara Barton. The LCMA recalled the compromise spirit of 1850 by inviting Robert Winthrop, who had seconded the South Carolinian motion in the House of Representatives for recognition of Calhoun's death, and Hamilton Fish, who had marked the occasion respectfully as governor of New York. The monument sponsors veiled the statue with a U.S. flag loaned by a Connecticut friend. The arrangements resembled the literary diplomacy of Paul Hamilton Hayne, whom the LCMA expected to grace the occasion with an original ode until he died in July 1886.[83]

Like the selection of Lawrence Keitt to speak at the cornerstone ceremony six years before he died in command of a South Carolina brigade at Cold Harbor, the choice of L. Q. C. Lamar as orator for the dedication ceremony neatly encapsulated the current viewpoint of the LCMA. The first white southerner to serve in the U.S. presidential cabinet since the war, the Confederate veteran personified the restoration of intersectional leadership. His participation framed the monument dedication as a pendant to the acclaimed eulogy Lamar had delivered on the death of Charles Sumner in 1874. The Mississippian embraced the opportunity to enhance his reputation as an intellectual statesman, and his address brought the Charleston proceedings the national attention that the LCMA sought.[84]

After an introductory tribute to the executive ability and breadth of social vision instilled by the vocation of a planter, Lamar selectively traced Calhoun's political career with a strong emphasis on his devotion to the Union. The future Supreme Court justice waved away debates over federal and state sovereignty with the observation that "in all nations in which there are any stirrings of constitutional life there is more than one fundamental principle or power." Both sides took reasonable positions. Conflicts between valid principles turned on "the law of development," which in the United States had resolved into the arbitrament of the battlefield. Lamar stressed that if Calhoun had lived longer, "his great talents would have been, as they had ever been before, directed to save this people from the horrors of disunion and war." He dwelled on Calhoun's leadership in the War of 1812 and his anticipation of civil service reform as a remedy for partisan excess. Lamar's review of the nullification controversy highlighted the compromise with Clay and Jackson, "a spectacle which cannot fail to excite the pride and admiration of all true Americans." The Civil War had prompted northern "misconception and distrust of the Southern people" that gravely distorted Reconstruction, but realization of the error had given way to "magnanimity on the part of the Northern people, unexampled in the annals of civil war and accepted by the South in a spirit not less magnanimous and great-hearted." Lamar looked ahead to realization of the American destiny that Calhoun had predicted in March 1846, shortly before the outbreak of the Mexican War started the chain of events that ended in the Civil War, when the South Carolinian successfully counseled the Senate to adopt a conciliatory policy toward England on the Oregon question and described a providential future of prosperity, moral improvement, and technological innovation.[85]

The tension in the dedication ceremony between exaltation of statesmanship and enthusiasm for soldiers did not escape notice. Dawson mused that "if the South Carolinians of fifty years ago . . . had been more like the people of South Carolina of today, the influence of the great statesman would not have been so general or so lasting as it was." Calhoun had thrived in an era when South Carolinians "were a people who believed in leaders" because "the upper class controlled." The Nullifier's intellectual ability exemplified the traits that elites valued, and ordinary people enjoyed the reflected glory of his career. "Carolinians were worshipping in him a personification or embodiment of South Carolina," Dawson noted. As a result, insistence on Calhoun's devotion to the Union struck a false note. "Calhoun was not a man of the nation," the editor insisted. "He was a man of the State, of the State of South Carolina, impressing its genius and its ideas on the General government." The LCMA's appeal to a national audience would not have much local impact because the organization honored Calhoun in terms irrelevant to most Charlestonians or other South Carolinians. Loyalty to the United States was no longer a debatable issue, although disagreements about federalism were bound to persist. Intellectual oratory now commanded less respect than the marching veterans. Dawson's reflec-

tions echoed Frederick A. Porcher's objections to Powers's portrait of Calhoun in a toga. Secession had given way to reconciliation, but both writers
pointed out that nationalist commemoration depended on an understanding of popular sentiment.[86]

The contrast between Lamar's address and Harnisch's statue troubled
the LCMA more than the dissonance between the speech and the parade.
Although the orator professed to sketch "the moral and intellectual image
of him whose outer form and lineaments are presented in the admirable
statue which we this day unveil," the two portraits differed sharply and
prompted opposite responses from the sponsors. The LCMA did not invite Harnisch to the dedication ceremony, and the well-illustrated record
of proceedings included no photographs of his statue. When the calendar
turned to the LCMA's annual meeting date on Calhoun's birthday in 1888,
the women did not announce their objective accomplished but instead
elected new officers. Amarinthia Snowden assumed the presidency on the
death of Mary Robertson; Harriet Porcher Stoney became treasurer.[87] Less
than seven years later, the LCMA commissioned a replacement for Harnisch's bronzework, which they melted into scrap metal. The new monument, they hoped, would better incorporate the themes they had stressed
since the war and better suppress the romantic nationalism they had promoted in the 1850s.

Harnisch faced a difficult task when the LCMA began to work exclusively
with him in 1879. Calhoun had already embodied a host of complex and
sometimes contradictory values in the era of controversy over Powers's
statue. Those layers of meaning had deepened considerably since the Nullifier's death. The LCMA had introduced the motif of women's participation
in the community of memory. That citizenship became so prominent after
the war that Lamar closed his dedication address with a tribute to Snowden's heroism in preserving the LCMA fund amid the burning of Columbia.
The narrative of defeat and regeneration embedded in the program for the
LCMA monument called for careful calibration between a plea of victimhood and an assertion of restored privilege. Harnisch chose to focus on
Calhoun as the heroic personification of the incipient Confederacy. His decision showed little sensitivity to the ways the LCMA had changed over the
last three decades, and his design prompted controversy in Charleston long
before the dedication ceremony. But the LCMA destroyed Harnisch's statue
only after the monument failed to meet the most basic requirement of Lost
Cause commemoration: it did not protect white supremacism.

Harnisch's assignment was in one important respect simpler than the problem addressed by the stymied design proposals of the late 1850s. The LCMA's monument was now clearly distinct from Calhoun's tomb. Henry Gourdin supervised the return of the remains to the west section of the St. Philip's churchyard on the morning before Easter in 1871. Nine years later, Thomas Green Clemson sought removal of the remains to the Pendleton cemetery where the family had buried the senator's widow immediately after the war, but other relatives protested that Floride Calhoun had wanted her husband to rest "near the monument which the noble daughters of Carolina have undertaken to erect." Drained of its political significance, the disposition of Calhoun's body had become merely grist for family quarrel. The LCMA was content to leave the embellishment of the tomb to the state legislature, which Floride Calhoun had entrusted with final authority. An 1883 appropriation of three thousand dollars led to the installation of a permanent sarcophagus without ceremony the following November.[88]

Harnisch's plan for the LCMA's monument was straightforward. He would depict Calhoun representing South Carolina in the Senate. A symbolic chair of government authority reflected the sovereignty of the state. The composition sought to capture the Nullifier immediately after he had risen to speak, his cloak falling onto his seat. In a gesture that classical oratory prescribed for the beginning of an address, the statesman pointed forward with his slightly upturned right index finger.[89] This focus on the transition from sitting to standing honored Calhoun both as a man of thought, conventionally seated, and a man of action, customarily standing. The design anticipated Augustus Saint-Gaudens's more effective treatment of corresponding themes in his *Standing Lincoln* (1884–87), which critics have praised since its unveiling as "that rarest of things—a true novelty in art."[90] Iconographically, at least, this Calhoun was Lincoln's older brother if not his father. Rather than introduce an antique scroll, Harnisch proposed placing allegorical figures of Truth, Justice, and Constitution around the base of the monument.

The keynote to the sculptor's conception was a fourth allegorical figure, History. As her sisters on the Charleston monument alluded to Powers's lost marble, History echoed Antonio Tantardini's statue on Odoardo Tabacchi's monument in Milan to Camillo di Cavour, which Harnisch described as his model for "the general plan of the whole." The parallel suggested a resemblance between the lives of Calhoun and Cavour—aristocrats, intellectuals, statesmen. As Cavour had expanded the small kingdom of Piedmont into a unified Italy, Calhoun's defense of South Carolina's sovereignty provided the foundation of the Confederacy. Harnisch's hero was the physi-

Albert E. Harnisch, model for Calhoun Monument. *Harper's Weekly*, March 12, 1887, 189. Courtesy of the Irvin Department of Rare Books and Special Collections, Ernest F. Hollings Special Collections Library, University of South Carolina, Columbia.

cal representative of a southern race as well as the personification of a constitutional principle. The figure stood with toes inward, one visitor to the studio explained, "like Southern people all over the world." The sculptor dressed his effigy in the long, double-breasted Prince Albert coat that W. J. Cash later called "a sort of uniform of the class" in the postwar South.[91] Here was the romantic nationalism Frederick Porcher had sought in 1850.

When the LCMA decided to replace Harnisch's monument, the official explanations focused not on objections to the approved design but on flaws in its execution. The casting was poor; the pose was "heavy and without animation"; the exaggerated pointing finger "amounted to a deformity." Other observers noted that the chair was too large and obscured the view from the back. One critic called the work "a statue of an arm-chair, with a tall gentleman standing beside it."[92]

Long before Harnisch executed his work, however, his plans excited attacks that struck more directly at the meaning of the monument. From the outset, the LCMA told the sculptor that its members had "hoped for something more imposing than the model suggests." When he traveled to Charleston in early 1882, his designs met a wave of condemnation. Detractors continued to call for a statue "at a proper elevation" atop a high, commanding column that would express the sponsors' claims to national and local leadership. Most protests focused on the emblematic figures derived from the Cavour monument. Letters to the newspapers savaged the allegories as "ridiculous," "inappropriate," "shabby-genteel," and "the style of ornamentation . . . seen on wedding cakes and candy castles."[93] Harnisch's decorative idealism, a strategy often admired in French and American monuments as well as Italian works, seemed frivolous to the South Carolinians. Truth, Justice, and Constitution were for them historical references to the trauma of Sherman's March, not conceptual aspects of an imagined southern nationality.

Stung by threats of legal action to block the commission, the LCMA leadership stuck to its decision and signed a contract with Harnisch in April 1882. A publicity campaign sought to restore public confidence. Dawson printed a favorable report after visiting Rome as well as complimentary letters from experts based in Philadelphia and Baltimore. Carson defended her recommendation by channeling to Harnisch a commission for a portrait bust of her father. But dissatisfaction with Harnisch's interpretation persisted. Four years after signing a contract, the LCMA debated instructing the sculptor to replace the allegorical figures with statues of William Lowndes, Langdon Cheves, Robert Y. Hayne, and Hugh Swinton Legaré. The switch would have undercut the ideological coherence of Harnisch's design; Legaré, a firm Unionist, openly regarded Calhoun as a "charlatan." But the proposal aptly reflected a desired emphasis on national leadership from South Carolina, and the LCMA gave up on the suggestion only because "the statue being based on one concentrated idea the substitution would necessitate an entire change of that idea," with consequent delay and expense.[94]

Harnisch's work received mixed reviews upon delivery. The *News and Courier* thought that "the statue unveiled to-day cannot be excelled as a representation of the real Calhoun as he stood in the Senate," although the now-lamented marble by Powers "suggested more fully the ideal Calhoun

... as he presents himself instantly to every mind." The *Columbia Register* considered the monument "an impressive figure" with an "excellent" front view if a "very bad" rear view because of "too much chair." A correspondent for the *New York Times* acknowledged that Harnisch's effort "might easily have been a more artistic work" but observed that "it will last a long time, and as it was built to perpetuate the name of Calhoun it will serve its purpose as well as if it were more beautiful."[95]

Public disappointment with commissioned sculpture was common in the boom of civic monuments that followed the Civil War, and the *Times* reporter's forecast might have proven accurate but for the response from an unexpected direction. "Blacks took that statue personally," recalled Mamie Garvin Fields. Born in Charleston one year after the dedication, Fields looked back more than ninety years later at Harnisch's monument as a postemancipation update of the message that the LCMA intended for free blacks on the Charleston Neck in the 1850s. Calhoun seemed to glare at each African American and say, "You may not be a slave, but I am back to see you stay in your place." According to Fields, "We used to carry something with us, if we knew we would be passing that way, in order to deface the statue—scratch up the coat, break the watch chain, try to knock off the nose." Historians have found no contemporary documentation to confirm these recollections of forcible resistance to a statue removed when Fields was eight years old. Standing atop a thirty-three-foot-high base, the fourteen-foot-tall statue would have been difficult to reach. A newspaper article about Charleston vandalism published near the time of the decision to replace Harnisch's work deplored the recent defacement of the Washington Light Infantry Monument located near City Hall but did not mention any damage to the Calhoun Monument. If perhaps not accurate in some ways, however, Fields's account did express an authentic black folk memory that protesters "beat up John C. Calhoun so badly that whites had to come back and put him way up high, so we couldn't get to him."[96]

The evidence is much clearer that African Americans undermined the monument with sarcasm. Harnisch completed only one of the four allegorical figures in time for the dedication, and the LCMA installed the effigy on the front of the base. White Charlestonians delighted in reporting that "the pickaninnies christened her Mis' Calhoun." Racist parody converged with satire of Harnisch's artistic ambitions in this mimicry. Adopting the Gullah label "Calhoun and he wife" for the monument added a fresh layer of contempt to the long-standing argument that the emblematic figures were "altogether meaningless." LCMA leaders proud of their efforts to ad-

Calhoun Monument, 1895. Courtesy of the South Carolina
Historical Society, Charleston.

vance white women's commemorative citizenship could only have been appalled at the female subservience implicit in the caricatured interpretation of the woman at Calhoun's feet.[97] The laughter directed at the statue helped to achieve what the violent protests recalled by Fields probably could not have accomplished. Vandalism often recognizes the sanctity of a challenged symbol, but public ridicule was devastating to the LCMA's assertion of dignity. A monument that encouraged white wags to indulge in misogynist blackface humor was intolerable to the Lost Cause.

The LCMA maintained a substantial balance in its treasury, in part because Harnisch's failure to complete the ensemble justified the withholding of final payment. Liquidation of his bronze figures also helped the organization recoup its investment. In 1894, the women empaneled a final gentlemen's advisory committee to find a new design. The search process identified an imposing column as the essential element of the new monument. Following the intersectional policy of its predecessor, the committee obtained a satisfactory plan from a New York architectural firm. For the bronze portrait statue to place atop the column, the LCMA solicited proposals from New York sculptors and accepted the lowest bid, submitted by thirty-four-year-old Scottish immigrant John Massey Rhind. The LCMA installed the new monument without ceremony in June 1896.[98]

The dominant feature of the replacement was its size. The granite pedestal and column were eighty-four feet high, with Rhind's colossal statue stretching thirteen feet higher. The location of the work exaggerated its apparent height. Rather than closing a long vista, the monument was only one hundred feet from the edge of Marion Square it faced; buildings on the boundary streets of the square screened the work from any distant view. The composition disdained allegory. A commentator emphasized that "the Rhind monument has no hint of a sibyl." The eye-level ornamentation underscored the LCMA's emphasis on Calhoun as an American leader rather than the prophet of a southern nation. Narrative relief panels depicted Calhoun as chair of the U.S. House of Representatives Foreign Affairs Committee at the outbreak of the War of 1812 and replying to Webster in the Senate.[99]

The new monument was extraordinarily self-referential, concerned as much with the history of the commemorative project as the significance of the person commemorated. Rhind made the mandatory allusion to Powers's lost statue by placing a scroll in Calhoun's hand and decorative bronze palmetto trees on the corners of the base. The inscription on the front panel consisted of Calhoun's dates and the phrase "Truth, Justice, and the Constitution." On the rear panel, two lines of the inscription blandly saluted Calhoun's "eminent statesmanship during the many years of his public life." Four lines celebrated the fund-raising of the LCMA and recorded that "its treasurer Mrs. M. A. Snowden having charge of all its assets secured them about her person and thus saved them during the memorable night of the destruction of Columbia, S.C. by Sherman on the 17th February 1865."[100] The allocation of space and disparity of detail betrayed that the monument sponsors had long ago lost their passionate admiration for Calhoun, the grandeur of the new column notwithstanding. The rear inscription acknowledged that the monument "replaces one formerly on the same spot which proved unsatisfactory," though the text did not specify that blackface parody was what the sponsors found decisively unsatisfactory. The LCMA's final act of construction aimed partly to clarify its vision of the postwar South but mostly to prevent Confederate commemoration from showcasing the instability of the color line.

¶

Upon completion of the monument, the LCMA donated the remainder of its funds to the Confederate Home to endow a Calhoun memorial scholarship.[101] The belated, partial fulfillment of Snowden's plan punctuated the relationship between the two commemorative projects. Forced to abandon its intersectional pretensions in a changing educational environment, the Confederate Home continued to modify its mission and eventually found a way to combine its local constituency with national leadership. In contrast, the LCMA's false starts culminated in the installation of Rhind's statue above Charleston. The figure was too far removed from the city to contribute effectively to the civic landscape and insufficiently artistic to promote wider respect for Calhoun. Subsequent enhancement of his reputation took other forms; the monument became a target for his critics.

The Confederate Home began to address the contradictions in its institutional strategy shortly after Snowden's death in 1898. Northern philanthropists no longer took much interest in a facility that accommodated fewer than twenty Confederate widows, who had little contact with the old-fashioned academy that dominated the administrators' attention. The Home rechartered in 1900 as the Confederate Home and College and soon began to receive substantial legislative funding. The College was essentially a normal school that provided its graduates exemption from the qualifying examinations for schoolteachers. This vocational approach put the Home in awkward competition with public institutions such as the Memminger School in Charleston and weakened its social prestige. After Henrietta Kelly closed her Charleston Female Seminary, the Ashley Hall School founded in 1909 served young women from elite families who wanted to prepare for college; future novelist Josephine Pinckney transferred out of the Confederate Home as soon as Ashley Hall opened. Confederate Home president Louisa Cheves Smythe Stoney proposed in the early 1920s that the Home sell its valuable Broad Street property and relocate to a site that would accommodate more students and permit the improvement of the educational program "until it becomes in truth, what it is in name, the Confederate College." But the proposal foundered, in part because the College of Charleston had begun to admit women in 1918. The Home closed its school in 1923. The facility then served for a while as a boardinghouse for female students attending the Memminger School or the College of Charleston before a shift of the residential focus to older women. The Home offered moderately priced lodgings on a variety of plans over the following decades, including a midcentury convalescent ward. Eventually the institution began to supplement its income and expand its influence by renting working space to artists and writers and entrepreneurs. Ashley Hall graduate Josephine Humphreys, the most important Charleston novelist of the late twentieth century, wrote *Rich in Love* in an office in the Confederate Home.[102]

The final Calhoun Monument was less flexible than the Confederate Home and could not negotiate a similar transition. After the initial publicity flurry that surrounded the replacement, northern commentators on art ignored the prosaic composition. The pillar was also too tall and forbidding to serve as a stage for urban life. Although the Nullifier's political legacy remained powerful in South Carolina for many decades, the monument was not an effective backdrop for political rallies or official speeches. Residents did not use it as a point of rendezvous; tourists did not flock there. Travel writers still paused sometimes at Calhoun's grave but never commented on the monument. The artists and authors who devoted themselves to passionate exploration of the Charleston landscape from the close of World War I until the outbreak of World War II gave almost no attention to this prominent feature of the city. As the College of Charleston expanded in the late twentieth century, Calhoun became an increasingly incongruous chaperone for the young men and women who claimed Marion Square as a playground. One group of students spent several years trying to project a Santa Claus hat onto the Nullifier during the holiday seasons.[103] My future wife and I stayed at the chain hotel located in the old Citadel building on New Year's Eve in 2006 and crossed through Marion Square at midnight. Every tree and bench in the park glittered with festive lights. The Calhoun Monument alone was dark.

The statue has not completely escaped notice, for it is the most explicitly political trace of the attempt to establish a proslavery republic. No twentieth-century engagement with the LCMA's legacy was more vivid than Mamie Garvin Fields's testimony that African Americans in Charleston saw the column as a monument to white supremacy and black resistance. The record of black vandalism directed toward the 1896 work was more definite than evidence of attacks on its 1887 predecessor. A historian who interviewed African Americans associated with the Avery Normal Institute reported several accounts of such protests. One former student recalled that a classmate in the 1930s threw stones at Rhind's bronze reliefs because Calhoun "didn't like us." Former slave Elijah Green, who dug Calhoun's final grave in St. Philip's churchyard, emphasized to a Works Progress Administration interviewer during the same period that "I never

Calhoun Monument through Holocaust Memorial, Charleston.
Photograph by Carol E. Harrison.

did like Calhoun 'cause he hated the Negro; no man was ever hated as much as him by a group of people." Lucille Odom's shudder at "John C.'s mean bronze-green face" in *Rich in Love* illustrated the LCMA's failure to secure the loyalty of white Charlestonians after the civil rights revolution. As the bronze statue darkened, local ironists took delight in the blackening of the proslavery ideologue, an update of the racial satire that had doomed Harnisch's statue.[104]

This backfire reached a climax with the dedication of the Holocaust Memorial in Marion Square in 1999. Visiting Charleston shortly afterward on a speaking engagement, novelist and essayist Jamaica Kincaid remarked to her audience and later to a national magazine readership that the proximity was fitting because "John Caldwell Calhoun was not altogether so far removed from Adolf Hitler." Proponents of a Charleston tribute to Denmark Vesey asked to place their memorial in Marion Square, partly to recall the original location of the Citadel but also to form a triangulation with the Calhoun and Holocaust Memorials.[105]

Without the luster of martial virtue that glamorized remembrance of Confederate soldiers, the Calhoun Monument was perhaps the clearest southern reminder of the ideas about race and slavery at stake in the Civil War. The glimmer of topics ordinarily suppressed by Confederate commemoration stimulated alternative community memories and encouraged thoughtful Charlestonians, like the fictional Lucille Odom, to ground their personal identities in an effort to uncover the partially hidden past.

Despite these unintended consequences, the Calhoun Monument was not entirely a failure from the standpoint of its sponsors. The initiative contributed to the founding of the Confederacy, the central goal of the project's varied advocates during its first decade. The LCMA turned women's voluntarism in Charleston toward commemoration, which became a lasting civic outlet of tremendous importance. The LCMA's institutional offspring incorporated some of the original themes of the Calhoun Monument, including heroic mortality and Victorian modernity, into the observance of Memorial Day and other tributes to Confederate soldiers. Much more than the direct aftermath of the secessionists' commemorative campaign, these postwar adaptations provided a solid foundation for the development of the Lost Cause.

The Evolution of the Lost Cause

THEY ARE A STUDY in the art of counterpoint. The
marble statue honoring the fallen Confederate soldiers of South Carolina stands in front of the principal entrance to the state capitol. Leaning on his rifle
as he looks directly down Main Street from a height of
forty feet, he commands the precise spot at which the
channels of government and business power meet in
Columbia. The bronze statue honoring the Confederate women of South Carolina sits diametrically across
the statehouse, about an equal distance from the
building, in a chair on a low pedestal. Her back to the
street, surrounded on three sides by high hedges, she
looks up from the Bible resting on her lap. The carefully coordinated inscriptions on the two monuments
emphasize that Confederate loyalty united the male
and female models of virtue. The men were "TRUE TO
THE INSTINCTS OF THEIR BIRTH, / FAITHFUL TO
THE TEACHINGS OF THEIR FATHERS, / CONSTANT
IN THEIR LOVE FOR THE STATE." The women were
"UNCHANGED IN THEIR DEVOTION, / UNSHAKEN
IN THEIR PATRIOTISM, / UNWEARIED IN MINIS-
TRATIONS, / UNCOMPLAINING IN SACRIFICES."
According to the inscriptions, this partnership led to

South Carolina Monument to the Confederate Dead, 1904. Courtesy of South
Caroliniana Library, University of South Carolina, Columbia.

mutual recognition of complementary contributions. The soldier monu-
ment declares that it has been "ERECTED BY THE WOMEN OF SOUTH
CAROLINA." The monument to women answers that it was "REARED BY
THE MEN OF THE STATE." Together, the monuments to the exemplary
Confederate man and the exemplary Confederate woman naturalize the
South Carolina statehouse—their house—and situate the public realm in
a timeless order of sexual differentiation and harmony epitomized by the
gendering force of war.

A look behind the statues shatters any notion that the Civil War so
simply perpetuated a martial reinforcement of distinctions ordained by
biology. As the attempt to merge the Calhoun Monument into the Confederate Home demonstrated, wartime convulsions intensified the fluidity of
gender norms. The monuments to Confederate soldiers and Confederate
women unveiled at the statehouse in 1879 and 1912 invite fuller examination of the Lost Cause as a public culture through which white southerners
debated shifting interpretations of manhood and womanhood.

The campaigns that produced these statues bracketed a remarkable institutional elaboration of Confederate remembrance. Columbia offers an
excellent vantage point for analyzing the proliferation of commemorative

South Carolina Monument to Women of the Confederacy, April 11, 1912. The figure was later turned to face the statehouse and relocated further from the building along the same axis. Courtesy of the South Caroliniana Library, University of South Carolina, Columbia.

associations, civic ceremonies, veterans' reunions, museums, publications, and welfare facilities as well as sculptural monuments. Gender ideology remained central throughout this varied activity, but the terms of discussion shifted over time. Early postwar commemoration adapted ideals of domesticity developed in the antebellum period. By the turn of the century, men and women more often used the vocabulary of social Darwinism to imagine relationships between the sexes in a regime of laissez-faire industrial capitalism. The application of evolutionary theory to Confederate remembrance accommodated considerable internal conflict and provided a historical synthesis for a wide range of racial, gender, religious, and class dynamics. The process of modernization invigorated the Lost Cause as an organic social myth.

The stresses of the war and its immediate aftermath shaped women's work in the South Carolina Monument Association (SCMA). Columbia organizers called for meetings to form the SCMA during the November 1869 state fair, the first such event since the war and an important forum for strategists aiming to counter the political revolution caused by the enfranchisement of African Americans. The inaugural elections under the 1868 state constitution had yielded a legislature and executive administration dominated by Republicans. The general assembly soon enacted a statute prohibiting racial discrimination in public accommodations, established a state militia in which African Americans served as armed citizens, and created a land commission empowered to purchase farms for resale to freedpeople.[1] The SCMA's founding was part of the partisan recruitment of opposition to Reconstruction.

Sponsored by the State Agricultural and Mechanical Society under the direction of former Confederate general and future Democratic governor Johnson Hagood, the 1869 fair coincided with the formation of several other resistance networks. New organizations included a Confederate Survivors' Association, headed by future Democratic governor Wade Hampton; a Young Men's Christian Association, directed by future Democratic Party chair Alexander Haskell; and the South Carolina Club, which promoted social interaction among young gentlemen and was guided by future Democratic paramilitary commander Martin W. Gary. Hampton delivered the main address at the first SCMA meeting on November 4. Although no transcript survives, he most likely suggested to the women, as he did to a similar Virginia group four years later, that their project reflected "no keen sense of private bereavement" but was "more sacred in its aims and more patriotic in its object." The campaign against Reconstruction called for women of the Lost Cause to remain actively engaged in politics.[2]

The SCMA chose a president who merged private and public interests in remembrance of the Confederate dead. A mother whose only son had died as the result of wounds sustained at Second Manassas, sixty-year-old Louisa McCord had been the most prominent female proslavery polemicist of the 1850s. She was also a leading southern theorist of women's place in civic life. In an essay deploring the women's rights movement as a corollary of abolitionism, she espoused the familiar mid-nineteenth-century argument that Christianity assigned distinct missions to men and women. Woman's religious duty, "even nobler than man's," was in this formulation "to love, to sway by love, to govern by love, to teach by love, to civilize by love!" McCord maintained that "woman throws away her strength, when she *brings herself down* to men's level. She throws away that moral strength, that shadow of divinity, which nature has given her to keep men's ferocity in curb." Although premised on sexual differentiation, this evangelical argument summoned women to transform men and sanctioned transgression of social boundaries. Leadership was a gradual melding of gender identities. Mary Chesnut thought that McCord combined "the intellect of a man and the strength and perseverance of a woman." In addition to her education and literary career, McCord stretched convention by managing her family plantation. During the Civil War, she followed the ideology of woman's mission to a controversial conclusion by serving as nurse and administrator at a Confederate hospital on the grounds of South Carolina College. She certainly understood the SCMA to be a political organization rather than a merely instinctual expression of women's grief. Six months after she assumed the presidency, she resigned in protest against the short-lived Union Reform strategy of cooperation with conservative Republicans, declaring that "to our beloved dead, principles are a nobler monument than marble."[3]

Before she resigned, McCord composed a public appeal addressed to the women of South Carolina that eloquently summarized the SCMA's principles. Her statement described the group as defined by emotional and tangible sacrifice, established to parallel as well as honor the soldiers' "great sacrifice of pure purpose." McCord announced that membership dues had been set "at the lowest point practicable" to broaden opportunities for participation to those "who, having little to give, have still the right, through tears and suffering, to join us in the fulfillment of this most sacred duty." She exhorted other South Carolinians to "give to us freely according to your means, give generously; give gratefully to the memory of those who gave their lives for us." Consistent with this objective, the group initially raised money almost exclusively through donations, disdaining bazaars and raffles. McCord expressly invited men as well as women to contribute, but the prospectus figured women as the leaders of the community project and self-sacrificing counterparts to fallen soldiers.[4]

This vision of women as representatives of South Carolina took on a special concreteness amid the effort to resist Reconstruction by forming institutions that would undermine the Republican government. The SCMA emblazoned on its official history the state motto that appeared on the first Confederate flag of South Carolina, *animis opibusque parati*.[5] From the outset the women sought to place their monument in a conspicuous public location. When soil instability frustrated the initial plan to set it atop a hill with a commanding view of the city, the SCMA reluctantly accepted the gift of a site outside the front gate of Elmwood Cemetery while continuing to raise funds for the statue, which they placed in storage upon its delivery in September 1875. After the Democratic "redemption" of South Carolina in the disputed 1876 election, the legislature granted the SCMA's petition for a site at the capitol and paid for relocation of the base from Elmwood Cemetery, ratifying the authority of the women to act on behalf of the state.

If the SCMA defied patriarchy by placing women alongside fallen soldiers on a plane of citizenship defined by sacrifice, the image of manhood
advanced by the organization contrasted equally sharply with the ideal of
mastery that slaveholding had fostered. The most obvious expression of
this alternative ideal was the statue that the SCMA ordered from Muldoon,
Walker, and Cobb for ten thousand dollars in July 1873. In the organizational history, SCMA secretary Isabella Martin identified the figure as "a
picket 'in for' a night's duty," wearing a cloak on his shoulders to ward off
the midnight chill and holding his rifle upright with bayonet fixed. At the
time the SCMA placed its order, about forty such single-figure sentinels had
been dedicated in northern communities; only one monument similar to
the Columbia design had been installed in the states of the former Confederacy, in a cemetery in Wilmington, North Carolina. The SCMA, which reported proudly that all members of the Muldoon firm and all workmen on
the Columbia job were Confederate veterans, clearly was not attempting to
emulate its northern counterparts. Instead, its design selection evoked an
intersectional wartime culture of sentimentality.[6]

The picket was a prominent character in this representation of the Civil
War because he embodied the soldier as an individual, not as a part merged
into a mass, and offered an opportunity to imagine his thoughts during his
long, lonely vigils. Popular songs emphasized that in those hours, the sentinel mostly dwelled on the sweetness of home. For example, in "All Quiet
along the Potomac To-Night," widely circulated on both sides of the line,
the night guard envisioned his children ("the two on the low trundle-bed /
Far away in the cot on the mountain") and then turned to his wife:

> The moon seems to shine as brightly as then,—
> > *That night* when the love yet unspoken
> Leaped up to his lips, and when low-murmured vows
> > Were pledged to be ever unbroken.
> Then drawing his sleeve roughly over his eyes,
> > He dashed off tears that are welling,
> And gathers his gun close up to its place,
> > As if to keep down the heart-swelling.

The extreme vulnerability of the isolated picket also encapsulated soldiers'
stoic acceptance of their uncontrollable fates in the staggeringly deadly
war. Martin reported that "the most striking characteristic of the statue"
was the "full manly strength" of the determined expression on the soldier's
face. This mid-Victorian ideal was defined by principled endurance of pri-
vation rather than aggressive exertion of force.[7]

The SCMA added a local twist to the intersectional gender construction by asking the sculptor to model the face of the statue from a photograph of Stephen Elliott. The choice was in some respects peculiar, for the monument explicitly honored men who died in the performance of duty, and Elliott lived until 1866, though he never fully recovered from wounds sustained late in the war. Moreover, Elliott had entered the Confederate army as an officer and risen to the rank of general, which conflicted with the statue's focus on the private as an emblematic figure. But as the commander at Fort Sumter for the first nine months after the fall of Battery Wagner in September 1863, Elliott's stoic perseverance through constant bombardment had come to personify a heroic manhood defined by steady fortitude rather than dashing battlefield charges. A poignant eulogy delivered before the state legislature by historian and politician William Henry Trescot capped this reputation by describing Elliott as a typical South Carolina soldier who "simply did his duty where his country put him." Another eulogist stressed that Elliott brought to Fort Sumter the strength he had gained in his wartime religious conversion, an experience that the sentimental image of soldiers often highlighted and that—like unglamorous, self-effacing toil—was central to prescribed ideals of womanhood. Even a quarter century after the dedication of the Columbia monument, remembrance of Elliott would prompt the reflection that "the bravest are the tenderest often and that man is at his best when some womanly thought ennobles him, just as womanhood is soundest with a touch of manliness to make it strong."[8]

The SCMA invited Trescot to expand on his portrait of the representative South Carolina soldier by commissioning the historian to write the monument's inscription. The result was a masterpiece of its genre, reprinted in magazine articles and literary anthologies and reproduced on at least a dozen other Confederate monuments around the South. More than a century later, V. S. Naipaul reported that it deservedly remained known in South Carolina as a text that "contained much of the South's idea of itself." Novelist and screenwriter Larry McMurtry called it "one of the noblest pieces of prose ever produced in the South."[9]

Consistent with Trescot's belief that "it ought to be true and simple and yet there is an element of ornateness that a monument inscription requires," the historian built his composition around an insistent parallel structure that highlighted the qualities of deliberateness and equipoise in the Confederate soldier. Arguing that the dead "HAVE GLORIFIED A FALLEN CAUSE / BY THE SIMPLE MANHOOD OF THEIR LIVES," he located that simple manhood in "THE PATIENT ENDURANCE OF SUF-

FERING, / AND THE HEROISM OF DEATH." The inscription on the front
of the monument echoed the popular songs of the Civil War by emphasiz-
ing the close connections between loved ones at home and soldiers who

> IN THE DARK HOURS OF IMPRISONMENT,
> IN THE HOPELESSNESS OF THE HOSPITAL,
> IN THE SHORT, SHARP AGONY OF THE FIELD,
> FOUND SUPPORT AND CONSOLATION
> IN THE BELIEF
> THAT AT HOME THEY WOULD NOT BE FORGOTTEN.

The inscription on the reverse side of the monument further elaborated a
vision of manhood consistent with the sentimental ideal. Trescot stressed
that moral purity, and particularly a strong sense of self-restraint, had
guided the soldiers through life and into the afterlife. He enjoined future
strangers looking at the monument to

> RECOGNIZE THAT THESE WERE MEN
> WHOM POWER COULD NOT CORRUPT,
> WHOM DEATH COULD NOT TERRIFY,
> WHOM DEFEAT COULD NOT DISHONOR.[10]

The dedication ceremony on May 13, 1879, not only praised the power
of self-restraint exhibited by the dead but tested its presence among the
living. Later described by journalist William Watts Ball as "one of the greatest days, it may be the greatest, that ever [Columbia] has known," the spectacle marked for many whites "the first time after the war and 'Reconstruction,' which had ended two years before, that South Carolinians with
a feeling of sureness that they were a free people let themselves loose in a
mighty jubilation." Excursion trains from around the state brought a crowd
estimated to include as many as twenty thousand people. Observers re-
layed breathlessly that the streets were alive "with military either marching in glittering bodies or strolling upon the pavements and commingling
with the civilians. The air has been continually resonant with the sounds
of thunderous salute, bugle call or martial music." The SCMA and its supporters took pride, however, that the excitement did not overwhelm participants' self-possession. The Columbia daily newspaper reported that of
the more than one thousand former soldiers in arms "not a man was intoxicated." The SCMA official history declared it "one of the largest, most enthusiastic, and at the same time most orderly, harmonious and satisfactory
demonstrations that Columbia has ever seen."[11]

The women sought to stimulate emotion if not boisterousness. The SCMA dramatized the pathos of the occasion by raising the statue into position on May 10 as the city bell tolled to summon white Columbia for observance of Memorial Day. Quoting one of the most sentimental ballads of the war, an observer wrote that "the tears swell as we recall the fact that this figure is typical of the brave and fallen youth who was 'somebody's darling.'" Newspapers reported that veteran soldiers cried at the dedication ceremony, which reached its climax in the unveiling of the monument by four young women orphaned by the war, each escorted by a young veteran who had lost an arm for the Confederacy.[12]

The tattered battle flags that the SCMA had urged veterans to bring as "votive offerings to the great memorial celebration" rivaled the monument as the focus of the melodrama. More than a dozen of the totemic objects linked women and men in a community of sacrifice. The two features of the flags that most commanded interest were the role of women in presenting standards to units and the stories of soldiers who gave their lives holding the banners. The official proceedings of the dedication recorded that seventeen color-bearers had been shot down at Chancellorsville while carrying the bullet-riddled battle flag of Orr's Regiment of Rifles, presented to the unit by the widow of its previous commander.[13] This motif of the fallen standard-bearer was widely popular in the sentimental culture of the war and its aftermath, in part for the same reasons as the lonely picket. The standard-bearer was also an exceptionally vulnerable representative of the ordinary individual soldier detached from the mass of the army. The soldier carrying the colors in battle did not have the same opportunity to contemplate his family, but he devoted himself to protecting a tangible trust from women at home.

John Preston's oration at the monument dedication confirmed that influential men shared the ideals of manhood advanced by the SCMA. The contrast Preston identified between "the wild enthusiasm with which [the soldiers] began the fight, and the stern religious courage with which they met all its terrible trials" tracked the narrative of male conversion emphasized in the antebellum writing of McCord, whom Preston's wife had succeeded as president of the SCMA. The former head of the Confederate conscription bureau, Preston personified military service as a submission to duty rather than an exercise of voluntarism. He emphasized that southern soldiers had no equals in "calm endurance and fortitude, in meek submission to and humble reliance on the God of all Truth." Preston's administrative position also made him a representative of the rights of noncombatants, such as the women of the SCMA, to address the meaning of the war. This point produced some controversy when his shrill defense of secession and resistance to Reconstruction drew objections that "denunciation and vituperation . . . come with ill grace from one who saw no active field service." Preston's defenders grounded his right to speak for the community in terms that applied equally to women: he had served the Confederacy faithfully in a capacity appropriate for his physical condition, and he had lost a son to the cause.[14]

Preston's oration more directly recognized women as entitled by their sacrifices to represent the public. He suggested that the Wayside Hospital at the Gervais Street railroad depot in Columbia, burned during Sherman's invasion, "would have been as grand a monument to these women as that granite and marble is to the dead soldier." In saluting women's wartime entry into a new segment of the labor force, Preston stressed not that the hospital initiative had demonstrated feminine solicitude and tenderness but that the "earnest, active, efficient, working sacrifice" had left "fair, delicate women, wasted, haggard, tottering beneath burdens which might have crushed the stoutest of us." He further pursued the motif of women's sacrifices by pointing out that the soldier statue looked toward the neighborhood most devastated in the burning of Columbia. More specifically, he observed, the monument was "placed on the spot where these women stood shelterless, in the black winter night, with their old men and half-naked children gazing thitherward at their crumbling houses . . . burned to the ground by those who had slain the men whose effigy overtops the column." Preston asked, "Is not this monument meant, in part, to commemorate that scene?" He rhetorically urged the SCMA to "go, ladies, and call your sculptor here, and bid him complete his half-told tale and carve there, in deep relief, your own images, crouching and shuddering, and huddling around the base."[15]

A jarring reminder of Confederate military impotence amid white South Carolinians' celebration of their victory over Reconstruction, this vivid picture of an implied component to the monument presented the collective ordeal of soldiers and female civilians as the epitome of the broader system of gender equivalencies and transferences embedded in the work of the SCMA. The marble memorial promised to stand as a permanent declaration that white southern men and women shared a common experience, an overlapping potential for religious virtue, and a unified public authority.

The SCMA's interpretations of manhood and womanhood faced immediate challenges. Upon the dedication of the soldier monument, one editorialist predicted sadly that "few who shall come hereafter to behold this shaft shall pause to read the fair inscriptions in comparison with the thousands who shall carry with them a vivid recollection of that warrior image there poised aloft, the teacher, the exemplar, of the spirit and lust of military glory." The writer called for continued emphasis on the Christian piety of the Confederate army but sighed that "we all feel our pulses bound and our natures aglow at the mention of the martial deeds of glory." The SCMA also encountered opposition to its model of female citizenship. When a lightning bolt destroyed the statue in June 1882, many men suggested that women had achieved the transitional objective of rehabilitating men and should now step aside. South Carolina College president William Porcher Miles declared that the statue had been "erected by the untiring zeal and devotion and self-denial of our women; let it be reerected by the public spirit and liberality of our men." The SCMA ignored this attempt to displace its sponsorship. In May 1884, the women installed a nearly identical replacement statue that amplified their claim to public authority, for they moved the monument from the east wing of the statehouse to a more prominent site in front of the main entrance.[16] Tensions between Lost Cause men and women deepened in the last two decades of the nineteenth century. The establishment of new associations for former Confederate soldiers reshaped the rivalry, which was especially evident in white southern gatherings for Memorial Day and veterans' reunions.

Memorial Day was the most dynamic early vehicle for Confederate remembrance, in part because the structure of the ritual accommodated conflict and change. In Columbia, as in the Charleston observance that featured the first reading of Timrod's "Ode," the holiday began in 1866 as a bombastic spectacle. Former Confederate officers and soldiers formed the center of a parade to Elmwood Cemetery accompanied by a military band. Renowned artillery commander Edward Porter Alexander, now professor of mathematics and engineering at the University of South Carolina, served as marshal. At the rural cemetery, Colonel Fitz William McMaster delivered a lengthy address in which he insisted that the South had "exercised a legitimate and constitutional right" and conceded sardonically that "Massachusetts, wielding the *brutum fulmen* of the West, has triumphed." After passage of the Military Reconstruction Acts in 1867, Columbia shifted to a more somber Memorial Day performance of victimhood led by the local Ladies' Memorial Association (LMA). The deeply political exercises remained open to tactical innovations. The superheated electoral campaign of 1876 produced "differences of opinion or a misunderstanding between the ladies . . . and their gentlemen friends" over the LMA's resolution to limit the decoration of graves to the Confederate dead, which some observers interpreted as an unduly pointed exclusion of the eight to ten Federal graves at Elmwood. The LMA canceled its public ceremony, citing fear of violence between advocates of fusionist and straight-out resistance to Reconstruction; the women privately decorated the graves of the Confederate dead. McMaster and a group of fellow Confederate veterans organized substitute exercises, which included decoration of the Union graves and a call for intersectional goodwill during the year of the national centennial. Democratic Party chair and straight-out proponent Alexander Haskell characterized this fusionist initiative as a "war of men against women." After the coalescence of the straight-out campaign and installation of the redeemer government, however, the ritual resumed its recent pattern with minor adjustment.[17]

As Haskell recognized, that pattern began with the auspices of women. Before the term "Memorial Day" fully took hold, newspapers often referred to the event as "the anniversary of the Ladies' Memorial Association." The proceedings reinforced not only women's civic engagement but also the overall gender ideals epitomized by the soldier monument. The first phase of Memorial Day, signaled by the tolling of the city and church bells for an hour in the morning, positioned Confederate memory as a bond between secular society and organized religion. Committees of women decorated Confederate graves at the principal churches of each denomination. Sometimes these congregations held services later in the morning. After 1879 the soldier monument at the statehouse was also an important site for ornamentation with ivy, moss, flowers, wreaths, and Confederate flags. During the early afternoon, women decorated twenty-eight Confederate graves scattered around Elmwood Cemetery and installed elaborate floral displays at the cemetery entrance and in the enclosure that contained the graves of 264 Confederate soldiers. When the city bell tolled again in the late afternoon, businesses closed to enable citizens to assemble at the rural cemetery. Newspapers routinely reported attendance by more than one thousand people, "representing all the best elements of our community," from a white population that in 1890 totaled only 6,563 residents of all ages. Ordinarily led by the governor after redemption, a procession moved to the

Confederate enclosure for a prayer. Schoolgirls placed flowers on each of the graves, after which the crowd dispersed quietly.[18]

The 1888 formation of a Confederate Survivors' Association for Richland County, the offshoot of a regional movement that consolidated one year later as the United Confederate Veterans (UCV), led to significant shifts in the structure of Memorial Day. The atmosphere of exercises became less solemn and more celebratory. The approximately fifty members of the association, which later took the name Camp Hampton, instituted an annual procession from the soldier monument to the cemetery, escorted by active military units and a city band. The ex-soldiers also sponsored evening addresses that drew large crowds. Columbia newspapers reported in 1894 that "the chief event of Memorial Day" was the appearance at the opera house by James Armstrong, "the famed, loved and admired soldier-orator of Charleston," whose presentation featured breathless tales of military adventure and humorous stories of camp life.[19]

The veterans made Confederate survivors the equal of wartime casualties as the honored heroes of Memorial Day. The association obtained a lot in Elmwood Cemetery, separate from the Confederate enclosure, to be made available to veterans. By the 1890s, observance of Memorial Day concluded not with the decoration of graves in the enclosure but with a community visit to Camp Hampton's "bivouac of the dead," now one of the sites embellished in the afternoon by the LMA. The veterans marched around the lot and received wreaths from women to place on the graves of former comrades. After 1901, the dramatic finale of Memorial Day exercises at Elmwood became women's presentation of "crosses of honor" to selected veterans. Irene Goldsmith Kohn, one of the Columbia women most active in Confederate commemoration, asked in exasperation, "Can we not . . . give some other day to the living and let that one day, May 10th, stand in sacred remembrance to our honored dead? Only in this way can we preserve its true significance."[20]

The veterans' ideal of the Confederate soldier was not the sentimental figure that the SCMA had honored. He was distinguished by his martial prowess rather than his vulnerability, and while he grandly appreciated the support he received from women at home, he was also sustained by his political claims and by loyalty to his fellow soldiers. The 1899 observance of Memorial Day featured the women's presentation of an obelisk in the Elmwood enclosure, dedicated expansively to "The Soldiers of the Confederate States." The main inscription emphasized that the constitutional prerogatives of white southern manhood had survived the war:

THE DEATH OF MEN IS NOT
THE DEATH OF RIGHTS THAT
URGED THEM TO THE FRAY.[21]

In addition to the assertion of rights, soldierly camaraderie characterized the masculine ideal of Confederate veterans' organizations. Innes Randolph's song "With the Boys of the Sixties" was the anthem of the movement. The ditty about an old soldier hurrying his wife as she helps him dress to go out "paradin' with the boys" matched a gendered revision of the social experience of the war. In the new account, men were gregarious; women were isolated. "His was the merry, ringing laugh of camp, the pleasing incident of the march, the daring and ruthless adventure, the battle, the shout of victory," recalled an evening Memorial Day address. "Her's was the keen anguish of a refined and sensitive nature, mourning over loved ones lost." The dichotomy reversed the polarity of the soldier monument, in which a women's collective had honored the solitary, brooding sentinel.[22]

The transformation of Memorial Day also moved race more squarely to the foreground of Confederate commemoration. In Columbia, the celebration of white supremacism centered on William Rose, a body servant to Maxcy Gregg during the Civil War. In this capacity, Rose attended the return of Gregg's remains to Columbia after the brigadier general died at the Battle of Fredericksburg. Rose regularly joined the Memorial Day military procession from the soldier monument to Elmwood Cemetery during the 1890s as an orderly of the Richland Volunteers. Newspaper accounts of the observance highlighted his annual presentation of a large wreath on Gregg's tomb. White southern women later became custodians of nostalgia for supposedly faithful slaves, but in its initial Columbia emergence, the commemoration of mastery supported a masculine trend in Confederate remembrance.[23]

The gendered upheaval culminated in the rise of the veterans' reunion as the most prestigious Confederate commemorative ritual during the 1890s and early 1900s. In 1899, for example, Columbia women rescheduled Memorial Day to October because local veterans attended a state reunion in Charleston on May 10. Veterans' reunions drew relatively little from the religious framework that was fundamental to the cemetery gatherings and concentrated less on the casualties of the war than on its survivors. Festivities provided a roseate image of the camaraderie of the Confederate army. The Columbia daily newspaper began its report on the 1901 state convention by reprinting "With the Boys of the Sixties" and observing that the poem accurately described the veterans fortunate enough to participate in the grand parade.[24]

Veterans' reunions showcased an ideal of womanhood that differed radically from the assertion of citizenship at the statehouse monument and on Memorial Day. The primary official roles for women were positions as "sponsors" for participating veterans' groups, along with the sponsors' attending maids of honor. These attractive young women played a conspicuous part in the conventions. Sponsors and maids took the stage in ritual presentations of virgins to veterans; they danced at reunion balls; they chatted informally with old soldiers and sometimes delivered addresses. "The reunion would lose half its charm without the presence of the sponsors," judged one observer. Fifty-nine-year-old C. Irvine Walker of Charleston, longtime commander of the South Carolina division of the UCV and leading champion of sponsors, summarized the belles' significance for the veterans when he acknowledged the formal introduction of the young women to the old soldiers at the 1901 state reunion. Faced with an "avalanche of beauty," every gray-haired man recalled his youthful vigor and wished that "he could welcome you, as he did the fair girls of Confederate times. How that was I will leave to your imagination and to your mothers to tell you. We have not forgotten, but the well known modesty of the men of Carolina prevents a public explanation." Elizabeth Lumpkin, an especially popular sponsor, provided the desired response two years later when the twenty-three-year-old told a state reunion that "there is one regret concerning the men we may love and marry—they cannot be Confederate soldiers!" An embodiment of proven male potency, the sponsor had no function as a religious or civic partner.[25]

Distinguished sociologist Katharine Du Pre Lumpkin later published a withering reminiscence of the Confederate veterans' movement in Columbia in her autobiography, *The Making of a Southerner* (1946). Seventeen years younger than her sister Elizabeth, she had attended the 1903 reunion as a six-year-old "thrilled by the spectacle of the Lost Cause but not quite taken in." When old enough to recite a poem at a meeting of a Confederate veterans' camp, Lumpkin learned about "the humdrum, everyday labor that went into preserving a Lost Cause." She found "no bands, no thrilling songs, no crowds, no excitement of any kind" but only "fifteen or twenty aged men, droning away at their business and making decorous use of numerous spittoons strategically placed among them." The political failures of her father, a fervent Lost Cause orator, showed Lumpkin that Confederate commemoration could not replace the collapsed plantation order. "More change had come to our Southern world than we had been prepared for," she concluded, "and this despite the labor of Lost Cause men." Recoiling from what she deemed a culture of stagnation, she focused her scholarly career on the process of industrialization that was reshaping the town in which she had spent much of her childhood.[26]

Many white southern women at the turn of the century disagreed with Lumpkin's sense that Confederate memory and modernity were incompatible. They sought not merely to reassert the historical interpretation and gender ideals advanced by the SCMA and the LMA but to update Confederate remembrance into a newer social vocabulary. As the veterans' challenge had cohered with the founding of a survivors' association, Lost Cause women of Columbia found an institutional vehicle for their response in the establishment of the Wade Hampton Chapter of the United Daughters of the Confederacy (UDC), organized in 1895 on the thirty-fifth anniversary of the secession ordinance.

The UDC represented a generational shift in white southern women's commemorative activism. The transition was a harmonious adjustment rather than a rupture. Twenty-two of the twenty-eight founding members of the Wade Hampton Chapter were also members of the LMA. But the UDC much more energetically sought to fit Confederate remembrance into the lives of women who had come of age long after the end of the Confederacy. The LMA limited itself to coordination of Memorial Day and occasional projects like the Elmwood obelisk. The UDC envisioned Confederate commemoration as a wider field of civic activity. Sally Elmore Taylor, the driving force of the Wade Hampton Chapter during its first decade, observed in 1899 that "in the last few years the South Carolina women have become, like other women of the time, restlessly active and actively useful in modes unguessed before by their grandmothers." Taylor linked this impulse to the dramatic expansion of women's higher education, noting that "the more that women are turned out of colleges, the more energies are thrown among us." The youngest charter member of the Wade Hampton Chapter was among the first women to attend South Carolina College when the school became co-educational in 1895.[27] In its major initiatives, a museum and a book, the Columbia chapter remembered the Civil War as a template for the work of such educated, middle-class women. That emphasis brought Confederate commemoration into line with a dominant American intellectual trend by replacing sentimental tropes of sacrifice and conversion with an equally millennial rhetoric of social Darwinism.

An anonymous 1901 article on "The Problem of the Feminine" in the organ of the statewide UDC division summarized the new evolutionary premises of Lost Cause women's gender ideology. The overview began with the biblical creation of men and women as "the complement and counterpart of the other—the two equally important 'halves' whose union constituted the perfect 'whole' of humanity." The degradation of women was part of the Fall from paradise. Prehistoric and ancient peoples began to define women through sex and work; woman was "the slave and drudge of man." With the rise of chivalry, "he now elected that she should become his plaything and mock divinity!" The fading of this quixotic extravagance merged a lasting appreciation for woman's potential influence with a renewed awareness of woman's indispensable labor. From that point onward, woman's position in society slowly improved until at last she might "present her reasons for laying claims to the 'rights' not accorded her." In the white South, however, the chivalric phase had persisted until the Civil War. The aspirations of antebellum women were "gently murdered, tenderly crushed." The postwar expansion of "the toiling sisterhood" turned the region toward an advance in "civilization," a keyword of pseudo-Darwinist ideology. Work was the theme that defined the UDC vision of womanhood. The title of the official organ of the South Carolina division was *The Keystone: A Monthly Journal Devoted to Woman's Work*. The publishers and editors of the Charleston-based magazine were Mary Barnett Poppenheim and her sister Louisa, both Vassar graduates born in the late 1860s.[28]

Although considerably older than the Poppenheim sisters, Sally Elmore Taylor typified the application of this evolutionary framework to the Lost Cause. For Taylor, the Confederate experience was a decisive phase of human development. "The contest itself cannot be shut into the records of military struggle," she told a state UDC convention. "We must go far back for the root of the matter. All the previous patriotisms of all the peoples of the earth were vitalized in that civilization which called men, women and children to the work of 1860." Secession had failed, but the work of Confederate civilization continued to beckon. White southerners were "a part of Universal History made the ethical and ethnical expression of a principle and a people." They awaited a millennium that would include a new prosperity. Taylor declared that "South Carolina is to go to court some day and she is not going in a calico dress." This promise of productivity began with Confederate women. Their material contributions were essential to the impressive performance of Lee's army, and women's work remained crucial to the progress of the race after Appomattox. Taylor was skeptical about women's suffrage, though she understood that gender ideology was changing significantly at the turn of the century. Shortly before the 1895 state constitutional convention that dodged the call for enfranchisement, she wrote that "some of us old fogy women snap at the new time woman, but the new one will have her day." She focused the Wade Hampton Chapter on projects that depicted the Confederacy as the seedbed of the work that characterized transformative modern womanhood.[29]

Taylor's proposal to the Wade Hampton Chapter in March 1896 to create a Confederate Record and Relic Room hinted at the tensions between the emergence of the UDC and the commemorative agenda favored by veterans. Part of a regional surge of interest in relic displays as a form of Confederate remembrance, the Columbia initiative coincided with the announcement of a large donation toward the museum project most eagerly anticipated by veterans, the "Battle Abbey" that would eventually be established in Richmond as the Confederate Memorial Institute. The institution founded by the Wade Hampton Chapter underscored the determination of local women that exhibitions should be available throughout the South. The women also resolved from the outset that the objects selected for display should not be limited to the military artifacts that the veterans had in mind for the Battle Abbey.[30]

The siting of the Relic Room reasserted the SCMA's insistence that white southern women were entitled to articulate community ideals in public spaces. The Wade Hampton Chapter initially arranged to display its collections in the South Carolina College library. When the school reclaimed the assigned room after five years, a delegation led by Taylor successfully petitioned the legislature in February 1901 for space in the statehouse. The new Relic Room, at the top of the capitol staircase, looked out at the Confederate soldier monument.[31]

Unlike the SCMA, however, the Relic Room grounded Confederate women's legacy of citizenship in the productivity rather than the sacrifices of the war years. The Wade Hampton Chapter strived to highlight "the skill and enterprise of the women of that time." The first shelf of the central exhibit case featured numerous examples of homespun thread and cloth woven for counterpanes, dresses, and underskirts. Other domestic productions included shoes, candles, mattress ticking, a straw hat, and the hosiery of a woman who, according to the catalogue, "planted the cotton, picked carded and spun it, and knitted the stockings." One display case held a "Confederate Loom," and atop another case rested two spinning wheels. Confederate currency signed in her youth by Wade Hampton Chapter member Malvina Waring documented the controversial entry of

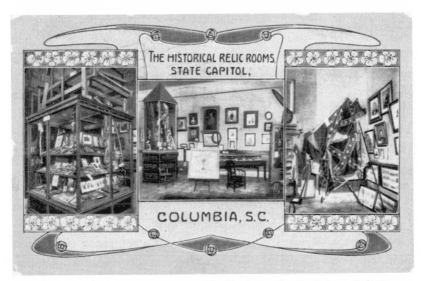

Confederate Relic Room, 1912. Courtesy of the South Carolina Confederate Relic Room and Military Museum, Columbia.

southern women into office work as "department girls" employed at the Treasury printing facility in Columbia. Waring emphasized that the Relic Room recorded women's ambition as well as self-sacrifice, "the genius of rare achievements" as well as "hardships bravely borne." The museum displayed photographs of women who had played leading roles in organizing Confederate hospitals and soldiers' aid societies, including Louisa McCord and Mary Amarinthia Snowden. Women's agency in the religious and sentimental experiences of soldiers received much less attention. The collection included several Bibles and prayer books owned by soldiers, but these items were scattered through the display and not connected to the Christian influence of women. The cataloged relics included the sheet music for patriotic anthems "God Save the South" and "The Southern Marseillaise" but not the homesick ballads with which Columbia printer Julian Selby scored the greatest local successes of wartime music publishing, "All Quiet along the Potomac To-Night" and "Rock Me to Sleep, Mother."[32]

The Relic Room enacted as well as recounted the doctrine that work defined a modern womanhood prepared to advance white southern civilization. The original installation of the collection in the college library aligned the UDC initiative with a field of employment in which women were assuming an increasingly prominent role, education. The Wade Hampton Chapter underscored this connection by simultaneously inaugurating a college essay contest on Confederate history. The women adhered to their educational vision after moving to the statehouse. Taylor reported that "we make this Hall a small College of History. We have twenty-two women as a Relic Room Committee; they serve as our professors of History to visitors, though we call them Hall openers." The prominence of several chairs in a photograph of the Relic Room from the early 1900s suggests that the staff likely took an active role in conversing with visitors about the relics. The absence of descriptive labels in the display cases made this expert assistance especially valuable. As the Relic Room expanded its holdings and hours of operation, responsibility for the institution became paid employment funded by the admission fees charged to visitors.[33]

The same emphasis pervaded the second major project that Taylor initiated within the Wade Hampton Chapter in 1896, a publication describing women's work during the Civil War. Taylor envisioned a two-volume work. The first book would collect membership rolls and other materials related to hospitals and soldiers' aid societies; the second would "represent the manufacturing and industrial efficiency of the women." The statewide UDC division made the undertaking a large-scale collaboration to which many women contributed personal narratives, documents, or editorial services. As at the Relic Room, the celebration of work implied opportunities for individual distinction. Taylor warned against an outdated self-effacing feminine modesty, stipulating that "the names of those who figure in the narratives submitted to the committee shall be given without reserve." On another occasion she observed that "these rolls are as necessary as those of the men who stood before the enemy to present State history in its completeness." Taylor headed a successful appeal to the South Carolina legislature for an appropriation that financed the printing of the first volume in 1903 through the purchase of several hundred copies for distribution to local libraries. The publication of the second volume in 1907 completed another monument to the civic authority claimed by white southern women as exemplars of Confederate virtues.[34]

Much as John Preston had endorsed the SCMA's gender ideals at the dedication of the soldier monument, Yates Snowden's introduction to *South Carolina Women in the Confederacy* demonstrated that prominent South Carolina men shared the revised ideal of womanhood proposed by the UDC. The frontispiece to the book featured a photographic portrait of Snowden's late mother, Mary Amarinthia Yates Snowden. Her son had spent most of his early career in journalism, but his reputation as an antiquarian would bring him an appointment in 1904 as head of the history department at the University of South Carolina. He recognized that the UDC aimed to record women's work "not only in making banners, 'binding her warriors' sash,' and those offices which the cold-blooded materialist classes as 'sentimental'; but woman as a potent factor in furnishing food and clothing for the men on the battle line, and for the wounded and dying in the hospital." He identified southern women's associations as tenacious counterparts to the well-funded northern Christian Commission and U.S. Sanitary Commission and indispensable adjuncts to the inadequate commissary and quartermaster departments of the Confederate army. The compilation offered rich material not only to the poet who would praise the beauty of women's devotion but also to the statistician and political economist who would explain how the Confederacy achieved its military successes. Snowden's essay reflected the extent to which unpaid domestic labor and paid employment had redefined white southern womanhood since the war. His emphasis on material productivity also made South Carolina women of the war era suitable forebears for the rapidly expanding manufacturing sector of the state economy.[35]

The social Darwinism that reinforced UDC ideas about gender and race also supported a renewed commitment to class stratification. Taylor, a member of one of the most privileged families in South Carolina, illustrated the Lost Cause exaltation of bloodlines by persuading the statewide division to place a marble tablet in the statehouse to commemorate her cousin and three comrades shot while carrying the colors of the 1st South Carolina Volunteers during the Battle of Gaines's Mill. Like sixteen-year-old James Hunt Taylor, the other soldiers were sons of wealthy families. In her appeal to the state UDC convention for the memorial, Taylor described the incident as an epitome of family leadership in South Carolina. More than merely members of an army unit, the standard-bearers revealed "the long story of womanhood, manhood, statesmanship and the result." The state's prospects depended on a genealogical transmission of exemplary traits. The well-born role models evinced "vitalities which acted through our past, underlie our present and which are bound to be emerging in our future." Even the melodramatic figure of the fallen flag-bearer now claimed commemoration not as a solitary vulnerable individual but as patriotic justification for the status of the elite.[36]

Lost Cause women in turn-of-the-century Columbia further expressed their vision of the class order in an enthusiasm for Confederate commanders that contrasted with the SCMA's focus on the common soldier. The dozens of Relic Room photographs cataloged in 1904 included fewer than ten enlisted men. One shelf of pictures featured forty-seven generals, six-

teen other officers, and two men of unspecified rank. The Wade Hampton
Chapter reserved its most fervent veneration for Wade Hampton III. One
of the eight cases in the Relic Room, topped by a marble bust, was devoted
entirely to Hampton; three portraits of him hung on the walls.[37]

The class implications of this adulation were not limited to Hampton's
role as personification of the continuity between the planter aristocracy
and the Confederate military hierarchy. The postwar politics of Hampton
and his followers also made him a symbol of the urban and industrial class
stratification deepening in South Carolina. For the Wade Hampton Chapter, the identification of their namesake with the consequences of laissez-
faire capitalism neatly fit a social Darwinism that expected women's work
to lead white southerners toward fulfillment of their racial potential. Men
rising in influence during the same generational shift that produced the
UDC would propose a different trajectory for the evolution of Lost Cause
gender relations.

The South Carolina Monument to Confederate Women, dedicated in April
1912, extended the gender tensions that had recently shaped Memorial Day
and veterans' reunions. When proposals for such monuments began to circulate throughout the South in the mid-1890s, women immediately saw
that efforts to place Confederate womanhood on a pedestal threatened to
cancel the citizenship developed through public indebtedness to women's
devotion to the Lost Cause. UDC members responded that a women's college or at least the endowment of scholarships would be a more welcome
commemorative form if men insisted on a permanent gesture. "Keep back
your shaft of granite; we do not want or need it," hissed one South Carolinian as plans for a state memorial advanced. The dissatisfaction made it
plain that men's commitment to a monument constituted a challenge to
women as much as a tribute to them. A veteran from Chesterfield County
sounded the keynote of the initiative when he declared that "it is always
safe to follow the women, but the boys of the '60s will not follow them in
this."[38] Much more than previous phases of the contest, the monument
project provided a vehicle for comprehensive elaboration of a masculine
commemorative vision. As the UDC had updated the religious ideals of the
SCMA and LMA into zeal for educated women's work, the men behind the
women's monument turned to social Darwinism for a Confederate remembrance inflected by the energies and anxieties of industrialization.

C. Irvine Walker personified veterans' support for a monument that would parallel the appointment of sponsors for UCV camps and divisions. The Charlestonian had come home from the war to a family-based partnership in a prominent printing and paper firm, but his life continued to revolve around the Confederate army and its postwar incarnations. Along with several other veterans, he organized the Carolina Rifle Club as part of the armed resistance to Reconstruction. He took a leading part in the campaign to reopen the Citadel, which ended successfully in 1882. He was the first commander of the South Carolina division of the UCV and eventually became commander in chief of the national organization. In ascending that ladder, he became the chair of the UCV committee on a women's monument in 1903. He muscled aside the fledgling Sons of Confederate Veterans (SCV), founded in 1896, which had sought to make its first substantial mark with a women's memorial and had indicated a willingness to accommodate women's preference for a home for needy Confederate widows. Walker fixed instead on a plan by which each southern state would install a bronze casting of a single monument. Addressing the UDC's national meeting in 1906, he argued that "the very uniformity of the crowning statues will show, as they should, that the South, as a whole, united in paying this magnificent tribute to the women of the South as a whole." The UDC remained diffident. At the same convention, the women "most enthusiastically adopted" a resolution calling on the UCV "to dispense with the offices of Sponsor and Maids of Honor" at the upcoming national reunion and ensure that "the entertainments for that occasion be such as are adapted to aged Confederate veterans."[39]

Walker also encountered frustration in advancing the project through the UCV. His committee stumbled in presenting the veterans with a design by Louis Amateis for a statue of a woman brandishing a sword and Confederate flag, beneath which was emblazoned the inscription "UPHOLD OUR STATE RIGHTS." The antisuffragist fervor that guaranteed rejection of "this brawny Southern Amazon . . . declaiming like a candidate for the Legislature" at the UCV national convention in June 1909 makes it surprising that such a politicized depiction of womanhood ever won Walker's endorsement. The fleeting approval doubtless reflected the vigor with which Amateis's design—like the obelisk installed at Elmwood Cemetery ten years earlier—stressed that southern men had fought and continued to fight to assert their rights. Soon after the setback, Walker endorsed a design proposed by twenty-three-year-old Belle Kinney, the daughter of a Confederate veteran. Commendation of the only woman sculptor to enter the UCV competition did not necessarily imply any shift in Walker's chauvinism.

UDC leaders saw his patronage of the Nashville ingenue as merely another demonstration that veterans were "so susceptible to a winning smile and pleasant manner!" The innocence, beauty, and love Walker complimented in the countenance of Kinney's exemplary young Confederate woman, who bestowed a palm on a dying warrior, were the same attributes he admired in the statuesque sponsors.[40]

Despite his influence among veterans in South Carolina and beyond, Walker played only a subordinate role in the making of the state monument to Confederate women. The dominant force was William Elliott Gonzales, editor of the *Columbia State* newspaper. Born a year after Appomattox, he promoted the perpetuation and transformation of the Lost Cause in the postwar generation of white South Carolina men as energetically as the Poppenheim sisters spread its influence among white South Carolina women of the same age. Gonzales's father, expatriate Cuban revolutionary Ambrosio José Gonzales, had served in the Confederate army after failing to stimulate antebellum annexation of the island by the United States, but the grandson and namesake of literary sportsman William Elliott did not indulge in mere filiopietism. His older brothers founded the *State* in 1891 as a Hamptonite organ of opposition to Ben Tillman's agrarian insurgency. The newspaper soon became a leading advocate of the industrial development reshaping South Carolina. The number of cotton-textile spindles in operation more than tripled during the 1890s, abruptly turning the state into the second-largest producer in the country. Within the next five years, capacity doubled again. By 1905, census data indicated that one in every six white South Carolinians lived in a company-owned mill village. In Columbia, one of the most active centers of development, the proportion was about one in three.[41] The enthusiasm of the *State* for the Lost Cause dovetailed with immersion in the economic and social transformation.

This context for commemoration partly resembled the situation in Fort Mill, South Carolina, which in 1895 dedicated the first monument to Confederate women to be installed anywhere in the South. The sponsor of that monument was Samuel E. White, founder of the cotton-textile manufacturing company that under the name of the allied Springs family would eventually become one of the largest corporations in South Carolina. The former Confederate officer applied profits of the Fort Mill Manufacturing Company toward the commissioning of the local soldier monument unveiled in 1891. Four years later, he expanded the site into a park embellished with monuments to the women of the Confederacy and "THE FAITHFUL SLAVES / WHO, LOYAL TO A SACRED TRUST, / TOILED

FOR THE SUPPORT / OF THE ARMY WITH MATCHLESS / DEVOTION, AND WITH STERLING / FIDELITY GUARDED OUR DEFENCELESS / HOMES, WOMEN AND CHILDREN, DURING / THE STRUGGLE FOR THE PRINCIPLES / OF OUR 'CONFEDERATE STATES OF / AMERICA.'" In 1900, he added a fourth monument that saluted Catawba Indians' support for the Confederacy. Insisting on grassroots backing for some stages of the overall project, White made Confederate Park a commemorative extension of the corporate paternalism imposed in the mill town. The nostalgic promise of community continuity was a familiar pattern. In Columbia as well, the campaign to raise a women's monument prompted at least some supporters to suggest that the logical complement would be a memorial to faithful slaves, presenting the Confederacy as an idyllic harmonious society and a beacon of moral values still applicable amid changing economic conditions.[42]

William Elliott Gonzales recognized, however, that industrialization was changing South Carolina more profoundly than White admitted. Gonzales's role at the *State* reflected the new fissures in white society. When lieutenant governor James Tillman extended his uncle Ben's flamboyant populist strategy to factory workers in the 1902 gubernatorial campaign, Narciso G. Gonzales's scathing criticism prompted the narrowly defeated candidate to murder the newspaper editor in front of the statehouse. The *State* gradually acknowledged the formation of an industrial underclass. In 1898, a correspondent described that process in evolutionary terms. A Methodist minister serving at a mill church predicted that the factory system would produce a physiologically distinct people unable to function elsewhere, like the eyeless fish of Mammoth Cave. The absence of gender differentiation in the mill regime of family labor proved and concentrated the degeneracy of industrialization. The specter of "hundreds of both sexes mingling miscellaneously behind the looms" threatened not only moral but genetic purity. Inbreeding of workers with defective tendencies portended "a monstrosity" more disastrous than Confederate defeat. "War destroyed many of [South Carolina's] inhabitants, but it did not develop a pernicious heredity," the pastor concluded. "Her heroes and her past greatness may live within the pages of history; they cannot be reproduced from a debased heredity." N. G. Gonzales had considered these fears excessive, but by 1905, his successor was ready to draw a quasi-racial line marked "civilization" between bourgeois whites and mill workers. William Elliott Gonzales editorialized that "the white man's superiority over the negro is in civilization; in morals and in education. It is not inherent in each individual. There are many whites as uncivilized, brutish and depraved as the lower stratum of blacks; such whites deserve nothing from their connection with a superior race; they contribute nothing to its supremacy." The Confederate monument championed by Gonzales would honor this ideal of civilization and its primary social predicate, the differentiation of gender roles.[43]

Gonzales was the key consultant to the legislator who sponsored the bill drafted by state archivist Alexander Salley authorizing the women's memorial, and the editor became the influential secretary and treasurer of the monument commission on which Walker served as a figurehead chair. The enactment provided for a state appropriation of seventy-five hundred dollars to be released "when the men of South Carolina have availed themselves of the privilege" of contributing an identical amount. Gonzales conducted the fund-raising drive on the front pages of the *State* from February to August 1909. His approach illustrated the boosterism that he would also show as a leader of the Columbia Chamber of Commerce. Vividly different from the metropolitan effervescence directed by the LCMA in the 1850s or the community of sacrifice envisioned by the SCMA in the 1870s, the appeal for the women's monument reflected the extent to which the expansion of textile manufacturing mapped into a proliferation of southern towns churning with commercial development and real estate speculation. Gonzales's daily exhortations challenged the pride and rivalries of contributing localities. One supporter felt obliged to clarify that receipts forwarded from Rock Hill reflected "a sincere sympathy with the effort to do honor to the noble women of the Confederacy and not an effort to outdo some other town or county." The campaign unhesitatingly promoted Gonzales's company as well as the memorial. Readers did not fail to notice that "the monument to the women is likewise a monument to the loyalty and influence of your paper."[44]

Gonzales's efforts succeeded impressively, as the *State* collected $11,500 in six months. A similar campaign several years earlier for a Hampton equestrian statue had raised less than $3,000 in eighteen months. Women rarely shared in the enthusiasm generated by the men's fund-raising drive. UDC chapters focused instead on the creation of a state home for destitute and infirm Confederate veterans on land owned by the state mental hospital. A closely divided legislature approved establishment of the welfare institution in February 1908 but denied a request of $4,000 to outfit the facility. Upon completion of construction in early 1909, members of the UDC helped to block an attempt by legislative opponents of the Confederate Infirmary to divert use of the building. The organization then launched

Confederate Infirmary, or Soldiers' Home. Courtesy of the South Carolina Confederate Relic Room and Military Museum, Columbia.

a fund-raising campaign for the necessary furnishings. Women argued that this project deserved priority over the simultaneous appeal in the *State* and that the retirement home would make a suitable memorial to Confederate womanhood. Gonzales answered that only a monument comparable in form to the soldier statue at the statehouse could adequately preserve the legacy of Confederate women. The Confederate Infirmary, often called the Soldiers' Home, opened on June 3, 1909, with dormitory accommodations for seventy-six residents. The Wade Hampton Chapter of the UDC served cake to the veterans and played bugle calls on a phonograph. State senator Francis Weston, longtime South Carolina commander of the SCV, noted in his inaugural speech that he had learned his reverence for the Lost Cause in the classroom of Isabella Martin, a charter member of the Wade Hampton Chapter. Her preferences notwithstanding, he served as local chair of fund-raising for the monument to Confederate women. Even the leading alternative to Gonzales's campaign became an advertisement for the proposed memorial.[45]

Gonzales also took the lead in the selection of an artist for the women's monument. Ignoring the UCV competition organized by Walker that would soon yield the successive endorsements of designs by Amateis and Kinney, the newspaper editor wrote in March 1909 to solicit the aid of Frederick Wellington Ruckstuhl. Although based in New York, the fifty-six-year-old sculptor was well known in Columbia. He had designed the Wade Hampton equestrian monument dedicated at the statehouse in 1906 and was presently working on a standing marble of John C. Calhoun for South Carolina to place in Statuary Hall in the U.S. Capitol; the legislature later installed a bronze cast of this portrait at the center of the statehouse lobby. Born in Alsace and raised mostly in St. Louis, the sculptor produced works of Union as well as Confederate commemoration but liked to stress his "constant sympathy for the South." His Confederate memorials for Baltimore (1903) and Little Rock (1905) won particular acclaim. When Gonzales provided a personal guarantee of the fifteen thousand dollars expected from the fund-raising campaign and legislative appropriation, Ruckstuhl accepted the commission. He visited Columbia in May 1909 to encourage public support for the project and delivered a lecture that echoed the boosterism of the daily appeals in the *State*. Embellishment of the statehouse grounds was "a mere commercial proposition and investment, with heavy profits," Ruckstuhl declared.[46] His broader hopes for the project similarly matched Gonzales's commitment to a gendered ideal of civilization.

A founder of the National Sculpture Society and later editor of the magazine *Art World*, Ruckstuhl was among the most outspoken theorists of public art in early-twentieth-century America. He insisted vociferously that universal, rigorous aesthetic laws governed artistic achievement. Discovery of those principles had been the work of centuries, and in the modern age, willful defiance of the rules branded an artist as "either an undeveloped or a degenerate." The convergence of those two retrograde categories was particularly appalling. When Ruckstuhl affirmed in a lecture at the University of South Carolina that he rejected "the new-fangled art fads and isms, such as impressionism, pointism, cubeism, tubeism, and all other kinds of lunaticisms that you may have heard of and which are now rampant in Paris," one of the most dangerous trends from his perspective was the influence of what he soon described as "savage, negro art, which has of late been 'honored,' even by exhibition in our museums . . . as *'splendid'* and *'inspiring'* examples of *'abstract art.'*" For Ruckstuhl, the avant-garde disregard for classically grounded academic standards reversed the millennial evolutionary processes of culture and society. Art was valuable, he told his Columbia audience, only insofar as it was "working for a civilization which aims to subjugate the animal in man and to place it under the control of his spirit." Subsequently amplified by his alarm over the Bolshevik Revolution but never wavering from his entrenched prewar precepts, Ruckstuhl's ideas about national artistic progress and degeneration have been identified by art historian Albert Boime as an important influence on the aesthetic policies of Adolf Hitler and the Nazi Party in Germany.[47]

Ruckstuhl encapsulated his vision of art and society in his design for the South Carolina Monument to Women of the Confederacy. The sculptor explained in an article for the *State* that his overarching plan for the memorial described the social structure best suited for collective advancement. A friendly South Carolina historian—almost certainly Yates Snowden—suggested that Ruckstuhl could "strike the popular chord" by depicting the Confederate woman "engaged in some characteristic work for the soldiers, such as sewing, knitting, nursing, or making hospital supplies." Paraphrasing the introduction to *South Carolina Women in the Confederacy*, the historian observed that the white southern paragon showed her devotion "not merely in the quiet endurance of hardship and suffering, but also and primarily in the work which she did." Ruckstuhl disdained this call for a readily accessible narrative illustration similar to the picket on night duty depicted in the soldier monument. The proposal "lowered my point of view to the mental grasp of the mass of men who are too harassed by labor ever to get the time to study the secrets of successful monumental art." A more complex composition, he argued, would enable "the great and wise" to instruct and edify the community. "The only things that raise a man, or a State, above the merely animal is lofty thought and noble form," Ruckstuhl maintained. "The average man all over the world is not yet very noble, and the noble few are constantly tugging at this mass of their brother men to lift them to a nobler level."[48]

The resulting design aimed to achieve the blend of realism and symbolism that Ruckstuhl admired in great monuments of Western art. His bronze group featured a woman "about forty years of age, but still handsome," wearing a simple dress and chiffon scarf at the end of the Civil War. He specified that she was from "the great middle class" rather than "one of the few very poor, or the few very rich," but her well-bred face was "full of the beauty and aristocracy and the refinement and strength of the perfect type of the Southern woman." She sat on a fantastically ornate chair of state and looked up from the Bible she held in her lap, "lost in a far-away meditation over the past and future of her people," according to the sculptor. He opined that "no higher activity than this, nor a more characteristic one, could be imagined." Behind the seated figure, a winged Genius of the State landed on earth to crown the woman with a laurel wreath. Two accompanying cherubs epitomized Ruckstuhl's faith in a cosmic regime of gender differentiation. A male cherub carried an armful of roses that "boy-like, he did not even bother to tie into a bouquet"; instead he rushed forward "full of enthusiasm" to present them to the Confederate woman. A female cherub advanced "timidly . . . as if half afraid to approach the great lady."[49]

The Confederate woman's demeanor was central to Ruckstuhl's inter-

F. Wellington Ruckstuhl, model for South Carolina Monument to
Women of the Confederacy. Courtesy of the South Caroliniana Library,
University of South Carolina, Columbia.

pretation. Absorbed in her ruminations, she remained oblivious to her
otherworldly visitors. Her impassivity denoted not only the allegorical
realm of the tribute but also a commendably selfless modesty. Ruckstuhl
claimed to aim for "sphinx-like seriousness" in her face, but the blank look
struck another sculptor as "without expression or feeling." More revealingly,
Ruckstuhl repeatedly described the woman as "listless." Listlessness was a
prime symptom of neurasthenia, the diagnosis that turn-of-the-century
male physicians treated as the natural consequence of overexertion by in-
appropriately ambitious women. Doctors theorized that female reproductive systems drained too much energy to permit long-term engagement in
mentally taxing activity. Defiance of these biological limitations would lead
to illness for individuals and catastrophe for the advanced civilization that
exposed women to the conflicting demands of intellectual and reproductive
labor. Ruckstuhl's image of nervous exhaustion not only disregarded but

deplored the UDC's appreciation for the Confederacy as the white southern gateway to educated women's work.[50]

Ruckstuhl's design celebrated motherhood as the highest calling of womanhood. The South Carolina monument participated in a significant change between wartime images of women, which had often focused on soldiers' wives or sweethearts, and Lost Cause gender ideals, which centered more exclusively on mothers. Monuments to Confederate women dedicated in Macon, Georgia (1911), Little Rock, Arkansas (1913), Raleigh, North Carolina (1914), and Jacksonville, Florida (1915), depicted Confederate women with young children. This trend fit into a broader cultural exaltation of motherhood that drew not only on antifeminism but also on white Protestant anxieties about the pace of family formation amid the tide of southern and eastern European immigration into American cities. Not coincidentally, Mother's Day became an annual national festival during the years that South Carolina was planning its tribute to Confederate women. One of the contributors to the Columbia project described it as "a monument to the women of the Confederacy—rather, the mothers of the Confederacy, truly to 'Mother.'"[51]

Ruckstuhl's treatment of this theme extended well beyond his decision to highlight a middle-aged woman. His symbolic program linked Confederate womanhood to the consummate Western image of maternity, for the woman pausing from her reading of scripture for the visit of a glorifying angel evoked traditional iconography of the Annunciation. The sculptor's allusion praised the actual mothering of white southerners and also the conception of regional memory that transformed Confederate defeat into Christian martyrdom. If the pose acknowledged women's contributions to Lost Cause remembrance, which had animated the monument campaign at least as much as their wartime support for the Confederacy, Ruckstuhl did not imply that the sacred legend was a manufactured product. Like the Virgin, the women of the Lost Cause had come as close as possible to divinity by accepting an assigned role as an inspirational embodiment of purity and devotion amid sorrow that looked ahead to resurrection.

Religious idealization reinforced Ruckstuhl's evolutionary schematization. The soldier monument at the South Carolina statehouse invited remembrance of each man who had died in the war. A newspaper editor commented at the 1879 unveiling that "we do not recognize its special resemblance to any one we have known, yet it recalls many faces." The tribute to women sought less to recall the historic achievements of particular individuals than to prescribe a moral standard. This contrast between specification and typification paralleled the influential theory that only males could contribute original physiological traits to offspring and that the female role in reproduction was passive conservation of the hereditary legacy. Male variability, latent in the generic soldier statue, led the racial progress consolidated by the female constancy that Ruckstuhl rendered artistically.[52]

Through such juxtapositions, the monument to Confederate women reframed and redefined the monument to Confederate soldiers. Compared with the seated woman lost in meditation while listlessly holding a Bible, the marble sentinel represented vigilance in anticipation of decisive action more than he had when he was understood as a sentimental stereotype of midnight reverie. The lonely fortitude honored in Ruckstuhl's monument erased remembrance that solitary reflection had been an important aspect of the male experience of the war at the same time that the image elided the organizational activism that had been one of the most memorable aspects of women's experience in the Confederacy. Contrary to John Preston's praise for the volunteers at the Wayside Hospital, supporters of the later project noted that white southern women had benefited from "none of the inspiration which a united host creates" and had struggled to carry on "not to the inspiring music of the military band or in that excitement of the battlefield which leads to self-forgetfulness, but on the deserted plantation."[53]

A crucial reversal was the abandonment of the promise implied in the soldier monument that women's devotion to the Lost Cause ensured lasting public authority. Ruckstuhl underscored their political exclusion by placing in the female cherub's hands a commission from the General Assembly, affixed with the state seal, "to show that the men ordered the monument by passing a law for its erection."[54] The device imagined the legislature not as representative of all South Carolinians but as a male body. The seated figure gazing into the past and future foresaw and fostered the resurrection of the former Confederacy, but her role was merely transitional. Returned to power after Reconstruction and restored to prosperity by industrialization, white men of South Carolina no longer needed the extraordinary interventions of middle-class or elite women. The winged figure reminiscent of the Nike of Samothrace announced that the struggle was over and the monument sponsors were victorious.

Gonzales's inscriptions for the women's monument, intended to echo the famous text of the soldier monument, tried to shift Trescot's somber cadences to this celebratory key. Only one of the three inscriptions described women's wartime activities, concluding blithely that "THE TRAGEDY OF THE CONFEDERACY MAY BE FORGOTTEN / BUT THE FRUITS OF THE NOBLE SERVICE / OF THE DAUGHTERS OF THE SOUTH / ARE OUR PERPETUAL HERITAGE." The other two texts focused on recovery from "THE ASHES OF RUIN." The main inscription began at the moment "WHEN REVERSES FOLLOWED VICTORIES / WHEN WANT DISPLACED PLENTY" and praised postwar women as models for twentieth-century southern society. Ruckstuhl identified the conclusion as the passage that best summarized the idea of the monument:

IN THE REBUILDING AFTER THE DESOLATION
THEIR VIRTUES STOOD
AS THE SUPREME CITADEL
WITH STRONG TOWERS OF FAITH AND HOPE
AROUND WHICH CIVILIZATION RALLIED
AND TRIUMPHED.

The triumph of "civilization" encompassed the economic regeneration of the South and the overthrow of interracial government. As Gonzales had made clear in the *State*, the motif of "civilization" continued to link those two phases of recent South Carolina history by lumping semiwhite mill operatives together with African Americans. Women's virtues served as a temporary rallying point for "civilization," but the actors responsible for its restoration and future were implicitly male.[55]

Joseph W. Barnwell's address at the dedication ceremonies for the monument, held on the thirty-fifth anniversary of federal recognition of Wade Hampton as governor, similarly saluted the women who "gave strength to the men and enabled them to withstand the temptations of the days of reconstruction and to look forward to the end when civilization should again triumph and barbarism be overthrown." He, too, warned that this exciting example should not distract modern women from domestic duties. The sixty-six-year-old Barnwell had fought in the Civil War as a Citadel cadet and championed the Hamptonite faction in state politics during the 1890s. Identifying himself at the outset as "a boy of the 'sixties,'" he organized his oration around the remarkable changes he had seen in South Carolina during his long life. He began with the observation that the seedbed of secession was "a very different State from the State we now know." The antebellum economy was almost entirely agricultural, without "the great cotton manufacturing industry" that in number of looms and spindles now stood second only to Massachusetts. Mills employed a workforce almost half as large as the white population of South Carolina in 1860. The low-country phosphate industry had also sprung up since the war. Slave labor, Barnwell noted more defensively, had ended.

"Among the vast changes of the last sixty years," the Charleston attorney told the women of South Carolina, "none has been greater than in the position of your sex." Work was the heart of that shift. "Field after field has been opened for your energies, and few occupations or employments are now closed to you which you care to enter," Barnwell reported. He claimed sympathy with the trend but worried that it threatened love, marriage, and childbearing. "Shall sentiment depart?" he asked. "Shall grace be banished and beauty be neglected or despised?" Confederate heroines were not "unsexed and denatured women," he emphasized. The orator urged women to "go on with your educational work . . . but do not forget that after all you are not, and cannot be, men, and that love and admiration are as well worth winning as an acknowledgment of superiority or cold respect." Family formation was the primary challenge of white southern civilization.[56]

The fund-raising strategy, artistic design, inscriptions, and dedication ceremonies for the South Carolina Monument to Confederate Women differed diametrically from corresponding features of the soldier monument on the opposite side of the statehouse. Appreciation for cross-class availability of permeable, interpenetrating gender traits gave way to bourgeois insistence on a stricter gender differentiation that defined manhood through gregarious assertion of rights and womanhood through maternal grace. The men's tribute also contrasted sharply with women's commemorative undertakings like the Confederate Relic Room, which defined manhood through command of power and womanhood through resourceful competence.

Beneath these important tensions, the Lost Cause maintained some consistent emphases from the soldier monument to the women's monument and between the initiatives of Sally Elmore Taylor and William Elliott Gonzales. White supremacism was the most obvious continuity. Men and women also agreed steadily that Confederate remembrance should feature prominent participation of women even if southerners disagreed about the parameters of that role. The early trope of religious conversion faded, but the Lost Cause remained vigorously Christian. The millennial expectations of social Darwinism offered a mechanism for reconciling orthodoxy with evolutionary theory. Faith in natural selection also united men and women who built a class structure for town life in the industrial age, including plantation heirs such as Taylor and Gonzales.

The combination of stability and adaptability made the turn-of-the-century projects of the UDC, the UCV, and unaffiliated enthusiasts more than a screen obscuring fundamental transformations in the region. The Lost Cause provided not merely ballast but a rudder for navigation of intellectual, economic, and social currents. If suffused with nostalgia, Confederate memory helped to define southern modernity.

Henry Timrod's poem "The Two Armies" (1863) limns the Confederate tale of yin and yang. Distinct legions of men and women stand together beneath the rebel flag: "One, facing battle, blight and blast, / Through twice a hundred fields has past" while "The other, with a narrower scope, / Yet led by no less grand a hope, / Hath won, perhaps, as proud a place, / And wears its fame with meeker grace." Soldiers fight "the ruffian foe"; the distaff brigade equally ably nurses the wounded and "by a thousand peaceful deeds / Supplies a struggling nation's needs." Political mobilization enhances feminine charm, as "many a sweetheart hides her blush / In the young patriot's generous flush." The male army conversely incorporates the influence of the female army, which "nerves the son's, the husband's hand" and "sometimes lifts the veriest clod / To its own lofty trust in God." The partnership promises Confederate victory and domestic bliss: "The triumph grasped, and freedom won, / Both armies, from their toil at rest, / Alike may claim the victor's crest, / But each shall see its dearest prize / Gleam softly from the other's eyes."[57]

Like much southern nationalist rhetoric, Timrod's verses describe Confederate commemoration more accurately than they match the realities of the Civil War. Proposals for gendered harmony pervaded the Lost Cause contributions of Louisa McCord and John Preston, Isabella Martin and William Henry Trescot, Elizabeth Lumpkin and C. Irvine Walker, Mary Barnett Poppenheim and Yates Snowden, Sally Elmore Taylor and William Elliott Gonzales. Representation of the Confederacy as an intimate union linked public memory to private hopes. Far more than the troubled apotheosis of John C. Calhoun, the familial narrative of the Civil War became a flexible, powerful civic myth for generations of white southerners.

Division of the imagined Confederacy into two armies established intellectual space for diversity and debate in commemoration. The female host not only sanctioned an alternative to male authority but also symbolized a less regimented discourse than the military ideal. Exemplary Confederate women were mothers, sisters, sweethearts, wives, and daughters, each with separate relationships to the exemplary Confederate soldier. The logical implication was systemic, creative tension within the Lost Cause. Arguments between men and women may have encouraged and certainly outlasted the postwar sniping among defeated officers that many subsequent historians have regarded as the core of Confederate memory. But the gendered disagreement did not undermine the cultural formation. Despite their criticism of the planning for a monument to Confederate women, many female South Carolinians participated conspicuously in the dedication ceremonies. Similar squabbles and reconciliations continued in future years. In 1921, the superintendent of the Confederate Infirmary resigned in protest against "constant interference and assumption of authority" by UDC members on the supervisory board. The retirement home endured, however, and by the mid-1940s was occupied entirely by Confederate widows, daughters, and nieces.[58]

The familial myth of the two armies presented Confederate remembrance as a productive enterprise. Whether through competition or cooperation, white southern men and women invented an array of commemorative rituals, voluntary organizations, public institutions, artifact collections, documentary records, and monuments. The Lost Cause merged with evolutionary theory to form a social identity that was durable as well as malleable. Confederate cosmology explained race, gender, religion, and class in a pattern that was politically useful because so many white South Carolinians found it satisfying.

Reconstruction assumed a special importance in this template. The overthrow of Republican government substituted for the victory that Timrod's poem had promised in the Civil War. Jubilant remembrance of redemption was one of the most significant similarities between the dedication ceremonies for the soldier monument in 1879 and the women's monument in 1912. Not surprisingly, South Carolina novelists interested in exploration of cultural narratives quickly identified the struggle against Reconstruction as a promising setting for intertwining dramas of personal and community regeneration. That literature, developing within the period bracketed by the call for the soldier monument and the completion of the women's monument, tested the potential and the limitations of the Lost Cause myth.

4 Imagining Home Rule

FICTION WAS A DECISIVE weapon in the campaign
against Reconstruction. Polemical lies and fraudulent electoral returns were as fundamental as violence
to the overthrow of Republican governments in the
former Confederate states. Discrete falsehoods cohered in a more elaborate fiction that Reconstruction
was an exploitation of the vulnerable white South per-
petrated by carpetbaggers, African Americans, and a
few scalawags, backed by an occupying federal army.
The gradual demolition of that myth was one of the
principal achievements of American historical scholarship during the middle and late twentieth century.

Vindication of the facts of Reconstruction led to a
deeper appreciation of its fictions, as historians asked
how the transparently partisan version of events could
have appealed to ostensibly disinterested northerners.
Fresh attention showed that the tale of a baneful oppression ended by the "redemption" of the South overlapped with other stories through which Americans
imagined the postwar order, particularly the reconciliation of North and South to forge a more perfect
union. The fictive narrative of a grassroots intersectional settlement served northern as well as southern

interests in Anglo-Saxon supremacism, exploitation of labor, and eviscera-
tion of government potential to redistribute wealth. The trope also appealed to postwar Americans for a variety of other reasons. Metaphorical
visions of the North and South joined together in a "romance of reunion"
brought the United States into line with newer models of organic nationalism and lent the nineteenth-century prestige of nationalism to the institution of marriage. Sectional reconciliation invited northern Protestants to
anticipate reunification of Christian churches divided by slavery disputes.
The prospect that former enemies could agree on a retrospective interpretation of the Civil War even reinforced faith in the existence of objective
truth. The dominant narrative of Reconstruction was a versatile fiction.[1]

South Carolina occupied a prominent position in this saga. Its leadership in secession ensured that the state would figure frequently in the
canon of sectional reconciliation. John W. De Forest, who based several
short stories and a novel on his experience as a Freedmen's Bureau agent
in South Carolina, borrowed a well-known Charleston surname for the title
character of his major contribution to reunion literature, *Miss Ravenel's
Conversion from Secession to Loyalty* (1867), and featured the low country again in *The Bloody Chasm* (1881).[2] And because its Republicans exercised power longer and more fully than their counterparts elsewhere in
the South, encountering a resistance that prompted substantial federal enforcement measures, South Carolina also became a prime site for mapping
the trajectory of postwar reform. Northern journalist James S. Pike's profile of *The Prostrate State: South Carolina under Negro Government* (1873)
was the most famous of many attacks on the premier laboratory of Reconstruction.[3] The narratives spun by De Forest and Pike came together spectacularly in what were long the most influential fictional or nonfictional accounts of Reconstruction, Thomas Dixon's novel *The Clansman* (1905) and
its adaptation into D. W. Griffith's film epic *Birth of a Nation* (1915), set in
the piedmont section of South Carolina that had been such fertile ground
for the rise of the Ku Klux Klan.

Fiction *from* postwar South Carolina has drawn little of the scholarly
attention devoted to fiction *about* postwar South Carolina, but the subset
has particular importance within the development of Reconstruction literature. The wide range of topics that northerners explored in romances of
reunion calls for examination of the extent to which stories of redemption
provided white southerners with a similarly flexible narrative framework
that could accommodate more than propaganda. South Carolina offers a
promising field of study because its white population was so energized in

opposition to Reconstruction and because literature stood at a dramatic juncture in the state after the war. Antebellum and wartime South Carolina's robust cultural life had featured several fiction writers of national importance, including Caroline Gilman, Susan Petigru King, and above all William Gilmore Simms, whose regional preeminence prompted the legend that a commercial convention during the 1850s had resolved that the South should have a literature and had further resolved that Simms should supply it.[4] Simms's shadow was especially imposing in his home state. When aspiring author Mary Boykin Chesnut asked a professor at South Carolina College in 1862 if she might borrow some novels, he replied that the school library owned only the works of Simms and Walter Scott.[5] This self-conscious state tradition stood in need of renewal after the defeat of the Confederacy and the death of Simms in 1870. The imagined struggle in Reconstruction to drive out an alien occupying force offered a deeply resonant theme for that literary project, for the parallel drama of the American Revolution had long provided the foundation of secessionist political rhetoric and the central topic in Simms's historical fiction.[6] South Carolinians who wrote about the partisan resistance to Republican government not only helped to concoct a fictional Reconstruction that exercised lasting political influence; they also participated in a fictional reconstruction of what had been one of the most stimulating intellectual centers in the antebellum United States.

Examination of South Carolina narratives of Reconstruction offers a fresh perspective on one of the most important literary texts produced in the former Confederate states during the late nineteenth century, Chesnut's chronicle of the Civil War. The book she drafted in the early 1880s on the basis of her diaries from the 1860s is set almost entirely in the period between secession and surrender but continues briefly after Appomattox to foreshadow the postwar order. Her denouement reveals her ideological doubts about redemption and illustrates her ability to transform the narrative models that she and other South Carolina writers had inherited from Simms and Scott. Parodying the conventions of the historical romance, Chesnut presented a tale of sectional reunion that was protomodernist in its construction of comedy and tragedy.

Chesnut's remarkable work was thoroughly typical in recognizing that white southern demands for "home rule" united the central issues of Reconstruction politics and the nineteenth-century novel. Her preview of postwar society played out at Mulberry Plantation, near Camden. Other writers advanced ideas about who might rule and how at fictional homes scattered throughout South Carolina. Similarly, the mansions of rival Democratic leaders Wade Hampton III and Martin Witherspoon Gary became important sites of collective memory. The domestic convention lent considerable power and flexibility to early tales of redemption, but the plantation ideal lost much of its regenerative force when state agriculture stagnated and Ben Tillman's belligerent populism challenged the genteel leadership style within which political fiction flourished. Although Democrats long continued to invoke the struggle against Reconstruction as precedent for resistance to black civil rights, South Carolina novelists had exhausted their enthusiasm for the topic within three decades of the Red Shirt campaign of 1876. Unable to update Simms's framework and unaware of Chesnut's example, tardily published in a form that suppressed much of her creativity, later novelists of home rule began to recenter Confederate memory from a narrative of resurgence to a narrative of persistence.

The five novels about Reconstruction written by white South Carolinians between the early 1870s and the early 1880s are in many ways utterly predictable.[7] The authors portrayed African Americans either as faithful followers of their former masters or as ignorant, corrupt tools of malevolent politicians. The tales of redemption betrayed no more sympathy for scalawags and carpetbaggers than Simms's tales of the American Revolution had expressed for Tories or British imperial officials, although a few writers saluted the integrity of federal army officers exasperated by the assignment to protect Republican scoundrels. Representation of soldiers' experiences as an apolitical antidote to sectionalized ideological tensions illustrated one of the strategies by which opponents of Reconstruction sought to erode northern support for federal reform measures in the South. But the early South Carolina fiction of Reconstruction addressed itself primarily to southerners rather than northerners. Like Simms's cycle, it drew creative energy from recognition that the resistance movement had significant potential for conflicts among its different elements. The solutions proposed for these problems sometimes included more pointed social criticism than might be expected.

Schematization of home rule as an endpoint for Reconstruction fiction outlines the possibilities imagined by early postwar South Carolina writers. Some novels culminate in the protagonist reclaiming a home from which he or she has been displaced. Other books end with a spotlighted couple's decision to make new home. In a final variation, the heroine and hero conclude by renouncing any permanent home.[8] This framework may not be equally useful in other contexts. But in the case of South Carolina fiction written during or shortly after Reconstruction, it effectively clarifies distinctions along a spectrum of restoration and reform. Attention to the final dwelling place of each narrative focuses analysis on the authors' visions of the local social order and especially their views of gender relations in a state that had built its reactionary antebellum politics on an exceptionally massive foundation of patriarchal law and custom.[9] Although the novels written under the state constitution of 1868 rarely engaged the debates surrounding the introduction of divorce in South Carolina and the extension of property rights to married women, the stories consistently foregrounded domestic relations and in several instances identified white southern readiness to expand the authority of women as an important symbol of redemption.

Sallie F. Chapin's *Fitz-Hugh St. Clair, the South Carolina Rebel Boy; or, It Is No Crime to Be Born a Gentleman* (1872) issued a call for reform even as it typified the conservative narrative of restoration. Fitz-Hugh St. Clair grows almost to manhood at the low-country plantation Glendaire, which after the Union capture of Beaufort falls into the possession of a rare disloyal slave. Fitz, who becomes the main financial support of his mother and siblings after his father's death while commanding Confederate troops at Second Manassas, goes to New York after the war to revive the family fortunes. His Christian resistance to the city's corruption brings him to the attention of his father's dearest friend, H. D. Winthrop, who owes his wealth and his angelic wife entirely to the moral guidance and generous loans he received from St. Clair's father when Winthrop slipped into a life of desperate dissolution after graduating from Yale. Winthrop enthusiastically repays these debts to the son of his late friend. Fitz marries Winthrop's daughter, and Winthrop's son marries Fitz's sister. Fitz declines a position in Winthrop's bank, however, to participate in the redemption of South Carolina and reclaim Glendaire.

Chapin's picture of the South as the dominant partner in the old Union was not likely to inspire northern sympathy. Her book aimed to appeal mostly to the group to whom it was dedicated, the children of the Confederacy. The daughter of a Methodist minister, Chapin revealed anxieties about these intended readers that extended beyond sectional politics. Her sermons against gambling and fornication and alcohol, which presaged her later prominence as a temperance activist, reflected a distrust of the white southern male work ethic typical of early postwar women's novels. Chapin also sounded a memorable alarm about the dangers of circuses and department stores. "No one ever heard of a great statesman being made out of a bandbox-boy, whose great ambition was to smell sweet, wear modified pink neckties, and moonlight-on-the-lake kids, and stand behind the counter to sell chignons, or measure ladies' busts to fit them with French corsets," she warned. "Imagine, if you can, John C. Calhoun in such a situation; and yet, to fill such places is the height of the ambition of many, (yes, too many) of our boys."[10] Her admonitions highlighted perils of urban consumer society that Chapin had observed in her native Charleston. Marketing and entertainment constituted a social foundation inconsistent with the hierarchy endorsed in Chapin's alternate title. Upon returning to Glendaire, Fitz aims to renew the old order through the development of mining and manufacturing. He is a modernizing reformer within the plantation tradition.

William J. Rivers's *Eunice: A Tale of Reconstruction Times in South Carolina* features a lead couple who make a new home free from the class stratification that Chapin defended. The title of the novel, which Rivers began shortly after the classicist resigned from the University of South Carolina faculty in 1873 to protest the enrollment of African Americans, translates to "good victory."[11] Eunice DeLesline's grandfather is a prominent secessionist, her father a Confederate colonel killed at Sharpsburg. The burning of Columbia, which Rivers had witnessed, introduces the main villain of the story, Union sergeant Isaiah Guelty. Coincidentally assigned to protect the home of the young woman whose inheritance he had fraudulently kept secret after preparing the will of her dying long-lost uncle, Guelty becomes obsessed with Eunice. His first attempt to ravish her is foiled by the DeLeslines' faithful slave, whom the Union soldier symbolically murders. After Guelty returns to Columbia during Reconstruction as a preacher-politician stirring unrest among African Americans, the action of the novel follows his pursuit of Eunice and her ultimate triumph, which is connected to the overthrow of the alliance between carpetbaggers and freedpeople that has dominated the state.

Rivers offered his prescription for the South by contrasting the two men who strive to protect Eunice, a beautiful young aristocrat of Huguenot ancestry. At the outset of the story, all characters assume that she is informally betrothed to Willie Barton, whose family is of the same high social status as her own and whom she has known since childhood. A lieutenant in the regiment that Eunice's father commanded, Willie is a likeable but immature young man who neglects his law studies to enjoy hijinks with the Ku Klux Klan. Eunice sensibly prefers Edmund Loyle, whom Rivers called

Lyle in his first draft before deciding that readers might miss his point. The successor to Eunice's father at the head of their Confederate regiment, Loyle is Rivers's ideal man of the postwar South. Though not born into the aristocracy, he is highly competent and prosperous. While he would prefer to get on with rebuilding his plantation, he is a natural leader in the resistance to Reconstruction. He favors exposure of radical misdeeds rather than clowning around with the Klan, and he organizes a rifle club to demonstrate the moral monitory force of Confederate veterans. The obstacles to his love for Eunice are first that he shares the widespread impression that Eunice is engaged to Willie and second that Willie's suit is particularly favored by Eunice's widowed mother, whose best friend was Willie's late mother and who cherishes the hope that Willie will accede to keeping the DeLesline family name alive after marrying Eunice. The Loyle family name is nothing special in South Carolina society, but Eunice's mother knows that Loyle would never agree to such an arrangement. Eunice eventually punctures her mother's dream and together with Loyle rids the state of Guelty and the rest of the radical political ring.

While Rivers's reservations about the rash and unreliable Barton imply criticism of the privileged men who had led South Carolina into the war, his portrait of Eunice associates redemption with changes in gender ideals. The protagonist lacks the shallow snobbery of her mother and the fragile dependence of a cousin, Helen Clarens, who appears several times in the story. The pathetic Helen has lost her mind after the deaths of her father, brothers, fiancé, and cousins in the war, and she now spends her time strewing flowers on a child's grave that she mistakenly believes is the burial site of her beloved. She begins to regain sanity only after she is narrowly rescued from a gang of freedmen who attempt to rape her as she passes through the cemetery. Eunice's fidelity to the Confederate dead involves no such weak sentimentality. She is characterized by "self-reliance, endurance, even an intrepidity akin to the exalting spirit of heroism." Rivers's most sexually charged description of her appears in the scene in which she demonstrates that she is a dead shot with a revolver. Eunice has worked in Confederate hospitals during the war and prepares to teach school until the recovery of her inheritance ends the family financial troubles. Her relationship with Loyle is to a considerable extent a partnership of equals. Her admiration for him includes "nothing we would call reverence," and he treats her with a respect lacking in Willie Barton's failure to consider her views.[12] Upon marrying, they decide to divide their time between their plantations, thereby combining the best of the Old South and the new order.

Celina E. Means's *Thirty-Four Years* (1878) imagined a more fundamental reorganization of white southern values by abandoning the goal of home that other narratives regained or remade. Means's title—the protagonist's age at the 1872 marriage that ends the story—encapsulates an important postwar social pattern. Agnes Moore is representative of a generation in which increasing numbers of white southern women would marry later than their mothers or never at all as a result of the Confederate demographic trauma and shifts in personal priorities.[13] Admired for her beauty, intelligence, Christian goodness, and ability to make a happy home, Agnes declines a barrage of proposals from planters, soldiers, members of Congress, and European nobles. When pressed, she acknowledges that she has loved someone who evidently did not understand her interest, but she does not rue her situation. Instead, she embraces single blessedness with resourceful improvisation.

That self-reliance, so contrary to her upbringing as the daughter of a wealthy cotton planter, is a legacy of the war. Means devotes most of her brief coverage of the period between Fort Sumter and Appomattox to a flamboyant example of female adventure, a type of tale that had become increasingly common in popular literature by the late stages of the conflict.[14] Setting out to rescue her beloved, a daring Confederate scout held in a Union prison in July 1861, Agnes charms Union commander Irvin McDowell into permitting her to visit the jail by putting aside her scruples about singing in public. She cleverly sneaks into the cell a set of women's clothes in which the prisoner makes his escape while a faithful slave maid is left in his place dressed in a Confederate uniform. By enabling the scout to report to General Beauregard, Agnes plays an important part in the Confederate victory at Manassas. After the war, Agnes continues to accept the necessity of assuming new social roles. Although she is "not especially fond of young ideas" and dislikes presenting herself to strangers, she unflinchingly responds to the loss of family wealth by becoming an excellent schoolteacher.[15]

In Means's narrative, Reconstruction signals a continuation of the opportunity introduced by the war to reorganize southern society. The main romantic triangle of the book points toward a key direction of change. In many ways, Agnes's most appealing suitor is Johnnie Carleton, who has been her dear friend and protector almost from the cradle. Johnnie is thoughtful, competent, and deeply religious. He is a rock of support for his mother and siblings, and his sterling qualities ensure his advance in politics and the army. But Agnes turns him down in favor of Herbert Grey, after which Johnnie promptly dies in battle. As their names suggest, both men are good Confederates. The son of an upcountry planter, Grey has become a lawyer since graduating from South Carolina College. He is, however, less reliable than Johnnie. When both men address a crowd on the subject of secession, Johnnie is reminiscent of George Washington, while Grey speaks with "a kind of lurid eloquence."[16] His failure to propose to Agnes for so long is largely the result of his overly prickly sense of pride. But impeccable as Johnnie may be, he is essentially Agnes's older brother. And contrary to earlier domestic epics like Susan Warner's *Wide, Wide World* (1850), the lesson of *Thirty-Four Years* was that the ideal mate did not offer the guidance of an older brother but the passion of a mutually constituted adventure in life.

Grey's questionable judgment becomes the pivot of the book when he takes the lead role in organizing the Ku Klux Klan in Spartanburg County. For Chapin, who wrote *Fitz-Hugh St. Clair* amid the federal investigation and prosecution of the Ku Klux Klan in upcountry South Carolina during 1871–72, the Klan was the fictional invention of northern Republicans who held power by inveigling voters with tales of white southern outrages. For Rivers, the Klan was typical of the rash impulses of the antebellum leadership group that South Carolina needed to replace. For Means, the Klan was an understandable but unwise expedient that responded to a breakdown of law with an equally lawless regime. Predictably, the lynchings led by Grey prompt imitations in which "low, irresponsible parties—here and there, perhaps, one of better condition" take advantage of opportunities afforded by the Klan disguise and mystique to engage in theft, intimidation, and personal revenge.[17] Federal enforcement turns toward Grey at the same moment he realizes that Agnes loves him. She agrees to marry him despite his error in organizing the Klan. Her common sense overcomes a male notion of honor that would have left Grey rotting in jail because he disdains to run, and she develops a plan of disguise that enables them to escape. They marry and flee South Carolina to live as missionaries in Greece.

The abandonment of home by the domestic heroine underscores the depth of the transformation Means hoped to see. Though she published *Thirty-Four Years* after the supposed redemption of South Carolina, Means plainly advocated a more thoroughgoing regeneration. The epigraph of the novel, in which British writer Anna Jameson called on legislators to consider "the relation between the two sexes, the passion of love," hinted at support for measures that would enable women to make marital decisions based less on economic pressure and more on the ideals of meaningful fulfillment for which Agnes held out. More generally, the departure of Agnes and Grey for the birthplace of Western political theory looked toward a fundamental reassessment of contemporary relations of power.

Chapin, Rivers, and Means offered a range of political variations on the theme of home rule, but all three authors sought to update a South Carolina literary tradition identified with Simms and Scott. Chapin ended *Fitz-Hugh St. Clair* with tributes to Simms and Timrod. Rivers headed each chapter of *Eunice* with a quotation from a South Carolina writer, the first of which was an epigraph from Simms. Means declared in her opening paragraph that she wished Scott could have written her story. Her project reflected an eagerness to shape popular interest in state history that later prompted her, as it had previously led Simms and Rivers, to write a primer of South Carolina history for young readers.[18] Chapin, Rivers, and Means, like their contemporaries Rose Ashleigh and Florella Meynardie, retold the struggle over Reconstruction through narrative forms previously applied to the American Revolution. Their stories centered on romances that paralleled the institution of a new public order. The authors shared the basic optimism that had characterized the dialectic structure of the antebellum romance and, in particular, Simms's version of South Carolina history. The novelists who wrote in the shadow of Appomattox depicted the Confederate defeat as grave but not disastrous. Fitz-Hugh St. Clair, Eunice DeLesline and Edmund Loyle, and Agnes Moore and Herbert Grey eventually triumph over the enemies who seek to thwart their marriages and oppress the South. Rose Ashleigh maintained in "The Cavalier and the Puritan" that since the war, former Confederates had won "a far greater victory than they fought for."[19]

The authors were not quite as successful as their characters, for none of the novels is a thoroughly satisfying work. The books vary considerably in intellectual ambition and compositional felicity, but each suffers from tendentiousness. As Simms's fiction often illustrates, rigid adherence to mid-nineteenth-century narrative formulas could produce wooden characters and plots. In their eagerness to explore complexities in the struggle for home rule, however, the first South Carolina novelists of Reconstruction offered hope for a revitalization of state literature that would parallel the political achievement of redemption. That promise would be realized in the work of Mary Boykin Chesnut.

It has become incongruous to think of Mary Boykin Chesnut alongside her South Carolina contemporaries Sallie Chapin, William Rivers, Celina

Means, Rose Ashleigh, and Florella Meynardie, although all of those authors published much more than the single newspaper sketch Chesnut sold during her lifetime. Chesnut has been keeping considerably more exclusive literary company ever since Edmund Wilson called her writing reminiscent of Chekhov and Tolstoy. Daniel Aaron invoked Emily Dickinson. C. Vann Woodward devoted the last major scholarly project of his illustrious career to editing Chesnut's manuscripts, for which Woodward received the Pulitzer Prize in 1982. By the end of the twentieth century, the foremost scholarly anthology of southern literature devoted more pages to Chesnut than to Kate Chopin or Allen Tate or Eudora Welty, among other regional standard-bearers. Michael O'Brien has compared her at length with Virginia Woolf. Julia Stern's monograph situates Chesnut in the epic tradition of Homer and Virgil and explores affinities with Shakespeare, Jane Austen, William Faulkner, and especially George Eliot.[20]

Local contextualization is nonetheless useful. Chesnut certainly understood herself to be the product of a distinctive state culture. She reported that a day spent in Charleston in March 1861 was "one of the pleasantest days of my life" because it involved "so many pleasant people, so much good talk—for after all, it was talk, talk, talk, à la Caroline du Sud."[21] Most of the major figures in the mid-nineteenth-century state intellectual community are characters in her chronicle. She was to greater or lesser degrees a friend and admirer of William Gilmore Simms, Louisa McCord, William Henry Trescot, Susan Petigru King, William Porcher Miles, James Henley Thornwell, Henry Timrod, and Paul Hamilton Hayne. She shared the antiquarian sensibility characteristic of writers from her home state, including a respect for genealogy. She brooded over the strengths and weaknesses of South Carolinians as a type, taking note of the new light shed by comparisons with the first families of Virginia. She knew that she was a representative of that type. Determined to make the best possible impression when President Jefferson Davis visited her house in Columbia in 1864, she turned instinctively to a hospitality that she acknowledged to be "high South Carolina."[22]

Association of Chesnut with the minor South Carolina novelists of Reconstruction also underscores her position as a postwar writer. Scholars have mostly treated Chesnut as a guide to the Old South. Historians have sifted through the revisions of the 1880s to understand the slaveholding elite that led secession in the 1860s.[23] A few readers have examined the ways in which Chesnut looked ahead to new forms of southern society and literature in a narrative that looked back at the collapse of the Confederacy. O'Brien's magisterial survey of intellectual life in the antebellum South as-

signs to Chesnut much of the burden of demonstrating that southern culture nurtured an imagination able to deal effectively with the challenge of
the Civil War. O'Brien argues that Chesnut realized that "failure required a
new technique of narration" and suggests that her creative response to defeat was "quasi-modernist" in its opacity, manipulation of the diary genre,
taste for irony, juxtapositions of trivial events and profound observations,
and deployment of multiple incompletely identified voices, several of which
belong to the narrator.[24]

Chesnut's modernist tendencies are further illuminated by her manipulation of the conventional models for historical romance developed by Scott
and bequeathed by Simms to the early South Carolina novelists of Reconstruction. If Chesnut was disappointed to learn that Scott was the only novelist other than Simms represented in the collections of the South Carolina
College library, she could not have been surprised. Of the several dozen
authors to whom Chesnut's book refers, Scott ranks second only to Shakespeare in the number of times his work is mentioned.[25] Chesnut attributes
these allusions to many different people, at times implying that Scott was
the common currency of a flawed southern culture. Woodward notes one
point at which Chesnut's account of her husband's fascination with *The
Bride of Lammermoor*, juxtaposed with her own admiration for Balzac's
Comédie Humaine, suggests a satirical commentary on the code of chivalry
and conception of tragedy informed by Scott. Fire-eater Louis Wigfall, who
promises a Charleston crowd in an April 1861 speech that he will master
the federal government, just as Fitz James quelled the Clan McAlpine in
The Lady of the Lake, turns out by the end of the war to be more like the
self-centered smith in *St. Valentine's Day* who can only "fight for his own
hand." This use of Scott anticipates Mark Twain's claim that the Wizard of
the North "had so large a hand in making Southern character, as it existed
before the war, that he is in great measure responsible for the war."[26]

Consistent with that subversive spirit, Chesnut shaped her materials
to present a trenchant parody of the historical romance. Chesnut's book
centered on the failure of the Confederacy, and the famous doomed romance between the aristocratic belle Sally Buchanan "Buck" Preston and
the rough-and-ready military officer John Bell Hood serves as the opposite
of the triumphant marital synthesis characteristic of Scott's narrative formula. But Chesnut also provided the book with a clear conclusion in the
traditional form of a marriage. Because the final pages of the chronicle are
among the sections for which both Chesnut's notes from the 1860s and her
revised version of the 1880s survive, it is possible to see how carefully she

constructed a denouement appropriate for her ambitious narrative. That resolution, a condensed preview of the postwar world, inverted the plot formula followed by other novelists of Reconstruction. Chesnut indulged in no fantasies of victory emerging from the ashes of defeat. The ending to her book bitterly condemned the New South that had consolidated in the years since the war and firmly rejected faith in "redemption." The satire through which she expressed these views expanded her political parable into a wider attack on the Victorian values codified in the conventional historical romance.

For Chesnut as for other postwar South Carolina novelists, the problem of home rule offered a vehicle for connecting public and private crises. Though Chesnut lived in several places over the course of her narrative, the home she invested with the most significance was Mulberry, the primary residence of her husband's parents, James Chesnut Sr. and Mary Cox Chesnut. Her descriptions of this grand Old South plantation three miles outside Camden prompted Edmund Wilson to compare it to the Bolkonsky manor in *War and Peace*. Behind the expansive hospitality were strains and tensions, for Chesnut was well aware as she revised her diary in the 1880s that both as a piece of property and as a site of family relations, a home was subject to division. Her husband, his father's only surviving son, had inherited a life estate in Mulberry through the 1864 will of James Chesnut Sr., who was ninety-two years old at the end of the Civil War. The will provided that at James Jr.'s death, title would pass to whichever male Chesnut descendant he chose.[27] But title is often less important than possession, as Blackstone pointed out, and the Chesnut kin who actually lived at Mulberry during the period covered in Mary Chesnut's book included a wider range of the family. When she returned to Mulberry in March 1861 after her husband's participation in the organization of the Confederate government, the white members of the household consisted of the elder Chesnuts; their unmarried forty-seven-year-old daughter, Sally; and their granddaughter, Harriet Grant.

Although seldom mentioned in the commentaries on Mary Boykin Chesnut, the only young adult ensconced in Mulberry assumed an important role in Chesnut's home life and literary imagination. Harriet Grant's mother was James Jr.'s sister Harriet Serena, who died when Hattie was born in 1835; her father was William Joshua Grant, with whom she may have lived at Mulberry for years before he died in 1855.[28] Chesnut's diaries from 1861, which are particularly complete, make clear that she found the abrasive personality of her husband's niece at least as exasperating as the

Mulberry Plantation, 1900. Courtesy of the South Caroliniana Library,
University of South Carolina, Columbia.

imperiousness of her father-in-law and the passive-aggressive innocence of
her mother-in-law. After one row, Chesnut frankly acknowledged her "sin-
ful hatred" of Grant, and after another, she resolved that "I shall never be
familiar with her again." When Chesnut was at Mulberry immediately after
the war, she found Grant "more detestable than ever." Competing interests
in the wealth of James Chesnut Sr. were a significant part of the "atmosphere of contention" enveloping the two women. By the end of the diary,
Chesnut had come to refer to Grant as "Hecate," and in the final surviving entry, she wrote that the witch had foreordained the death of James
Chesnut Jr. in the war and was nonplussed that he had lived to preside
at Mulberry "as if every thing belonged to him (as it does)." But Chesnut
clearly realized already in 1865 that Harriet's influence on James Chesnut Sr. would have devastating consequences for his land-rich, cash-poor
son. By the time Chesnut revised her journal in the 1880s, she and her husband had been ruined financially by the obligations that the elder Chesnut's
wartime will imposed on his son to make payments to the women of the
family, including a sizable bequest to Harriet Grant.[29]

In the revised narrative, Grant emerged as a prime example of Chesnut's flair for seeing incidents of daily life in synchronized movement
with the national drama. The chronicle reported in April 1862 that a civil

war was taking place within the Chesnut family. The younger residents of Mulberry—notably Grant—wanted a more secure inheritance than the slaves and bank stock promised by James Sr.'s current will, as the heirs feared that those assets would become worthless after the war. The patriarch was making "a heroic resistance" and trying to transmit his land to his son, Chesnut reported, "but what can an old man do?"[30] She enhanced the importance of that family squabble by presenting her distaste for Grant through a political lens. She suppressed from the section of her book covering 1861 all of the references to their personality clashes and instead highlighted Grant's role as a leader of Camden society. This emphasis was consistent with the local prominence of the wealthy young lady. Emma Holmes, a well-to-do Charleston refugee, recorded in her Civil War diary that "I used to stand quite in awe of Hattie when I first knew her . . . and had heard so much of her talents and cultivation that if anyone had told me that I would ever be on such sociable terms with her, I would have thought them daft."[31]

As recounted by Chesnut, Grant's public services are comically unsuccessful and vaguely ominous. She organizes the tableaux and concert that accompany the presentation of a flag to the Kirkwood Rangers and takes her place on the ceremonial platform in the guise of "a veiled prophet" because of a temporary facial blemish. As president of the Camden Ladies' Aid Society, she quickly drives the association into debt and disarray by making underclothes for the Kershaw Guards instead of aiding hospitals. She then vanishes for most of the book, reappearing late in the war in "a most abusive and insulting letter" that sneers at her antithesis in Chesnut's story, the ideal southern belle Buck Preston. Grant is a central character in the section that covers the end of the war and especially the weeks after Chesnut returns to Camden in early May 1865. By this point Grant has become, Chesnut reports, "an enemy in my own camp," the outspoken advocate of a thoroughgoing Reconstruction that the young woman proposes to begin with the hanging of Jefferson Davis for treason. Her expectations of postwar northern investment in southern railroad and telegraph lines prompt Chesnut to scoff incredulously that Grant is "crawling to their feet," naively believing that "these Yankees have poured out all this blood and money to put us just where we were before!"[32]

Grant's significance as the scalawag of Mulberry is heightened by her role as a representative of the commercial community. Readings of Chesnut's work have not explored the extent to which it foregrounds a rivalry of planters and merchants. Grant's father had served as cashier of the Bank of Camden from its founding in 1836 until his death. Chesnut declared that "My ancestors were farmers—*hers* on the gouty side—Philadelphia merchants. I *prefer* my plain Carolina farming gentry to the *monied* gentry of Yankeedom." As Chesnut knew well, similar fissures were important in local politics. The municipal race held in Camden in March 1844, for example, featured slates called the planters' ticket, the merchants' ticket, the mechanics' ticket, and the clerks' ticket. During the following decade, high-stakes debates over transportation policy drew forth the argument that "if Rail Roads are only to be made for the convenience of Planters, Merchants display but little judgment or wisdom in aiding in their construction."[33] Chesnut's loyalties in this contest were clear. Although she did not hesitate to criticize planters like her father-in-law or her uncle Alexander Hamilton Boykin, she generally saw in them a dignity wholly lacking in the merchants and lawyers she scorned, including John McPherson DeSaussure, William E. Johnson, Anthony Kennedy, and James Irwin Villepigue. She ridiculed the "boundless ambition" of "militia idiot" Joseph B. Kershaw, grandson of the merchant who founded Camden. Chesnut especially resented the Kershaw family's fondness for recalling that the original Chesnut in South Carolina worked in his youth in the store of the original Kershaw. "The Kershaws, I think, have that fact on their coat of arms," she noted.[34]

Chesnut was even more scathing toward the "pretentious descendants" of Charles John Shannon Sr., who had commendably lifted himself from humble beginnings to become "a rich merchant." "That is," Chesnut felt obliged to add, "rich for Camden." While she considered the father "one of our most respectable citizens," she found his children intolerable. Daughter Mattie formed an impulsive, ill-fated friendship with Harriet Grant. Charles John Shannon Jr. skulked through the war before announcing in May 1865 that he "would be found ready enough to take up arms when the time came." He next appeared "lying drunk on the Yankees' bed." His equally fraudulent brother claimed to speak French but asked why a tea caddy labeled "Thé" was marked "The." In contrast with James Chesnut Jr., who took "off his hat grandly, like a prince of the blood," Sam Shannon touched "his hat like a footman." William M. Shannon, his father's successor as president of the Camden branch of the Bank of South Carolina, was "a clear case of genealogical, aristocratic mania" who gullibly believed that the family into which he married was a branch of the royal house of Stuart. Chesnut returns repeatedly to Shannon's "treachery" in shouldering Edward Boykin aside to assume the captaincy of the Kirkwood Rangers, only to leave the army after a year and spend the rest of the war "safely housed in a bombproof—a bank president paying himself three thousand dollars a year in gold while all the rest of Confederate mankind are starving and before the enemy's guns."[35]

The significance William Shannon shared with Grant as a negative exemplar in Chesnut's narrative reflected his postwar as well as his wartime career. The series of newspaper articles about Camden history that the lawyer published in the *Kershaw Gazette* in April 1876 infuriated Chesnut. She poured out forty-three manuscript pages of point-by-point rebuttal to Shannon's praise for Joseph B. Kershaw as "our favorite citizen" and claim that "the success, the tone, and the prosperity of this community are more indebted to [the Kershaws] than to any other family." As Chesnut's biographer notes, after the publication of these articles, Shannon "undoubtedly stood as a surrogate for Camden itself in her mind."[36] Her frustration soon deepened when Kershaw received the most valuable piece of local patronage in the aftermath of the Democratic return to power in South Carolina, a circuit court judgeship that he held for most of the rest of his life, while James Chesnut Jr. waited in vain for a reward for his support of Wade Hampton.

The zenith of the Camden rivalry between merchants and planters was the apotheosis of Shannon that followed his death in one of the most celebrated duels ever fought in South Carolina, and supposedly the last. As soon as E. B. C. Cash put a bullet in Shannon from fifteen paces on July 5, 1880, newspaper editors and politicians portrayed the encounter as a moment of transition in the values of the South. Cash was the imperious planter determined to avenge the allegation that his late wife had received a property conveyance intended to defraud her brother's creditors; Shannon was the conscientious attorney who had declined to apologize for the processes of commercial law and had agreed to the duel only because he feared that his sons would otherwise fight it on his behalf. The polemics gained traction from the political activism of Cash, for the depiction of him as a barbarous relic discredited those who agreed with him and Martin W. Gary that the postredemption Democrats had shown too much favoritism to "elegant, smooth mannered, oily tongued bondholders, bond speculators, banks and members of financial boards."[37] That populist argument would win a wide following in South Carolina in the next decade, but the disgust with dueling that swept through the state and prompted swift legislative action after the Cash-Shannon interview was a clear victory for the Hamptonite faction. Shannon emerged as a martyr for the progress of the New South.

Mary Chesnut was appalled by this canonization. Shannon's second in the encounter, fellow bank president William E. Johnson, reported that Chesnut's antipathy toward Shannon explained her husband's failure to intervene before the duel to save the life of his longtime friend and colleague in the Camden legal community.[38] The final manuscript revisions that Chesnut began in 1881 took a far more caustic view of the New South than the Cash-Shannon legend promoted. Like her fellow postwar novelists, she used the marital fortunes of her major characters to project forward the future of South Carolina at the conclusion of her narrative. The couple personifying the planter class does not gel. Chesnut reports that Buck Preston is leaving the country for an extended European trip with her family, unattached and evidently incapable of advancing from flirtation to fulfillment.[39] This inability to sustain commitment mirrors Chesnut's portrait of her nephew, Johnny Chesnut, the person she scrutinized most intently as a model for a fictional character and the man she considered an appropriate match for Buck. The son of James Chesnut Jr.'s older brother, Johnny was the member of the rising generation who stood to inherit Mulberry on the death of his uncle. Mary Boykin Chesnut adored him, but she also despaired that he personified a South Carolina elite that was no longer as "active-minded" as it had been in the Revolutionary generation. Johnny was "the very perfection of a lazy gentleman who cares not to move unless it be for a fight, a dance, or a fox hunt." Buck teases him at one point that "you will never marry. There is one insuperable bar to that. You must first ask some woman to marry you. Nobody is going to ask you."[40] The intimation that Johnny would die without extending the Chesnut family line was accurate, for the young planter died in 1868. Meanwhile, the person who closed the war with a brilliant marriage foreshadowing the reconstructed order was Harriet Grant.

Grant's marriage was an astonishing symbolic opportunity for Chesnut, for the match was not only an intersectional union but also a bridge to the Revolutionary era. In the Simmsian tradition of parallels between the War for Independence and the sectional conflict, Chesnut often described the Civil War as a struggle over the legacy of the Revolution. She relished the thought that during the 1850s, she had "lived on the battlefield" where the colonists met Cornwallis in Camden.[41] Her conviction that South Carolina partisans had contributed decisively to the eventual triumph of the patriot cause encouraged her to hope that their descendants would enjoy similar success. She developed the Revolutionary theme most extensively in situating Mulberry within the national cult of Washington remembrance. The Chesnut ancestor who first moved the family from Virginia to South Carolina was the widow of a Virginian killed in action in Washington's unit during the French and Indian War. The president had visited the son of this former comrade, himself a fellow Revolutionary veteran, while touring the South during Washington's first term in office. In the hall at Mulberry hung Gilbert Stuart portraits of Washington; his host, John Chesnut; and Mary Chesnut's future father-in-law. James Sr.'s wife had even stronger Washington connections: her father had served on the commander's staff in the Revolution, and she was close to the Custis and Washington families in Philadelphia. The intersectional marriage between James Chesnut Sr. and Mary Cox that had flourished at Mulberry represented for their daughter-in-law the heart of the old republic, including a planter preponderance in the balance of power.

The marriage of Harriet Grant inverted this union. Chesnut described the prenuptial festivities in the next-to-last entry of the chronicle, dated "Black 4th of July—1865." The groom was the grandson of a signer of the Declaration of Independence, "the American patent of nobility." Richard Stockton was a New Jersey native but had fought for the Confederacy, which Chesnut identified as an extension of his grandfather's commitment to sovereignty vested in the consent of the governed. If the northerner's military service vindicated the Confederacy, however, his romance of reunion with Grant betokened the defeat of the planter class. Commercial forces were now ascendant. The southerners who managed to exercise power—like the shrewish Harriet in her marriage or William Shannon or Joseph Kershaw in public life—would come from the ranks of merchants. Chesnut's account of the fate of Mulberry encapsulated the fall of the plantation regime. A federal unit sacks the house in a raid after Joseph Johnston surrenders his army to Sherman. After the war, the home becomes a sentimental and financial millstone. The dying James Chesnut Sr. cannot bear to live elsewhere, but the cost of repairs promises to be overwhelming. Harriet Grant suffers none of these frustrations. She dismisses the depredation of Mulberry as "only the fortunes of war." Her inheritance will come in cash. She and her husband prepare to visit the North immediately after the wedding. "New York and South Carolina being equally Yankee land now," she declares, "how much nicer to live in New York."[42]

The marriage of a southern Yankee and a northern Confederate with which Chesnut ends her book stretches the popular formula of the reconciliation romance to the point of absurdity. The bounty to be weighed against all of the suffering recounted in the narrative falls to its least deserving character. This conclusion is as neatly packaged as anything in Scott or Simms, but the cohesion has the logic of a nightmare. Insistent on the pathos and finality of Confederate defeat, Chesnut offers no grounds to imagine that the outcome has been for the best or that events might yet fall into place acceptably. Instead of the notion of progress embedded in the formula of the historical romance, she substitutes a bleakly ironic sensibility. This assault on established plot patterns supports the view that her narrative style reflected protomodernist experimentation rather than "her inability to sustain a viewpoint."[43] Chesnut's marriage denouement indicates that inherited literary conventions and their underlying Victorian values are no longer adequate in the postwar world. The parody vividly illustrates a process by which a creative author might transform both the historical events she has witnessed and the cultural models available to her.

The modernist tendencies that shaped Chesnut's black comedy also informed her view of Reconstruction as a racial tragedy. The entry in the chronicle that details preparations for Harriet Grant's wedding immediately follows an entry in which Chesnut and her friends ridicule the occupying Union military commander's exhortation of freedpeople to "respect the marriage tie." This juxtaposition dramatizes the repeated apprehension that the northern victors will reduce white southerners to the status of their former slaves. Similar analogies were common in early postwar South Carolina rhetoric, including novels of Reconstruction. Florella Meynardie's *Amy Oakley; or, The Reign of the Carpetbagger* (1879) was an especially vivid image of racial fluidity. Wrongly suspected of a crime, the orphaned protagonist spends much of the book disguised as a black servant in the household of a childhood friend. One of the weaknesses of the upper-class male foil in Rivers's *Eunice* is a readiness to pass as an African American. Willie Barton speaks fluently in dialect and dies in blackface. Redemption ends the danger that white will become black. Rivers's hero, Edmund Loyle, advocates a racial policy of "parallelism, instead of crossing lines at all angles."[44]

Chesnut's darker forecast for the white South highlights the motif of the mask that she regarded as the hallmark of the African Americans she watched intently. Even after Lee's surrender, she reflects, "the shining black mask they wear does not show a ripple of change—sphinxes." Although fascinated by African Americans' stagecraft, she finds that "they carry it too far" and risk dehumanization. She worries that the war will similarly force ex-Confederates to forsake genuine freedom and follow new scripts. Chesnut's entry for July 4, 1865, extends the image to postwar gender ideals.

For her prenuptial party, Grant arrays herself as a May queen, the character that antebellum southern belles ritually surrendered to enter into marriage. James Chesnut Jr. takes a knife "like a Goth" to slash the garlands from the body of his niece and enjoins her to "dress like a Christian woman—not in masquerade." But as an unnamed speaker points out, the protest is futile. Grant would merely be acting a different part as a Christian woman. The rite of passage into authenticity is obsolete in a society with such a heroine. Chesnut's fragmented authorial voice transforms the metaphor of the mask into a narrative strategy. As Julia Stern notes, "Chesnut herself has donned the sphinx-like mask of inscrutability behind which, she had complained in 1861, her slaves hid *their* feelings about the war's potential significance."[45]

Chesnut's uses of the historical romance and the figure of the blackened white southerner link her to more obscure South Carolina novelists of the early postwar era. Chesnut was the most imaginative of this group, but she shared with her contemporaries a set of literary inheritances and ambitions, including a readiness to look critically at the state as it responded to the shock of defeat. Her impressive contribution to the fiction of home rule indicated that the intellectual vitality of antebellum South Carolina had not only survived the war but achieved a new energy in response to Reconstruction and redemption.

That evidence long remained hidden. Chesnut's work did not begin to appear in print until the *Saturday Evening Post* serialized excerpts from it in 1905 as *A Diary from Dixie*. A book edition appeared under that title in the same year, almost two decades after Chesnut's death in 1886. During that interval, the romance of reunion remained a vigorous form of American literature. The conquest of strong-minded Yankee women by former Confederate soldiers in Henry James's *The Bostonians* (1886) and Owen Wister's *The Virginian* (1902) developed a new variation on the intersectional plot and pointed toward Thomas Dixon's *The Clansman* (1905). This influential tribute to the Ku Klux Klan, building on Dixon's *The Leopard's Spots* (1902), might have been expected to have enjoyed particular popularity in the state where Dixon set his melodrama in the fictional town of Piedmont. But the best seller and its stage adaptation proved controversial among white South Carolinians, not to mention the protests from African Americans. Dixon's repeated declaration that Ben Tillman had inspired him to write *The Clansman* situated the novel squarely on one side of the

rift that had divided state Democrats since the mid-1870s. Tillman identified closely with the continuing Reconstruction legacy of white paramilitary racial violence, while his Hamptonite critics preferred to believe that
the campaign of 1876 had restored racial paternalism through a more law-
ful process of energizing white voters and merely intimidating black voters.
The *Columbia State*, the chief Hamptonite newspaper, pummeled Dixon
for crediting the Klan rather than the Red Shirts.[46] Turn-of-the-century
South Carolina writers similarly revisited the local experience in a fresh
round of Reconstruction fiction. These works provide valuable context for
understanding crucial editorial decisions in *A Diary from Dixie*, much as
earlier Reconstruction novels illuminate Chesnut's drafts of the 1880s.

South Carolina novelists' argument with Dixon insisted on the cen-
trality of the state in the national drama of division and reunion. Writing in the shadow of Hampton's death in 1902, his admirers maintained
that the sectional conflict had concluded uniquely in South Carolina, as it
had begun there, and that the Red Shirt resolution offered singular lessons
for the country. Like their forerunners of the early postwar period, they
saw the struggle for home rule as a promising topic for state literature.
But the South Carolina novels of Reconstruction written during the first
decade of the twentieth century could sustain neither the self-confidence
nor the critical engagement that characterized the works of the 1870s. The
later authors were as competent and committed to their common project as
their predecessors. James Walter Daniel, a Methodist minister in Laurens
County, was an antiquarian and historical novelist squarely in the Simmsian
tradition. Edward L. Wells, a veteran of Hampton's Legion, turned to Reconstruction fiction between his histories of *Hampton and His Cavalry in
'64* (1899) and *Hampton and Reconstruction* (1907). Theodore Jervey was
a longtime president of the South Carolina Historical Society and worked
as a newspaper editorialist before settling into a legal career. He published
several substantial books about history and current affairs in addition to
his thoughtful Reconstruction novel. Phoebe Hamilton Seabrook was an
accomplished schoolteacher whose educational career brought her from
Beaufort to Virginia to Illinois to Washington, D.C.[47] These authors were
as well prepared to continue the state literary tradition as Sallie F. Chapin,
William J. Rivers, Celina Means, Rose Ashleigh, and Florella Meynardie.
But their books demonstrated a collective inability to envision redemption
as the South Carolina epic that Simms had found in the Revolution. The
path that Chesnut had extended so brilliantly in her manuscript chronicle
was at a dead end by the publication of the first edition of her work.

J. W. Daniel's *A Maid of the Foot-Hills; or, Missing Links in the Story of Reconstruction* (1905) offered the most direct response to Dixon and the clearest argument that redemption should figure as prominently in state literature as it did in state history. Daniel declared that appreciation of "the real spirit of the times, as shown in the humor, amusements, fun, and so-cial enjoyments of the oppressed populace," was essential to understanding "the heroic deeds by which the people finally threw off the yoke of oppres-sion." If regional humor was one "missing link" in the solemn literature of Reconstruction, another was "the failure to give the great Red-shirt move-ment its proper place in the picture of those stirring scenes through which the prostrate South passed." Of course the Red Shirts had hardly been for-gotten in South Carolina, where the revolution of 1876 had been a center-piece of white remembrance for three decades. Daniel's point was that au-thors outside of South Carolina had failed to recognize the significance of the sequence in which former Confederates wore the white robes of the Klan, the red shirts of redeemers, and the blue uniforms of U.S. soldiers. Dismissing *The Clansman* as "very much distorted and embellished by the fertile brain of the writer," Daniel maintained that "the story of Reconstruc-tion in South Carolina ought to be told from her own point of view."[48] Con-sistent with his interest in local folklore, he designed *A Maid of the Foot-Hills* as a retelling of the postwar South Carolina legend of Manse Jolly.

Daniel's version of the Jolly story demonstrates the diminished vitality of the redemption narrative. Manson Sherill Jolly was a Confederate vet-eran who became an outlaw in upcountry South Carolina after the war. He was said to have murdered a number of soldiers in the Union occupation force, perhaps in retribution for the wartime deaths of his brothers, but he left the state permanently for Texas in 1866, well before the passage of the Military Reconstruction Acts or the subsequent Enforcement Acts, and drowned there in 1869. In Daniel's account, the thinly veiled Mance Holley refuses to submit to the authority of African Americans in uniform and vows to kill one hundred of them after black Union soldiers shoot his only surviving brother in the back. His private campaign parallels the formation of the Klan and later the Red Shirts, though Holley is too much of a lone wolf to belong to either organization. Contrary to the Hamptonite pretense of peaceful white paternalism, Daniel explicitly endorses Klan lynchings during Reconstruction and the continuation of the practice in the early twentieth century. The minister's objection is that these tactics are neces-sary but not sufficient to restore home rule. The complementary contribu-tion of the Red Shirts is the perfection of white solidarity. Holley and his allies accordingly instill Democratic loyalty in the town scalawag, and in a series of colorful episodes, Holley escapes the grasp and secures the admiration of white northern soldiers ordered to capture him. At the end of the novel, he decides to "slip away to some other part of the country and be at rest."[49] The force behind redemption does not remain in the state. The couple whose marriage symbolizes the triumph of home rule contribute little to the political success and cannot infuse its momentum into their exemplary household. Clarence Armstrong, the New South figure who marries the maid of the foothills, is a Confederate veteran who has lost an arm in the war (despite his surname). He is offstage for much of the book, attending Washington and Lee, and never demonstrates the authority of his former commander and protector, Holley.

Edward Wells's unpublished novel "The Voodoo Doctor: A Story of Reconstruction in South Carolina" (1901) similarly excludes its most effective redeemer from the marriage that defines the future of the white South. The title character is a former Confederate scout who leads his local rifle club and masquerades as a black conjurer to infiltrate a rigged Republican jury in a criminal trial that parallels the election of Hampton. The helpless defendant is the protagonist of the story; he is struggling to reinvigorate the heroine's family plantation, Runnymede, symbolic home of constitutional liberty. The climactic racial disguise differs from the blackening of white southerners that Meynardie, Rivers, and Chesnut deemed degrading. White ability to pass as black is for Wells a demonstration of racial superiority, complicating the debt his voodoo doctor owes to the trickster figures of African American oral tradition that Joel Chandler Harris had recently popularized. The racial ruse presents redemption as a process that neither besmirches nor empowers the lead couple of the novel.

The heroines imagined by Daniel and Wells are no more impressive than their mates and contrast sharply with the women who heralded the regeneration of the white South in earlier novels. Julia Jackson, the title character in *A Maid of the Foot-Hills*, combines her vigor as Holley's niece with a gentility derived from girlhood associations with Huguenot benefactors, but she is far less important to the plot than Eunice DeLesline in William Rivers's *Eunice* or Agnes Moore in Celina Means's *Thirty-Four Years*. Jackson's contribution to redemption is limited to some fast horseback riding and the sewing of red shirts. Edith Milfort of "The Voodoo Doctor" is likewise pronounced an ideal southern woman for her beauty, grace, and sunny disposition, but her competence does not extend beyond equestrian skill. She is the first lead heroine in a South Carolina novel of Reconstruction whom white vigilantes must rescue from African Americans intent on rape, an experience that Julia Jackson would soon share.

Theodore Jervey's *The Elder Brother* (1905) details the postredemption stultification that Daniel and Wells imply. The novel focuses on two brothers who come of age after the war in a halfheartedly disguised Charleston. Rupert Gordon is the noble natural leader that his name implies— strong, handsome, and sound in judgment if not intellectually gifted. As a journalist for a fictionalized version of the *Charleston News and Courier*, he brings steady purpose and stainless integrity to the rise of the straight-out Democrats as well as the muscle that the romanticized campaign requires. He easily wins the belle of local society, Madge Herndon, the daughter of a parvenu turpentine factor. But the triumph of home rule proves less than entirely satisfactory. An attractive flirt who slips readily into conjugal subordination, Madge continues the trend away from heroines who symbolize the potential for new social order. More surprising is the decline of the virile Rupert. He retires from political journalism to take over the family planting interests, only to grind slowly toward bankruptcy. His health begins to fail, and his occasional comments on public affairs exercise little influence.

Rupert's less charismatic younger brother, Berwick Gordon, personifies the frustration of white South Carolinians who thought they had achieved their goal in 1876. Political contests in the black-majority city repeatedly expose divisions within the white population that threaten to return the balance of power to African Americans. Responses to this situation tax consciences already strained by memory of Reconstruction, during which Rupert had dimly foreseen that "if the negro was to be overthrown by fraud and violence, would not the whites turn these same weapons later against themselves?"[50] But unlike Chapin, Rivers, and Means, Jervey offers no program of reform. The climax of the novel revolves around Berwick's romance with Alice Bohun, the younger sister of a straight-out strategist whose shrewdness and Huguenot name quickly propel him to the forefront of politics. Alice is serious-minded and intelligent, but she is emotionally frigid and ultimately a good deal less independent in her thinking than the heroines of *Eunice* or *Thirty-Four Years*. When an anguished Berwick sides with an Episcopal bishop who proposes admitting black delegates to the diocesan convention, Alice merely parrots the politically useful racism of her brother. She rejects Berwick's marriage proposal, but he nevertheless ends the book still pining for her. Contrary to the golden future promised by redemption, Jervey reports a chronic paralysis.

The exhaustion of the redemption saga is a central theme of Phoebe Hamilton Seabrook's *A Daughter of the Confederacy: A Story of the Old South and the New* (1906). The preface to the book promises to avoid "the unpleasant incidents which have grown almost characteristic of the Southern novel," most notably in the works of Dixon. When the protagonist's family faces a tax auction of their Beaufort townhouse to benefit the school-building program of the Freedmen's Bureau, a good-hearted station agent from the North donates money to save their home. That young man sublimates his unrequited affection for the heroine, Di Marmion, and becomes an eminent justice on the U.S. Supreme Court. Seabrook does depict some unscrupulous northerners, among them the clergyman from Quincy, Massachusetts, who marries Di's widowed grandmother and sets up a profitable business lending money to ex-slaves. But mostly Seabrook emphasizes that, as Di's wise mother tells the child, Yankees are as good as any other set of people. The novel vigorously disapproves sectional grudges in a subplot centered on Di's older sister, who spurns a well-mannered federal admiral. Saddened by her sister's stubborn loneliness and skeptical from the outset about secession, Di lets no such political considerations prevent her marriage to a northern minister.[51]

More remarkable than this sectional reconciliation are the perils Seabrook identifies with memory of the war. The crisis of the book is Di's decision to reject a hard-drinking former Confederate captain because "the army had left its traces on his character—as alas! on so many of his companions." Seabrook also inserts into the story a disheartened ex-Confederate who "had taken to the hermit's cell instead of facing the battle of life in its din" as well as a community still angered by unhappy wartime experiences with Confederate foragers.[52] The shadow of the war ruins Di's sister and repeatedly threatens other characters. A man who collects bomb shells on old battlefields nearly kills himself and several guests when one of his prizes explodes while on display.

Although more skeptical about white southern Civil War commemoration than its title suggests, *A Daughter of the Confederacy* is a less penetrating view of South Carolina than earlier Reconstruction novelists presented. Like Means's *Thirty-Four Years*, Seabrook's work was the sort of book that Mary Chesnut ridiculed for its "piety and pie-making."[53] But Means's domesticity framed a forceful critique of white social relations. *A Daughter of the Confederacy* was less lively both in its prose and its ideas. The protagonist is hardly a thoughtful or adventurous new woman of the New South. Di's challenge to convention does not extend much beyond seeking the bishop's permission to dance, which he readily provides as long as Di does not plan to enter into a sordid ballroom. Seabrook's hopes for the future are vaguer and less passionate than her longing for an idyllic antebellum past. Di's marriage to an insubstantial character in the story does not invest the return of home rule with implications for white society beyond the restoration of sectional peace. The prevailing mood of the book is resignation.

The tentativeness of turn-of-the-century Reconstruction narratives corresponded to discouragements that had characterized South Carolina public life since the 1870s. The decline of state agriculture had by the first decade of the twentieth century thoroughly undermined the Simmsian image of the plantation as a site for the renewal of Providence. Like Rupert Gordon in *The Elder Brother*, Di Marmion's gallant father in *A Daughter of the Confederacy* presides over the failure of the family planting interests. Beyond the economic breakdown flared the Hamptonites' frustrations over the rise of Tillman. The agrarian rebellion had shattered the illusion of harmony among white citizens and ended the pretension that the state united political leadership, social status, and cultural refinement. Redemption had failed to fulfill its millennial expectations. Turn-of-the-century South Carolina novelists did not treat the Reconstruction saga as a vehicle for exploring this reversal of fortune, for they did not match the self-criticism any more than the self-confidence of their predecessors. They described the malaise of the state but drew no moral conclusions from the collapse of planter power Chesnut had forecast. The initial publication of Chesnut's work would further dramatize the limits to the triumph of home rule.

A Diary from Dixie surprisingly shared in the failure of redemption to offer a narrative center for renewal of South Carolina literature. By the time work began toward publication of the book, Chesnut's literary executor, Isabella Martin, secretary of the South Carolina Monument Association throughout the life of that organization, secretary of the Ladies' Memorial Association of Columbia for decades, and a charter member of the Wade Hampton chapter of the UDC, had long ago lost the youthful irreverence that endeared her to Chesnut during the war. She regarded publication of Chesnut's manuscript more as a responsibility to the Confederacy than as a fulfillment of her friend's literary aspirations. "You owe it to *Our Country*," she implored Myrta Lockett Avary when the Virginian visited Columbia to research a follow-up to her edition of the memoir of a Confederate officer's wife.[54] Avary's enthusiasm for the Chesnut project was more commercial

than political. She saw it as a useful step in her cultivation of a relationship with the Appleton publishing firm, which in turn had its own plans for
marketing the book for northern sales as an inside look at the Confederate
high command. These varied motives produced a text that departed significantly from Chesnut's draft and in important ways resembled the turn-of-
the-century South Carolina novels of Reconstruction.

Martin was a forceful figure in the editorial negotiations. She and the
more hesitant Avary carried on an increasingly exasperated correspondence with Appleton editor Francis W. Halsey and eventually W. W. Appleton over the firm's high-handed imposition of an introduction drafted by
Halsey as well as such Civil War chestnuts as deciding whether to call the
first large-scale battle Bull Run or Manassas. Martin was especially exercised about use of the term "Civil War," against which she noted the UDC
was taking "concerted action" because the phrase failed to recognize the
sovereignty of the Confederacy. Beneath these disputes, however, the prin-
cipals shared a good deal of common ground in their conceptions of the
venture. Martin vetoed Halsey's proposal to dedicate the book "To the Men
and Women of the North Who Would Understand," but she no less than
he expected the publication to impress on northern readers the military
achievement of the Confederate army and the desperate conditions that
Confederate patriotism withstood on the home front. She liked the title
that Appleton planned for the book, "With the Heroes of Dixie."[55]

Although she was Chesnut's chosen literary heir, Martin showed a limited interest in her friend's artistic ambitions. Her diffidence was not, as
historians have often implied, the result of a lack of sophistication. Daughter of an influential Methodist minister, she headed a school in Columbia
for twenty-five years after the war and then taught English and philosophy
at the college level for twenty years. She typified late postwar South Carolina intellectual life as thoroughly as many writers of state Reconstruction
novels and was reasonably well prepared for her editorial duties. But she
valued Chesnut's text far more as an eyewitness record than as a creative
achievement. She knew that Chesnut had intensively revised it long after
the war and had left multiple drafts of many segments, but Martin certainly did not wish to present the chronicle as a semifictional reconstruction. She also took a narrow view of the potential significance in material
she dismissed as merely personal or local. She considered "the War parts of
the Diary the only thing of general interest." It was Avary who argued for a
fuller publication of the manuscript on the grounds that "there is more to
it than war history—there is psychological interest, soul development, the

woman's personality, her keen criticism of people and things, her *bon mots*; the world should not be cheated of these."[56]

The "keen criticism of people and things" especially troubled Martin. A draft preface summarizing her views pointedly noted that "among [Chesnut's] contemporaries who survive her, dissenters would rise up against any claim that her criticisms of men and measures are representative of their own attitude in the sixties. We who are her sponsors in this publication do not endorse all her views and utterances." Chesnut's perspective was limited, the draft explained, because "she saw the heroes of Dixie at close range, but it was in their moments of relaxation rather than in their hours of supreme stress, peril and greatness." Even Martin's broadest claims for Chesnut came about as deflections of the author's stern judgments. Martin suggested that "the South would accept best [Chesnut's] criticism of persons and happenings" if the introduction pointed out that "her satire arraigned not merely Southern, but human, nature."[57] Although apt, this praise deliberately downplayed the extent to which Chesnut focused specifically on the pretensions and social patterns of the community in which she lived.

Such an approach left no room for the postwar denouement that Chesnut had carefully crafted. Harriet Grant, a dominant figure in the closing pages of the original diary and even more so in the last revision, does not appear at all in *A Diary from Dixie*. Martin left no recorded comment on a conclusion in which the marriage of the Confederate heiress brought the commercial forces of a divided South into ascendancy in partnership with the triumphant North. Instead, the editors invented an entirely different ending that also foreshadowed redemption. This finale invoked the very model Chesnut had so imaginatively rejected. The next-to-last paragraph of *A Diary from Dixie* purports to quote a letter Chesnut received in late July 1865 from Martin in Columbia: "General Hampton is home again. He looks crushed. How can he be otherwise? His beautiful home is in ruins, and ever present with him must be the memory of the death tragedy which closed forever the eyes of his glorious boy, Preston! Now! there strikes up a serenade to General Ames, the Yankee commander, by a military band, of course." The brief final paragraph of the book records a conversation in which two of Chesnut's acquaintances "were talking of a nation in mourning, of blood poured out like rain on the battle-fields—for what?" Chesnut provides an answer in the last lines of *A Diary from Dixie*, an unidentified quotation from none other than Walter Scott: "Never let me hear that the blood of the brave has been shed in vain! No; it sends a cry down through all time."[58] The juxtaposition transparently implies that memory of the brave Preston Hampton—and a quarter of a million men like him—will eventually rouse his dazed father to overcome calamity and expel the Yankee forces occupying Columbia.

This conclusion is breathtaking in its disregard for the author's design. The quotation from Walter Scott does appear in the final surviving entry of the original diary, but in the very next line, Chesnut added her epitaph to its romantic optimism: *"In vain*, alas, ye gallant few!" Chesnut did not include that unflinching comment in her revised version, but the quotation appears in a less prominent location and is expressly attributed to Scott, whose authority Chesnut challenged throughout her narrative.[59] The purported quotation from Martin is based on several lines in one of five letters from various correspondents that Chesnut copied at the end of her notebooks. The original letter does not refer at all to Hampton's home, which the closing passage of *A Diary from Dixie* uses as the harbinger of redemption.[60]

But Martin and the other editors could not so easily restore the optimism that propelled Reconstruction narratives of the 1870s and early 1880s. Competing with the final paragraphs of *A Diary from Dixie* was a photograph that powerfully suggested a different trajectory for South Carolina. The picture was an evocative view of the ruins at Millwood, the Hampton family seat on the outskirts of Columbia. Hampton's father had built the plantation house into a showcase modeled partly on the Charleston Hotel, a parallel landmark of expansive hospitality and up-to-date architectural taste. The house burned during Sherman's occupation of Columbia in February 1865. Nothing remained of the mansion but a row of tall, fluted columns, overgrown with weeds by the turn of the century. The illustration in *A Diary from Dixie*, expressly identified in the caption as a recent photograph, showed that the restoration of "home rule" had not returned the South Carolina elite to its antebellum power but had taken place within a severely diminished scale of home. Hampton's admirers may also have seen the ruins as a foreshadowing of the political divisions associated with the burning of his postwar home, alleged to have been an act of Tillmanite arson. Certainly white South Carolinians regarded the plantation shards as a claim of irremediable Confederate grievance. A countermonument to the myth of postwar regeneration, the image of Millwood circulated widely in the early twentieth century through the new medium of postcards. State archivist Alexander Salley included a version of the *Diary from Dixie* illustration in a select exhibition of historical photographs at the Jamestown

Millwood ruins. Courtesy of the South Caroliniana Library, University of South Carolina, Columbia.

exposition of 1907. Martin chose Millwood as the most meaningful place in Columbia when asked by Yates Snowden to write a newspaper sketch of a noteworthy site in her home county.[61]

Identification of South Carolina as a permanent ruin belied the celebration of redemption. Early Reconstruction novels had predicted that the South would rise again. Chesnut had described an unattractive but dynamic postwar South Carolina in which merchants flourished as planters lost wealth and power. Later writers in contrast saw no meaningful future for the state. Despite Martin's zealous Confederate patriotism, *A Diary from Dixie* confirmed that the postwar resurgence personified by Wade Hampton was, in another term the UDC regarded warily, a Lost Cause. Local memory would develop differently upon acknowledgment of this fate.

A Diary from Dixie marked an end to redemption as a recurrent motif in South Carolina fiction. An unpublished coda would have appalled Mary Boykin Chesnut almost as much as the editorial distortion of her manuscript. Written between 1912 and 1916 by John Preston Arthur, the son of

an antebellum Columbia mayor, "Through Southern Eyes" was a fictionalization of the Cash-Shannon duel that idealized the self-sacrificing lawyer
based on William M. Shannon. The novel showed little critical engagement
with the transition from Old South to New South. Arthur limited his reform program to a belated, uncontroversial denunciation of dueling. His
aim was to unify white southerners and demand white northern deference.
A politically radical heroine from Massachusetts endangers herself by encouraging the self-development of a freedman who has renamed himself
John C. Calhoun upon enrolling in the integrated University of South Carolina. After the inevitable attempted rape, the inevitable intersectional marriage prompts the bride's mother to observe that "sectionalism will persist
till the North comes to look at Southern problems through Southern eyes."
The effort to renew South Carolina literature through the narrative of Reconstruction had disintegrated into mere propaganda.[62]

Martin acknowledged a new direction in state intellectual life when she
suggested that Appleton commission Harriott Horry Rutledge Ravenel to
write an introduction for *A Diary from Dixie*.[63] Ravenel was a friend of
Chesnut, whom she had followed by a few years at Madame Talvande's
school in Charleston. Born in 1832, she had lived through secession and Reconstruction as an adult. Her husband, St. Julien Ravenel, was a Confederate surgeon and medical chemist, a designer of the *David* torpedo boat,
and a key figure in the postwar development of the low-country phosphate
industry. Despite those links to the war and the rebuilding of the state,
Ravenel consistently looked back to earlier eras. Her debut novel *Ashurst;
or, The Days That Are Not* (1879) took place entirely in antebellum South
Carolina. She followed with biographies of two of her famous ancestors
from the eighteenth and early nineteenth centuries, Eliza Pinckney and
William Lowndes. Her most important book, *Charleston: The Place and
the People* (1906), played an influential role in reorienting the South Carolina literary imagination to an emphasis on the years before the escalation
of the sectional conflict. She devoted nine-tenths of the five-hundred-page
survey of city history to the century and a half before 1830. She ended the
tome with a short chapter on the period from secession through the occupation of the city by Union forces in February 1865, reluctantly conceding
that "in order to finish the story of Charleston, some mention of the war in
which her old life ended must be made, briefly as possible."[64]

Ravenel's wistful view of her home city closely resembled the most pol-
ished portrait of postwar South Carolina in early-twentieth-century fiction,
Owen Wister's *Lady Baltimore* (1906). Grandson of the Pierce Butler who

brought Fanny Kemble to the South, Wister combined a personal investment in the prestige of the Charleston elite with an old-stock northeastern
writer's recognition that a highly romanticized South Carolina could provide a safe blind from which to criticize newcomers and upstarts throughout the United States. The novel is the classic depiction of Charleston as
"the last citadel of good-breeding," a society governed by severely formal
old women of Huguenot ancestry who mourn quietly in church for the husbands and sons lost in the war and "also for the Cause, the lost Cause, that
died with them."[65] Wister's elegiac myth permits no postwar resurgence of
the white South Carolina tradition, doomed to a graceful contraction even
as its antimaterial ethos unites the low-country hero and upcountry heroine of the novel. Reconstruction does not end decisively in 1876; it is an
indignity that in some ways continues forty years after the war. The story
incorporates a recent northern intrusion on southern autonomy, the decision of Wister's friend Theodore Roosevelt to appoint an African American
to the position of customs collector for Charleston. Wister identifies the degrading force of commerce as an even more dangerous sectional intervention. When a boorish second-generation immigrant Wall Street financier
enters into Charleston for the first time, his newfangled automobile runs
over and kills General Hampton, the heroine's aged pet dog.

South Carolina fiction about the postwar period increasingly came to
focus on the timeworn texture of rural life rather than the forward-looking
politics of home rule. The last noteworthy fictional recounting of the Red
Shirt revolution by a state novelist, Elliott Crayton McCants's *White Oak
Farm* (1928), demonstrated this trend. Hampton's campaign is an exciting
event in the youth of McCants's protagonist, Pembroke Gautier, and a
memorable moment in Gautier's lifelong love for the daughter of the leading local merchant. But redemption is merely a prelude to the embrace of
an agricultural vocation in which Gautier makes his inherited backcoun-
try plantation into a prosperous farm and a happy home. Gautier supports
Hampton, but public and private narratives never converge. Reconstruction does not enter into the politics of the community or the private fortunes of self-made individuals. As Tillman emerges, Gautier reflects that
"it did not greatly matter, so far as I was concerned, who became governor,
but that which affected the plantation touched me vitally." He accepts the
defeat of Hampton as the necessary end of the Old South and regards the
political future with "a feeling of apathy."[66]

The disappearance of Reconstruction politics from South Carolina fiction most certainly did not eliminate the topic from local culture. In the

year after the initial publication of *A Diary from Dixie*, the state dedicated an equestrian monument to Wade Hampton on the grounds of the capitol before a crowd reported to be the largest ever assembled in Columbia. Although plaques on the base of the monument listed the Civil War battles in which Hampton had fought, the portrait depicted him not as he looked in the war but as he did in his campaign for governor. Newspaper coverage left no doubt that the tribute honored Hampton primarily for his role as the "chieftain of Carolinians when the prostrate State was given the spirit to arise and stand."[67] In the following years, Red Shirt reunions, histories, and reminiscences refreshed memory of redemption. U.S. senator Ellison D. "Cotton Ed" Smith treated his 1938 reelection campaign against prolabor governor Olin D. Johnston as a replay of Reconstruction, focusing on Johnston's support for a Roosevelt administration that had welcomed African Americans into the Democratic Party and had northern allies who called for federal antilynching legislation. Smith celebrated victory at the Hampton monument dressed in the red shirt that served as the symbol of his campaign, exulting that "we conquered in '76, and we conquered in '38." The scene dramatized the extent to which the Hamptonite narrative of redemption favored by most of the state literati had lost specific coherence and merged into the Tillmanite version of the story.[68]

As the ruined Hampton family seat became emblematic of the failed promise of home rule, the preservation of Martin Gary's house illustrated the narrower remembrance of redemption that eventually prevailed. The former Confederate general bought Oakley Park in 1875, well into the advocacy of paramilitary violence that would culminate with his notorious "Plan of Campaign, 1876." Situated on an eminence overlooking the Edgefield courthouse square, Oakley Park was more of a public building than a home. Gary never married. Instead "the Bald Eagle of the Confederacy" enjoyed a series of postwar relationships with attractive women whom he and his brother called "White Sulphur goddesses," met on Gary's frequent vacations at that West Virginia resort or at Saratoga or Hot Springs. He used the antebellum plantation mansion as the office for his law practice, in which his partner was a nephew with whom he lived. Another nephew in the household was the young John Gary Evans, future governor of South Carolina, who donated the estate to Edgefield in 1941 with the proviso that the UDC would manage its interior as the Red Shirt Shrine and would be welcome to hold meetings there. The family connection between Tillman's mentor and Tillman's protégé underscored the lineage of South Carolina populism, but Oakley Park offered little aura of domesticity. Evans never

Oakley Park. Courtesy of the South Caroliniana Library, University of South Carolina, Columbia.

lived there after his youth, and the house was devoid of furnishings when the UDC received it. Publicity invariably focused on Oakley Park as the headquarters of the Red Shirt movement, where Gary met with fellow straight-out strategists and stood on a second-floor balcony to deliver commanding addresses to crowds of Red Shirts assembled on his property.[69]

This memory of redemption may have encouraged white South Carolinians to resist African American or federal demands for civil rights, but it did not present a vision of communal regeneration. Unlike the early novels about Reconstruction, this commemoration of militant racial supremacism did not explore tensions within white society or fuse public and private life. This defense of home rule did not propose local reforms or stake a claim to national leadership. Collapsed into the ruins of Millwood or the politicking of Oakley Park, the plantation ideal could not match William Elliott Gonzales's industrialized invocation of redemption as a rapture in which civilization rallied and triumphed. Postwar agriculture instead provided a setting for the quietism of McCants or the declension narratives of Jervey and Seabrook.

Displaced Hamptonites eventually concluded that persistence offered a more promising keynote to Confederate memory than redemption. Wister's comedy of manners proposed an alternative to the Simmsian romance. The death of the heroine's dog parodied local remembrance of heroic revolution in 1876, but her successful marriage signaled the indomitable tenacity of South Carolina gentility. The crucial adjustment was the recognition that perpetual siege could become a basis for rejuvenation. *Lady Baltimore* sold well, although Wister could not have foreseen how thoroughly a reputation for Old South perseverance would soon underwrite the national prominence of Charleston through the promotion of historical tourism. If South Carolina literature of Reconstruction contributed less to the reconstruction of state literature than champions of home rule expected, a narrative of postwar stagnation turned out to have valuable applications in Confederate commemoration.

Fortification and Siege

MY FRIEND TED PHILLIPS typified the last great South Carolina antiquarians in centering his interest on the so-called Charleston Renaissance, the cultural effervescence and historic preservation movement of the twentieth-century interwar period. His compeer Harlan Greene shared this enthusiasm. Greene's novel *Why We Never Danced the Charleston* (1984) revolved around a homosexual romantic triangle that featured a character based on Ned Jennings, the avant-garde artist and Charleston Museum curator who committed suicide in the Confederate Home in 1929. The aged narrator, looking back a half century later, stressed that local young men felt engulfed by the past. "History haunted us all," he recalled, "especially those of us born in a sleepy old southern town that had Fort Sumter for a legacy. It rose up from the harbor to stain the sky. We could see it from our school windows, red in the morning. We were used to it, the symbol of the city, its epitome."[1]

Greene's treatment of Fort Sumter as the quintessential civic emblem challenges the most insightful scholarship on the development of "Historic Charleston" as a municipal identity in the tourist boom of the

1920s. Historians have emphasized that the intellectual and economic promoters of local memory tended to highlight the colonial and federal periods. Research has focused on the preservation campaigns mounted for
the Joseph Manigault House (1803), an impetus for the formation of the
Society for the Preservation of Old Dwellings in 1920, and the Heyward-
Washington House (1772), acquired by the Charleston Museum in 1929. The
narrative culminates in an institutional permanence established through
the Board of Architectural Review long dominated by Albert Simons, who
despised mid-nineteenth-century design, and the 1947 founding of the
Historic Charleston Foundation, which reached maturity with the preservation of the Nathaniel Russell House (1811). Scholars have suggested that
this celebration of colonial and early national Charleston broke with or at
least abstained from veneration of the Lost Cause.[2]

Greene highlighted Fort Sumter as part of a protest against the exclusion
of the Charleston Renaissance from the modernist Southern Renascence
canon marked by fascination with corruption, violence, and irrationality.
His account of a demimonde formed through sordid midnight trysts on
the Battery paralleled his admiration for John Bennett, whose folklore collection *The Doctor to the Dead* (1946) was a late harvest of the Charleston
Renaissance. The grotesque legends, gleaned several decades earlier from
local African Americans, are saturated with imagery of decay and putrefac-
tion. Mold creeps through the crackling paint on every rotted wood-frame
window. This version of Historic Charleston was foul rather than quaint,
like the vultures at the city market that were famous long before DuBose
Heyward wrote the lyrics to "The Buzzard Song" for *Porgy and Bess* (1935).
Fort Sumter, "the fortress of rubble that birthed and buried, and is now
the symbol of Charleston's history," documented for Greene the inescapable awareness of Renaissance artists and writers that their parents had
initiated an orgy of death.[3] This argument is not entirely convincing, but
the antiquarian impulse once again offers a valuable corrective to scholarship, including not only the academic excision of the Lost Cause from Historic Charleston but also the assumption that "Civil War ruins appertain to
issues other than that of urban modernity."[4] Fort Sumter, the most famous
of Civil War ruins, was in many ways a product of urban modernity.

Confederate memory is crucial to understanding the strand of modernism that emerged in Charleston during the 1920s in place of the withering
introspection that made the Civil War a touchstone for William Faulkner
and Robert Penn Warren. The Lost Cause thrived in the local renaissance.
DuBose Heyward and Herbert Ravenel Sass wrote novels about the war,

and popular historical writers Harriette Kershaw Leiding and Katherine Drayton Simons devoted much more attention to the conflict than Harriott Horry Rutledge Ravenel had at the turn of the century. The Ladies' Memorial Association burnished Timrod's example by commissioning an original ode each year for the well-attended Memorial Day exercises at Magnolia Cemetery. Heyward read the work of his mother, Janie Screven Heyward, at the 1918 observance. Josephine Pinckney wrote the ode for 1927, the same year she published her verse collection *Sea-Drinking Cities*. Other prominent members of the Poetry Society of South Carolina who contributed odes during the 1920s included Helen von Kolnitz Hyer, Alston Deas, and Sam Stoney. Among the Memorial Day orators active in the Charleston Renaissance were historian Yates Snowden and attorneys Augustine T. Smythe and Harold Mouzon.[5]

The secretary of the Carolina Art Association when he spoke in 1931 and later its longtime president, Mouzon articulated a widely shared understanding of the war and identified the current challenge of remembrance. "The South fought for the right to live its own life and fulfill its own destiny," he told the crowd at the cemetery. Those values stemmed from the rhythms of agricultural life, which created time "for the enjoyment of the arts, for freedom of the soul, and for the simple pleasures of home and family, for friendship, for hospitality, for good taste, for manners and the social graces." The rural foundations of southern culture had largely eroded. He sighed that "men who but lately walked their own farms and tilled their own soil now punch a time clock and spend their days endlessly screwing the same nut on the same bolt, and their reward is to ride in a Ford car and pass their evenings listening to a radio." Mouzon emphasized that this degradation was not limited to laborers. Corporate management encouraged the goal of "selling one's personality, of selling one's self, surely of all forms of prostitution the saddest." Industrialization had produced a pervasive standardization of American life. Towns throughout the South as well as the North featured "the same drug stores full of Coca-Cola and ham sandwiches, the same asphalt, the same filling stations, the same houses full of the same plumbing, the same movie theaters showing the same pictures." Neither the agricultural regeneration anticipated by the early Reconstruction novelists nor the textile manufacturing championed by Progressive-era boosters offered a solid economic basis for protection of Confederate beliefs "in the dignity of the individual man, in the home and family, in religion, in the decencies and graces of life."[6]

Mouzon's analysis summarized the critique of American economics and mass culture that propelled interwar regionalist movements in the art colonies of Santa Fe and Taos and the college towns of Austin, Lincoln, Norman, Missoula, Nashville, and Chapel Hill as well as the New York of Lewis Mumford and Waldo Frank. The Charleston Renaissance similarly proposed a decentralized United States in which organic traditions would temper the individualism of laissez-faire capitalism and provide spiritual sustenance. As the western regionalists found renewal in their contacts with American Indians, whites of the Charleston Renaissance claimed creative custody of African American culture. Bennett's folklore collection was a characteristic production, as were the marketing of sweetgrass baskets and the study of Gullah. The Society for the Preservation of Negro Spirituals, which numbered among its members Heyward, Pinckney, Sass, Smythe, and Stoney, performed low-country slave songs while costumed in antebellum planter garb. This viewpoint imagined the Confederate army as a white southern folk movement committed to protection of the local community and stewardship of African Americans. The Society for the Preservation of Negro Spirituals gave a "complimentary concert" for a national United Daughters of the Confederacy (UDC) convention and donated two gala performances to the campaign to restore Robert E. Lee's birthplace. In class politics as well as racial attitudes, the Charleston Renaissance stood at the extreme right wing of the modernist regionalist movements. While other southern and western regionalists tried to repair the Turnerian myth of frontier democracy or replace it with clearer understanding of exploitative power relations, Charleston intellectuals celebrated a hierarchical yet harmonious society reminiscent of an idealized early modern England.[7]

The Charleston Renaissance was most distinctive among the interwar regionalist movements in turning to mass tourism as a substitute for the failures of agriculture and industry. An immense municipal investment in historic preservation loomed behind Mouzon's exhortation that "the preservation of the things for which they fought" was "the only true memorial." The economy of Historic Charleston depended on a national reputation for preservation of buildings and values, for aristocratic resistance to standardization and materialism. The local interpretation of the Civil War was central to this claim. The Confederacy had never surrendered Fort Sumter, and Charleston remained a bastion of Old South character.[8] When Rhett Butler announced at the end of the movie *Gone with the Wind* (1939) that he was going home "to see if somewhere there isn't something left in life of charm and grace," Hollywood endorsed a civic image that Historic Charleston had promoted relentlessly. The city was ready for the tourists who followed in Butler's footsteps: in honor of the local premiere, the Charleston Museum opened a tie-in exhibition featuring dresses in the fashion of Scarlett O'Hara that attracted twenty-three thousand visitors in three months. Charleston had learned to be prepared for such opportunities. Three days after the premiere, the executive secretary of the chamber of commerce told the weekly luncheon of the Lions Club that "a city is a product which must be sold in a highly competitive market."[9]

Fort Sumter illustrated key tensions in the latest version of Confederate memory. Civil War tourism updated the mid-Victorian rhetoric of evangelical domesticity and the late Victorian rhetoric of millennial Darwinism that had connected the Lost Cause to religion and family. The military installation in the harbor became a shrine of mid-twentieth-century American civil religion, an enjoyable and edifying destination for vacationing pilgrims of all ages. The commercial and recreational framework of tourism was problematic for this spiritual ambition. Charlestonians and visitors wondered if the community had turned to the "selling one's personality" that Mouzon considered the saddest form of prostitution.

The intersectional balance at Fort Sumter further distinguished the site from previous Lost Cause assertions of national significance. Confederate memory in interwar Charleston drew on cooperation with national professional networks and the federal government, as other local preservation initiatives enlisted the aid of the American Institute of Architects, the Carnegie Corporation, and the Works Progress Administration. Such administrative collaborations paralleled literary tributes to secessionist South Carolina as a model for the United States. The arrival of the National Park Service to take charge of Fort Sumter marked the institutional culmination of this strategy. The shaping of Fort Sumter National Monument was the single largest restoration project in mid-twentieth-century Charleston. Federal historical interpretation initially reinforced the landscape of Confederate memory built up in the city since the death of Calhoun. But intersectional partnership also heightened the vulnerability of the Lost Cause to a national ideological upheaval. The centennial anniversary of the first shots of the war exploded into a symbolically significant episode in the acceleration of the civil rights revolution. The ensuing transformation of Civil War memory would repudiate the Charleston Renaissance premises for veneration of Fort Sumter.

The history of tourism at Fort Sumter began with the bombardment that crowds gathered to watch from housetops on the Battery in the early morning of April 12, 1861. Mary Boykin Chesnut reported that "all the agreeable people South seemed to have flocked to Charleston at the first gun."[10] Steamboat captain Thomas J. Lockwood, soon to become a celebrated blockade-runner, started offering trips to Fort Sumter for a dollar on the day after Major Robert Anderson's garrison ceremoniously lowered the U.S. flag and sailed north. Two local studios quickly began to exhibit and sell photographs taken at the fort. In the years following Anderson's triumphant restoration of the flag to its position, journalists J. T. Trowbridge, Whitelaw Reid, and Russell Conwell produced widely circulated reports on their visits to the pulverized ruin.[11] An early Charleston guidebook reported in 1872 that "the most renowned" attraction for travelers was Fort Sumter, where army renovations were under way. Harbor sloops provided convenient transportation for relic hunters, and the officer on duty "offers every facility to strangers." That military hospitality gradually faded. Except for large-scale reunions of veterans, travelers to Charleston during the late nineteenth and early twentieth centuries ordinarily took in Fort Sumter from the Battery. Pennsylvania journalist Alexander K. McClure, noting that the installation was by 1886 primarily a navigation beacon, rhapsodized that "a light-house relieves the squatty summit of the memorable fortress to light the path of the commerce and wealth of peace." William Dean Howells saw the "shadow on the waters" from an East Battery veranda where "my host pointed it out to me, his fellow-citizen of whatever sort, who must wish to visit with my eyes, if by no nearer approach that most venerable monument of our Civil War."[12] Interwar boosters would develop a substantial infrastructure to influence such ruminations from the Battery and facilitate pilgrimages to the fort.

Henry James cast the most elaborate tourist gaze toward Fort Sumter in the years leading up to the Charleston Renaissance. At the age of sixty-one, he had returned to the United States for the first time in twenty years with plans to write a travel book "absolutely personal to myself and proper to my situation." The view from the Battery in February 1905 offered him abundant personal material. His younger brother Wilky had suffered a near-fatal wound at Morris Island while serving as Robert Gould Shaw's adjutant in the 54th Massachusetts Regiment's charge on Battery Wagner; Wilky's long and incomplete convalescence at home was a formative event for the James family. William James had delivered the principal address at the 1897 dedication of the Shaw Memorial in Boston, in which he noted that the postwar construction of jetties to deepen Charleston Harbor had put the site of Battery Wagner permanently underwater. The novelist left

"The House-Tops in Charleston during the Bombardment of Fort Sumter,"
Harper's Weekly, May 4, 1861, 273. Courtesy of the South Caroliniana Library,
University of South Carolina, Columbia.

that metaphor to his older brother and recorded no reflections on Wilky's
cause or comrades. After spending three days in Richmond, he was eager to
see more of the imprint of slavery and secession. He wrote in *The American
Scene* (1907) that "I was to find myself liking, in the South and in the most
monstrous fashion, it appeared, those aspects in which the consequences of
the great folly were, for extent and gravity, still traceable." His expert guide
in Charleston was his friend and admirer Owen Wister, who had recently
completed a first draft of *Lady Baltimore*.[13]

The view from the Battery furnished the keynote for James's visit. "Filled
as I am, in general, while there, with the sadness and sorrow of the South,"
Wister told him, "I never, at Charleston, look out to the old betrayed Forts
without feeling my heart harden again to steel." James could not agree.
"The far-away dimness" of Sumter, almost four miles from the Battery, "was
a blow even to one's faded vision of Charleston viciously firing on the Flag."
The faintness of the fort matched the remoteness of the war. "To justify

hardness, moreover, one would have had to meet something hard," James added, and "the depleted cerebral condition" of Charleston made it difficult to conceive that "such a place had ever been dangerously moved." He understood that the slaveholding South could not have been limited to the "unmitigated mildness" he now saw, but the former Confederacy had become a "practically vacant cage." He wondered "how, in an at all complex, a 'great political,' society, can *everything* so have gone?—assuming that, under this aegis, very much ever had come." The logical question was, "had the *only* focus of life then been Slavery?" James occasionally detected "the ghost of the grand style" or an antique "air of reality" in knocking about town, but he confirmed his answer in Magnolia Cemetery, where he "kept finding the mere melancholy charm reassert itself where it could—the charm, I mean, of the flower-crowned waste that was, by my measure, what the monomania had most prepared itself to bequeathe." With such a legacy, the cultural prospect of the white South was dim. James observed that W. E. B. Du Bois's *The Souls of Black Folk* (1902) had been "the only 'Southern' book of any distinction published for many a year."[14]

Charlestonians worked to claim an impressive share of the national tourism expansion after World War I by offering an alternative to such views. Modernization of logistics was important to this process. James followed long-standard travel arrangements. He arrived by rail and stayed for three nights at the Charleston Hotel, a monument of the antebellum commercial heyday. The immense growth of automobile traffic fostered a new tourism. The highly seasonal trade revolved around the well-publicized gardens on former plantations near Charleston, especially Middleton Place, Magnolia Gardens, and Cypress Gardens. The increase in the number of travelers led to the development of new accommodations. Charleston celebrated the opening of two hotels in the spring of 1924, the first large lodgings in decades. The Francis Marion Hotel drew from a wide base of community support; it aimed to serve business travelers, and its position on what was now known as Marion Square, facing the Calhoun Monument, promised to benefit merchants on King Street. The Fort Sumter Hotel was the first facility in Charleston to advertise itself as primarily a tourist hotel. The seven-story building, with accommodations for 350 guests, stood directly on the western extension of the South Battery. "There is no spot in the United States, perhaps, more suitable to the site of a tourist hotel than that upon which the Fort Sumter is built," one newspaper opined. In conjunction with the formal opening, the chamber of commerce held a public meeting at the hotel to initiate planning for the establishment of a permanent tourism and convention bureau for Charleston. The selling of "America's Most Historic City," a motto introduced by mayor Thomas Porcher Stoney in 1924, required an up-to-date promotional management as well as the latest amenities.[15]

Self-conscious interweaving of past and present was fundamental to the tourism experience marketed by the Fort Sumter Hotel. Lead developer Edward J. Murphy obtained the prime Battery tract through a city donation during the mayoral administration of Stoney's predecessor and bitter rival, John Patrick Grace. The Irish Americans represented by Murphy and Grace recognized that Stoney's old-stock vision of Historic Charleston mirrored the nativism and anti-Catholicism that the Ku Klux Klan was riding to a crest of power. The Fort Sumter Hotel was thoroughly contemporary in style. The owners brought in an operating group based in New Jersey, including the Asbury Park mayor who guided the interwar development of that boardwalk playground. The design of the hotel announced ambitions to tap into Florida's vast tourism trade. Atlanta architect G. Lloyd Preacher evoked a villa with a Spanish tile roof. The stucco was painted "an unusual and distinctive pink," and the terrace furniture was green with orange trim. Publicity focused less on the proximity of colonial houses or churches than on the facilities for card parties, mah-jongg, dancing, yachting, and hunting as well as the privileges of two country clubs. At the same time, the hotel's name recognized that "when a visitor comes to Charleston, especially if he has not been before, one of the objectives that occurs at once to his mind is to get a view of historical Fort Sumter." Commercial adoption of the emblem suggested that the pleasures of the resort gained resonance from an awareness that "within sight of eye and four miles across a beautiful sheet of water . . . grim-visaged Sumter stands a melancholy witness of heroic deeds."[16]

The introduction of regular cruises from a wharf near the hotel to Fort Sumter extended the synthesis of lighthearted recreation and historic dignity. Daniel Ravenel, who inaugurated daily tours in 1926, personified the merger of tourism and Confederate memory. He expanded the steamship agency inherited from his uncle into a broader travel business, and his wife was the younger sister of Mary B. Poppenheim, recently president general of the UDC and later lead author of the official organizational history. Ravenel's initiative lasted only one season, but in 1928 mariner Shan Baitary formed Fort Sumter Navigation Tours, which continued until World War II. One key to Baitary's success during the first several years was the popular commentary of octogenarian William Robert Greer, reputedly

the last surviving Confederate veteran to have served at Fort Sumter during the Civil War. Greer naturally focused his remarks on the southern defense of the installation during 1863–65; he closed presentations with the
summation, "Fort Sumter—never captured, never surrendered." The most
conspicuous Confederate veteran in town, especially after the deaths of
C. Irvine Walker in 1927 and James Armstrong in 1930, the son of a Belfast
native was a living reminder that local memory need not celebrate old-line
families exclusively.[17]

The development of daily tours to Fort Sumter coincided with a commemorative adornment of the site, rarely garrisoned by the army after the
end of World War I. One of Robert Anderson's daughters began the process in 1919 by leaving the federal government a bequest of twenty-five
thousand dollars to place a statue of Anderson in the fort. Always eager to
encourage creative alternatives to portrait statues, the U.S. Commission of
Fine Arts persuaded the estate to convert the bequest into a bronze flagpole
with a medallion relief of Anderson, which highlighted the importance of
Fort Sumter in the history of national reverence for the Stars and Stripes.
Shortly after Congress accepted the flagstaff in March 1928, the Charleston chapter of the UDC obtained permission from the War Department to
install a bronze tablet honoring the Confederate defenders of Fort Sumter.
An officer of the army unit stationed at Fort Moultrie accepted the two tributes in a ceremony at Fort Sumter on the eve of the seventieth anniversary
of the outbreak of the war. The flagstaff saluted Anderson and the men of
his command who "withstood the destructive bombardment and withdrew
with the honors of war." Greer unveiled the UDC plaque to Confederate soldiers who "Defended This Harbor Without / Knowing Defeat or Sustaining
Surrender." The firm of Albert Simons and Samuel Lapham, the leading
architects of the Charleston Renaissance, designed both works.[18]

A veteran travel writer's account of a trip to Fort Sumter indicates how
effectively the new trappings supported a Civil War narrative of blame-
less sectional reconciliation rather than Wister's denunciation of treason or James's meditations on slavery. Baitary and a competitor were
together bringing almost ten thousand visitors to Fort Sumter each year
when William Oliver Stevens published a script for northerners contem-
plating an automobile getaway during the southern blossoming of spring.
Stevens judged the two-hour harbor outing "the best dollar's worth to be
had in all Charleston." Baitary kept up a steady commentary as his "roomy
and comfortable-looking motor pleasure boat" passed the convergence of
the yellowish Cooper River with the darker Ashley River. Although Greer

Edward Hopper, *The Battery, Charleston, S.C.* (1929). Whitney Museum of Art; Josephine N. Hopper Bequest. © Heirs of Josephine N. Hopper, licensed by the Whitney Museum of Art. Digital Image © Whitney Museum of Art.

had died recently, Baitary doubtless used much of the same material as he led the group around the fort, and a sense of living memory lingered in the tour. Stevens expressed satisfaction with the Union and Confederate memorials that ensured "honor for all to whom honor is due." The author recognized the opportunity to ballast his jaunty sophistication with some patriotic devotion. "This is, in the annals of our nation, sacred ground," he declared. The visit ended at the flagstaff, where Baitary delivered a speech "summing up the story of Sumter and expressing the satisfaction that we are again a united people under one flag." The guide lifted his cap before the flag, and the sightseers followed suit. The leisurely return cruise by way of the new Cooper River bridge provided time and diversions with which to relax after a memorable emotional experience.[19]

The Battery also sharpened as a commemorative viewpoint after the opening of the Fort Sumter Hotel, as the municipal government continued to supplement its array of Civil War cannons. Each gun featured an explanatory marker, and guidebooks added commentary. When Edward Hopper made an automobile trip from New York to Charleston in 1929, the Civil War buff recorded his visit with an oil painting of an eleven-inch Dahlgren gun pointed at Fort Sumter that Confederates had salvaged from the USS *Keokuk* after sinking that ironclad steamer in the repulse of Admiral Samuel DuPont's attack in April 1863. A plaque affixed to the cannon by the UDC saluted its second difficult salvaging by Lost Cause enthusiasts, who raised the trophy from the sands of Sullivan's Island at the turn of the century.[20]

The most important enhancement was a new monument to the Confederate defenders of Charleston, often called the Fort Sumter Memorial. In a September 1928 will, Andrew Buist Murray, the adopted son and eventual business successor of rice-milling magnate W. Jefferson Bennett, left the city one hundred thousand dollars with which to commission the work. Whether or not a response to congressional approval of the Anderson memorial flagpole four months earlier, the bequest added to Murray's long-standing support for waterfront improvements and recalled his brief Confederate military service on James Island. After his death in December 1928, his executors appointed trustees who adopted a much more self-consciously professional procedure for design of the monument than the process followed at any previous Confederate memorial in South Carolina. Headed by the son of the last Confederate commander of Fort Sumter, the trustees engaged National Sculpture Society president Adolph Weinman to serve as an expert consultant. Weinman set up an advisory jury that recommended award of the commission to Hermon A. MacNeil, a distinguished former president of the society. The trustees endorsed the selection and announced that the Massachusetts native and longtime New Yorker would "have a free hand with the design." The coordination with a national professional organization contrasted sharply with the making of the Magnolia Cemetery monument to Confederate defenders of Charleston, for which a German sculptor had executed local veteran James Gadsden Holmes's design for a Confederate flag-bearer marching into battle.[21]

The neoclassical bronze unveiled in October 1932 at the southeast point of the Battery showed that the local Lost Cause had also left behind the passionate literalism of the cemetery statue. MacNeil's composition featured a heroic male nude holding an archaic shield and striding forward to protect an Athena-like embodiment of the city, who pointed seaward toward Fort Sumter. Like MacNeil's professional credentials, his Beaux-Arts design testified that Charleston was a cosmopolitan cultural community rather than the "flower-crowned waste" that James had lamented or, more to the point, the "Sahara of the Bozart" that H. L. Mencken had ridiculed in 1920. Epic male nudity, rare in American war memorials until World War I, dominated the allegorical monuments that sculptors Daniel

Hermon Atkins MacNeil, Fort Sumter Memorial. Courtesy of the South Caroliniana Library, University of South Carolina, Columbia.

Chester French, Charles Niehaus, Henry Hering, C. Paul Jennewein, and Pietro Montana offered as alternatives to ubiquitous doughboy statues.[22] The monument inscription enjoined viewers to "COUNT THEM / HAPPY / WHO FOR THEIR / FAITH / AND THEIR / COURAGE / ENDURED A GREAT / FIGHT," but MacNeil's analogy to World War I memorials made clear that the Confederate fight was great not merely because it inspired devotion and valor but because its cause was just, like the ideals for which Americans had recently fought in Europe. Although intersectional comity prevailed within the federal fort, the memorial on the Battery defended the righteousness of the Lost Cause. Proclaiming a holiday for the dedication, Charleston mayor Burnet R. Maybank elaborated that "those who fought for the Confederacy fought for the principles of true Americanism, namely, the right to preserve their state rights and personal liberties; to pursue their normal occupations without the incubus of meddling and impractical bureaucratic control; and to throw off the shackles of fanatical oppression."[23]

The choice of orator for the dedication of the monument similarly illustrated local eagerness to combine Confederate memory with current intellectual trends. A native North Carolinian brought to national attention by Mencken during the 1920s, journalist Gerald W. Johnson was the foremost supporter of his mentor's crusade against southern provincialism. His *The Undefeated* (1927) presented Gutzon Borglum's attempt to carve a grand Confederate memorial on Stone Mountain as the story of an inventive artist with a sublime topic subverted by the venality of Atlanta businessmen. Johnson was currently working on *The Secession of the Southern States* (1933), commissioned by a leading publisher with hopes for a broad readership. He was friendly with DuBose Heyward and Josephine Pinckney, and he had won plaudits from *Charleston News and Courier* editor William Watts Ball for a magazine essay praising Confederate veterans for postwar sacrifices that made possible the recent successes of southern entrepreneurs and authors.[24] His appearance at the dedication, followed by brief remarks from W. Robert Greer, demonstrated the ambition of Charleston civic leaders to position the city at the forefront of regional sophistication.

Johnson described Fort Sumter as a symbol of the American democracy challenged during the Great Depression by fascism and communism. The Confederate defenders of Charleston fought for "their right to live their lives as they chose to live them." Slavery was for Johnson merely an incidental flashpoint of the sectional conflict, for "no rational man, with even a superficial knowledge of those days now pretends to believe that the men who held the shattered battlements of Sumter against tremendous odds were fighting for slavery." Slaveholders were few, he maintained, and planters' profits were tenuous; the heroism of Fort Sumter demanded a deeper motive. The peculiar institution, a school of civilization and source of material support for African Americans, was most significant as a foundation for distinctive white southern insight into the ongoing global crisis. Communists and fascists "promise us economic freedom if we will but surrender our political freedom; but in the South they are talking to men who know what that means," Johnson asserted. "The negro slaves in the South enjoyed a far larger degree of economic freedom than did their masters; but we have no desire to occupy their place." He concluded that "here where Sumter stood, no tyranny shall rise."[25]

The dedication ceremony linked the intellectual aspirations of the Charleston Renaissance to the promotion of tourism not only by embellishing the Battery but also by marking the opening of a widely publicized gathering of authors at the Fort Sumter Hotel. The sequel to a 1931 conference in Charlottesville, Virginia, that brought together William Faulkner, Ellen Glasgow, Allen Tate, and other southern luminaries, the Charleston meeting was more notable for its politic welcome to influential book review editors from New York and Chicago. The program built on the success of the Poetry Society in inviting and entertaining literary tourists such as Amy Lowell, Harriet Monroe, John C. Farrar, and Donald Davidson. The host committee arranged for visits to Magnolia Gardens and Middleton Place, a luncheon at the Miles Brewton House, and a cocktail party at the Heyward-Washington House. One night, Sam Stoney told Gullah tales and imitated "a negro sermon"; the next evening, the Society for the Preservation of Negro Spirituals gave a concert. Prominent on the carefully designed itinerary was an excursion to the original seat of the Civil War, which according to a newspaper report "proved highly enjoyable, the majority of the group seeing Fort Sumter for the first time at close hand."[26] Historic Charleston had made substantial progress in offering visitors an alternative to the outlook on the Battery assumed by James and Wister a quarter century earlier.

The writers' excursion underscored the importance of Fort Sumter to Lost Cause literature of the Charleston Renaissance. DuBose Heyward and Herbert Ravenel Sass both published Civil War novels that featured climactic battle scenes in the harbor. Heyward's *Peter Ashley* (1932) leaned toward the Menckenian critical realism reinforced by the regionalists at the University of North Carolina, while Sass's *Look Back to Glory* (1933) more nearly echoed the agrarian ideas associated with Vanderbilt University. The two friends' books were nevertheless remarkably similar. Both stories revolved around native South Carolinians who returned to the low country on the eve of the Civil War after years abroad. The protagonists rediscovered home, fell in love, fought duels with romantic rivals, and tried to stay aloof from frenzied secessionism but ultimately sacrificed misgivings to cast their lots with the doomed Confederacy. Neither narrative imagined southern defeat as the shattering of youthful illusions that Margaret Mitchell portrayed in *Gone with the Wind* (1936) or the formalist tragedy that Allen Tate envisioned in *The Fathers* (1938). For the Charleston authors, the Civil War marked not the annihilation of the Old South but the ruin of a tradition that might yet be restored as a social force rather than merely a prism of individual consciousness.[27]

Heyward and Sass came readily to their positions as renovators of the Lost Cause. In addition to their low-country lineage, the authors shared strong self-identification as heirs to the legacy of Simms, who is a character in both Civil War novels. Heyward looked back on Simms's work as a childhood favorite and gave the hero of his novel *Porgy* (1925) the name of Simms's best-loved character. Sass, a prolific nature writer, took up Simms's metaphorical position at the edge of the swamp.[28] Simms had encouraged the poetic ambitions of Sass's father, whose tribute to "The Confederate Dead" (1901) served as the text for a marble tablet in Saint Michael's Episcopal Church, the epicenter of local identity in Charleston and an example of persistence as a motif in Lost Cause tourism. Guidebook writers delighted in recounting the story that the parish removed the eighteenth-century church bells after the steeple became a target for Union bombardment. They were sent to Columbia, where Sherman's invasion resulted in damage to the bells. The church shipped the remains of the set to London for recasting from the original molds, a tidy tale of depredation and renewal. One of Heyward's early literary efforts was a hometown treatment of the "Swamp Angel," the dreaded Morris Island cannon that Herman Melville described in a wartime poem as "a coal-black Angel" avenging humiliations inflicted under the aegis of "the white man's seraph," Saint Michael.[29]

Heyward started working intermittently on *Peter Ashley* shortly after the completion of *Porgy*, but the thinking behind his Civil War novel began with World War I. Heyward was in Paris in August 1914, and his first publication was a newspaper report to Charleston on French mobilization. Disqualified from military service by the effects of polio, he enlisted as a "four-minute man," delivering short speeches to promote the purchase of war bonds. The dominant theme of *Peter Ashley* is the impact of war on the social and cultural order. The title character was born into a low-country rice family, raised in a mansion overlooking the Battery by a Huguenot uncle, and educated at Harvard and Oxford. Summoned home upon secession, the youth arrives on the day that Citadel cadets prevent the *Star of the West* from restocking the food supply at Fort Sumter. Military preparations have already knocked the underpinnings from the cultivated world enjoyed by his uncle, Pierre Chardon. Simms has turned from literature to military engineering; the fashionable Battery promenade has become a bristling battery. Ashley initially hopes to revive the suspended *Russell's Magazine*, but Chardon sees that "our civilization has ended" and that the world now belongs to the soldier.[30]

The propagandist of World War I maintained that this loss was not without countervailing gains. The narrative of intellectual narrowing describes a worldly wisdom in devotion to home. Heyward repeatedly underscores the limitations of individual free will. Planters reinforce their stoicism with ritual gambling; the protagonist's major literary effort is an account of Race Week. Ashley comes to understand that "willingly or unwillingly we all eventually conform to an unknown and preordained pattern." The unimpeachable Chardon similarly realizes that "it was as inevitable that Peter should go in eventually as that he had long ago obeyed his own blind impulse." Chardon's experience in the Mexican War was devastating but hardly meaningless; he emerged with "a realization of the impermanence of life, the fragility of happiness, the ridiculous futility of arguing with Destiny." Like him, future iterations of the civic type might eventually live nobly with serious wounds.[31]

Implicit in this hope was an argument that slaveholding did not define white southern culture as fully as Henry James had maintained. Heyward echoed current scholarship in Ashley's assessment that slavery "was, to say the least, outmoded; that while it continued to work in fact, it was wrong in theory, and that sooner or later it was doomed." Southern historian Charles W. Ramsdell had recently provided fresh intellectual currency to the notion that the peculiar institution had passed its peak of profitability and if not for the Civil War would soon have withered away for economic reasons, an argument that Gerald W. Johnson avidly endorsed. *Peter Ashley* never indicates that wealth and power lurk behind the supposedly impersonal forces to which the protagonist yields. The Confederacy inspires enthusiasm among the shopkeepers, artisans, and small farmers who form "the great middle class" even though "scarcely any of them owned slaves."[32]

After the climactic bombardment of Anderson's garrison, *Peter Ashley* jumps to its conclusion in the autumn of 1861, when Peter and his company depart for the front. Pierre Chardon looks on, haunted by the closing lines of a poem that James Matthewes Legaré wrote before his early death in 1859: "Dawn in the meadows of the heart. / The birds sing out a last refrain, / And ready garnered to the mart, / I see the ripe and yellow grain." The young men follow a road whence advanced "down the years always, like the wand passed from hand to hand of runners in a race, the tradition of gentility, hospitality, loyalty to one's own."[33] Like MacNeil's bronze allegory on the Battery, unveiled on the same day that Heyward's novel appeared, the evocation of the pastoral landscape and the passing of the torch in John McCrae's "In Flanders Field" (1915) asserted a parallel between the Confederate War and World War I. Despite the carnage, the low-country tradition personified by Chardon remains a solid foundation on which to rebuild.

Chardon's main historical avatar is his Unionist friend James Louis Petigru, who agrees in *Peter Ashley* that "youth must run with the pack, or die of loneliness" but finds that age brings different opportunities. "We fulfill a civic function," the lawyer explains to Ashley. "We are Charleston's ex-

cuse for considering itself broad-minded. If anyone accuses them of in-
tolerance, they have merely to say, 'Intolerant? Ridiculous!—why, there's
Petigru, there's Chardon.'" The self-deprecation adds a characteristically
wry gloss to the interwar apotheosis of Petigru. The University of South
Carolina named the building that housed its law school for him in 1919.
Susan Pringle Frost made the restoration of his law office one of her pet
projects. Guidebooks recycled his quips and directed tourists to his grave in
the Saint Michael's churchyard, which honored the "antique Courage" his
legend represented: "In the great Civil War / He withstood his People for
his Country / But his People did Homage to the Man / Who held his Con-
science higher than their Praise." William Oliver Stevens pointed out that
the local hero transcended the ostensible tension between individual and
community. "Solitary as Judge Petigru was in his allegiance to the Union
and his hatred of secession, yet in a sense he was a true Charlestonian,"
Stevens noted. "Stiff-necked independence was the characteristic quality
of this city from its earliest days. . . . Petigru only went a step farther down
the selfsame path by seceding from the seceders."[34] The incorporation of
Petigru into the Lost Cause argued that the open mind of cosmopolitan
Charleston had not entirely closed in the sectional conflict and that the
civic tradition of independence was sufficient to resist the mass culture of
the twentieth century.

Petigru appears in *Look Back to Glory*, but Sass's historical paragon was
John C. Calhoun. That admiration also drew on a broader resurgence of
interest. W. W. Ball made "Back to Calhoun" the theme of his call during the years after World War I for a state constitutional convention that
would base its reforms on the 1808 constitution praised in Calhoun's theo-
retical writings on government. The newspaper editor expressed satisfaction that skewed legislative apportionment prevented upstate mill workers
from advancing labor or regulatory reform without a "concurrent majority"
of Ball's fellow capitalists in the rural low country. He called for adaptation
of other features of the antebellum constitution, including an increase in
the offices to be filled by legislative appointment rather than election; these
positions would be unpaid to restrict government to "men of independence
and character." Demanding massive fiscal retrenchment at the outbreak
of the Depression, he maintained that the state should provide free public education only through six or seven grades for the vast majority of residents. His frank promotion of class interests prepared him to break with
the New Deal over emergency relief measures and the gold standard well
before the Democratic recognitions of African Americans that prompted

the editor to lead the white southern migration toward the Republican Party. Sass, a longtime member of the *News and Courier* staff before turning to freelance writing and a regular contributor throughout Ball's tenure, exulted that "Ball is Calhoun brought down to date." *Look Back to Glory* similarly maintained that the creative heyday of the South began when "the realism of John C. Calhoun had supplanted the sentimentalism of Thomas Jefferson." By rejecting the illusion of human equality and implementing a limited democracy, "the plantations of the Low-Country, the city-state of Charleston, had to a great extent directed the later course of the Republic." Although northern mishandling of the sectional conflict could not be undone, Sass explained in a December 1933 radio address, his novel sought to show that "we may be able to cut cross-country and get on the right road again."[35]

Calhoun's mistake, according to Sass's protagonist, was his commitment to a particular form of inequality. Returning to the low country after fifteen years abroad at Oxford and a series of mid-level diplomatic posts, Richard Acton laments to his brother, "We saw that there must always be slavery, because the strong will always rule the weak, but we didn't see that the time for our kind of slavery had passed."[36] This error was the consequence of abolitionism. Sass maintained in his 1933 radio address that the antebellum South was moving steadily toward emancipation until William Lloyd Garrison launched "his unfortunate campaign of unwise and irresponsible meddling." Not even the prosperity of the Cotton Kingdom would have halted this trend, "which had practically the whole outside world and an increasing part of the South itself behind it if only the Northern Abolitionists had been content to let the South handle its own difficult and dangerous problem and to let Nature take its course." Apart from northern political opportunists, *Look Back to Glory* suggests, the prime beneficiaries of this delay in emancipation were the African Americans supported by the peculiar institution. Sass was particularly proud that his novel "perfectly frankly" addressed "the problem of sex-relationship," which in his narrative results from comely slaves who seduce planters to obtain favorable treatment.[37]

Sass sounded the agrarian call for "restoration of the equilibrium between urban and rural life." He argued that the antebellum South had developed a "well-balanced agricultural-industrial system" that offered a model for the United States in the Great Depression. Acton makes his return at the family seat in the country, Avalon, named for the revitalizing retreat of the once and future king. Charleston, the setting for the final section of the book, is "the heart, the capital of the plantations." Close contact with nature awakens a reverent pantheism. Acton's response to the sensual Diane Rowland is the adoration of a goddess. He realizes ecstatically at the outset of the Union ironclad attack in April 1863 that "he couldn't separate her from the country itself: the country, the soil, the trees, the fragrances, the songs, the memories for which he was going into battle. The green plantation woods, the shimmering rice-fields, the moss-draped oaks of Avalon, the high-walled streets of Charleston—in a little while now they would be gay with bignonia and sweet with honeysuckle—all these were Diane."[38] Her other admirers similarly sustain themselves during the repulse of DuPont's fleet by thinking of her.

The central conflict of *Look Back to Glory* pits South Carolinian political realism against state leaders' inflexible commitment to their code of honor. Acton sees that the South has good cause and constitutional authority to secede and would be better off outside the Union, but he doubts that the South could prevail in a war to establish its independence. His rival, James Hail, refuses to bend his dignity to such calculations. Engaged to Diane through a remarkable series of marital postponements, Hail is handsome and well mannered; he wins the jousting tournament at which the local gentry test their knightly skills. Before the war he serves as a political lieutenant to Calhoun's courageously principled successor Robert Barnwell Rhett, "who more than any other living man, was responsible for that secession of South Carolina which had brought on the war." Upon the outbreak of hostilities Hail enlists in Hampton's Legion and distinguishes himself as a cavalry officer. Acton is a mere private posted to Fort Sumter. His love for Diane had led to a duel in which the crack pistol shot passed up his chance to kill Hail because Diane would not approve, and he has tried to resign his hopes for her. But when Hail comes to Fort Sumter on a military errand during the stalemated summer of 1864 while Acton is serving sentinel duty on the parapet, the two men quickly agree to "end it now" in hand-to-hand grappling. They plunge together over the wall of the fortress. Hail dies instantly on the iron fragment of a cannon ball. Acton lives only long enough to be assured of Diane's love. He reflects shortly before his death that "somewhere there was a parallel between his own individual futility and the great futility that had been South Carolina."[39]

Like the ominous departure for Virginia at the close of *Peter Ashley*, the mutual destruction of Hail and Acton describes a Lost Cause that might yet prevail. Secessionist punctiliousness had thwarted Calhounian realism. But the North had not defeated the South, much as the Union never cap-

FORTIFICATION AND SIEGE 183

tured Fort Sumter. Acton despairs only when he imagines that "new gen-
erations of South Carolina, chastened by disaster, enlightened by bayonets,
would learn that the South Carolina of their fathers had never existed."
Historians influenced by Union triumph might instead describe "a South
Carolina of error, of treason, of rebellion, of slave-driving, of oppression,
of braggadocio and fire-eating, of ignorance and stupidity and iniquity."
Sass's novel aimed to avert this calamity. The surviving principles of the
Old South presented "the only way in which we can save ourselves in our
present dilemma."[40]

Peter Ashley and *Look Back to Glory* testified to the authors' faith in the
commercial profitability of Confederate memory as well as the political and
social viability of the ideals the novels celebrated. Both writers tried to sell
their properties to Hollywood, which demonstrated its interest in southern sagas of the Civil War through the auditions for *Gone with the Wind*
held in April 1937 at the Fort Sumter Hotel, where George Cukor found
a descendant of Robert Barnwell Rhett to play the role of India Wilkes.[41]
Heyward and Sass also tried to tie their novels into the local promotion of
tourism. They combined their extended battle scenes to "make a little book
out of it, attractively arrayed, which would have undoubtedly a good and
continuous local sale among the tourists." The resulting *Fort Sumter* (1938)
featured a brief introduction and epilogue that set the separate narratives
in a frame favorable to the Confederacy. The issue in April 1861 was not
whether secessionists would fire on the American flag but whether Anderson would "evacuate the fort to the state of South Carolina and the newly
formed Confederacy, or would he remain there flying the Stars and Stripes
and invite civil war?" The lesson of April 1863 was not that the U.S. Army
had properly positioned Fort Sumter to block attacks by outgunned ships
in the narrow harbor but that Charleston was indomitable and that even
the subsequent Union demolition of Sumter "proved not to be synonymous
with defeat."[42]

Visitors confirmed that the Charleston Renaissance intensified the
cross-fertilization of local tourism and literature that *Lady Baltimore* had
begun a generation earlier. Counseling prospective travelers, William Oliver
Stevens recommended Heyward and Sass rather than Simms, Timrod, or
Hayne, who "make feeble and dusty reading today." Jonathan Daniels suggested the resonance of the Civil War novels in his thoughtful travel book
A Southerner Discovers the South (1938). Setting out from Raleigh, North
Carolina, the newspaper editor visited Virginia and then headed west to
the Mississippi River, looping back through the deepest South until he

turned up the Atlantic coast and made Charleston his final stop before returning home. The ardent New Dealer knew his reactionary counterpart W. W. Ball well, and he understood that "the technique of Charleston is the same as that so successfully pursued by Miss Greta Garbo," a modern public relations campaign that projected an image of graceful, reclusive world-weariness. But Daniels's goal was not to debunk. He aimed to find the usable essences of the South, and in Charleston he highlighted the same sites and figures as Heyward and Sass. At the conclusion of his chapter and almost the end of his long journey, he depicted himself peering out at Fort Sumter from the Battery. "And beyond Sumter somehow I looked back to Calhoun and Petigru," he fancied. Although both men were natives of the upcountry, "they above the others — and there were others — gave content and weight to the aristocratic tradition of the Low Country and Charleston." That noble and pleasant ideal, Daniels believed, offered the best way for the contemporary city to serve the region and the nation "while it eats its past."[43] The sojourner's imaginative vision of Fort Sumter illustrated the vitality of Confederate memory in interwar South Carolina and suggested the local readiness for resumed expansion of tourism after World War II.

W. W. Ball led Charleston Renaissance warhorses Sass, Josephine Pinckney, John Bennett, Sam Stoney, and Susan Pringle Frost into his revolt against the New Deal, but Depression-era mayor Burnet R. Maybank and his many supporters remained attentive to the usefulness of federal spending. When Charleston added a historical commission to its tourism infrastructure in the mid-1930s, Sass served as secretary and proposed that the commission should install historical markers throughout the city. Maybank obtained Works Progress Administration (WPA) funding for three hundred bronze tablets. The group realized from the outset that Fort Sumter presented an especially important opportunity for partnership with Washington. Daniel Ravenel and Charleston Museum director E. Milby Burton, like Sass appointed to the commission in 1935, lobbied federal officials to transform the little-used fortress into a historical site. The National Park Service, to which Roosevelt had in 1933 transferred responsibility for preservation of the battlefield parks and national monuments previously maintained by the War Department, sent two representatives to Charleston in 1936 to meet with the historical commission and chamber of commerce. Their field report agreed that the situation offered extraordinary potential, but the deteriorating international outlook militated against deactivation of the installation. The army reoccupied Fort Sumter in March 1941, and nine months later, Pearl Harbor brought the suspension of harbor tours for the duration. But World War II clearly indicated that Fort Sumter was no longer likely to play a significant role in protecting the United States from foreign attack. The facility was too small and inconvenient for any other military purpose, opening the way for its conversion to the full-time service of historical tourism.[44]

As chair of the historical commission, Ravenel returned in 1946 to the project he had begun by launching regular tours of Fort Sumter twenty years earlier. He and Burton again pressed the National Park Service to seek transfer of the fort to its jurisdiction, and the army soon acquiesced. Maybank, now a U.S. senator, introduced a joint resolution calling for the establishment of Fort Sumter National Monument. After the uncontested passage of the legislation, Harry S. Truman signed it in April 1948. Maybank's celebratory press release promised that "the unbowed pride of the Confederacy, the grand old fort which never surrendered under the Confederate flag, stands ready to rise now to even greater heights in the eyes of men who will come across miles and miles of plains, mountains and oceans to visit her in her glorious new role as a national shrine."[45]

Maybank's charge to the National Park Service underscored that the senator and his constituents would closely monitor the commemoration. Johnson Hagood, a retired brigadier general of the American Expeditionary Force named for an uncle who held the same rank in the Confederate army, specified further that "the Federal government in its guide book, should not be permitted to use the description given in the *Encyclopedia Americana*, which is punk." That encyclopedia entry had been written many years earlier by a Union veteran active in the turn-of-the-century development of Civil War battlefield parks. The reference work indicated that South Carolina "inaugurated war against the United States" when the state seized the federal arsenal, customshouse, and post office after Anderson "skillfully transferred" his command from Fort Moultrie to Fort Sumter during the week that followed the adoption of the secession ordinance, "believing that he was about to be attacked." Turning to the Confederate defense of the fortress, the narrative noted that DuPont's ill-conceived April 1863 assault prompted Union authorities to reevaluate the necessity of a seaborne attack. The ensuing bombardment from Morris Island quickly rendered Fort Sumter "entirely useless." Without artillery, the fortress was "held merely as an infantry outpost." The garrison of 450 Confederates and surrounding shore batteries withstood a poorly organized assault by 400 sailors and marines in small boats shortly after the fall of Battery Wagner. As operations during the summer of 1863 had practically ended blockade-running in or out of Charleston, however, the Union was content with "desultory fire" to prevent rearmament of Sumter while northern arms advanced elsewhere. Federal patience culminated in the progress by Sherman that prompted Confederate evacuation in February 1865, after which Anderson restored the American flag "with imposing ceremonies."[46]

As Hagood recognized, this distillation conflicted with the Lost Cause view of Fort Sumter in several important respects. Even the fictional Union loyalist Pierre Chardon in *Peter Ashley* considered Anderson's secret shift to Fort Sumter and spiking of the guns at Fort Moultrie "a fatal blunder" that secessionists understandably deemed an act of war. Anderson's clever ruse foreshadowed the dishonest trickery by which Seward and Lincoln, "deliberately playing upon the credulity of the South and making ready for war," induced the Confederacy to fire on Fort Sumter.[47] The perfunctory encyclopedia treatment of DuPont's attack similarly ran counter to Sass's insistence that the battle was "one of the most important engagements" of the Civil War. According to the UDC tablet dedicated in 1931, Fort Sumter was a scene of "Continuous Siege and Constant Assaults" rather than a sideshow marked by "desultory" action after September 1863. The WPA guide to South Carolina drew on standard local sources to report that the Confederates' evacuation after "567 days of continuous military operations against them" ended "the longest siege in modern history." Characterization of Union operations as a "siege," a term withheld by the *Encyclopedia Americana*, defied protests that Fort Sumter and Charleston were not truly under siege because the city maintained rail connections. For champions of Confederate commemoration, such semantic pettiness missed the grandeur of the site. Hagood even maintained that the events of April 1861 "would not warrant Fort Sumter's being preserved as a national monument" because the Confederate bombardment was "mild and did no material damage to the fort." The Union bombardment of 1863–65, in contrast, "was one of the fiercest in history." The World War I commander concluded that the Confederates' heroic defense of Fort Sumter "stands along with Verdun and Gallipoli."[48]

The National Park Service stepped warily into this cross-fire. William W. Luckett arrived in late 1948 as superintendent of Fort Sumter National Monument, and Frank Barnes became the staff historian a few months later. Together with regional Park Service historian Roy Appleman, they prepared planning documents, leaflets, tour scripts, and texts for historical markers that outlined a narrative Barnes elaborated in the official handbook published in 1952. Barnes made clear from the first page that "both the 'first shot' of April 1861 and the long siege of 1863–1865 are commemorated today by Fort Sumter National Monument."[49] He devoted approximately equal space to both events, and in both sections he adopted perspectives favorable to the South, although in a evenhanded tone rather than a Lost Cause panegyric.

The guidebook manifested the Park Service's narrow approach to the invitation that Fort Sumter presented to explain the outbreak of the Civil War. Except for an account of the planning and building of the fort in response to the War of 1812, Barnes did not discuss any events prior to the Ordinance of Secession. He did not comment on the origins of secession, and he did not suggest that the long-term political movements leading to the Charleston proclamation may also have shaped the crisis that flared when Anderson shifted base. Barnes fixed a rigid focus in place as well as time. He made little use of Kenneth Stampp's *And the War Came* (1949), which charted a surge of northern public opinion that instilled some Unionist backbone in James Buchanan and sustained Lincoln in a firm call for protection of federal property and execution of federal law even though war was the foreseeable consequence. Barnes indicated instead that Lincoln approved a supply mission as "the nearest thing to preserving the *status quo*." He hinted that Buchanan and Seward misled the South during negotiations. Although he could not entirely avoid the topic of presidential decision making, Barnes focused mainly on Anderson. The handbook characterized Anderson as not only a southerner for whom "preservation of peace was of paramount importance" but also a soldier with "a duty to perform."[50]

The Park Service was readier to present broad conclusions about the Confederate defense. Barnes labeled the Union campaign a siege without any quibbles over military definitions. He acknowledged that activity sometimes slackened and that army commander Quincy Adams Gillmore considered seizure of the fort unnecessary after its practical demolition. But Barnes described in detail other officers' continued plans for an assault and confirmed the remarkable intensity of three prolonged periods of bombardment. The fortress was "stronger than ever militarily" upon Confederate evacuation. That evacuation was not a defeat, for "the fortunes of war had accomplished what 3,500 tons of metal, a fleet of ironclads, and thousands of men had failed to do." Although reluctant to explore what

Anderson's defense of Fort Sumter meant to the northern public during the secession winter, Barnes did not hesitate to declare that the Confederate defense of Fort Sumter "became a symbol of resistance and courage for the entire South."[51]

The guidebook showed that the National Park Service, like the Commission of Fine Arts in the 1920s, saw tourism to Fort Sumter as an excellent opportunity to promote devotion to the American flag. Barnes's coverage of the surrender negotiations in April 1861 highlighted Anderson's insistence on the privilege of saluting the Stars and Stripes. A full-page illustration documented the jubilant restoration of the flag in April 1865. Barnes's brief account of that ceremony again demonstrated his effort to foster national unity through deference to white southerners. He did not mention that the event was a festival of emancipation in which William Lloyd Garrison took a prominent part, joined by Denmark Vesey's son, black war heroes Robert Smalls and Martin Delany, and three thousand recently liberated African Americans joyfully jammed together on the small island. Barnes culled from abolitionist Henry Ward Beecher's oration a quotation that looked to "win parted friends from their alienation." He ended this climactic section of the handbook on a dramatic note: "That night, with tragic coincidence, an assassin's bullet felled Abraham Lincoln in Washington."[52] The conjunction of the two events underscored the link between the sacred aura of the flag and the bloodshed of war.

National Park Service officials worked closely with local tourism promoters to realize the legacy of the Civil War in harmonious and productive cooperation between the federal government and white South Carolinians. The superintendent located his headquarters in the chamber of commerce building in downtown Charleston. Luckett explained in an internal memorandum that "the Service should in time take a leading part in fostering historical conservation in old Charleston" and that isolated headquarters at Fort Moultrie on Sullivan's Island "would not be likely to impress Charlestonians favorably." Park Service officers welcomed expert assistance from the historical commission and offered expert assistance when the city made a reenactment of the Fort Sumter bombardment the showpiece of the Azalea Festival, the central promotional event of the tourism season. The staff sought to establish strong relations with local schools and assiduously cultivated the local press. Charlestonians in turn recognized that the National Park Service's promotional prowess would benefit tourism throughout the city. When Luckett arranged for the army to celebrate the transfer of the facility by making Fort Sumter the kickoff site for the National War Trophy Safety Campaign, a nationwide deactivation of old artillery shells, the event drew coverage in newspapers throughout the country as well as *Life* magazine.[53]

The common interests of the Park Service and Charleston boosters included a mutual eagerness to encourage family tourism. The continued growth of automobile ownership, the expansion of highway construction, and the increased availability of paid vacations facilitated a wave of middle-class travel intended to implement the domestic ideology of the baby boom era. Ford advertised one of its sedans in 1949 as "a living room on wheels." The National Park Service sought to fuse the nuclear family with the nation at Civil War battlefield parks and other historic sites that combined adventure, education, outdoor stimulation, and patriotic inspiration. This policy converged with the strategic goals of Charleston tourism promoters. The early development of that trade had been remarkable but also limited. With gardens as the dominant attraction, travel to Charleston remained highly seasonal and offered little of interest to children. The establishment of Fort Sumter National Monument promised to help Charleston move toward becoming a year-round destination that would appeal to families more likely to stay in a motel than a hotel. The site was only one part of a broader diversification program, but the combination of a harbor outing and a Civil War shrine offered a solid contribution to competitiveness in a rapidly growing market.[54]

The operational goal immediately chosen by the National Park Service, "that Fort Sumter be restored as a stabilized ruin of the 1860–1865 period," aimed to create a theater of Civil War memory for imaginative engagement with the past. The preservation project involved a great deal of demolition, for the army had largely rebuilt the fortress during the 1870s and made many modifications over the following seventy years. Some of those changes were irreversible. Gillmore, assigned to repair the installation that his artillery had destroyed, leveled the surviving walls to half of their original fifty-foot height to match demolished walls that he replaced. The two-story concrete Battery Huger, added shortly before the Spanish-American War, covered more than half of the original parade ground. But the Park Service tried to undo what it could. Workers razed fourteen buildings and other structures that did not date to the Civil War, including barracks, a lighthouse keeper's residence, and two radio towers, and they removed a variety of cisterns, casemates, and gun emplacements. Another challenge was the recovery of areas that the army had filled with earth, rubble, obsolete ordnance, and other debris, substantially raising the ground level of

Fort Sumter from the southwest, 1948. Courtesy of Fort Sumter National Monument, Charleston, S.C.

the fort to reinforce the artificial island. "This is the story of much of the ruin of the western half of the fort: buried after 1865," one of Barnes's successors observed in 1956. Partial excavations exposed a powder magazine, the remains of a circular stair tower, and fragmentary barracks. The digging also yielded artifacts for a temporary museum that the Park Service opened inside Battery Huger.[55]

The centerpiece of the makeshift gallery was the storm flag that Anderson had flown during the bombardment and the larger garrison flag he had saluted at his surrender and raised on his return. In 1905, Anderson's family presented the banners to the War Department, which displayed them in the secretary of war's reception room alongside the Appomattox surrender table and other Civil War treasures. The *New York Times* protested in 1911 that very few visitors to Washington could see the Fort Sumter colors, "the most famous relic next after the Constitution of the United States." The flags remained in a similar display after the War Department moved to the Pentagon during World War II, but in 1954 the Defense Department transferred them to the National Park Service. Placed on public display at Fort Sumter National Monument, the banners powerfully supported a primary theme of the shrine. The staff advertised the acquisition by temporarily removing the tattered flags from their protective case for a photograph that appeared in *National Geographic*, the most widely circulated travel magazine of the 1950s.[56]

Fort Sumter National Monument figured prominently in federal planning for observance of the Civil War centennial. The National Park Service assigned the site priority funding under Mission 66, the ten-year plan to improve facilities by the agency's fiftieth anniversary in 1966. This support enabled the staff to expand dramatically on previous picking and shoveling by bringing in heavy equipment in 1959 to remove nineteen thousand cubic yards of rubble and fill. The excavation uncovered original brickwork and part of the parade ground and found sixteen more cannons. The mounted navigation beacon, for decades the most useful feature of the fort unrelated to tourism, was moved to another point in the harbor. Mission 66 funding also provided for construction of a permanent museum in Battery Huger, to be dedicated at the hundredth anniversary. Admissions trends rewarded the federal investments. The number of visitors brought to Fort Sumter by concessionaire Gray Line Tours nearly quintupled from 10,773 in 1950 to 51,800 in 1960. Meanwhile, the U.S. Civil War Centennial Commission (cwcc) began working on a pyrotechnic reenactment of the April 1861 bombardment immediately after the federal agency launched operations by hiring public relations entrepreneur Karl Betts as executive director in the spring of 1958. Betts predicted that "the trek toward battle sites during the Centennial is expected to result in the greatest tourist movement in history."[57]

Fort Sumter also loomed large in South Carolinians' planning for the anniversary of the Civil War, or as the state legislation establishing a co-ordinating agency styled the conflict, the "American War between the Confederated States of America, South, and the Federal Union of the United States of America, North." The well-practiced Charleston tourism industry looked forward to welcoming a flood of visitors. A three-day extravaganza organized by the Citadel for the anniversary of the repulse of the *Star of the West* was one of the most prominent events in the national kickoff of the cwcc campaign in early January 1961. The countdown immediately began for commemoration of the firing on Fort Sumter in April. The cwcc had arranged to meet at that time in Charleston for its fourth annual assembly of state centennial commissions, Civil War roundtables, other commemorative groups, and individual buffs. Host to countless conventions, the city was especially well prepared for this gathering. "Even if it lost the war, the South is bound to emerge victorious from the centennial, in terms of tourist dollars, at least," predicted the *News and Courier*.[58]

Fort Sumter from the southwest, 1991. Historic American Buildings Survey.
Courtesy of the Library of Congress, Washington, D.C.

The selection of Charleston for the CWCC meeting added to a long record
of local success in leveraging federal resources to develop a strong position
in the national travel market. That relationship had not compromised but
strengthened the Lost Cause. The National Park Service account of the
long siege was fully consistent with the Confederate memorials throughout
the city. Sightseers found little interpretive tension between Fort Sumter
National Monument and the Confederate museum in the Market Hall,
opened by the Charleston chapter of the UDC at the same time that the
Wade Hampton Chapter established the Relic Room in Columbia. The
Civil War centennial promised to set a triumphant capstone atop the fortification of Confederate memory through mass tourism.

The CWCC assembly turned out to be the most disastrous Confederate defeat in South Carolina since 1865. In early February 1961 the New Jersey
Civil War Centennial Commission notified Betts that one of its members
preparing to travel to Charleston was an African American, former state
legislator Madaline A. Williams. After much delay, Betts responded that

the assembly headquarters, the Francis Marion Hotel, would not permit Williams to lodge as a guest or attend the conference banquets. He claimed the situation was "entirely outside our jurisdiction and we, therefore, cannot concern ourselves with it." The New Jersey delegation announced that it would not attend the assembly, and other state commissions soon joined the boycott. The standoff lasted for weeks. The city of Trenton, where the Swamp Angel had been on display since 1876, spurned an appeal from Charleston to trade the relic for another Civil War cannon. Forced to clarify in part his civil rights policy, recently inaugurated president John F. Kennedy directed Betts and CWCC chair Ulysses S. Grant III to see that guests would be treated equally at any accommodations arranged by the federal agency. When the CWCC continued to disavow authority, the White House moved the meeting to the desegregated Charleston Naval Base. The New Jersey commission accepted this compromise, hoping that it was a harbinger of direct federal action against Jim Crow. Extensive newspaper coverage of the protracted controversy mocked local promoters' earlier hopes for national attention. The incident exposed the instability of a Confederate memory that rested on tourism. In a country that celebrated interstate circulation as a form of citizenship, the constitutional right to travel was a potent weapon against white supremacism, as the Freedom Riders would begin to demonstrate a few weeks after the CWCC assembly. Moreover, the federal infrastructure for the Lost Cause was subject to interpretive shifts shaped by the racial politics of the country rather than the views of white South Carolinians alone.[59]

Local centennialists deepened the parallels between the Fort Sumter crises of 1861 and 1961. Led by chair John A. May, a state legislator from Aiken County, the South Carolina Confederate War Centennial Commission (SCCWCC) organized a secession from the national assembly. The Confederate States Centennial Conference (CSCC) met at the Francis Marion Hotel rather than join the conference at the naval base and scheduled independent luncheons and dinners, though Grant, Betts, and other CWCC officials attended the opening CSCC banquet. U.S. senator Strom Thurmond told the southern delegations that "Calhoun believed that local problems require local solutions because local people know best how to handle local problems" and that the United States should not repeat its failure to follow that advice in 1861. The *Columbia State* claimed that "in a sense the War Between the Sections of 1961 is worse than that of 1861–1865" because the conflict over segregation was unlikely to produce a unifying national memory. "More good blood was shed in the original war than any in modern times," argued the newspaper. "More bad blood has been shown in the commemoration than in almost any such supposedly mutual event."[60] The editorial endorsed the secession of the cscc, concluding that separate Union and Confederate centennial observances would be preferable to a national commemoration.

Former U.S. senator, secretary of state, and Supreme Court justice James Byrnes pointed out the danger to the Lost Cause that resulted from reliance on an intersectional agency to remember the war. The most widely influential South Carolina politician since Calhoun and an important New Deal supporter, Byrnes was keenly aware of the leverage that federal resources provided the state. But he told the cscc that "in my humble opinion it was a mistake" to establish the cwcc because the Civil War lent itself to interpretations too different to combine in a single institution. The rupture at the national assembly opened debate over the history of the sectional conflict as well as the future of Jim Crow. Byrnes stood behind the Confederate memory advanced by the novels of Heyward and Sass. "Slavery was on the way out," he maintained, "and had there been no war, ways and means would have been found to abolish it." Lincoln's attempt to resupply Fort Sumter was "equivalent to a declaration of war" and part of a deceptive policy by which the president "deliberately goaded the Confederate government into firing upon the Fort." Byrnes similarly stood behind his recent efforts as South Carolina governor to avoid the integration of public schools. Since redemption, he asserted, "the Negro has made greater progress in the South than any place on earth." *Brown v. Board of Education* (1954) was shortsighted because "certainly in this state their schools are as good and in many instances, are superior to the schools of white children."[61]

Such insistence on Confederate virtue had long faced challenges from a varied commemorative tradition advanced by African Americans and white allies who tried to address the racial meanings of the sectional conflict. John Bennett's *Doctor to the Dead* recorded several fantastic strands of this countermemory. The title legend recalled a brilliant white Charleston physician of the 1850s who stubbornly refused to accept the truth of death. After his necromancy culminated in a tragic love affair with a revenant, he adopted even stranger behavior symbolized by his long black cloak, "made from the castoff funeral draperies of John C. Calhoun's obsequies." Young boys hooted him in the street and threw pebbles at him. The stench from his unholy experiments at last drove the police and neighbors to storm his house to investigate, but as the crowd broke down his door, the weird genius appeared on the second-floor balcony, spread his long arms draped in his Calhounian cloak, and flew away forever "like a soaring buzzard."[62] Disparagement of the Confederate legacy also took more straightforward forms. Federal judge J. Waties Waring, the old-stock white Charlestonian who called for school integration in the Clarendon County litigation consolidated at the U.S. Supreme Court with *Brown v. Board of Education*, drew support for his iconoclasm from historical scholarship that praised abolitionists for attacking the most salient moral problem of their era. When Waring declared, in striking down the white primary in 1947, that "it is time for South Carolina to rejoin the Union," he derided claims that the Lost Cause was a beacon for the rest of the country. Robert Lowell's "For the Union Dead" (1960) called attention to the racial legacy of the Civil War struggle in Charleston Harbor by juxtaposing the faces of the black infantrymen depicted on Augustus Saint-Gaudens's great Shaw Memorial with the faces of the black schoolchildren shown in television coverage of the civil rights struggle.[63]

The Charleston confrontation in 1961 foreshadowed a reinforcement of this countermemory with the power of the U.S. government. South Carolina segregationists dismissed Howard Fast's emancipation novel, *Freedom Road* (1944), as "an end product of a typical New York ideology," but they could not treat so blithely the federal historical interpretations on which the Lost Cause had come to depend. Shortly after the Francis Marion Hotel fiasco, the cwcc voted to fire Betts and accepted Grant's resignation. Kennedy appointed as chair Allan Nevins, an eminent Civil War historian who had actively supported the president's election after years of association with Adlai Stevenson. Nevins and the cwcc immediately began to focus on preparations for a substantial celebration of the issuance of the Emancipation Proclamation. The sccwcc's May protested that the cwcc was "going to use the Emancipation Proclamation as a vehicle to promote so called Civil Rights." Although he warned that "we in the South will vigorously oppose any effort to turn the Commemoration of the Civil War into a political issue," the cwcc would be less deferential to the Lost Cause during the remainder of the centennial than the National Park Service had been at Fort Sumter.[64]

The upheaval within the cwcc demonstrated the extent to which the Lost Cause had diverged from professional scholarship on the Civil War since World War II. The leader of the effort to sack Betts and develop a centennial program more responsive to current racial politics was Bell I. Wiley, a white southern expert on the Confederacy who taught at Emory

University. Avery Craven, another white southern CWCC member whose distinguished scholarship on secession was sympathetic to the slaveholding South, observed that his fellow academic Daniel Hollis of the University of South Carolina was "the only sane person" to serve on the SCCWCC. Scholars continued to debate vigorously the origins and meanings of the Civil War, but the spectrum of viable argument no longer included the interpretations that Byrnes had rehashed at the Charleston national assembly. No scholar still imagined that southern slavery was beneficent, and no scholar believed that the institution would have ended soon in the Deep South without the northern antislavery movement. Very few scholars still thought that Lincoln had tricked a peaceable Confederacy into starting the war. Nevins applied one of the most freighted policy labels of the period when he wrote in 1959 that surrender to secessionists' demands for Fort Sumter would have been delusive "appeasement."[65] Strengthened through the Charleston Renaissance by professional networks of artists, preservationists, and journalists, the Lost Cause had lost the support of the professional network at the apex of American historical education.

No less significant was the way in which the takeoff crash of the Civil War centennial shook public respect for any reverential commemoration of the American past. The candid politicization of remembrance, ripping the mask from long-standing pretensions to the expression of community consensus, was one reason for deepening cynicism. The combination of unabashed profit seeking and commemorative piety also proved difficult to sustain. Thomas L. Connelly, an emerging author of Confederate military history, scoffed that "there is something magical about the figure 100, possibly the fact that it so closely resembles a one dollar mark." The CWCC and the SCCWCC tried to balance the promotion of a tourist spectacle with effusive appeals to religion. The CWCC opened its program with a national day of prayer after mailing out twenty-five thousand copies of a booklet "designed to organize the churches of America behind the five-year Civil War program." Memorial services for the Confederate dead of the Citadel on that Sunday fell between a costumed ball on Saturday night and a lavishly staged reenactment of the *Star of the West* incident on Monday. Influential journalist Murray Kempton typified discontent with current American commemorative practice when he wrote shortly before the pyrotechnic display at Fort Sumter that the centennial was "by far, the emptiest and most tedious event ever inflicted upon a free people." Kempton doubted that the anniversary would accurately depict either the Union or the Confederacy, but such skepticism was especially ominous for the embattled Lost Cause.[66]

The frustrations of Ashley Halsey Jr. at the cwcc national assembly encapsulated the alienation of Confederate memory from the national institutions in which it was comfortably ensconced until 1961. The Charleston native was an heir to the local antiquarian tradition—his uncle had succeeded to Daniel Ravenel's seat on the historical commission—and a Civil War buff. He was active in the North-South Skirmish Association, a group of men who dressed in Union or Confederate uniforms for marksmanship competitions. As associate editor for the *Saturday Evening Post*, he sponsored a centennial series of Civil War essays. His contributions were whimsical looks into miscellaneous nooks and crannies of the war. One piece examined the claims of various Confederates to have fired the first shot at Fort Sumter, puckishly awarding the honor to Halsey's grandfather for a shell that hit the fort five weeks before the April 12 bombardment. A Confederate officer apologized to Anderson for "the accidental shot," but Halsey vouched one hundred years later that "the shot was no accident. . . . Grandfather was not the patient type." The cwcc engaged Halsey to give the principal banquet address in his hometown, and Betts advertised the talk as "perhaps the outstanding event on the entire program." When the cscc seceded from the assembly, however, May arranged for Halsey to speak earlier in the day to the southern delegations. His diatribe about federal civil rights policy and "the amazing effrontery" of the New Jersey commission as well as the biracial ancestry he imputed to Abraham Lincoln sparked yet another nationally publicized crisis for the cwcc. Grant and Betts prevailed on him to control his temper at the evening banquet, and according to one sympathetic listener, "he pulled his punches on this occasion and made about as flat and uninteresting talk as I ever heard." The Lost Cause evidently had nothing left to offer but die-hard segregationism.[67]

The displacement of Confederate memory proceeded gradually after the Charleston assembly of the cwcc. The National Park Service made no immediate changes in its interpretation of Fort Sumter, where tourism increased markedly during the anniversary years. In 1970, the Park Service began to fly the first and second Confederate national flags over Fort Sumter for the first time since the war, alongside the South Carolina flag and the U.S. flags of 1861 and 1865, at the behest of a wealthy South Carolinian with influence in the Department of the Interior. Ashley Halsey continued his centennial *Saturday Evening Post* series for a while before collecting his contributions in a book. He went on to make his deepest mark after the assassination of John Kennedy prompted a surge of support for gun-control legislation. Halsey became a leading voice of resistance to regulation as the editor of *American Rifleman*, an organ of the National Rifle Association. Adapting the Lost Cause tradition of parallels between the American Revolution and the Civil War, he suggested that British attempts to seize the patriot arsenal at Concord foreshadowed the Fort Sumter crisis. Halsey concluded that "both wars, then, sprang in their full-blown form from efforts to disarm Americans who would not be disarmed." Explicit racism was beginning to give way to a right-wing libertarian strand in Confederate commemoration.[68]

Glory (1989), the most influential Civil War movie since the release of *Gone with the Wind* fifty years earlier, eventually sealed the civil rights revolution in remembrance of the struggle for Charleston Harbor. The cinematic account of the 54th Massachusetts made the regimental assault on Battery Wagner, an event rarely recalled in Historic Charleston guidebooks of the mid-twentieth century, one of the most famous episodes of the entire war. The National Park Service had not mentioned the 54th Massachusetts in the text of the cast aluminum marker installed at Fort Sumter in 1950 to point out the location of Morris Island; it noted instead that Confederates held Battery Wagner through a siege of fifty-eight days and that federal cannons on Morris Island shelled Fort Sumter from 1863 to 1865. But a new panel installed in 1995 reproduced in full color a nineteenth-century chromolithograph that depicted black standard-bearer William H. Carney holding the American flag aloft at the top of the parapet alongside the dying Shaw. The image celebrated the galvanizing impact of black gallantry on white northern recognition of black citizenship, an update to the political import of military heroism that the Lost Cause had once claimed for the Confederate garrison. A report on Fort Sumter for the Historic American Buildings Survey in 1991 rejected the original parity in National Park Service commemoration of the long siege and the outbreak of the war, remarking that the Confederate defense was not a story of national significance.[69]

The most extensive change in the commemorative infrastructure of Fort Sumter was the construction of a new mainland terminal for the harbor ferry, which offered an opportunity to add the interpretive visitor center that Mission 66 had established as a characteristic gateway to National Park Service sites. The agency situated the visitor center in a waterfront plaza adjacent to the South Carolina Aquarium, a continuation of Charleston efforts to develop tourism attractions of interest to children. The centerpiece of Liberty Square was a commemorative fountain honoring Septima

Clark, an African American schoolteacher and civil rights leader. The permanent exhibit of the Fort Sumter National Monument Visitor Education Center, completed in February 2002, similarly reflected the racial revolution. The project coincided with a broad campaign to refocus National Park Service interpretation of Civil War sites. Congressional legislation enacted in 2000 directed the secretary of the interior "to encourage Civil War battle sites to recognize and include in all of their public displays . . . the unique role that the institution of slavery played in causing the Civil War." The Park Service responded with a variety of publications and programs and revised many of its interpretive installations. The superintendent of Fort Sumter National Monument described the Liberty Square visitor center as "the point of the sword" for the nationwide initiative.[70]

The exhibit obliterated the interpretive wall the National Park Service had once built around the origins of the war. Rather than beginning the Fort Sumter story with South Carolina secession accomplished, the set of illustrated text panels started with the rise of slavery in the colonial low country. The interpretation described white settlers' eagerness to translate the Caribbean plantation system to mainland North America and emphasized the wealth that rice planters extracted from the labor and agricultural expertise of African slaves. From the federal constitutional convention through secession, the narrative centered on slaveholders' economic self-interest as a driving force in national politics, with South Carolinians at the forefront of southern belligerence. In contrast with the indulgent slaveholder paternalism that the Lost Cause remembered, the National Park Service emphasized the brutality of slavery and the strict policing of everyday life impelled by whites' fear of black rebellion. The exhibit recognized resistance to oppression as the central motif of the dynamic culture that African Americans created in slavery. Frederick Douglass's testimony that "the songs of the slave represent the sorrows of his heart" repudiated the white nostalgia of the Society for the Preservation of Negro Spirituals, which had lasted long enough to perform during the *Star of the West* centennial festivities. Neither in politics nor in society did the National Park Service identify secession as the product of any distinctive values worthy of honored remembrance.[71]

Presented to more than three hundred thousand tourists during the year after the opening of the visitor center, the Park Service's interpretation was thoroughly conventional by the turn of the millennium.[72] A half century of scholarship had helped to make similar ideas familiar in many forms, including schoolbooks from the elementary level onward. The intellectual siege of the Lost Cause was more comprehensive than the Union encircle-ment of Fort Sumter during the war. Confederate memory was now thor-oughly on the defensive, even in South Carolina. The most significant attack would take aim at a commemorative legacy of the tempestuous Civil War centennial, the Confederate battle flag raised above the statehouse dome.

6 The Desertion of Tradition

THE SURGE OF PROTEST against state displays of the Confederate battle flag at the turn of the millennium posed a fundamental challenge to American habits of remembrance. In the years after New York City patriots pulled down an equestrian statue of George III to celebrate the declaration of independence, public attention rarely focused on deliberate retraction of earlier acts of commemoration. Many milestones and heroes slipped into oblivion, but the process less often involved repudiation than the corrosive force of time and the substitution of other memories. More typical than the fate of the George III statue was the career of the monument that the South Carolina legislature erected in 1766 to William Pitt in gratitude for his role in the repeal of the Stamp Act. Although dedicated to the understanding that the colonists were, in Pitt's phrase quoted in the inscription, "true sons of England" whose differences with Parliament might be resolved amicably, the tribute remained at Charleston's central intersection until 1794. Removed because complaints about the obstruction of traffic added weight to a flutter of enthusiasm for the French Revolution, the statue soon assumed a new place of honor in front of the Orphan House, an inadvertently apt site for the abandoned public memory that American independence might have been unnecessary.[1] Attacks on the Confederate battle flag struck at a commemorative shadow that had not faded as gently. These emotionally charged campaigns suggested that some memorial gestures warrant more explicit rejection than the accretion of community indifference that is the lot of so much American commemoration.

Conflict over the Confederate banner heated up across the South during the late 1980s and reached apparent resolution by the early twenty-first century. Mississippi voters in a 2001 referendum defeated a proposal to remove the Southern Cross from the state flag. In contrast, Georgia adopted new designs for its state flag in 2001 and 2003. Alabama removed a Confederate banner from the statehouse dome in 1993 and installed a different military standard in a display with the three Confederate national flags at the Confederate monument on the capitol grounds. South Carolina similarly lowered the unbordered, rectangular Confederate naval jack from the Columbia dome in July 2000 and raised a white-bordered, square version of the Southern Cross, used by many units in Lee's army, in front of the capitol at the state monument to the Confederate dead.

The most vigorous and revealing of these struggles, the controversy over the Confederate flag in South Carolina presented a remarkable grassroots debate over collective memory. In the decade leading up to the removal of the flag from the dome, the *Columbia State* daily newspaper published well over eleven hundred letters to the editor and guest editorials on the issue in addition to hundreds of columns by staff or syndicated writers and news stories about public opinion. Citizens' engagement escalated through three successive peaks. The first period of intensive concentration began with legislative consideration of a proposed Heritage Act in the spring of 1994 and lasted through the Republican primary election in August, in which a record turnout of voters urged the party to keep the flag atop the capitol. Republican governor David Beasley opened a second major phase of debate in November 1996 by calling for passage of the Heritage Act in the first gubernatorial address to be televised statewide in thirteen years. The ensuing flurry of discussion subsided in the first few months of 1997 after the House of Representatives blocked Beasley's proposal. The state branch of the National Association for the Advancement of Colored People (NAACP) launched the third and most absorbing round in July 1999 by securing approval at the group's national convention for a boycott of travel and tourism in South Carolina. In the next twelve months, the *State* published well over four hundred guest editorials and letters to the editor about the flag in addition to scores of regular columns and news stories. The newspaper rarely appeared for two consecutive days without an opinion piece on the issue until Citadel cadets changed the Confederate flags at the statehouse on July 1, 2000, pursuant to legislation modeled closely on the Heritage Act proposed six years earlier. Public debate subsequently continued more sporadically under the prodding of ongoing NAACP sanctions.

The depth of passion in South Carolina surprised no one. "Let's face it," sighed one legislator. "We're still fighting the Civil War."[2] Countless commentators noted the persistence—or obstinacy—of the first state to secede from the Union and the last to take down the rebel flag. Champions of the flag fervently insisted that they were preserving a long-standing Confederate "heritage," and their adversaries complained that nostalgic reverie paralyzed the state. "Wake up, Rip Van Winkle. We lost," jabbed one letter to the *State*. Academic analysis has similarly tended to assume that debates over the Confederate flag pitted "traditionalists" against modernizing critics. A book-length study of the controversy in South Carolina reports that the groups that rallied around the flag were "direct descendants" of the Lost Cause movement that pervaded southern culture for almost a century after Appomattox, now working through different organizations and responding to the fresh challenge of a multicultural society but emotionally and intellectually faithful to an inherited bond with the Confederate past. The leading scholar of the Confederate flag similarly concludes that its defenders' political muscle shows that "the traditional South is not disappearing any time soon."[3]

The image of old wine in new bottles fairly describes the reversal of South Carolina political parties' racial profiles and electoral fortunes. The controversy made Confederate honor the political property of the Republican Party, the organization that the Lost Cause had in no small part cohered to defeat during Reconstruction and its aftermath. Legislative machinations over the flag fit within a broader story of the consolidation of Republican dominance in a former Democratic stronghold of the white South. Factional alignments and personal rivalries within the party strongly influenced the flow of events, as did more structural considerations like the use of race in the drawing of legislative districts. The Republican invitation to voters in the August 1994 primary to express an opinion on the flag was a particularly straightforward use of the issue for party-building purposes.[4]

Beyond the most obvious racial politics of the flag, however, the claim for continuity from the Lost Cause era to the millennial defense of the Southern Cross fails to recognize important shifts in the foundations and uses of Confederate memory. The raising of the flag above the South Carolina statehouse in March 1962 reflected its recent emergence in a popular culture of recreation and consumption starkly different from and in some ways antithetical to the memorial culture of the Lost Cause. When state display of the flag came under attack, its defenders could not rely on the gender, religious, and class structures that had sustained earlier Confederate commemoration. To the contrary, those patterns of white southern social organization more often characterized the mobilization against the flag, which was in large part an exercise in collective remembrance of the civil rights movement of the 1950s and 1960s. The defense of the battle flag on the basis of common soldiers' individual integrity similarly paralleled the Lost Cause glorification of Confederate heroism less than it drew on American tributes to Vietnam veterans. Shaped by mass consumerism and the legacies of the civil rights movement and the Vietnam War, the rally around the flag differed diametrically from the communal versions of modernity that had dominated the Confederate image from secession through the Southern Renascence. The most vital form of Confederate commemoration now projected the disintegration of traditional social institutions into an atomism best exemplified by the consumer marketplace.

By the end of the twentieth century, the Confederate battle flag stood apart from the dense memorial framework joined to it at the beginning of the century. Flag defenders sometimes claimed that the attack on the flag was the first step in an assault on all public remembrance of the Confederacy. Letters to the *State* warned that flag opponents "won't stop their crusade until every school and street named for a Southern hero has been renamed, every Confederate monument demolished, every Confederate grave desecrated, and flying the flag declared a hate crime." No such expansion of targets even began to take place. One leading critic of the flag laughed that "you'd have to tear down half the state." An isolated local call for removal of the Confederate monument in Walterboro in 1997 attracted little attention or support.[5] The monuments and place-names across South Carolina had long ago lost the potency that might merit serious protest. Champions of Confederate memory struck a more resonant chord when they worried that the flag was not their first but last line of defense. One supporter called it "the only visible thing we have to show for the sacrifices our ancestors made," although the capitol grounds alone offered monuments to Confederate soldiers, Confederate women, and Wade Hampton; a magno-

Confederate Memorial Day at Elmwood Cemetery, 1955. Courtesy of the South Carolina
Confederate Relic Room and Military Museum, Columbia.

lia tree planted as a memorial to Robert E. Lee; carefully preserved and
highlighted evidence of William T. Sherman's attack on Columbia; and a
marker pointing out the position of the statehouse on the Lee Highway.[6]

Charleston attorney Samuel W. Howell IV situated the unique vitality of
the flag in the most poignant comparative context. Howell wrote in March
1997 that he would gladly agree to removal of the flag from the statehouse
if South Carolina revived Confederate Memorial Day with the energy and
earnestness the occasion had once inspired. Government offices and businesses would close; citizens would decorate monuments and graves; soldiers would parade; public leaders would deliver orations. But that world of
Confederate remembrance had long ago disappeared. Even in Charleston,
where several thousand citizens had gathered annually at Magnolia Cemetery for decades after the war to join in Memorial Day exercises, attendance had dwindled by the early 1950s to about one hundred participants,
"mostly elderly ladies wearing the Stars and Bars of the Confederacy like
a shibboleth."[7] Unable to restore his ideal of community, Howell chose to
take his stand behind the battle flag like another thwarted Charlestonian,
the hero of DuBose Heyward's novel *Peter Ashley*.

The impulses that placed the Southern Cross atop the South Carolina statehouse in March 1962 differed dramatically from the traditions
followed to the end by the aging women in Magnolia Cemetery. As John
Coski has chronicled, the divergence of the battle flag from other forms
of Confederate remembrance originated on southern college campuses. In
the 1920s, Coski reports, chapters of the Kappa Alpha Order—a student
fraternity founded in 1865 at the school where Robert E. Lee presided—
began to sponsor dances that "assumed the characteristics of modern 'retro'
fads." Confederate flags festooned halls in which students in gray uniforms
drank mint juleps with young women wearing vintage dresses. *Gone with
the Wind*, also a flapper appropriation of the Lost Cause, added to the
popularity of these Old South balls after publication of the novel in 1936
and release of the film in 1939, by which point intercollegiate athletics were
becoming a forum for more fervent and enduring display of the battle flag.
The ironic, mildly rebellious undercurrents to college students' use of the
banner as a party decoration recurred when the flag entered another realm
of white youth culture, the segregated U.S. armed forces. White southern
servicemen used Confederate flags in World War II for nostalgic identification with home and pranks that tweaked military authority. The trend
peaked a few years later in a national Confederate flag fad that mixed mis-
chievous incidents with lasting incorporation of the emblem into commercial and recreational settings. Tracks affiliated with the National Association of Stock Car Auto Racing quickly adopted the flag as a logo after the
establishment of NASCAR in 1949, recognizing that the emblem perfectly
fit the image of white southern moonshining speedsters that the racing
series sought to promote.[8]

This revitalization of the Confederate battle flag infused it with new
political potential. The second Ku Klux Klan, founded in 1915 by a young
man who closely followed popular culture, had devoted no particular attention to the Southern Cross. But the Klan revival that began in the late
1930s often used the flag to symbolize its fidelity to Confederate principles.
John D. Long, a thirty-seven-year-old lawyer serving his first term in the
South Carolina legislature, sponsored a March 1938 resolution that installed the battle flag alongside the state and federal flags in the House
of Representatives shortly after southern Democrats in Congress staged a
record-breaking filibuster to block federal antilynching legislation that the
NAACP had conspicuously supported by regularly flying outside its New
York City offices a black banner announcing, "A Man Was Lynched Yesterday." The prominence of the battle flag in the Dixiecrat presidential cam-

paign of 1948 marked its maturation as a symbol in mass politics. College students carried the banner into the nominating convention of the National States' Rights Democratic Party, and the Dixiecrats' extensive use of the battle flag during the campaign reinforced the youthful, peppy image projected by presidential nominee Strom Thurmond. Together with the broader flag fad of the early 1950s, the Dixiecrat example ensured that advocates of "massive resistance" to the racial integration ordered by the Supreme Court in *Brown v. Board of Education* would turn to the Confederate banner to express their defiance. Now a member of the South Carolina Senate, Long sponsored a successful April 1956 resolution to drape the battle flag alongside the federal and state flags in the chamber of the upper house on the last day of a legislative session that a newspaper reporter described as "dominated by one note—maintain at all costs segregation in the public schools of South Carolina."[9]

By the Civil War centennial, the Southern Cross was a common feature of white student life, mass consumerism, and segregationist politics. Some white southerners rued the transformation of the flag, much as many Americans expressed reservations about the new practice of "reenacting" Civil War battles in which men had died gruesome deaths. When a textile manufacturer reported booming sales of a beach towel that replicated the battle flag in February 1958, the South Carolina legislature adopted a resolution deploring the towel as "a veiled attack, parading in the garb of legitimate advertisement, on the valor, courage and sacrifice of the Men in Gray." The legislature made it a criminal offense to sell merchandise imprinted with a representation of a Confederate flag or to "publicly mutilate, deface, defile, defy, jeer at, trample upon, or cast contempt" on a Confederate flag. The statute did little to impede the distribution of souvenirs and other commercial ephemera during the Civil War centennial, which promoters welcomed as "one of the most mouth-watering marketing situations to come along in years." The federal Civil War Centennial Commission (CWCC) encouraged the robust exercise of free enterprise as essential to a popular and fiercely anticommunist festival, but even eighty-year-old CWCC chair Ulysses S. Grant III complained on his arrival in Charleston for the anniversary of the firing on Fort Sumter that "I don't think this advertising use of that banner that meant so much is proper. . . . I don't believe some of the advertising I've seen is carrying out the heritage your forefathers fought for."[10]

The United Daughters of the Confederacy (UDC) committed itself to turning back the waves of popular culture, only to marginalize the organization through its futile efforts. Although its influence in white southern society had peaked a generation earlier, the UDC remained by far the largest and most powerful Confederate commemorative organization when it denounced use of the battle flag by "college groups" as well as "political groups" shortly after the Dixiecrat campaign. The flag fad of the early 1950s quieted this insistence on restriction of the flag to ceremonial uses, as the popularity of the Confederate emblem delighted many UDC members. With the arrival of the Civil War centennial, however, the UDC firmly endorsed the principle that the sanctity of the banner precluded its use in many settings. The UDC's 1961 national convention adopted a flag code that prohibited incorporation of Confederate flags in "clothing of any kind," including athletic uniforms, or in any merchandise "designed for temporary use and discard."[11] The guidelines were hopelessly ineffectual in preventing the Southern Cross from appearing on bathing suits and women's underwear during the Civil War centennial. The battle flag had become defined by a proliferation far beyond the boundaries that the UDC deemed consistent with respect for the emblem.

John A. May, the legislator responsible for installing the battle flag above the South Carolina statehouse, personified the newer approach to Confederate remembrance. Flamboyantly styling himself as "Mr. Confederate," May sometimes wore a Confederate uniform in the capitol, where he represented Aiken County off and on from 1935 through 1966. On other occasions, he dressed as "a walking Rebel exhibit," in the words of an acquaintance of the early 1960s, replete with battle flags on his necktie, tie clasp, and cuff links.[12] In addition to collecting Confederate knickknacks and memorabilia, May played an active role in invigorating the Sons of Confederate Veterans (SCV), the younger and historically feebler sibling of the UDC. A moribund organization on the eve of the Supreme Court decision in *Brown v. Board of Education*, the SCV had begun to develop into a substantial enterprise for the first time under the guidance of Mississippi archsegregationist William D. McCain, the adjutant in chief of the organization from 1953 to 1993.[13] During the Civil War centennial, May suspended his law practice to immerse himself in his work as national commander in chief of the SCV and chair of the South Carolina Confederate War Centennial Commission. For the ceremonies opening the centennial observance in Charleston in April 1961, he wore a top hat, a gray suit, and a brightly colored vest emblazoned with the Southern Cross.[14]

May would have attracted attention at the Charleston ceremonies regardless of his costume, for his position on the South Carolina commis-

Strom Thurmond wearing Southern Cross at Confederate States Centennial Conference, April 11, 1961. Courtesy of South Carolina Political Collections, Ernest F. Hollings Special Collections Library, University of South Carolina, and Evening Post Publishing.

sion placed him at the center of the storm that erupted when the segregated Francis Marion Hotel refused to host a black member of the New Jersey delegation to the national assembly of the CWCC. May vehemently defended Jim Crow policy in the confrontation. Shortly after the Kennedy administration resolved the impasse by moving the federally sponsored meeting to the Charleston naval base, May arranged with a state administrator to add the Confederate banner to a flagpole atop the statehouse portico in recognition of the festivities that would begin in the next few days. May also supplied a battle flag to several fellow legislators and socially prominent Charlestonians who sneaked into Fort Sumter in the dark of night and raised the standard in time for the exact anniversary of the first Confederate shots at 4:30 on the morning of April 12.[15]

May took a leadership position in the Confederate States Centennial Conference (CSCC) that met in downtown Charleston while the CWCC's depleted national assembly convened at the naval base. The coalition of southern states remained an important vehicle for negotiation with the federal commission when Kennedy replaced the Eisenhower appointees who had directed the CWCC during the Charleston fiasco and the new leadership began planning to focus on commemoration of the Emancipation Proclamation. At a meeting of the CWCC and state commissions in Washington in early February 1962, May presented a CSCC resolution protesting any initiative "that could, or would, be considered by any section of our nation as propaganda for any cause that would tend to reopen the wounds of the war." Upon returning to South Carolina, he promptly introduced a legislative resolution on February 14 calling for addition of the Confederate battle flag to the pole on top of the statehouse that had been refit for the display of the U.S. and South Carolina flags five weeks earlier. The House of Representatives immediately approved, punctuating its endorsement with a resolution that praised May's work as chair of the state commission and the regional CSCC. Both measures soon sailed through the Senate, and the battle flag was installed above the dome before the end of March 1962.[16]

Mays's initiative was more akin to the placement of a bumper sticker on the statehouse than to an extension of the prevailing American flag culture. Popular treatment of the U.S. flag in the early 1960s revolved around a rigid set of ceremonial and ritual practices, including recitation of the Pledge of Allegiance, singing of the "Star-Spangled Banner," and protocols for handling and display of the national banner set forth in the flag code formulated in 1923 and endorsed by Congress in 1942. Schools and military units taught that reverence for the American flag was essential to good citizenship. Ironic appropriations of the Stars and Stripes comparable to the uses that had recently popularized the Southern Cross were rare, which was part of the satirical appeal of the Confederate flag in settings like the armed forces. In 1958, the Museum of Modern Art even declined to acquire Jasper Johns's coolly detached pop art masterpiece *Flag* (1954–55) because the trustees feared that the work "would offend patriotic sensibilities." American veneration of the flag was the very heart of what Robert Bellah famously identified in 1967 as a "civil religion" also centered by the Gettysburg Address, Memorial Day, and Arlington National Cemetery on sacralization of the vast bloodshed of the Civil War.[17]

White southern passion for Confederate military banners had played an important part in making the distinctive American flag culture during the Civil War, but placement of the Southern Cross atop the capitol dome in 1962 did not reproduce nineteenth-century sentiments. Kitsch imprinted with the battle flag continued to abound. State senator Earle E. Morris Jr. attracted brief notice in 1965 by decrying the "commercialization and abuse" of the flag, and sympathetic newspaper reports indicated that "protests have been arising spasmodically throughout the South recently as the

flag becomes a decoration for a score of trinkets and articles of clothing."
The legislature did not approve Morris's proposal for a commission to study
the problem, however, and the initiative mostly illustrated the extent to
which South Carolinians had forgotten that the state had extended the pro-
tections of the U.S. flag code to Confederate flags in 1958.[18] Law enforcement officials evidently made only one effort to enforce those restrictions,
predictably in response to the burning of a Confederate flag by a University
of South Carolina student in a protest held on Lincoln's birthday in 1969
in support of a request by African American students that the school administration ban the display of the flag and the singing of "Dixie" on campus. Even on that occasion, however, authorities declined to prosecute the
student on the basis of the patently unconstitutional statute and furnish a
forum for further challenge to the Confederate aegis.[19] Without the benefit
of the legal, ritual, and educational practices that had fostered American
respect for flags since the Civil War, the Confederate battle flag generated
supporters in the quarter century after the centennial partly through racial
politics but also through the presence of the emblem on T-shirts, baseball
caps, and shot glasses and in entertainments such as sporting events or
performances of the southern rock band Lynyrd Skynyrd. For example,
the popular television comedy *The Dukes of Hazzard* (1979–85), which revolved around a pair of happy-go-lucky good old boys, prominently featured a Dodge Charger nicknamed the "General Lee" and emblazoned on
the roof with the Southern Cross.

The consumer foundations of the Confederate battle flag in the late-
twentieth-century controversy were epitomized by the most prominent
South Carolina champion of the flag, state senator Glenn McConnell of
Charleston. An attorney by training, McConnell started a new career in the
late 1980s as proprietor of a shop called CSA Galleries. The store carried
a wide variety of Confederate-themed merchandise, much of which featured the Southern Cross. Most reminiscent of the Lost Cause were prints
of Civil War scenes that broadly imitated the pathos of the less expensive
prints widely circulated a century earlier, though brandishing Confederate battle flags much more frequently. The Southern Cross also appeared
on key chains, beer steins, ashtrays, and a dizzying assortment of other
wares. For the womenfolk, CSA Galleries offered dolls and memorabilia
based on *Gone with the Wind*. And converging with McConnell's avid participation in Civil War reenactment, the shop sold simulated Confederate
uniforms and reproduction accoutrements.[20] The reenactment pastime,
which dominated the meager attempts to develop a ceremonial culture

around display of the Southern Cross in response to the intensification of protests, underscored Confederate flag supporters' substitution of recreation for the quasi-religious authority of American flags. The consumerist mode of commemoration would shape debate no less than the racial theme of commemoration when flag defenders mobilized against demands for removal of the Southern Cross from the statehouse dome.

Like the practices that reinforced enthusiasm for the Confederate battle flag, the grounds of opposition to it shifted from the Lost Cause era to the late twentieth century. Hostility to Confederate commemoration rested for decades on disapproval of the proslavery rebellion against the United States. The observation that "you cannot separate slavery from the flag, bottom line" remained the single most common historical argument against state display of the Southern Cross in the debates at the end of the century. The NAACP boycott resolution of 1999 pointed to it as the first reason that South Carolina should not honor the flag. Many white South Carolinians agreed that "the cause for which our ancestors fought, although with great courage and valor, was evil." Professional historians engaged in the protest focused almost exclusively on the Confederate determination to preserve slavery.[21] But the millennial struggle against the flag also drew on newer sources of momentum, for it invoked remembrance of the civil rights movement as well as remembrance of the Civil War. Attention to the South Carolina that raised the battle flag in the 1960s instead of the 1860s brought the controversy into the realm of many citizens' personal recollections and provided opportunities to interlace individual and regional experience. This emphasis broadened the appeal of the campaign while clarifying that the challenge to Confederate commemoration did not extend beyond the flag.

The later approach contrasted with the earliest recorded protests against state display of the battle flag, which took place in the first legislative session in which African Americans returned to the General Assembly after seven decades of exclusion. Representative I. S. Leevy Johnson, one of three African Americans elected in 1970, and his fellow members of the Richland County delegation conducted public hearings in July 1972 on a proposal to remove the battle flag from the capitol. The president of the Columbia YWCA stressed that the flag "connotes the subjugation of minority groups, the idealization of slavery, and the unwillingness to be governed by the constitution of the United States." The president of the state branch of the

NAACP urged removal of the flag as a unifying measure in the current social tumult, noting that "the people who fought under that flag fought more militantly than any revolutionary force in the country today to divide this nation." The head of the South Carolina Council on Human Relations endorsed the initiative as consistent with Governor John West's announced intention to eliminate vestiges of discrimination in the state. Newspaper reports of the hearing do not indicate that the speakers dwelled on any use of the battle flag by more recent opponents of civil rights.[22]

In the major phase of the flag controversy, the frame of historical reference was more complex. Public memory of the Civil War had received fresh stimulus from the movie *Glory* (1989) and Ken Burns's television documentary series *The Civil War* (1990). But public memory of the civil rights movement had truly begun to crest. The campaign to establish a holiday honoring Martin Luther King Jr., which achieved success on the federal level in the mid-1980s and in every state except South Carolina by 2000, was the most conspicuous of countless initiatives. Other milestones included the television documentary *Eyes on the Prize* (1987); the movies *Mississippi Burning* (1988) and *Malcolm X* (1992); the dedication of Maya Lin's civil rights memorial in Montgomery, Alabama (1989); and the opening of the National Civil Rights Museum in Memphis, Tennessee (1991). Commemorations in South Carolina repeatedly revisited the *Briggs v. Elliott* school desegregation litigation initiated in Clarendon County and consolidated at the U.S. Supreme Court with *Brown v. Board of Education*, the integration of all-white state universities, and the Orangeburg Massacre of 1968.

Memory of the civil rights movement added two important arguments against the Confederate battle flag to the call for repudiation of the pro-slavery republic. South Carolinians did not need to know about May's role in the contentious Civil War centennial to infer that the installation of the flag atop the statehouse was "an act of defiance by politicians against an emerging civil rights movement." Many participants in the debate deemed legislators' motives in the 1960s more disturbing than secessionists' motives in the 1860s. "I would rather be ignorant of what the Confederate flag stands for [in Civil War history] than to be ignorant of why it was put up," maintained one reply to the argument that the Confederacy had formed to defend states' rights.[23] The situation in South Carolina was in this respect much like that in Georgia, which had incorporated the Southern Cross into the state flag during a legislative session devoted to planning resistance to *Brown v. Board of Education*, and in Alabama, where Governor George

Wallace had raised the battle flag above the capitol in April 1963 when U.S. attorney general Robert F. Kennedy visited Montgomery to discuss the integration of the University of Alabama. The only state that did not modify its display of the battle flag at the turn of the millennium, Mississippi, had added the Southern Cross to its state flag in 1894.[24]

Condemnation of the battle flag as an artifact of resistance to the civil rights movement also emphasized the use of the symbol by extralegal white supremacists. Mobilization against the flag gained region-wide momentum in 1987 from a dramatic reminder of the mass protests of the 1960s, a widely publicized confrontation in Forsyth County, Georgia, in which more than five thousand white reactionaries—some waving Confederate battle flags—harassed approximately twenty thousand marchers for calling attention to that community's exceptionally disturbing racial record. A few weeks later, James Clyburn of the South Carolina Human Affairs Commission, the state's principal antidiscrimination agency, renewed the demand for removal of the Confederate flag from the capitol dome. In March 1987, the NAACP's Southeast Regional Conference called on South Carolina, Alabama, Georgia, and Mississippi to discontinue official use of the Southern Cross. The protests stressed that the battle flag was an emblem of anti-integrationists. Clyburn indicated that African Americans would much rather see the Stars and Bars atop the statehouse than the Southern Cross. State senator Kay Patterson, who had led efforts to remove the battle flag from the legislative chambers of the capitol since his election to the House of Representatives in 1974, suggested the same substitution in an address to the SCV. For African Americans, Patterson reported, the battle flag symbolized "the Klan activity, the muggings, the hangings from trees, the shootings and killings." The readiness of black leaders to accept state display of the first national flag of the Confederacy marked a shift from the earlier emphasis on the shadow of slavery. At the peak of the debate, flag opponents circulated an image that depicted a hooded Klansman with the Southern Cross at the statehouse, again suggesting that violent resistance to civil rights had more polemical traction than the violent defense of slavery.[25]

Identification of the battle flag with extralegal white supremacism did not focus exclusively on the civil rights era. Some contributions to the debate associated the flag with the entire history of white terrorism since emancipation. That violence had not disappeared at the end of the twentieth century. Beasley's television address in November 1996 responded in part to the burning of thirteen black churches in South Carolina during the preceding five years and a recent incident in which three young African Americans had been shot by two Klansmen returning from a Confederate flag rally. But the center of gravity for the many references to the Klan was not in the distant past or in the present but in the bloody death struggle of the Jim Crow order. A newspaper reporter for the *Charleston Post and Courier* who traveled throughout the South to find shared themes in the various flag controversies concluded that "the battle flag was waved by the Ku Klux Klan during the 1950s and 1960s, back when the Klan was more prone to murder than marching. To the people who remember those horrible years, the argument that the flag has nothing to say about race is a hard sell."[26]

The depictions of the civil rights movement outlined by the flag protest were incomplete and in some ways unsatisfying. Identification of the Klan as the chief antagonist of racial progress highlighted the denial of basic human dignity to African Americans and the courage with which they transcended violence. But that emphasis isolated resistance in a set of extremists thoroughly disdained in the contemporary United States, situating the civil rights movement in a past embodied by archaic opponents of law. In contrast, attention to state legislators' motives for placing the battle flag on the statehouse focused on a legacy of legally sanctioned discrimination. But this narrative implied that the movement had ended with the achievement of legal equality. Neither link between the Confederate flag and the civil rights movement directed attention to the economics of racial injustice. The flashbacks to famous events of the 1960s affirmed public consensus about racial harmony without opening questions that remained deeply controversial.[27]

The two most elaborate rallies against the flag in South Carolina vividly presented the campaign as a commemoration of the civil rights movement. The anniversary of Martin Luther King Jr.'s birthday in January 2000 provided the occasion for the largest social protest in state history. A crowd estimated at forty-six thousand people gathered at the capitol to support removal of the flag from the dome as a continuation of King's legacy. The rally called national attention to South Carolina as both the only state to fly the Confederate flag from its capitol and the only state that had not made King's birthday a holiday. In April 2000, Charleston mayor Joseph Riley led a group of marchers from his city to Columbia to protest the flag less than one month after President Bill Clinton and luminaries of the civil rights movement had participated in a well-publicized thirty-fifth anniversary partial retracing of the 1965 march from Selma to Montgomery. Riley's trek from Marion Square to the statehouse covered more than one hundred miles and lasted four days. Newspaper coverage stressed that "King Day at the Dome" and the "Get in Step" march were extraordinary fusions of past and present in which veterans of the civil rights era remembered their experiences for younger listeners.[28]

Echoes of the civil rights movement also influenced defenders of the dome. Flag advocates denounced violent white supremacism and complained that the Klan had "hijacked" the Confederate emblem. Polemicists maintained that King surely would have supported the capitol display of the battle flag as an expression of cultural pluralism. "At what point in the Palmetto State do we realize we have a diverse heritage?," pleaded state senator John Courson, an architect of the Heritage Act. Flag critics needed to learn "toleration and an appreciation for differences," agreed Glenn McConnell, who piloted legislative authorization of the African American History Monument on the statehouse grounds and chaired the commission that supervised the project through its dedication ceremony in March 2001.[29]

The Heritage Act adopted in 2000 acknowledged the attacks on the flag based on remembrance of the civil rights movement while standing firm in commemoration of the Confederacy. The removal of the flag from the capitol dome to the soldier monument distinguished the new tribute from the gesture of the early 1960s and anchored the flag more securely in the Civil War era. The legislation also sought to dissociate the state display from the Klan by substituting the square-cut battle flag for the more readily available rectangular banner ordinarily used by Klan members. Like flag defenders' attempts to turn allegations of racial bigotry on their opponents, the Heritage Act revealed the commemorative priorities of the millennial South. A tribute to the Confederacy might withstand public scrutiny, but not if understood as an open affront to remembrance of the civil rights movement. Celebration of the civil rights movement was now a more powerful orthodoxy than celebration of the Confederacy, and the culture of remembrance mobilizing against the flag in many ways inherited the structural traditions of Confederate commemoration rather than the supposed heirs to the Lost Cause who rallied in defense of their logo.

The Lost Cause helped to define norms of gender, religion, and class in the white South for almost a century after Appomattox. Remembrance of the Confederacy intertwined with fundamental social institutions of family,

Flags over the South Carolina statehouse, April 12, 2000.
Courtesy of Flashnick Visuals.

church, and social hierarchy to shape the distribution of power. Hardly
a monolith, that tradition sustained considerable debate among competing advocates of Confederate memory whose creative differences yielded
a variety of significant voluntary organizations, community rituals, and
works of art and literature. The antiflag campaign at the end of the twentieth century reconstituted important parts of this cultural formation even
as it differed diametrically from the Lost Cause precedent on the fundamental subject of race relations. The defense of the flag, in contrast, resembled the Lost Cause almost solely in its racial politics. Rejecting the
communal bonds through which Confederate commemoration had once
thrived, flag champions envisioned an atomistic society in which individual
consumers determined the value of the common past much as buyers set
the price for any commodity.

No feature of the Lost Cause distinguished it more thoroughly in the
judgment of its adherents than the central role of women. White south-

ern women took the lead in forming organizations like ladies' memorial associations and the UDC, supervising the interment of fallen soldiers, establishing widespread observance of Memorial Day, sponsoring the construction of civic monuments, founding museums for the display of Confederate artifacts, and undertaking other initiatives. These ventures served many different purposes for participating women. Some ends were quite orthodox, such as reinforcement of the patriarchal family through salutes to male valor. Other ends were more daring, including women's use of Confederate commemoration to participate in public political debates before suffrage and challenge prevailing ideals of manhood and womanhood.

Women's role in the flag controversy differed sharply from the pattern established in the Lost Cause. Women played leading roles in the campaign against the flag, sometimes from positions dramatically removed from the earlier reliance on Confederate remembrance as an outlet for engagement in public life. Gilda Cobb-Hunter, minority leader of the state House of Representatives, and Paula Harper Bethea, board chair of the state chamber of commerce, demonstrated that black and white women now wielded authority formerly monopolized by men. Women responded to continued gender discrimination by attacking rather than promoting Confederate commemoration. One letter to the *State* described the flag as "a painful reminder of the injustices I have suffered as a woman as a result of the 'good ol' boy' system." Women acting more consistently with older gender roles also spoke out against the flag. Mary Simms Oliphant guarded the Lost Cause flame for decades in a series of updates to her grandfather William Gilmore Simms's history of South Carolina, but her granddaughter reported in 1994 that inheritance of Oliphant's custodial reverence for history had not included the family interpretation of the war. As history clearly showed that the Confederacy had fought for slavery, the battle flag belonged in a museum.[30]

The most notable revision of the Lost Cause model of voluntaristic domesticity involved Jamie Renda, a suburban Republican descended from a slaveholding family that included a Confederate captain. After watching a Disney television movie about the civil rights movement with her young daughters on the eve of Martin Luther King Jr.'s birthday in 1999, Renda decided to become active in the campaign against the flag. She formed United 2000, an organization designed to serve as a nonpartisan clearinghouse for different groups interested in removal of the flag from the statehouse dome. United 2000 took the lead role in organizing the King Day at the Dome rally in January 2000, a spectacular example of the extent to which the onetime constituency of the UDC now mobilized against the flag in remembrance of the civil rights movement.[31]

Conversely, women played little part in the defense of the flag. The UDC, which had dwarfed the SCV in membership and influence for three-quarters of a century, surrendered its long-standing role as the leading Confederate commemorative organization. By the turn of the millennium, the SCV claimed to have somewhat more than the UDC's approximately twenty-five thousand members, and the men's group was much more geographically concentrated and energetic. The UDC sometimes claimed that its charter precluded the group from intervening in political disputes, but the founding generation of women had joined in highly politicized controversies over commemorative initiatives. When invited to participate, UDC leaders tended to ignore the supposed ban and endorse compromise. UDC president general June Murray Wells, a Charlestonian, declared in January 2000 that she wished the statehouse displayed the Stars and Bars because it encompassed the women and children of the Confederacy, while the Southern Cross merely represented the men in the army. The tepid support of the leading women's commemorative organization typified the overall gender gap in the flag debate. A 1999 public opinion poll showed that women were much more likely than men to favor removal of the flag from the capitol dome. Although women comprised only one-quarter of the identifiable authors of unpaid contributions to the flag debate in the *State* from 1991 to July 2000, they wrote well over half of the letters and guest editorials that explicitly called for removal of the flag not only from the dome but also from the statehouse grounds.[32]

Defense of the flag spurned the institutional legacy of Lost Cause women. The central element of that legacy at stake in the flag controversy was the Confederate Relic Room in Columbia, founded by the local UDC chapter in the 1890s. Although contemporary American culture offered many examples of museums fusing the memorial and educational functions envisioned by the Relic Room, including the National Civil Rights Museum, flag champions loudly rejected the suggestion that the Relic Room could effectively substitute for display of the flag at the statehouse. "Encasement means entombment," chanted McConnell. "The flag will not be taken down and put in a museum and forgotten about. That is not going to happen, period," vowed Courson.[33] This stance underscored that the banner atop the capitol dome was a fungible, routinely replaced commodity rather than a historic artifact like the many Confederate banners already owned by the Relic Room.

Flag defenders' contempt for museums also reflected distrust of the broader educational enterprise in which white southern women had placed their faith in the early twentieth century. The UDC had counted on schools and museums as well as youth groups like the Children of the Confederacy to perpetuate reverence for the cause and had closely monitored the process. Flag defenders moaned that "if the school system would tell what really happened during the war instead of pumping this garbage about slavery into kids' heads, this issue wouldn't even be brought up."[34] But they did not try to restore the earlier mechanisms of remembrance. Sporadic calls for a Confederate History Month comparable to Black History Month generated little interest. This set of priorities was pragmatic. Flag defenders' interpretation of the Civil War commanded little support among educators at any level. One of the public officials who took a strong stand against the flag was the South Carolina superintendent of education, the only woman to hold a position elected on a statewide basis. Beyond an awareness of the academic consensus that closed the schoolhouse door to the Confederacy, flag defenders' claims to accurate historical understanding drew on an ideal of self-education divorced from the intergenerational institutions the UDC had supported. Letters to the editor in support of the flag, which often accused opponents of historical ignorance, indicated that the exemplary citizen did not learn historical truth in school but in the leisure time of the adult individual, through books and archives deliberately neglected by the dominant forces in society.[35]

Flag defenders' strategies abandoned Confederate veterans' patriarchal response to feminism. Veterans had tried to turn back the feminist tide by sponsoring monuments to Confederate women and by making the election of attractive young female sponsors a central part of Confederate reunions. Flag champions did not style themselves as husbands or fathers but only as sons who inherited Confederate identity without the power to propagate it further. Metaphorically located in the nuclear family throughout the Lost Cause era, Confederate commemoration was in the flag controversy rhetorically centered on the sterile homosocial realm of the army. Addresses often compared flag defenders to Confederate soldiers. McConnell urged supporters to "stand and fight at the dome." "This is our 'summer of '64,'" the state SCV commander told members at the peak of debate. The posture of combative masculinity proved crucial to the passage of the Heritage Act, which divided the coalition that called for removal of the flag from the dome. When the Black Legislative Caucus and the NAACP announced their opposition to the substitution of a Confederate flag display at the soldier monument directly in front of the statehouse, Republicans seized the opportunity to frame the measure as defiant resistance to the boycott through which the civil rights organization had brought pressure to bear on the legislature. "I'm simply not going to be bullied anymore," declared House Speaker David Wilkins as he exhorted party members to vote for the measure.[36] This pugnacity presented a less socially engaged model of manhood than the ideals that men and women had promoted in the Lost Cause era.

Religion was a second vital feature of the Lost Cause more typical of the millennial attack on the Southern Cross than its defense. The battle flag had been the foremost site for the sacralization of Confederate memory during the Civil War. In the years after Appomattox, white southerners developed a vast set of Confederate symbols, shrines, rituals, myths, and heroes. This cultural formation not only served fundamental moral and spiritual purposes associated with religion but intertwined with the strategies of particular religious institutions. Ministers ranked among the most influential promoters of the Lost Cause. Interpretation of Confederate experience played an important part in denominational development in the postwar South, including the perpetuation of regional divisions in white Protestant evangelical churches.

Religion was similarly central to white southerners' late-twentieth-century opposition to the flag. The call by the annual conference of the United Methodist Church for removal of the Southern Cross from the dome helped to mark the transition from intermittent public discussion of the issue to full-scale debate. Beasley's reopening of the question in November 1996 built on his broader effort to mobilize white evangelical Christian voters and expand the place of religion in public life. Beasley reported on his prayers, quoted the Bible, and urged his television audience to "show Judeo-Christian love that will bring the races closer together and teach our children that we can live together in mutual respect."[37] Though he failed to sway some key elements of his party, the governor correctly anticipated the response of organized religion. More than six hundred white and black ministers endorsed his appeal. Scores of letters supporting removal of the banner from the dome agreed that "the Bible instructs us on how to handle the flag issue." Beasley called the debate "the most spiritually uplifting experience in this state in my lifetime."[38]

The religious mobilization against the flag did not correspond exactly to the ecclesiastical underpinnings of the Lost Cause any more than women's role in the campaign reproduced presuffrage gender models. The sacralization of Confederate memory had centered on rituals and symbols. The sacralization of civil rights memory in the flag debate emphasized recognition of sin in social relations. Reconciliation of the races was now a key step in the reconciliation of humanity to God. But both religious uses of remembrance featured ministers in prominent roles that advanced denominational interests and built on a tradition of interaction between history and theology in the white southern imagination.

Despite that regional pattern, religion formed almost no part of the defense of the flag. Only sixteen ministers signed the clerical petition in support of the display on the dome. Even the few proflag ministers often concentrated on secular arguments.[39] A scattering of polemicists stood by the old-time argument that the Southern Cross was the Christian symbol of a Christian army that fought for a holy cause. State senator Arthur Ravenel tried the backhanded reasoning that "if God didn't want that flag up there, he'd of let lightning strike it," perhaps unaware that a lightning bolt had demolished the Confederate soldier monument in 1882. The overwhelming bulk of proflag commentary on the subject denounced "pseudo-religious posturing." "The church should concern itself more with saving souls instead of creating new areas of division and controversy within the state," asserted a typical letter.[40] Flag defenders presumably included many devout Christians, a significant percentage of whom doubtless favored a vigorous religious influence in public life. Attorney general Charlie Condon was merely the most prominent and politically opportunistic flag champion to compare the presumed antimajoritarian protest against the Confederate standard with the presumed antimajoritarian protests that had restricted group prayer in public schools.[41] But the Southern Cross could not reverse secularization when flag defenders regarded state display of the emblem as strictly a secular matter. If women's desertion of Confederate commemoration ripped out the heart of the Lost Cause, the rupture with the churches destroyed its soul.

The white southern class order had been the backbone of the Lost Cause. Confederate commemoration inscribed an ideal of deference in white southern culture comparable to the army's command structure. Robert E. Lee personified the conflation of social and military rank, a metaphor reinforced in South Carolina by admiration for Wade Hampton. Veterans' reunions and similar celebrations offered occasions for the prescribed hierarchy to relax into interclass harmony. The Lost Cause offered no cultural support, however, for antagonism toward white southern elites. Soldiers in arms may have grumbled about "a rich man's war and a poor man's fight," but the Lost Cause had little room for such dangerous sentiments.

The flag debate clearly associated class privilege with opposition to the display on the dome. The campaign against the flag drew on strong support from business interests and placed corporate executives in symbolic positions of leadership. Presidents and board chairs of the largest companies in the state were the plaintiffs in a lawsuit organized by the mayor of Columbia that sought to follow the strategy that had succeeded in Alabama by challenging the legislative authorization for the display at the statehouse.[42] Family history was another significant venue for social status in a debate about heritage. Flag critics were much more likely than their adversaries to base authority to speak for South Carolina on an ancestry that boasted not only a record of Confederate service but also claims to inheritance of high social status. Letters and guest editorials calling for relocation of the flag came from contributors who described themselves as the descendants of Huguenots, slaveholders, nineteenth-century political leaders, and Confederate generals, field officers, and surgeons. No defender of the dome relied on similar credentials.[43]

Class structure in the attack on the flag often took the form of pride in a tradition of white gentility. An eighth-generation state resident argued that "it is time to put an end to the notion that being a South Carolinian is equivalent to driving a pick-up truck with the Confederate flag and rifles on the rear windshield. Let us show the rest of the country what the majority of us really represent: gentility, grace, and dignity." "No gentleman would expose a symbol that caused such pain and anger in his neighbors," agreed a schoolteacher. Many letters pointed to manners rather than morality as a reason to take down the flag. One contributor underscored the distinction by calling on readers to remember childhood lessons to "at least pause and pretend to care about other people." Flag critics enlisted Lee, the Lost Cause paragon of white southern gentility, in support of their cause. "Can we not learn from genuine heroes like Lee . . . to put good manners ahead of this exclusive and peculiar pride?," asked one of many debate participants who maintained that Lee would have opposed a commemoration that upset community harmony. A guest editorial reported that "there is no doubt he would politely ask that his flag be lowered." Other arguments invoked Hampton's authority for the same position.[44]

Flag supporters occasionally protested the conscription of Lee and "socially demeaning" newspaper descriptions of participants in flag rallies, but they largely ceded superior class standing to their opponents. The turn-of-the-millennium flag defense differed from the self-image put forth in 1972 by a South Carolinian with "reasonable wealth" and "a nice home" who beseeched "the black minority, the marijuana minority, the poor, the jobless, the food stamp people, the general do-gooders, to please leave the darned flag alone."[45] Later flag champions continued to identify African Americans as their main nemesis but now went on to rail against hostile elites, including business elites, media elites, religious elites, academic elites, and political elites such as U.S. senator Strom Thurmond and seven other former governors who supported the call for removal of the flag from the dome. "This is a case of the people vs. the leaders," said McConnell. "I'm going to stick with the people." Some flag defenders delighted in flouting the genteel decorum that their opponents sought to establish. Arthur Ravenel, scion of a socially elite low-country family, referred to the NAACP in a public address as the "National Association of Retarded People" and not only refused to apologize to the civil rights organization but protested that "I made a rhetorical slip, and they want to lynch me for it." Like McConnell's warnings of "cultural genocide," Ravenel's brash appropriation of the lynching image figured flag supporters as a highly vulnerable group despite their claims to speak for a majority of voters.[46]

Flag defenders' vision of the Confederate army bore little resemblance to the band of gentleman privates admired by Mary Boykin Chesnut or the marble tablet that the UDC installed in the statehouse in 1897 to honor the four socially prominent young men killed at Gaines Mill while carrying the colors of Gregg's 1st South Carolina Regiment. The Confederate army consisted of "poor farmers defending their homes," reported Condon. McConnell told the same television audience that "96 percent of the people in South Carolina did not even own slaves," which almost doubled the actual percentage of white residents belonging to nonslaveholding families in 1860. No one who expressed enthusiasm in the *State* for display of the flag atop the dome acknowledged descent from a slaveholding family. To the contrary, many grandchildren and great-grandchildren of Confederate soldiers expressly denied any connection to the master class and denied that elites made up any significant portion of the army. Flag supporters shared little of the Lost Cause fascination with the Confederate high command. When relocation became inevitable, they immediately rejected the suggestion that the equestrian statue of Hampton would be a suitable place for the battle flag. That opposition turned primarily on the greater visibility of the soldier monument in front of the statehouse but also reflected the conviction that the Confederate saga centered on private soldiers from humble social backgrounds rather than powerful generals. Admirers of the rank and file bristled at the suggestion that slaveholders might have controlled supposedly independent yeomen. An SCV officer deemed it "absurd" to suppose that "thousands of working-class southerners" endangered themselves to preserve slavery.[47]

In January 1997 prominent flag partisan Clyde Wilson—then my colleague in the history department at the University of South Carolina— warned that removal of the Confederate banner from the statehouse dome would abandon the cultural distinctiveness necessary to produce literature, manners, "or anything else except consumption and triviality." The debate over the flag shows instead that the campaign to lower the Southern Cross relied on much the same traditions through which the Lost Cause had contributed to regional creativity in the late nineteenth and early twentieth centuries. The embrace of the civil rights movement transformed and re-energized these gender, religious, and class patterns in a configuration that Fred Hobson has described as "the white southern racial conversion narrative." Opposition to the Confederate battle flag expanded onto a public scale the defining regional story of self-perceived progress from bigotry to enlightenment pioneered by white southern autobiographers like Katharine Du Pre Lumpkin and James McBride Dabbs in the late 1940s and early 1950s. Attachment to the Southern Cross took its place among the racial sins for which ordinary white citizens atoned in conversions that turned more on remembrance of the civil rights movement than participation in it. Eugene Downs's letter to the *State* neatly encapsulated the narrative. "When I was a boy, I had a Confederate flag on my bedroom wall," Downs recalled. "I was very proud of it. And as much as it shames me now to admit it, I—reflecting the sentiments of others—was happy when Dr. Martin Luther King was assassinated. I have since learned that Dr. King was a great man. But I know the source of reverence for the Confederacy. It is racism."[48] The climactic expression of this genre was the King Day at the Dome promoted by a Confederate descendant whose account of her youth included the standard childhood racial sins confessed by Hobson's authors. The massive rally that Jamie Renda traced to the television movie *Selma, Lord, Selma* was a cultural production as remarkable as the dedication ceremony for the Confederate soldier monument held at the same location in 1879.

Wilson's fears notwithstanding, commitment to the battle flag was more closely associated with "consumption and triviality" than was opposition to the banner. Separated from all foundations of the Lost Cause except for self-conscious whiteness, contemporary Confederate commemoration was also isolated from a nonelite white southern creative tradition that from the era of Huck Finn through the era of Elvis Presley had drawn on racial heterodoxy as well as religious and gender patterns antithetical to the proflag campaign. Beyond the display at the statehouse, Confederate commemoration remained heavily dependent on the marketplace. The most noteworthy spillover of the proflag campaign was legislative authorization of the sale of state license plates emblazoned with the Southern Cross, an official identification of the citizen as consumer. In May 2000, the Republican legislature instituted a state holiday on Confederate Memorial Day in exchange for future recognition of King's birthday, but the public response was feeble. Only ten of the state's forty-six counties adopted the Confederate holiday during the next five years. Few schools or businesses observed the occasion. Attendance at ceremonies in Columbia and Charleston attracted small crowds comparable in number if not in demographic composition to the gatherings of elderly women who had foreseen the end of the Memorial Day ritual at Magnolia Cemetery in the early 1950s. The s c v, the core of participation in the attempted renewal of Memorial Day, continued to honor the Confederacy more vigorously through the purchase of car decals, logo clothing, and other merchandise.[49]

Removed from Lost Cause traditions, the Southern Cross fell from the capitol dome in the face of the shared memory that most deeply excited white and black South Carolinians at the end of the twentieth century, celebration of the successful civil rights movement of the 1950s and 1960s. The decision to continue display of the banner on the statehouse grounds did not simply express a residual popular respect for the Confederacy reinforced by Republican political calculations and enthusiastic consumerism. The shift of the battle flag to the Confederate soldier monument also drew support from the shared memory that Americans associated most darkly with social alienation: the specter of the Vietnam War.

The defense of the battle flag abandoned the moral premises of the Lost Cause as well as its social foundations. Jefferson Davis outlined the original values of Confederate commemoration in 1878 when he told a Memorial Day gathering in Macon, Georgia, that "heroism derives its lustre from the justice of the cause in which it is displayed." The former president warned his fellow admirers of Confederate soldiers not to "impugn their faith by offering the penitential plea that they believed they were right." Davis insisted that the South *was* right to secede and fight the Civil War. The dozens of Confederate monuments dedicated throughout South Carolina from the

1860s into the 1920s demonstrated the consistency with which the Lost Cause followed these precepts. The inscriptions on three county monuments echoed Davis by quoting the same verse of Father Abram Ryan's poetry: "The world shall yet decide, / In truth's clear, far-off light, / That the soldiers who wore the gray and died / With Lee, were in the right." Other monuments invoked concepts of "state sovereignty" or "constitutional liberty" to assert the justice of the Confederate cause. The monument of Clarendon County proclaimed that Confederate soldiers took up arms "to defend cherished principles of civil rights."[50]

Davis's emphasis on the political dimension of military service was much closer to the mainstream of American commemoration in the century after the Civil War than the oft-quoted Memorial Day suggestion of Oliver Wendell Holmes Jr. that "the faith is true and adorable which leads a soldier to throw away his life in obedience to a blindly accepted duty, in a cause which he little understands, in a plan of campaign of which he has no notion, under tactics of which he does not see the use." Called on to honor soldiers who had fought and died in the moral quagmire of the First World War, for example, Americans tended to depict doughboys as crusaders striving to save the world for democracy or to end all wars, in contrast with the European allies' stark remembrance of suffering and death. The Lost Cause similarly clung firmly to the ideological predicate for martial heroism. The Confederate monument in a federal forum like Arlington National Cemetery might assert only that rebel soldiers fought "in simple obedience to duty as they understood it." Outside of such problematic settings, however, white southerners usually remembered Davis's admonition. In a 1957 address to the South Carolina Senate, John Long observed that "no cause is lost whose principle is right." The Senate unanimously adopted a resolution proposed by Long declaring that "this Flag symbolizes the divine cause of human freedom for which our forefathers fought" and that "the Battle Flag of the Confederacy inspires our dedication to the resurrection of truth with glorious and eternal vindication."[51]

Davis's approach to Confederate commemoration aligned squarely with the dominant military landmark in twentieth-century American public memory, the Second World War. The example of Nazi Germany provided an undisputed illustration that soldierly commitment and competence could not bring honor to the adherents of an evil cause. That precedent featured prominently in the millennial debate over the battle flag. Many letters to the *State* argued that South Carolina should furl the standard of the proslavery republic as Germans had repudiated the banner of Aryan supremacy.

Although quick to contest the identification of the Confederacy with slavery and dismiss the Nazi analogy, flag defenders did not demonstrate the same ideological zeal that pervaded Long's speech or the inscriptions on Lost Cause monuments. To be sure, polemicists repeated and sometimes updated the well-worn claims that the Confederacy represented a historical alternative to the expansion of the federal government. The Southern Cross thus became the banner of tax relief. The Lincoln administration sought to "enslave all men under an all-powerful central government," wrote one flag defender, as "anyone earning a paycheck is reminded when he sees the federal withholding taxes." But proflag politicians seldom focused on such claims even when they heartily shared a post-Reagan disdain for government and especially the federal government. Aware of the commitment to slavery expressed in such documents as the South Carolina Ordinance of Secession and the Confederate Constitution, the chief defenders of the flag defined the Confederate cause not in terms of southern policy but in terms of the supposedly autonomous motives and experiences of individual soldiers. McConnell rejected substitution of a Confederate national flag for the Southern Cross because "the soldiers' flag is the battle flag, not the governmental flag." The meaning of the Southern Cross had been defined "at Gettysburg, at Chancellorsville, at Secessionville, at Fort Sumter and in the *Hunley*," not at the South Carolina secession convention in Columbia and Charleston, the drafting of the Confederate Constitution in Montgomery, or the meetings of the Confederate government in Richmond.[52]

The attempt to distinguish soldiers from the government that enlisted them drew directly on the Vietnam War commemoration that escalated shortly before the Confederate flag controversies. Movies, television programs, and books about Vietnam proliferated rapidly in the fifteen years after the fall of Saigon. Communities across the country built monuments to Vietnam veterans. The Vietnam Veterans Memorial, unveiled on the National Mall in 1982, was the most widely seen and passionately discussed noncinematic work of art unveiled in the United States during the final two decades of the twentieth century. In this negotiation of collective memory, the faction that sought to depict American intervention in Vietnam as "a noble crusade" made little headway. Public remembrance instead focused overwhelmingly on the ordeal of the individual soldier, epitomized by the iconic list of names on the wall in Washington. Taking its cue from the emergence of posttraumatic stress disorder as a medical diagnosis for the continued suffering of Vietnam veterans, commemoration centered on a quest for "healing" of the nation as well as the individual survivors.

The public wound in need of healing was, in most accounts, an estrange-
ment between civilian society and Vietnam veterans angered by the extent to which elites had avoided combat service, the protests that American
military intervention in Southeast Asia was immoral, the suspicions that
substantial numbers of soldiers had participated in atrocities like the My
Lai massacre, the eventual abandonment of the effort for which so many
Americans had suffered and died, the failure to provide veterans with adequate medical treatment or social services, and the reports that soldiers returning from Vietnam often met with derision rather than gratitude from
civilians. Commemoration acknowledged the integrity and sacrifices of
American soldiers but mostly declined to justify the presidential and congressional decisions to go to war.[53]

Vietnam remembrance provided a template for defense of the Confederate battle flag at the turn of the millennium. "I think you ought to be able
to honor people who thought they were doing their duty without honoring the cause they fought for," observed southern intellectual John Shelton
Reed. "That's the compromise we've reached on Vietnam. There are people
who think that was an evil, imperialistic war, but I don't see them protesting the Vietnam Memorial."[54] Similar expressions of sentiment in South
Carolina far outnumbered arguments that Confederate soldiers had nobly
represented decentralized government or any other ideal of community.
"I'm proud of the men who fought for their beliefs with blood, sweat and
tears," declared a letter to the *State* that typically saw no need to discuss
the content of those beliefs. Some participants in the debate specifically
indicated that display of the flag, if not necessarily on the capitol dome,
reflected a "justifiable pride" in soldiers' commitment even though the collective cause that brought them to the battlefield was morally wrong. Suggestions that commemoration should express a public evaluation of that
cause prompted warnings to "remember how the Vietnam veterans were
treated." After the United States invaded Iraq in March 2003, supporters of
the Southern Cross again pointed to state display of the Confederate banner as a promise that the American public would not decline to honor soldiers who fought in a controversial war.[55]

Defense of the battle flag also resembled the Vietnam model of remembrance more closely than Lost Cause precedent in other important ways.
Flag advocates' self-identification with a Confederate army comprised almost entirely of nonslaveholders built on the class tensions surrounding
the Vietnam War and its most transformative institutional legacy, the all-
volunteer military. Supporters of the Confederate flag "are the ones who

have fought in every war this country has engaged in for the last 40 years," seethed a 2003 letter to the *Charleston Post and Courier*. "There is a very harmful battle being waged right inside the borders of this country. It is the open hostility that is being promoted against the average blue-collar working guy and it needs to be addressed, and stopped." The image of a working-class homage to a working-class army differed sharply from the Lost Cause claims of universal white southern mobilization in support of the war. Commemoration in the post–Vietnam War era also ended the Lost Cause boasts of Confederate martial prowess, which Long had illustrated in 1957 when he called the battle flag "the symbol of the only nation known to history whose soldiers wore themselves out whipping and chasing the armies of the enemy and thus lost a war by utter exhaustion and collapse." Later admirers of the battle flag occasionally alluded to the accomplishments of the Confederate army, but like Vietnam War memorials, flag advocates tended much more frequently to base tributes on soldiers' courage through suffering and death. Assertions of battlefield superiority had lost standing in American culture, and defeat no longer needed to be explained away. When relocation of the flag became inevitable and legislative discussion turned to alternatives to the dome display, McConnell's proposal directly appropriated the rhetoric of the Vietnam Veterans Memorial by calling for a "healing pool" lined with statues of Civil War soldiers reminiscent of the figures by Frederick Hart installed near Maya Lin's therapeutic wall in Washington, D.C.[56]

The shift of the Southern Cross to the state monument to the Confederate dead linked the banner to the manifestation of the Lost Cause tradition most frequently cited by flag defenders, William Henry Trescot's inscription on the 1879 memorial. The connection was in some ways appropriate. Writing in the shadow of Reconstruction, Trescot had worried that a forthright statement of continued white southern commitment to Confederate principles would risk renewed enforcement of the federal victory. He concentrated instead on the personal virtues and experiences of the Confederate dead. Philosophically opposed to the providential view of history that characterized most Lost Cause eulogists, he avoided religious allusions much as millennial defenders of the Southern Cross regarded its display as a secular matter. He emphasized the loneliness of the soldiers who had suffered "IN THE DARK HOURS OF IMPRISONMENT, / IN THE HOPELESSNESS OF THE HOSPITAL, / IN THE SHORT, SHARP AGONY OF THE FIELD" and who now lay "BURIED IN REMOTE AND ALIEN GRAVES." But these images set up Trescot's fundamentally sentimental resolution that the soldiers "FOUND SUPPORT AND CONSOLATION / IN THE BELIEF / THAT AT HOME THEY WOULD NOT BE FORGOTTEN."[57] The installation of the battle flag contradicted this nineteenth-century climax. Championed as the symbol of the army alone—not the Confederate republic or its civilian society—the flag offered instead the late-twentieth-century conclusion that in their crisis, the Confederate soldiers stood by themselves. Isolated from the domestic institutions of the Old South, they were images of alienation as complete as the depictions of American soldiers separated from all support and supervision while on nightmarish patrols in the jungles of Southeast Asia.

The reliance of the Confederate flag defense on post-Vietnam shifts in American military commemoration was much grimmer than the origins of contemporary flag enthusiasm in consumer and recreational practices, but both impulses shared a pronounced social atomism. The abandonment of Jefferson Davis's insistence on the justice of the southern cause detached flag defense from political responsibility at the same time that Confederate commemoration departed from its earlier grounding in gender, religious, and class relations. Flag champions dissolved the Civil War, like the Vietnam War, into as many private wars as there were soldiers, into whose inner experiences nobody else could enter with full understanding. Commemorative judgments were in this situation as subjective as marketplace values, the sum of individual assessments rather than the expression of communal ideals. "How people view this flag is like how they view beauty. It is in the eye of the beholder," explained a flag supporter. Confederate memory had become "the essence of anarchy," as Lincoln called secession.[58]

"We did what General Lee should have done at Gettysburg. We flanked on them," crowed McConnell after the legislature moved the flag display to the soldier monument over the objections of the Black Legislative Caucus and the NAACP.[59] The analogy was in some ways curiously inapt, for flag admirers were on the defensive during the millennial controversies, not on the attack as Lee had been in his invasion of the North. Flag supporters had followed tactics that Lee ably illustrated against many Union charges: sharp counterpunching, followed by a sidestep to more defensible ground. But McConnell's comparison was in another sense inevitable, for it came directly from the movie *Gettysburg* (1993), a commercially successful adaptation of Michael Shaara's novel *The Killer Angels* (1974), which sympathetically depicted Civil War soldiers on both sides of the battlefield.

McConnell's choice of a historical precedent reflected not only the influence of Hollywood on even a passionate Civil War buff but also flag defenders' immersion in modernity rather than tradition. In *Gettysburg*, Lee represents an inability to leave inherited models behind. He sees his current military situation through a reliance on the example of Napoleon and a faith that southern soldiers will most likely succeed by fighting as their regional culture has taught them to fight—in a gallant charge. He therefore fails to follow the prescient advice of General James Longstreet, who recognizes that the Civil War has begun to anticipate that archetype of modernity, the Western Front, and that long-cherished southern ways are doomed.

McConnell took a similar antitraditionalist position in the disagreement among flag admirers that followed the relocation of the Southern Cross to the soldier monument. Made of cotton, like many Confederate standards of the Civil War era, the new banner clung to its flagpole rather than catching the breeze. The colors also tended to run after rainstorms. Noting that "pink stars aren't seemly," McConnell ordered the substitution of a nylon flag. Visibility was more important than verisimilitude for the retailer of reproductions. When Courson insisted on representation of Dixie as the land of cotton, not the land of synthetic fibers, the flag supporters compromised on a silk-cotton blend.[60]

In these incidents, McConnell epitomized the desertion of Lost Cause tradition that had characterized enthusiasm for the flag ever since college fraternities introduced Old South balls during the Prohibition era. The cutting edge of that impulse remained consumerism and recreation, which provided lively venues for flag debates after legislators left behind the issue. Rabid flag advocates who felt betrayed by the Heritage Act immediately found a new champion in barbecue entrepreneur Maurice Bessinger, who hoisted immense Confederate battle flags above his nine Piggie Parks in the Columbia area on the same day that the Southern Cross came down from the capitol. The substitution of the chain restaurant for the statehouse was consistent with a commemorative campaign that had already severed most of the Lost Cause institutional moorings. For the next several years, the Piggie Parks became the preeminent South Carolina forum for public expression of opinion about Confederate commemoration. Columbia residents unwilling to endorse Bessinger's views informally boycotted his restaurants despite the excellent reputation of his barbecue. Proflag diners patronized the enterprise.[61]

Like disappointed defenders of the dome, opponents of the continued display of the flag at the capitol expressed their dissent in recreational and consumer arenas. Intercollegiate sports became the main field of resistance to the Heritage Act, as the NAACP tourism boycott evolved into a policy adopted by the National College Athletic Association and leading regional athletic conferences not to hold basketball tournament games, football bowl games, or several other lucrative types of championship events in South Carolina while the state continued to display the flag on the capitol grounds. The world of college sports, in which the battle flag had won much of its popularity during the mid-twentieth century, became the source of the most widely discussed appeals to remove the banner from the pole near the soldier monument. The most sustained public debate of the issue in the first decade of the new century followed a remark by the University of South Carolina's football coach that the legislature should remove the flag from the capitol grounds.[62]

Institutions of government played a minor role in the continuing controversy after passage of the Heritage Act. Ministers occasionally conducted antiflag vigils at the capitol, as they had in the 1990s. An African American who called himself the Reverend E. X. Slave carried out a direct protest in April 2002 by propping an extension ladder against the flagpole and setting the flag ablaze while dressed in a black Santa Claus costume.[63] But the legislature devoted little attention to the issue, though twenty-two of the twenty-six African Americans in the House of Representatives had voted against the Heritage Act in 2000. This hesitancy reflected the difficulties encountered by the millennial campaign to move the flag, now compounded by the diminished availability of an attack based on remembrance of the civil rights movement and the increased availability of a defense based on popular support for soldiers regardless of the cause for which they fought. Some of the most determined opponents of the flag display, including several African Americans who voted for the Heritage Act in the Senate, evidently concluded that in its new position, the flag would gradually become as ineffective in inspiring enthusiasm for the Confederacy as the soldier monument had long ago become.

Whether the flag disappeared altogether from the capitol grounds in another extraordinary act of repudiation or merely faded into public neglect, the shift of the debate from government to barbecue and sports underscored the displacement of traditional social institutions and modes of commemoration in contemporary promotion of Confederate memory. In arguing that rampant exploitation of the national emblem could deepen reverence, Confederate flag admirers had to some degree anticipated the trajectory of the U.S. flag. Modest commercial appropriations of the Stars and Stripes gave way in the last third of the twentieth century to much bolder and more pervasive use of the American flag for a wide variety of purposes. The notion that wearing even the most informal leisure clothing emblazoned with a flag logo might express patriotism, as defined by the consumer, became a commonplace. The Museum of Modern Art eagerly added Jasper Johns's *Flag* to its permanent collection in 1973. But the overall pattern still differed significantly from the Confederate precedent. Ritual practices reinforcing respect for the U.S. flag remained stringent in many ways, and a primal identification of the flag with violent death continued to be renewed. The terrorist attacks of September 11, 2001, prompted a marked reassertion of the quasi-religious veneration of the flag. Designer Ralph Lauren generated large revenues by selling casual apparel decorated with the Stars and Stripes, but he also helped to fund a thoroughly conventional shrine at the Smithsonian Museum of American History for display of the preserved standard that had inspired Francis Scott Key to write the "Star-Spangled Banner" during the War of 1812.[64]

Much closer was the parallel between the Confederate battle flag and its fraternal twin, the state flag of South Carolina. Both banners were products of secession. The South Carolina legislature adopted the design proposed by fire-eater Robert Barnwell Rhett Jr. for the standard of the self-proclaimed sovereignty on January 28, 1861, a few days before the opening of the Montgomery convention at which Rhett's fellow South Carolina radical William Porcher Miles began his ultimately successful campaign for adoption of the St. Andrew's Cross as the ensign of proslavery Christianity.[65] An invocation of South Carolina memories dating back to the Revolutionary War, the white palmetto tree and crescent on a field of blue expressed from the outset the martial resonance that the Southern Cross developed after Confederate commanders adopted it. Like the Southern Cross, the palmetto and crescent served as a banner for many South Carolina units in the Civil War, and into the 1890s it remained sufficiently associated with the sectional conflict for the legislature to consider a proposal to change the field to purple in recognition of the blood that Confederate soldiers had shed. Routine official use defined the banner for most of the twentieth century, beginning with a 1910 statute that provided for its display at government buildings. At the end of the century, however, the state flag became "downright trendy and definitely marketable." The palmetto and crescent appeared on an astonishing array of merchandise. State residents frequently purchased banners to fly from their homes or boats. A journalist reported that the palmetto and crescent ranked with the lone star of Texas as the "most embraced" state emblem. Nowhere else in the United States did commercial appropriations of a flag comprise a larger part of what might plausibly be called a collective identity. That enthusiasm rarely touched on the Civil War origins of the state flag, and at least one retailer speculated that the controversy over the Southern Cross had spurred interest in a visually striking but less ideologically problematic banner. Surely more influential was the immense popularity of such corporate symbols as the Nike swoosh and the Apple apple.[66]

The transformation of the South Carolina flag from a separatist standard into a marketing phenomenon neatly counterpointed the removal of the Confederate battle flag from the capitol dome under pressure of a tourism boycott. In the business jargon of the day, the state had protected its brand. For South Carolina now was a brand more than it was a "soul" constituted by a "rich legacy of memories," as Ernest Renan famously defined the sort of nation that secessionists had hoped to establish and the Lost Cause had tried to perpetuate.[67] Tourism was the largest industry in the state, and the leading source of revenue reflected an appetite for exciting images that characterized the era as thoroughly as the production of staple crops had once fostered affection for the land. Confederate commemoration, long the richest part of the state legacy of memories, offered a preview of a postnational pattern of allegiance. Popularized by consumerism even before Dick and Mac McDonald built their first set of golden arches in 1953, the Southern Cross eventually achieved a global circulation. Although the model of social relations defended by the proslavery republic had collapsed in the Civil War, the model of social relations pioneered by the Confederate battle flag in the mid-twentieth century was on the rise at the sesquicentennial anniversary of the war. The winds of history had not blown as Henry Timrod predicted in "Ethnogenesis," but South Carolina strained to catch "the softened breeze" in the logo that fluttered atop the statehouse.

7

The Steampunk
Confederacy

THE OPENING OF Horace L. Hunley's tomb in
November 1863 was a gruesome moment of a sick-
ening war. "The spectacle was indescribably ghastly,"
General P. G. T. Beauregard later recalled. The bodies
of Hunley and the crew of his eponymous submarine,
which had sunk nose-first into the floor of Charleston Harbor on October 15 and remained stuck in the
mud for three weeks, were "contorted into all kinds
of horrible attitudes." The suffocated Hunley stood
upright, his stiffened arms raised above his head in a
desperate attempt to open a manhole cover; the un-
lit candle in his hand showed that the crew had died
in complete darkness. The drowned men lying on the
bottom of the vessel clutched each other in panic.
"The blackened faces of all presented the expression
of their despair and agony," Beauregard shuddered.
After workers hacked Hunley's bloated corpse into
pieces and moved the remains from the submarine
to an oversized wooden coffin, the New Orleans businessman was buried with military honors at Magnolia
Cemetery, followed the next day by the crew. William
Gilmore Simms turned over to them the plot he had
received in appreciation for delivering "The City of

Conrad Wise Chapman, *Submarine Torpedo Boat H. L. Hunley, Dec. 6, 1863.*
Courtesy of the Museum of the Confederacy, Richmond, Virginia.

the Silent" at the cemetery's 1850 dedication. The *Charleston Mercury* reported that Hunley's last letter to his friends revealed "a presentiment that
he would perish in the adventure," the grim fate of a previous crew, and observed that "that presentiment has been mournfully fulfilled."[1]

Like many rank-and-file troops angered by commanders' calculations of
military risks and possible returns, Confederates in Charleston expressed
dismay with Beauregard's hesitant acquiescence in a proposal to try "the
fish-boat" again. Sailors' nickname for the *Hunley*, "murdering machine,"
echoed Beauregard's judgment that it was "more dangerous to those who
use it than to [the] enemy." One bold critic painted the word "COFFIN" on
the vessel as it sat in dry dock at Mount Pleasant for cleaning and refitting. The most eloquent protest came from the young painter Conrad Wise
Chapman, whose artistic training and political connections had brought
the infantry volunteer an assignment from Beauregard to make a pictorial record of local military operations with particular attention to Confederate innovation in the art of war. Among his drawings for this task,
Chapman executed a careful rendition of the *Hunley* at Mount Pleasant
in early December 1863, which he incorporated shortly afterward into an
oil painting. In the foreground of the small canvas, Conrad depicted the
bucket and tools used to wash away the smell of death, paint over the graf-

fiti, and prepare the "peripatetic coffin" to receive another crew. An open hatch aired out the stench. A ghostly Hunley stood next to the creation that had killed him two months earlier, absorbed in conversation with a seated sentinel who resembled Chapman. The juxtaposition of brushwork projects was forceful. Slaves working under army command might efface the traces of Hunley and recycle his tomb for the national project, but the artist would safeguard memory of the individual human being. Even thirty-five years later, Chapman displayed lasting bitterness in recalling that when dispatched a third time, the vessel predictably "never came back, nor was anything ever heard from it."[2]

As Chapman acknowledged only diffidently in his recollections, the *Hunley* and its crew under the command of army lieutenant George Dixon sank the Union frigate *Housatonic* on that final voyage in February 1864, which ensured that the submarine would be heard from in commemoration even though the men did not return. The *Hunley* became one of the most important vehicles through which Confederate memory addressed the process of technological change, the vortex of modernity. Celebration of southern ingenuity was not static. Remembrance of the *Hunley* shifted in synchronization with realignments of American technological culture. For the first three decades after the war, the sinking of the *Housatonic* was a subordinate element in recognition of the Confederate transformation of naval warfare through the widespread use of underwater explosives, known since the era of Robert Fulton as torpedoes. Chapman's notes on the *Hunley* in 1898 coincided with the emergence of a new narrative prompted by the recent invention of practical submarines. Some white southerners tried to extend to the submarine the claims to progress so successfully advanced in the case of the torpedo, but Confederate folklore mostly emphasized the stark contrast between the *Hunley* and the new machines. The career of the Civil War vessel modeled a Confederacy doomed to die yet destined to a mystic rebirth. The revolutionary introduction of the nuclear submarine in the 1950s led to a third major phase in *Hunley* commemoration. The development of atomic energy spurred attempts to trace a reassuring patriotic lineage for the exercise of potentially catastrophic power amid the tensions of the Cold War. Nowhere was that effort more pronounced than in Charleston, a town dominated by a naval base that was home to a fleet of nuclear-powered submarines armed with ballistic missiles.

The finding of the *Hunley* wreck near the Charleston coast in May 1995 and its salvage in August 2000, one month after South Carolina finally furled the battle flag atop the statehouse, led to an update in this remembrance of Confederate technology. On the defensive throughout the protracted flag controversy, champions of Confederate memory turned to the *Hunley* to launch a counterattack. Ridiculed as shortsighted traditionalists, they sought to rebrand Dixie in accordance with the contemporary values revealed by the millennial rally around the flag. They succeeded spectacularly. Conservation and display of the submarine became one of the most expensive public works projects in South Carolina during the early twenty-first century and the first new commemorative site of national significance to glorify the Confederacy since the dedication of the Stone Mountain memorial in 1970.

The climactic phase of *Hunley* remembrance departed from previous versions of the narrative. Confederate commemoration again celebrated southern technological innovation, but claims for the introduction of submarine warfare abandoned Civil War veterans' claims that the opening of torpedo warfare marked the ascendancy of the nation-state. Confederate commemoration again treated the *Hunley* as a legend, but no longer as a Lost Cause parable of frustration and redemption. Confederate commemoration again honored Dixon and his crew, but the attributes of fame changed significantly from the early 1960s to the late 1990s. These contrasts reflected a fundamental shift in conceptualizing the relationship between past and present.

The insistence of millennial Confederate memory that the *Hunley* was "literally fifty years ahead of her time" closely resembled the simultaneous steampunk fad, which used the mid-nineteenth century as a standpoint from which to imagine futuristic contraptions historically realized in later periods and different forms. Adapted from a steam boiler, the hand-cranked vessel aptly fit the pseudo-Victorian aesthetic.[3] Costumed reenactment and virtual-reality apparatus similarly shifted remembrance from myth to fantasy. As the defense of the Southern Cross had demonstrated the consumer basis of contemporary American social organization, the follow-up promotion of the fish-boat addressed a culture enthralled by new devices for communication and entertainment. Once more aligning commemoration with technological change, South Carolina relaunched the *H. L. Hunley* as the flagship of the steampunk Confederacy.

Like many advocates of new national identities over the last several centuries, white southerners before and after Appomattox identified Confederate technological innovation as evidence of political legitimacy.

Such claims described the polity as an agent of modernity, a force for material progress and attendant social and cultural transformation.[4] Late-nineteenth-century champions of the Lost Cause praised several achievements of southern resourcefulness. The rapid development of ordnance factories had laid a foundation for the industrial aspirations of the New South. The conversion of the USS *Merrimack* into the CSS *Virginia* had impressed observers on both sides of the Atlantic as the inauguration of an ironclad era in military shipbuilding. The wartime innovation for which Confederate apologists most vigorously and persuasively claimed credit was the extensive deployment of underwater explosives. "The system of torpedoes adopted by us was probably more effective than any other means of defense," Jefferson Davis concluded in his history of the war. "The destructiveness of these little weapons had long been known, but no successful modes for their application to the destruction of the most powerful vessels of war and ironclads had been devised. It remained for the skill and ingenuity of our officers to bring the use of this terrible instrument to perfection." Northern as well as southern writers agreed with Davis's assessment.[5] Whether fixed in the water or delivered by a vessel, the torpedo was the most important Confederate technological breakthrough of the war.

This claim to achievement featured technical, strategic, political, and moral dimensions. The prominent participation of Matthew Fontaine Maury, the most distinguished scientist in the Confederacy, lent prestige to southern advances in torpedo engineering, which included improvements in the electrical wiring of underwater mines and the design of better fuses for explosives triggered by diffusion of acid rather than an electrical charge. The devices played an important role in military maneuvers. Davis counted fifty-eight Union vessels destroyed by southern torpedoes. Commentators pointed to the mines floating in the James River and Charleston Harbor as the main reason the Union did not make more headway along those waters. Maury's nephew Dabney H. Maury, the commanding general in Mobile when Farragut damned the torpedoes there, argued that if the Confederacy had understood underwater explosives at the beginning of the war as well as it did at the end, the South could have protected New Orleans and all other port cities from Union invasion.[6] Such conclusions suggested political implications that extended beyond the American sectional conflict. A defensive weapon, the torpedo would be invaluable to any country attacked by a strong navy. As the Confederacy had offset much of the Union naval advantage, including its dominance in the new ironclad vessels, the torpedo promised a reallocation of the international balance of power between invaders and their weaker neighbors.

The expanded deployment of torpedoes was a Confederate victory in ethics at least as much as engineering. The primary impediment to the use of torpedoes before the Civil War was the widespread agreement that the explosives were not a civilized form of warfare. The Confederacy blew that argument out of the water, insisting on the right of the nation to any available means of self-defense as a fundamental law of morality. In so doing, white southerners extended a broader argument that the proslavery republic embodied the hard-nosed realism demanded by modernity while the antislavery North embraced a sickly sentimentality that in the case of warfare had died with medieval knights in armor. All observers noted that the Union had capitulated to the Confederate viewpoint by establishing a torpedo bureau within the U.S. Navy shortly after the war. Union admiral David Dixon Porter illustrated the beguiling logic of military innovation when he wrote in a popular magazine in 1878, "It is now conceded that governments subserve not only their own interests, but those of mankind, by using a weapon that will soonest decide the result of war."[7] The torpedo was a solid example of an argument dear to the Lost Cause—that the Confederacy continued to live in important ways in the postwar United States.

Charleston was a prominent setting for this story, not only because the torpedoes floating in its harbor discouraged Union attack but also because Beauregard took a strong interest in the development of a torpedo boat. This narrative began with the development of a spar torpedo by Confederate engineer Francis D. Lee and climaxed in the October 5, 1863, attack on the most powerful Union warship, the *New Ironsides*, by a Confederate torpedo ram with an appropriate biblical name for the occasion, the *David*. Although this David did not sink its Goliath, Union commander John Dahlgren later found it necessary to retire his flagship to Port Royal for extensive repairs that amply proved the potential of a torpedo attack. The incident also dramatized the moral controversy over torpedoes, for the Union navy captured *David* commander William Glassell and threatened to try the Confederate officer for the capital crime of "using an engine of war not recognized by civilized nations."[8] But the Union eventually exchanged Glassell and turned to development of its own torpedo rams while hastening to improve defenses against future attacks from the *David* and its predictable imitators. The *Hunley* was one of those imitators. Horace Hunley's death on October 15 may well have resulted from eagerness to emulate or surpass Glassell's success ten days earlier. Although originally designed to deploy a torpedo toted on a long cable, the *Hunley* eventually sank the *Housatonic* with a modified version of Lee's spar torpedo.

Chronological priority was not the only reason that the *David* loomed larger than the *Hunley* in Confederate memory during the late nineteenth century. Local pride was a minor factor. The *David* was from beginning to end a project that centered on Charleston and its elites. Francis Lee had been the architectural partner of E. C. Jones before the war. George Alfred Trenholm provided early funding for Glassell's attempts to build a ram, and Theodore Stoney financed the construction of the *David* along plans outlined by St. Julien Ravenel. Yates Snowden solicited and edited the postwar narrative by Glassell that became a standard source of information about torpedo warfare in Charleston.[9] In contrast, the team that built the *Hunley* worked in New Orleans until the fall of that city and then moved to Mobile, where they completed the vessel sent to Charleston. But the response to Hunley's death indicated that he had made friends in the city, and Charleston elites would take a strong interest in the submarine by the turn of the century.

Military analysts rather than Charleston socialites accounted for most of the emphasis on the *David*. Jefferson Davis's memoir saluted the attack on the *New Ironsides* but did not mention the sinking of the *Housatonic*. Beauregard put Glassell's raid at the center of an important article about torpedo operations in Charleston. Alfred Roman's authorized history of Beauregard's military operations in Charleston highlighted the commander's conviction that the steam-powered torpedo ram was the most promising weapon available to him. Former Confederate engineer John Johnson underscored the same point in a postwar volume he prepared for the history board formed in 1864 to chronicle the novel military operations in Charleston, much as Beauregard had earlier detailed Chapman to prepare a pictorial record. The commander had foreseen the type of naval vessel now evident everywhere, Johnson observed in 1889, when Beauregard pleaded with Richmond to commission swift ironclads armed with spar torpedoes that would expand on the example of the *David*. "With one of those vessels here the blockade could be raised in less than one week, and the army of Gillmore captured very shortly afterward," Beauregard had reported in November 1863. "Half a dozen of these steamers would raise the blockade of our Atlantic and Gulf coasts, and enable us to recover the navigation of the Mississippi River."[10]

Beauregard and his subordinates were not arbitrary in identifying the *David* rather than the *Hunley* as the symbol of the future. Although hastily improvised, the *David* was at least a steam-powered ship. The *Hunley* relied on the muscle power of the seamen working its crank. Its maximum speed was four miles per hour, about half the speed of the *David* and only

a third of what postwar analysts deemed the minimum for an effective torpedo ram.[11] The submersibility of the *Hunley* did not impress these commentators. In a published lecture on submarine boats first presented in
1875 at the new torpedo station in Newport, Rhode Island, naval officer
Francis Barber stressed the basic point that the *Hunley* was not a submarine at all when it attacked the *Housatonic*. Drawing on the testimony
of *Housatonic* crew members, all but five of whom survived the incident,
Barber noted that Union sailors spotted the *Hunley* on the surface of the
water several minutes before the Confederate vessel rammed the blockader.
The *Hunley* remained awash throughout the attack and drew considerable
small-arms fire, which may have caused its sinking. On the occasions when
the *Hunley* did submerge, its corpse-riddled performance was appalling by
prevailing standards; Bavarian submariner Wilhelm Bauer had recorded
134 underwater voyages without an accident in the 1850s. The *Hunley* "was,
for all practical purposes, a failure," summarized an Annapolis instructor.
The "very unsatisfactory results" offered no encouragement for the development of submarine boats, concluded a former Confederate engineer.[12]

The greater postwar interest in the *David* than the *Hunley* also reflected
differences between the *New Ironsides* and the *Housatonic*. Ships are important characters in naval stories, and the *New Ironsides* was the lead
actor in the Charleston theater. The well-armed ironclad was a forerun-
ner of the battleships that captivated the transatlantic military imagination
after the Royal Navy launched the HMS *Dreadnought* in the early twentieth century. Admiral Porter called the *New Ironsides* the best offensive
vessel he had ever seen. Beauregard reported that it "threw more metal,
at each broadside, than all the monitors together of the fleet; her fire was
delivered with more rapidity and accuracy, and she was the most effective vessel employed in the reduction of Battery Wagner." Johnson, who
included in his volume an appendix devoted specifically to the *New Ironsides*, calculated that the ship had fired thirty-three hundred rounds at
Battery Wagner between July 18, 1863, and the Confederate evacuation of
that installation on September 8.[13] Though Beauregard exaggerated in recalling that the *New Ironsides* never fired another shot after the attack of
the *David* on October 5, Glassell's raid prevented the vessel from inflicting
a similar bombardment on Fort Sumter or spearheading another attempt
to invade Charleston. The achievement of the *David* contributed substantially to the Lost Cause pride that the Confederacy never lost Charleston,
even if the army evacuated Fort Sumter and the city in February 1865 as
Sherman advanced on Columbia.

The *Housatonic*, in contrast, was a useful new ship but merely a wooden frigate in a theater where the ironclad had become the basic unit of military calculation. George Alfred Trenholm's firm offered a bounty of one hundred thousand dollars for the sinking of the *New Ironsides* or the uss *Wabash* and fifty thousand dollars for the sinking of any monitor; the *Housatonic* commanded no bounty. Unable to steam past artillery fire in a possible invasion, the *Housatonic* was simply one participant in the large Union blockading squadron. Postwar commentators interested in the fortunes of the Confederacy rather than the prosperity of Charleston rarely regarded the local blockade as a primary factor in the outcome of the war because Confederates had largely shifted to Wilmington, North Carolina, the import-export business that flourished in Charleston until the intensification of Union military operations in low-country South Carolina during the summer of 1863. Whether a national threat or a community nuisance, the Charleston blockade did not loosen one iota with the sinking of the *Housatonic* in February 1864. The *Hunley* had accomplished nothing to stave off Confederate defeat, let alone match the *David* in shaping a tale of Confederate victory.[14]

Insignificant in the arc of naval technology or the arc of the Civil War, the Confederate submarine became a dramatic incident within a broader memory of torpedo warfare. The *David* had prompted so many attempts to build similar ships that the name became generic, like that of the uss *Monitor*. This practice routinely extended to the vessel that wartime military records identified as the *H. L. Hunley*. Even Ben H. Teague, the leading collector of Civil War relics in South Carolina, called the submarine the *David* in an article he wrote to welcome a national reunion of his fellow Confederate veterans to Charleston in the spring of 1899.[15] At precisely that moment, however, new technological developments were beginning to offer fresh commemorative perspectives on the *Hunley*.

The subordination of the *Hunley* story to the rise of the torpedo did not fade from popular memory because the late-nineteenth-century interpretation was historically inaccurate. The same basic narrative, with a sweeping intellectual contextualization, later became the core of Alex Roland's authoritative study *Underwater Warfare in the Age of Sail* (1978). The historian of military technology treated the *David* as emblematic of the triumphant torpedo and found no reason even to mention the *Hunley*. But the torpedo, like the sharpshooter, was a morally unsettling symbol of the transformations wrought by the Civil War, and the innovation had limited appeal for broad audiences. The submarine, conversely, could clearly captivate the popular imagination, as Jules Verne demonstrated in *Twenty Thousand Leagues under the Sea* (1869). The invention of practical submarines in the late 1890s by John P. Holland and Simon Lake electrified that potential enthusiasm. The heady realization of ancient human dreams to travel through the sea like a fish soon drew further intensity from the nearly simultaneous realization of ancient human dreams to travel through the air like a bird. The age of wonders prompted a look back at the steps that had led to such achievements. At the same time, the pervasive brutality of industrial factory labor fostered considerable wariness of new technology.

The commemorative marble fountain installed in White Point Garden by the Charleston chapter of the United Daughters of the Confederacy (UDC) in May 1899, in time for the national convention of Confederate veterans, illustrated remembrance of the *Hunley* as the submarine began to emerge unevenly from the shadow of the torpedo. Inscriptions on the monument honored Confederate seamen who were "first in marine warfare to employ torpedo boats" and credited Lee, Ravenel, and Glassell for their roles in attacks that sustained no casualties; the monument also noted that more than thirty men had drowned on the *Hunley*. A newspaper history published for the dedication devoted more than twenty paragraphs to the period from Lee's development of the spar torpedo through the attack on the *New Ironsides* and only five paragraphs to the *Hunley* and the sinking of the *Housatonic*. Another retrospective observed that the *Hunley* deserved mention "not so much on account of any peculiarity in its construction, nor on account of the injury it inflicted on the enemy, but as a lesson of simple patriotism." But the monument also saluted Horace L. Hunley as "inventor of submarine boat," and the newspaper report on the dedication put forward the novel claim that "it was in Charleston that the first submarine torpedo boat was constructed and used."[16] The Lost Cause had begun to stake its claim to one of the most exciting American technological innovations of the last several years.

The most forceful assertions of this claim came from Confederate veteran William A. Alexander, a mechanical engineer who had participated in the building of the *Hunley* in Mobile and served briefly on its final crew until he was ordered back to Alabama shortly before the attack on the *Housatonic*. Alexander decided to publish his reminiscences of the *Hunley* in 1902 amid the flurry of publicity that surrounded the new submarines. His widely circulated memoir would remain one of the most frequently cited sources of information about the Confederate fish-boat. In addition to providing technical details and thrilling anecdotes, Alexander advanced the proposition that the *Hunley* was "the first submarine boat successfully operated in naval warfare." In one of several articles to borrow Alexander's narrative and his conclusion, *Harper's Weekly* suggested a few years later that submarines were not entirely a product of the "flying-machine, wireless telegraph age" because the *Hunley* had previously proven their military effectiveness, and "its general plan has been followed in the most modern submarines." Lost Cause publications sometimes echoed these assertions. In September 1914, the month of the first U-boat sinking of a British cruiser, a former Confederate naval officer called the *Hunley* "the first submarine craft in the world worthy of the name."[17]

But even ardent white southerners rarely supposed that the submarine, like the torpedo, had followed a line of technological development that led through the Confederacy. The *Hunley* was one of many disconnected experiments with underwater vessels in the decades after Robert Fulton's *Nautilus* built systematically on David Bushnell's foundational *Turtle* of the Revolutionary War. Holland and Lake had studied all of their predecessors as keenly as possible, but neither inventor found much use in the *Hunley* either before or after Alexander published his account. Holland indicated that one key to turn-of-the-century progress had been to ignore all of the failures of the mid-nineteenth century, including the *Hunley*. Lake's history of submarines featured a chapter on "Comedy and Tragedy in Submarine Development" that contrasted his successful 1897 exhibition of the *Argonaut* with the disastrous career of the *Hunley*.[18]

The shelf of submarine histories published in the first decade of the twentieth century shared a similar understanding of the process of technological development. These books devoted careful attention to Bushnell and Fulton and sometimes Bauer but passed quickly over the *Hunley* as a dramatic story with no greater engineering significance than the *Alligator*, the *Intelligent Whale*, or other mid-nineteenth-century submarines. The historians made plain that the most advanced submarine launched in 1863 was not the *Hunley* but *Le Plongeur*, the much larger French vessel that sparked Jules Verne's imagination at the 1867 international exposition in Paris. Apart from its influence on the cultural image of the submarine, *Le Plongeur* marked the beginning of productive attention to the development of a submarine engine. Its compressed-air engine proved unsatisfactory, but the architects of *Le Plongeur* had made a systematic experiment with the central problem of submarine construction. "The engine is the most important element in the submarine," observed Lake. Even if it chanced to sink an enemy ship, an underwater vessel without an engine was no more a submarine in the contemporary sense than a bicycle was an automobile or a hot-air balloon was an airplane.[19]

The antithesis of technological modernity, the *Hunley* achieved fame through a consistent exaggeration of the number of Confederate seamen it killed. Early histories presented twentieth-century writers with several choices. Beauregard, who had followed the project closely, indicated in 1878 that the submarine sank three times, including the raid that destroyed the *Housatonic*. Duncan Ingraham, the senior Confederate naval officer in Charleston, agreed with Beauregard even though the admiral's distrust of "new-fangled notions" might have inclined him to credit additional negative information. Charles H. Olmstead, an army officer stationed in Charleston in 1863, corroborated their accounts in an 1883 narrative. Alexander echoed Francis Barber's tally of four sinkings and thirty-two deaths. The nineteenth-century outlier was Thomas Scharf's *History of the Confederate States Navy* (1887), which claimed that the *Hunley* sank six times: once in Mobile, twice in Charleston under the command of Lieutenant John Payne, once under the command of Horace Hunley, yet again in an accident with the Confederate ship *Indian Chief*, and finally in the attack on the *Housatonic*.[20]

Scharf's total was dubious from the outset. No documentation supported three of the alleged incidents. Payne supposedly had escaped twice from identical fatal swampings that took place within one week, an effective narrative device for suggesting uncontrollable repetition but not a reasonable accounting for the time needed to salvage and clean the *Hunley* after a disaster. Yet the extreme estimate became widely accepted among Lost Cause enthusiasts as well as other writers. Augustine T. Smythe Jr., whose mother headed the UDC chapter that dedicated the 1899 monument, described six sinkings in a 1908 essay. Fellow Confederate naval veteran C. L. Stanton reported in 1914 that he frequently heard similar stories, which added up to almost fifty lives lost on the submarine. Stanton, a wartime friend of Payne, tried to correct the record to three sinkings, but five years later, an instructional program published in *Confederate Veteran* for use at meetings of the Children of the Confederacy stood stubbornly by the more spectacular six disasters. During the first half of the twentieth century, no other telling of the *Hunley* story reverted to the three sinkings reported by the knowledgeable witnesses Beauregard, Ingraham, Olmstead, and Stanton.[21]

248 THE STEAMPUNK CONFEDERACY

White southerners recognized that such accounts of the *Hunley* were "almost impossible" or "almost fantastic" or "sound incredible."[22] But the story of the Confederate submarine was now something of a tall tale, in which truth depended on exaggeration. In the mid-1910s, the claim emerged from Charleston that P. T. Barnum had offered a reward of one hundred thousand dollars shortly after the war to anyone who located the *Hunley* wreck for inclusion in Barnum's famous display of frauds and freaks. DuBose Heyward presented a lengthy poem about the supposed sixth and final crew in *Carolina Chansons: Legends of the Low Country* (1922) alongside folklore about ghosts and buried pirate treasure. In his subsequent *National Geographic* essay about Charleston, the novelist continued to report six *Hunley* sinkings over the protest of leading local historian E. Milby Burton, who pointed out in a prepublication review of the manuscript that no evidence supported such an epic total.[23]

The widespread adoption of the darkest narrative underscored that, in the words of the history prepared for the Children of the Confederacy in 1919, the various *Hunley* crews "knew that they were facing certain death." A few years later, *Confederate Veteran* excerpted a poem that envisioned the submarine, again called the *David*, as a "leaking little biscuit box" and indicated that the crew "and Dixon knew / That if they sank the enemy they'd sink the David too." Heyward agreed that "the crew, sealed in their metal coffin, hoped only to reach and destroy a Federal battleship before they were suffocated or drowned."[24]

This view of the *Hunley* differed fundamentally from the celebration of technological progress through which nineteenth-century writers had understood Confederate development of the torpedo and through which Alexander described Confederate development of the submarine. Remembrance of the torpedo had claimed Confederate victory, but the early-twentieth-century legend of the *Hunley* dramatized Confederate defeat. Like some other versions of the Lost Cause, the narrative situated the ordeal of the white South in a Christian framework that emphasized the inevitable frustrations of humanity. The first sinking of a warship by a hapless Confederate submarine was not a tribute to skillful engineering but a sign of the mysterious ways of Providence. The modern submarine vindicated the sacrifices of the *Hunley* rather than adapting its ideas. The parable warned that worldly celebration of technological innovation was a poor measure of humanity.

Theodore Jervey's novel *The Elder Brother* (1905) incorporated this religious image of the *Hunley* into a cosmic order of sectional reconciliation.

Depicting the hero, Rupert Gordon, and his fiancée in a twilight stroll along the Battery, Jervey reflected on the "dark and vague and deep" waters that surrounded his characters. On Morris Island, scene of "the most terrible bombardment to which any work was ever subjected," the thunder of artillery had given way to the even more relentless boom of the surf. "If spirits meet when death has freed the soul from its earthly ties," Jervey exclaimed, "what rare gatherings of the dauntless might there be on those waters!" At the edge of the beach, Robert Gould Shaw had fallen on the rampart of Battery Wagner at the head of the 54th Massachusetts Regiment in an event that northerners commemorated as one of the most Christlike sacrifices of the war. Jervey imagined the abolitionist martyr in communion with "the dauntless seven who dared and met an almost certain death within the 'fish' boat" and who now rested "out under the dark flood, full many a fathom down." The differences between Union and Confederate dissolved in a peaceful reconciling grave.[25]

Emphasis on the acceptance of death aboard the *Hunley* sharpened conjecture about the motives of the crew members. The motif of inevitability helped Lost Cause apologists dismiss the reasoning that the bounties offered for the sinking of Union shipping had encouraged avaricious volunteers to take the risk. Some writers maintained that Confederate patriotism had impelled the crews; others pointed to a determination to personify the highest socially sanctioned level of physical courage. Dabney Maury, who may have known George Dixon in Mobile, suggested that survivor's guilt was an important factor. "He had taken active part in the construction of this vessel, had caused other men to perish in her by dangers he had not shared, and now bravely demanded this opportunity," Maury reported.[26]

The first *Hunley* novel, Cyrus Townsend Brady's *A Little Traitor to the South* (1903), was the most elaborate foray into the idiosyncrasies of motivation. An Annapolis graduate who wrote maritime adventure fiction, Brady typified the turn-of-the-century northern romanticization of the Old South as an aristocratic land of honor and valor. In the preface to the novel, he saluted the Confederate submariners as American heroes. His adaptation replaced Dixon at the helm with the fictional Harry Lacy, scion of an old South Carolina family. Before the war, Lacy's weakness for gambling and liquor had tarnished the fine name he inherited. During the war, his guilt-ridden death wish helped him achieve an admirable record of gallantry. "I'd rather die than live," he explained, "but I would like to go out of existence doing something fine and noble." The Confederate submarine, which had sunk on all five of its outings and killed more than thirty men, offered a splendid finale. When the "little traitor" of the title tricked her lover into missing a chance to command the "floating, or sinking, death trap," Lacy led the attack on the *Housatonic* in one last redemptive flourish. "Nothing in life had so become Lacy as the ending of it," the narrator concluded. "He was not to be pitied for that he died the death of his choice."[27]

The two world wars reinforced identification of the *Hunley* with certain death for its crews. Although Lost Cause enthusiasts expressed pride in anticipating the U-boat successes of World War I, they also sought to distance the *Hunley* from the Hun. The president of the Confederated Southern Memorial Association reported in 1916 that the White Point Garden monument honored "the first victims of torpedo, or submarine warfare," a tribute "worthy of note when submarine warfare is so disastrous."[28] During World War II, a national journalist reassured readers that "if you think there is something peculiarly, fatalistically Japanese about 'suicide' submarine crews, consider the six crews of Americans who, in succession volunteered to man the world's first war submarine." This reading of the *Hunley* story argued that American culture contained and could therefore conquer the kamikaze spirit it now confronted in Asia. A contributor to the UDC monthly magazine similarly maintained in 1946 that the *Hunley* had invented "the so-called 'suicide' tactics that played a much publicized part in World War II." Two years later, a Mobile chapter of the UDC dedicated a white marble cemetery obelisk to the men who died on the submarine. The selection of a commemorative motif that excluded William Alexander, who had helped to build the *Hunley* at the Parks and Lyon machine shop and made Mobile his home for a half century after the war, testified to the failure of Alexander's straightforward story of technological progress.[29]

If Lost Cause tales of the *Hunley* reflected a Christian skepticism about the importance of technological achievement, the Metropolitan Museum of Art used Conrad Wise Chapman's wartime painting of the Confederate submarine to express more secular reservations about technological culture in a landmark survey of American art organized for the 1939 New York World's Fair. The largest show the museum had ever mounted, *Life in America* collected paintings from 145 lenders to present a historical overview that began with a portrait of Pocahontas and ended with a portrait of Woodrow Wilson. The curators described the Civil War as a watershed conflict between a static South and a dynamic North. Unlike some contemporary writers, they did not romanticize the agrarian alternative to the modern United States. Calhoun's commitment to slavery made him "prophet of the disaster which he dreaded, yet helped to prepare." William Aiken

Walker's *Calhoun's Slaves* (1888), a portrait of two field hands who had long outlived their master to achieve a threadbare dignity as free men in the still-troubled realm of King Cotton, was one of several canvases that depicted the black experience of that cataclysm. At the same time, the curators were no more roseate about industrialization. The exhibition catalog bluntly declared that the spread of the factory system had resulted in "denial of freedom and satisfaction for the ordinary man." Placing the first paintings of railroads immediately after the section on the Civil War era, the curators introduced the pivotal industry with a portrait of notorious robber baron Cornelius Vanderbilt and noted that "his career as a capitalist resembles that of a big-game hunter." Two of the first railroad paintings focused on completion of the transcontinental railroad as a death knell for the great American herds of buffalo. Turning repeatedly to Walt Whitman for guidance, the curators defined faith in an America caught between the tragic trajectories of the plantation South and the industrial North. Their prime image of a synthesis between tradition and progress was the clipper ship, "the envy of the world" because of "the exactest craftsmanship, and daring innovations in design." Rewarding for laborers and profitable for merchants, the clipper ships disappeared only when American shipbuilding declined with the national concentration on domestic trade.[30]

The catalog essay singled out Chapman as one of the revelations of the exhibition, "an unpretentious artist" committed to craftsmanlike documentary precision while on detail as Beauregard's pictorial historian. Chapman's canvas of the *Hunley* corresponded perfectly with the curators' overarching interpretation. The successor to Fulton's *Nautilus* demonstrated Confederate "ingenuity and determination" but also illustrated the dangers of a technological innovation blinded by the lack of an adequate cultural compass. The *Hunley* "had a nasty trick of plunging to the bottom and drowning the men within, who could not see where they were going." The record of five sinkings, followed by the mutually fatal final attack on the *Housatonic* while not submerged, was utterly disastrous. An embrace of technology without tradition or craft, the Confederate submarine was the polar opposite of the antebellum clipper ship.[31]

Yearning for an organic democratic society, much like the high-art celebration of folk culture during the 1930s, *Life in America* drew piquancy from its deliberate contrast with the theme of the 1939 New York World's Fair, the World of Tomorrow. The glittering fair offered previews of nylon, color photography, air-conditioning, television, and Smell-O-Vision. The lyrical exhibition looked back at George Caleb Bingham's flatboat men,

Thomas Eakins's scullers, and Winslow Homer's seascapes. In this context, Chapman's ambivalent portrait of inventor and invention stood out enough for at least one prominent reviewer to name it among the most memorable of the three hundred works in the show.[32] The image cast a dark chill over the technological utopia promised by the futuristic fair. The *Hunley* had once been the world of tomorrow for the Confederacy, a world of tomorrow that ended in shipwreck and death for all aboard.

The invention of the atomic bomb threatened a vastly more comprehensive technological catastrophe than anything the Metropolitan Museum curators imagined in 1939. Submarines assumed a crucial position in the transformed world that took shape during the years after Hiroshima and Nagasaki. From a military standpoint, nuclear-powered submarines armed with ballistic missiles soon ranked among the most strategically important of all weapons. The constantly circulating undersea vessels served as silent reminders of the omnipresent atomic specter and the readiness of the nation-state to launch posthumous apocalyptic retaliation. The nuclear-powered submarine was also vital to American propaganda during the post-Sputnik period of Soviet leadership in the space race. Nuclear propulsion had opened the oceans to technological exploration scarcely less dramatically than rocket ships had opened the skies. At the end of World War II, a submarine might travel underwater at eight knots for one hour or, by reducing speed to only three knots, remain submerged for up to thirty-six hours. In preparation for the Eisenhower-Khrushchev summit meeting during the U-2 crisis in May 1960, the uss *Triton* completed the first entirely submerged navigation of the globe, cruising for eighty-three days at an average speed of about eighteen knots, well below its short-run peak. Three months later, the uss *Nautilus* matched one of the climactic achievements of Jules Verne's *Nautilus* by passing under a polar ice cap. Such performances testified not merely to national military prowess but more ebulliently to the American capacity to fulfill human aspirations.[33]

From the christening of the *Nautilus* in 1954 through the release of the Beatles' movie *Yellow Submarine* in 1968, submarines enjoyed an extraordinarily high public profile that combined the challenge of nuclear responsibility with the fun of adventure. The film adaptation of *Twenty Thousand Leagues under the Sea* produced by Walt Disney in 1954 emphasized this twinned theme by depicting Captain Nemo's power source as a technology that could revolutionize the world or destroy it. The submarine generated breathtaking excitement and profound scientific advances, but Nemo exploded it in a familiar mushroom cloud at the end of the movie because he feared that the world of the 1860s was too belligerent to use the invention safely. A concluding voice-over assured audiences that "when the world is ready for a new and better life, all this will come to pass." That day had evidently arrived. By the summer of 1959, tourists could enjoy "atomic submarine" rides installed at Disneyland with the assistance of General Dynamics, maker of the USS *Nautilus*.[34]

Despite the divide between the atomic age and the past, promoters of nuclear submarines avidly invoked history. More revealing than the selection of the *Nautilus* for the name of the first new vessel was Eisenhower's decision to scrap altogether the U.S. Navy custom of naming submarines for sea creatures. The administration turned instead to such American paragons as George Washington, Patrick Henry, and Theodore Roosevelt for the names of the first nuclear-powered submarines armed with ballistic missiles. In a tribute to intersectional harmony typical of patriotic culture during the years leading into the Civil War centennial, the USS *Robert E. Lee* complemented the USS *Abraham Lincoln*. The new policy proclaimed that in exercising its awesome new power, the United States remained guided by the principles personified by its established exemplars.[35]

Remembrance of the *Hunley* gained fresh momentum and dignity from this commemorative strategy. The second *Hunley* novel, published in 1956, opened with author Francis Van Wyck Mason's observation that the story of the Confederate heroes demanded retelling "in these days of atomic submarines capable of traversing oceans without refueling or resurfacing." His version of George Dixon recruited volunteers with the exhortation that "we, who will serve aboard the *Hunley* will be initiatin' a new fo'm of naval warfare; one which may well determine not only the outcome of this war, but of wars to be fought by our descendants." In 1958 the commander of the *Nautilus* accepted for the ship library a collection of documents about *Hunley* history that an enthusiast had assembled. Two years later, the UDC presented the General Dynamics showcase library in Groton, Connecticut, with a plaque honoring Horace L. Hunley and a model of his vessel to display alongside models of contemporary nuclear submarines. U.S. senator Strom Thurmond of South Carolina pressed the federal government to name a nuclear submarine for Hunley, which led in 1961 to the launching of the USS *Hunley*, the first ship built specifically as a tender for nuclear submarines. The navy later named another submarine tender for George Dixon.[36]

This approach shifted gradually away from the gleeful enumeration of *Hunley* calamities. Ceremonies at the donation of the *Hunley* documents to the *Nautilus* recounted the familiar tale of six sinkings, a figure still cited commonly into the 1960s. But the motif of certain death ceased to shape a Confederate parable. Mason's *Our Valiant Few* described Horace Hunley as an impassioned if imperfect inventor who went to his death muttering about the improvements necessary for the next version of the submarine. Southern novelist Shelby Foote pushed a more buoyant interpretation in the segment of his Civil War narrative published in 1963. Unlike the other popular Civil War chroniclers of the centennial era, Bruce Catton and Allan Nevins, neither of whom considered the topic worth mentioning in their multivolume sagas, Foote devoted several pages to the *Hunley*. According to him, "She was, in short, the world's first submarine," and he reported that Beauregard had greeted the vessel with the optimistic predictions that the commander had in fact made about the *David*. Foote acknowledged that the *Hunley* was "accident-prone" and severely punished errors by its crews. But he indicated that carelessness had caused the only two sinkings before the *Hunley* set off, "a surface vessel now like any other," on the mission that destroyed the *Housatonic* as well as the submarine.[37]

The new interest in the *Hunley* centered on a heritage of personal character more than a lineage of technological innovation. Mason's protagonist was a newspaper editor from an old Charleston family courageously trying to expose corrupt southern merchants who profited from trade across the blockade by importing luxury goods rather than essential military supplies. Violently run out of town, the crusader eventually made his way back via Mobile with Hunley, Dixon, and the submarine. He volunteered to serve on Dixon's mission because a temporary weakening of the Union blockade would ensure the passage of a steamer carrying his unfairly exiled wife and documents that proved his allegations. In Mason's rendition, the sinking of the *Housatonic* achieved this objective. The journalist was the only crew member to escape from the lost submarine, his valor reinforcing the credibility of his documents. The *Hunley* served as a vehicle for the preservation of community virtue.

The most direct application of the *Hunley* precedent to the advent of nuclear submarines followed the most devastating blow to the prestige the United States had invested in the vessels, the shocking sinking of the USS *Thresher* in the Atlantic Ocean in April 1963 with the loss of all 129 men aboard. Within seven weeks, veteran Hollywood screenwriter Francis Cockrell had produced a script about the *Hunley* for use as the debut episode of

The Great Adventure, a CBS television series of historical dramatizations that would premiere in the fall. Cockrell's script provided for the episode to begin with a montage of nuclear submarines that ended with footage of the USS *Hunley*, "a tender created to service these fabulous nuclear-powered vessels—also the first of her kind. . . . But the *second* naval vessel to bear her name." The scene then dissolved to the salvage of the Confederate submarine from Charleston Harbor in November 1863 and the removal of Horace Hunley's body. The rest of the episode followed Dixon in recruiting and training a fresh crew, modifying the vessel with the aid of his fellow engineers William Alexander and James Tomb, and successfully attacking the *Housatonic*. The program, which aired in September 1963, exhorted Americans in the wake of the *Thresher* disaster to emulate the resolution that Dixon had demonstrated in the aftermath of Hunley's death.[38]

Cockrell gave several members of Dixon's crew fictitious names with obvious resonance. The name "Hampton" invoked South Carolina leadership in the Civil War. The name "Aiken" invoked South Carolina leadership in the Cold War. No community in the United States was more thoroughly transformed by the new military technology than Aiken, epicenter of the enormous Savannah River Site built by DuPont and the federal government during the early 1950s for the production of nuclear materials used in weapons manufacture. John A. May, longtime state legislator from Aiken County, was an important local force in promoting the project and reassuring constituents that the social and economic shifts unleashed by massive federal spending would not destabilize what had until recently been a deeply stagnant rural area. The self-proclaimed Mr. Confederate presented a striking variation on the intersection between *Hunley* commemoration and anxieties about the atomic age. As chair of the state Confederate War Centennial Commission, he arranged for engineering students at Clemson University to make a full-scale replica of the *Hunley* in 1961 for the parade held on the one hundredth anniversary of the firing on Fort Sumter. After the replica toured the state in similar centennial events, he transferred it to the outdoor museum he had built on his estate, Mayfields. The twenty-five miles from Mayfields to the Savannah River Site implied a reassuring proximity between the *Hunley* tribute and the upheavals that threatened to accompany Cold War military maneuvering.[39]

The city of Charleston experienced a similar Cold War transformation that more directly shaped remembrance of the *Hunley*. The dogged efforts of U.S. representative L. Mendel Rivers led in 1956 to authorization for the expansion of Charleston Naval Shipyard to maintain nuclear submarines, and two years later, the navy transferred to Charleston a squadron of vessels armed with Polaris missiles. Rivers argued that a leading factor in the shift of resources from Key West was "the attitude of this community to Navy personnel," who at this point numbered almost seven thousand sailors and another seven thousand civilian employees. The base expanded further in the early 1960s with the transfer of another Polaris squadron and the construction of a dry dock capable of supporting simultaneous maintenance on three nuclear submarines. Analysts soon ranked Charleston with Norfolk, San Antonio, and San Diego among the metropolitan economies most heavily dependent on military spending.[40]

Naval officers exercised considerable influence in civic affairs and stimulated energetic remembrance of the *Hunley*. The local commanding officer initiated the making of a thirty-inch model of the submarine by a well-known specialist for display in the Charleston Museum, which also began to display models of a nuclear-powered submarine and a Polaris missile. Retired admiral Robert Bentham Simons, who had returned to his hometown to teach history in local high schools and research family genealogy, was particularly active in *Hunley* commemoration. He prodded the UDC to put up a new marker at the Magnolia Cemetery graves of Hunley and his crew on the centennial of their deaths. Simons also tried to arrange for the Charleston Museum to receive the full-scale replica commissioned by May for the Civil War centennial.[41]

Thwarted by May's transfer of the *Hunley* replica to Mayfields, director E. Milby Burton of the Charleston Museum began working in 1966 with the president of the Citizens and Southern Bank of South Carolina toward the establishment of a *Hunley* museum in the basement of an eighteenth-century building that the bank acquired to house its trust department. With funding from the bank, Burton commissioned students at a nearby technical college to make another full-scale *Hunley* replica, in which the museum installed several mannequins to demonstrate the positions of the crew. Painted seawater green and decorated with depictions of creatures indigenous to Charleston Harbor, the basement was a close space with a low, barrel-vaulted ceiling. Burton added copies of Chapman's paintings, models of ironclads and the *Housatonic*, and Civil War torpedoes from the museum's collections. At the push of a button, a recording narrated the sinking of the *Housatonic*. The Cold War was never far away, for the basement museum doubled as a nuclear fallout shelter.[42]

The opening of the Charleston Museum branch in July 1967 marked an important step in the institutionalization of *Hunley* remembrance. The museum averaged between forty thousand and fifty thousand visitors per year during the late 1960s and early 1970s, increasing to a peak of seventy-seven thousand visitors in 1977. When Citizens and Southern closed the basement display site in 1981, the Charleston Museum moved the replica to a prominent position at its spacious new headquarters. Meanwhile, a commission working toward the establishment of a South Carolina State Museum in Columbia acquired the replica at Mayfields after May's death. The commission brought it to the capital in 1980 and featured it in the publicity campaign that led up to the museum's opening in 1988. Together, the Charleston Museum and the State Museum forged institutional commitments to promoting *Hunley* remembrance that outlasted the heyday of popular interest in nuclear-powered submarines. Carrying forward the cultural influence of the military long after Cold War anxieties had begun to ease, the museums fostered a reverential attitude toward the *Hunley*. Narratives of its career gradually stabilized at the documented three sinkings. A brochure produced by the Charleston Museum advertised the vessel as the "first submarine successfully put to military use," with the clear implication that such a first must be significant. By the late 1980s, a journalist writing about the museum display simply asserted that "military historians consider what happened in 1864, a revolutionary new development in naval warfare."[43]

In addition to creating institutions with self-interest in the importance of the *Hunley*, the Cold War burst of attention to the submarine created another lasting commemorative legacy, a challenge to find the wreck in Charleston Harbor. In 1870, a newspaper article reported that divers had seen the *Hunley* lying on the bottom next to the *Housatonic*. For decades, retellings of the *Hunley* tale ended with that image of the former combatants paired in death. In the early twentieth century, divers explored and dismantled much of the *Housatonic* wreck as authorities sought to clear the shipping channel, but no evidence indicates that anyone searched for the *Hunley* again until the era of the nuclear submarine. At the urging of Robert Bentham Simons, the Navy planned a well-publicized 1957 effort to find the ship. Local scuba diving hobbyists soon joined in the search, and an automobile-supply salesman announced as early as 1964 that a piece of iron he had found in the harbor might have come from the *Hunley*. Enthusiasm waxed and waned over the following years and involved different individuals, but Simons had defined a reasonably continuous if not necessarily coordinated project. Clive Cussler, a maritime adventure novelist in the tradition of Cyrus Townsend Brady and Francis Van Wyck Mason, became a prominent participant in the enterprise in 1980. He returned to Charleston more than a decade later, and in May 1995, divers working in his employ located the submarine buried in the sandy bottom slightly seaward of the *Housatonic* wreck. Their success opened the climactic chapter in remembrance of the *Hunley*.[44]

Earlier foundations of *Hunley* commemoration had largely disintegrated by the time Cussler's divers found the submarine. The gradual perfection of the self-propelled torpedo during the half century before World War I had long ago rendered the spar torpedo a quaint and obscure dead end in the history of technology. The deindustrialization of the American economy had quieted many of the qualms about factory labor that influenced attitudes toward mechanization in the first half of the twentieth century. Nuclear-powered submarines had lost their glamor to space travel even before arms-reduction diplomacy and later the collapse of the Soviet Union eased popular anxieties about an atomic apocalypse. The transfer of the *Hunley* upon salvage in May 2000 to the former site of the Charleston Naval Shipyard, shuttered five years earlier, encapsulated these and other important shifts in the cultural frame of Confederate memory. The recovery team installed the wreck in a conservation laboratory set up in an abandoned warehouse used most recently as a soundstage for the making of a television movie, *The Hunley* (1999), that had been prompted by media attention to the rediscovered vessel. The desolate site in the sprawling edge city of North Charleston, only a few miles from state senator Glenn McConnell's emporium of Confederate kitsch, aptly symbolized the postindustrial, post–Cold War, postmodern landscape in which the commemorative initiative would take shape.

Most immediately, the *Hunley* project developed in the wake of intense controversy over the Confederate battle flag in South Carolina. The Republican mobilization in defense of the flag atop the capitol dome in the spring of 1995 spun off a quick state response to the discovery of the submarine. Within three weeks of Cussler's announcement, the legislature established a nine-member commission charged with ensuring that the vessel remained in South Carolina and directing state plans for its preservation. Flag champion McConnell, the measure's chief sponsor, became chair of the *Hunley* Commission. Under his leadership, promotion of the *Hunley* consistently followed flag defenders' strategies for adapting Confederate commemoration to a society transformed by the civil rights movement and the Vietnam War. The notion that Confederate military personnel aboard the *Hunley* shared in responsibility for Confederate proslavery objectives reflected "agendas driven by bias or prejudice." "We cannot let those who subscribe wholly to political correctness use the race card as the trump card on all matters of heritage and history," McConnell maintained. The crew members who died on the *Hunley* deserved praise for their "duty, bravery, ingenuity and sacrifice."[45]

The addition of "ingenuity" to the boilerplate Confederate virtues distinguished the new undertaking from the flag campaign and marked a self-conscious updating of Confederate remembrance. Although popular attention to the *Hunley* during the Cold War had receded from the previous emphasis that the "leaking little biscuit box" was a death trap, grander claims about the submarine's technological sophistication began to develop with the flag controversy and inflated exponentially upon discovery of the vessel. Underwater archaeologist Mark Newell and submarine enthusiast Mark Ragan, whose competing bids to find the *Hunley* shared similar neo-Confederate sympathies, asserted separately in September 1993 that the vessel was "ahead of its time." When Cussler announced the success of his effort, Newell called the submarine "a great example of the technological wizardry" of the South. On the day a salvage crew lifted the wreck from the water, Ragan declared that "the *Hunley* was cutting-edge technology in the 1860s, as advanced for that period as our spacecraft are today." Other promoters of the project indulged in similar hyperbole. State attorney general Charlie Condon told Congress in July 1995 that the vessel was "a scientific breakthrough that changed the course of naval warfare." McConnell maintained that "maritime history and the technology man uses to conquer the sea changed for all times" with the sinking of the *Housatonic*. Writers relying on the press releases of the conservation team routinely made comparable assertions. Charleston newspaper reporters Brian Hicks and Schuyler Kropf wrote that at the time of its completion, the *Hunley* "was the most technologically advanced weapon ever built."[46]

These claims were of course shameless exaggerations. Submarine historian Thomas Parrish more accurately noted that the *Hunley* "did not involve any technical advance on the work of Robert Fulton." As lead *Hunley* designer James McClintock was well aware, the cutting edge of submarine technology by the 1860s was the problem of engine propulsion. McClintock reported after the war that he "spent much time and money" trying to develop a motor for the *Hunley*. He failed, after which he fell back on a crank. Even the nicest features of the final design were mere wrinkles, not breakthroughs like an engine or even a periscope. Moreover, that design exercised no influence over any future technological developments, contrary to millennial claims that "the *Hunley* is to submarine warfare what the Wright brothers' airplane is to aviation." Unlike the Wright brothers' airplane, the *Hunley* disappeared into the sea in February 1864, after which little detailed information about the vessel was available until Alexander published his memoirs in 1902. Knowledge about the *Hunley* did not advance the development of the modern submarine; to the contrary, the development of the modern submarine advanced knowledge about the *Hunley*. Not surprisingly, a longtime submarine specialist in the U.S. Navy's historical research branch remarked that "I'm hard-pressed to think the *Hunley* was terribly important technologically."[47]

If the *Hunley* replicated technology that Fulton had demonstrated more than sixty years earlier, the effort to conserve the Confederate submarine was much closer to the technological forefront of the day. Even the most commonplace tools of the operation—including portable computers, cellular telephones, and the cable television networks that presented programs about the *Hunley*—had matured only within the past few decades. More specialized equipment, such as shipboard magnetometers and navigational programs or the apparatus used in DNA analysis and metals conservation, was often newer. Indeed, the project claimed not merely to apply the latest innovations but to develop original knowledge. Concerned that X-ray examination of the vessel might alter the DNA in the skeletal remains of the crew members, conservators conducted experiments on the genetic consequences of electromagnetic radiation and presented the results at professional meetings. One senior official called plans to remove sea salt from iron through the use of superpressurized water potentially "a turning point in the history of archaeology and conservation." The theme of technological innovation closely linked the supposed *Hunley* story of the Civil War to the *Hunley* story of the twenty-first century. "The *Hunley* technologically was just on the cutting edge," summarized McConnell. "She was when she was built, just like she is now on the eve of conservation."[48]

The new argument for the significance of the *Hunley* reimagined the relationship between past and present. Earlier commemoration had understood the present as heir to the past. The postexcavation venture recognized the present as fabricator of the past. "The fourth crew of the *Hunley*," as McConnell liked to call supporters of the conservation project, had raised the sunken vessel and now proposed to "complete the journey." The twenty-first-century pilots choosing that final destination regarded their work as integral to the historical importance of the Confederate submarine. Seeking the "reconditioning" of the *Hunley*, not merely the preservation of its wreck, they reenacted the refitting that Chapman had depicted during the war.[49] They summoned a gleaming arsenal of advanced technology to show that the fish-boat was a marvelous craft rather than an iron coffin, and they emphasized that it remained a uniquely valuable vehicle for scientific research. Obligingly, every new book and documentary about the Confederate submarine devoted substantial attention to its rediscovery and conservation. The highly visible processes of commemoration reinforced interpretations of the *Hunley* that departed sharply from precedent.

The insistence on the technological achievement of the *Hunley* superficially resembled Lost Cause pride in Confederate torpedoes, but the difference between the two commemorative eras was much deeper than the shift in attention from underwater explosives to submarines. Late-nineteenth-century remembrance of the *Hunley* retraced a chain of technological progress linked to the status of the nation-state. The moral imperative of national self-defense justified the use of the weapon, and the Confederate government was the key lever of innovation through the establishment of the torpedo bureau and the efforts of military engineers. In contrast, twenty-first-century remembrance of the *Hunley* undercut the nation-state. Innovation resulted from Hunley's entrepreneurial instinct to take advantage of the Confederate authorization of privateers and reap financial rewards for disrupting the Union blockade. A television documentary produced by *National Geographic*, a financial partner of the conservation project, characterized the impetus as "one part patriotism and two parts profit motive." The government was an impediment to progress, most notably when Beauregard seized the vessel from its builders and assigned command to a naval officer, who promptly sank it with the loss of five crew members. The Confederate failure to compensate the entrepreneurs was important to the historical interpretation by which the state of South Carolina asserted ownership of the vessel after salvage. Although controlled by military personnel in the *Housatonic* attack, the submarine remained private property, according to the *Hunley* Commission, not part of the Confederate war machinery forfeited to the United States.[50]

That argument failed in its immediate objective, as the federal government retained title to the *Hunley*, but South Carolina received permanent custody of the vessel and proceeded to organize the conservation effort as a model for the privatization of the polity. Rather than following the provisions of state law that assigned responsibility for underwater artifacts to the Office of the State Archaeologist, the legislature entrusted the project to the special *Hunley* Commission, which in turn delegated day-to-day operating authority to the Friends of the *Hunley*, a nonprofit corporation. Though championed as a vehicle to attract tax-deductible private contributions to the project, the Friends relied almost entirely on public funds. A prizewinning investigative report concluded in May 2006 that about 85 percent of *Hunley* spending originated in tax revenues. State appropriations channeled through the commission were only the most obvious funding source. The project also depended heavily on grants from the Department of Defense and contributions from a wide variety of state agencies for rent, security, employee benefits, videotaping, and other services. These public resources did not carry commensurate public accountability. The legislature exempted the *Hunley* Commission from the state procurement code, and the Friends claimed similar exemption, awarding lucrative public relations contracts to a prominent Republican political consultant without soliciting competitive bids. The Friends also claimed exemption from the Freedom of Information Act, a position the corporation litigated at considerable expense before turning over some requested documents to moot a lawsuit brought by a citizen gadfly who sought to establish the applicability of the disclosure statute. The Friends controlled all revenues from the sale of fleece vests, golf balls, coasters, mouse pads, and other *Hunley* tchotchkes despite the federal agreement with South Carolina that specifically allotted those funds to the state. After the newspaper exposé generated controversy, the state audit agency concluded that the organizational structure of the *Hunley* project precluded an official audit of its revenues and expenditures. Confederate remembrance had successfully evaded most of the mechanisms governing traditional public agencies.[51]

Privatization sought to supplant the Confederate vision that shaped the early Lost Cause. The Commission and the Friends eventually transferred much of the responsibility for conservation of the *Hunley* to Clemson University, which agreed to make the commemorative effort the centerpiece of a new Charleston campus centered on engineering research applicable to repair of bridges and other infrastructure as well as renewable energy and similar environmentally attractive fields. Like the *Hunley* venture, the Clemson University Restoration Institute depended heavily on public funding. The goal, however, was for the Restoration Institute to become the nucleus of a corporate research park. That plan offered a striking update of Thomas Green Clemson's appeal to use the funds raised by the Ladies' Calhoun Memorial Association as the starting point for a college that would perpetuate Calhoun's political principles. Both Clemson and the state university later bearing his name regarded remembrance as a fulcrum for community development. In the 1870s, however, the citizens envisioned for the commemorative school were young South Carolinians. In the twenty-first century, the citizens envisioned for the commemorative research park were multinational corporations. The attack of the *Hunley* conservation project on government institutions made its political application of the Confederate submarine diametrically opposite to the political legacy of the torpedo.

Open intervention of the present into the past also characterized stark differences between *Hunley* remembrance in the early twentieth century and the early twenty-first century. Lost Cause tales of a doomed but successful vessel translated Confederate defeat into Christian mystery. *Hunley* enthusiasts of the millennial era sought to unify their narrative by situating the submarine in another set of mysteries. The location of the wreck was the keynote mystery, solved after off-and-on searching by a variety of adventurers over almost forty years. Promoters of *Hunley* remembrance also maintained that the vessel had been shrouded in secrecy through the war. Writers relying on publicity releases from the Friends described the *Hunley* as "the secret hope of the Confederacy." Little evidence shows that the Confederacy protected information about the *Hunley* more assiduously than information about any routine military operation, and the fish-boat was thoroughly familiar to Charleston socialites as well as Confederate soldiers and sailors, some of whom kept the Union fleet well informed about the vessel. But the claim that the *Hunley* had been a secret weapon reinforced the argument that it was technologically advanced, like the Manhattan Project. The guide leading the first tour of the conservation laboratory told visitors, "This was a top-secret, a top-top-secret piece of military hardware."[52]

The climactic mystery, and a prime theater for the supremacy of the present, was the explanation for the final sinking of the *Hunley*. This question had rarely interested the Lost Cause faithful who understood the submarine to have sunk almost every time a crew embarked. But the new commitment to the vessel's technological sophistication made the exact fate of Dixon and his crew a challenging puzzle that the conservation project proposed to solve through massive deployment of advanced technology. The laboratory was "basically just a large forensic scene," reported a senior archaeologist. Participants frequently compared the undertaking to popular television series in which police officers used technology to crack difficult mysteries. Patricia Cornwell, a best-selling author of forensic thrillers, donated five hundred thousand dollars to the *Hunley* project and sponsored a staff seminar led by representatives of the Law Enforcement Innovation Center at the University of Tennessee, the Georgia Bureau of Investigation, and the Oak Ridge National Laboratory.[53] Whatever the final result of investigation, it was clear that as in most crime novels and television programs, the lead role in the mystery would be played by the detectives rather than the victims.

The gulf between Cold War praise for George Dixon's character and later fascination with his personality similarly inserted the present conspicuously into the past. In depictions like the *Great Adventure* television program, Dixon was an exemplary leader who forged his military unit in the tradition of the war-movie genre. In the flood of *Hunley* publications and dramatizations that followed the discovery of the wreck, Dixon was instead most memorable for a romantic narrative composed by Mark Ragan in 1995. In the Battle of Shiloh, a minié ball struck Dixon and bent the twenty-dollar coin he was carrying in his pocket. Plausibly convinced that the gold piece had prevented the ball from severing his femoral artery, Dixon had it inscribed "My Life Preserver" and carried the ostensibly lucky charm with him on the night of his death. Ragan resurrected a 1904 newspaper story that claimed that Dixon's sweetheart had given him the coin when the 21st Alabama Infantry Regiment left Mobile in March 1862 and told him to hold onto it in remembrance of her, which would have been an unusual use of cash as a keepsake. Ragan and his fellow *Hunley* enthusiasts also credited the lore of a southern family that the unnamed sweetheart was Queenie Bennett, who was fourteen years old in March 1862. With vigorous promotion, the tale became a fresh focus of twenty-first-century Confederate remembrance. McConnell called the finding of the "legendary" coin in Dixon's skeletal remains tantamount to finding Cinderella's golden slipper and estimated its market value at between 8 and 10 million dollars, considerably more than the highest price ever paid at auction for any coin up to that time.[54]

Whether Dixon in fact received the gold coin from a sweetheart and whether that woman was in fact Queenie Bennett, the broader point was the sudden attention to his personal life. The new Confederate idol needed "human interest" at least as much as exemplary values. If sufficiently engaging, his habits did not necessarily have to be particularly commendable. Dixon was evidently a riverboat dandy who carried onto the *Hunley* a showy diamond tie pin; his limited worldly possessions at the time of his death included a single trunk containing nine linen shirts, three pairs of cashmere trousers, an imported straw hat, and another diamond pin. The Friends of the *Hunley* smiled that he "cherished nice things."[55] Millennial commemoration yearned to depict the Confederate officer's unofficial side, love struck or foppish. He was not so much a hero as a historical celebrity, dependent on the Friends of the *Hunley* as his publicity machine.

Forensic reconstruction of the *Hunley* crew members' faces further re-envisioned the object of commemoration. The only wartime list of Dixon's final crew was a letter sent by a Charleston torpedo officer answering Dabney Maury's request in mid-April 1864 for the names of the other men aboard during the February attack. The response provided two full names, three surnames with first initials, and one surname, leaving one man completely forgotten; at least one of the names may have been wrong.[56] This documentation—eagerly sought, incompletely supplied, left unresolved—serves as a small but representative example of the complex experience of identifying the vast numbers of dead bodies during the Civil War. *Hunley* enthusiasts in the millennial era would try much harder than Confederate officers to identify the crew members, relying on DNA analysis and extensive genealogical research. Most remarkably, the project aimed to reconstruct the faces of the dead on the basis of DNA samples and skeletal remains. McConnell promised "98% accuracy" in the controversial process. Like the story of Dixon's gold coin, the effort sought to create personalities for the crew members. "Smoking a pipe is a personal characteristic that should be portrayed in these men," decreed the anthropologist who headed up the reconstructions, after studying the dental remains. "It's part of who they were." No longer was it enough for them to have been Confederate martyrs. After the burial of the crew's remains, the Friends of the *Hunley* newsletter expressed satisfaction that "the world was not watching strangers being laid to rest, but rather people whose faces we now know and personal histories we can remember."[57]

The unapologetic intrusion of the technologically advanced present into the realm of the past, vividly illustrated by the facial reconstructions, furnished the plot for the most significant new *Hunley* novel, Stan Clardy's *TimeLight* (2003). The title referred to a central addition to the Confederate narrative, the claim that Dixon had signaled success by shining a blue light after sinking the *Housatonic*. A freelance writer proposed this story for the first time in 1987 on the basis of three documents: the testimony of a *Housatonic* survivor that when the USS *Canandaigua* came to the rescue he saw a blue light on the water just ahead of the arriving Union vessel; the report of Confederate officer Olin Dantzler two nights after the *Hunley*

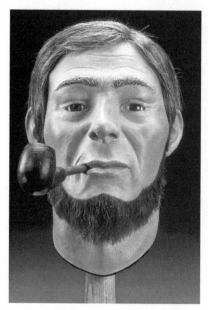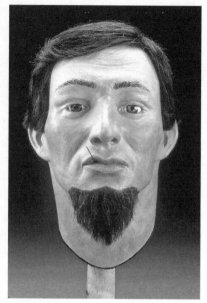

Facial reconstructions of *Hunley* crew members C. Lumpkin and Frank Collins. Courtesy of the Friends of the *Hunley*.

disappeared that "the signals agreed to be given in case the boat wished a light to be exposed at this post as a guide for its return were observed and answered"; and the hearsay recollection of an elderly Charlestonian after the war that Dixon had told Dantzler "when they bid each other good-bye, that if he came off safe he would show two blue lights. The lights never appeared."[58] Poorly as this evidence supported the tale loaded atop it, *Hunley* promoters treasured the blue light. The Friends of the *Hunley* named its newsletter the *Blue Light*. The supposed incident was crucial because it implied that the sinking of the *Hunley* was not immediately and inevitably linked to the sinking of the *Housatonic* and that the submarine had worked well in the attack, even if misfortune struck later. These claims faced severe challenges apart from the weakness of the supposedly underlying evidence. The discovery of the *Hunley* in close proximity to the *Housatonic* and the failure to find a source of blue light aboard converged with commonsense skepticism that Dixon would have shined such a signal while surrounded by Union vessels and more than four miles from the Confederate shore. In April 2006, a senior project archaeologist bravely pronounced the story of the blue light improbable in the *Blue Light*. But the Friends continued to feature Dixon's triumphal gesture in the official summary of *Hunley* history.[59] In Clardy's novel, the blue light became a portal for travel across time.

TimeLight begins in an Orwellian 2019 in which the United States prohibits sympathetic remembrance of the Confederacy. Following a seizure of power by oppressive "unity activists" during the 1990s, devotees of constitutional liberty have gravitated toward a secretly subversive collection center for Confederate monuments removed from sites throughout the South. When the facility receives the White Point Garden memorial for the *Hunley*, an impressively innovative submarine that almost sank the *Housatonic* but failed for lack of sufficient speed, protagonist Henry Bellingham meets two men who share his admiration for the Confederacy and his disaffection with the current condition of the United States. Albert Gray, a brilliant African American scientist who has secretly invented a time machine, believes that the *Hunley* attack on the *Housatonic* is an accessible point in time at which intervention could change the lamentable course of history. Upon learning that Bellingham is an engineer who has designed computer simulations of improvements that would have enabled the *Hunley* to succeed, Dr. Gray sends Bellingham and Woody Miller back to Charleston in the days surrounding the submarine's arrival from Mobile. They work their way into the *Hunley* circle, and Bellingham introduces several decisive adjustments. Miller becomes a member of the crew, dying after Dixon's blue light signals the sinking of the *Housatonic*. Bellingham returns to 2019 with his new Confederate fiancée. Now the oppressive regime did not secure power in the 1990s. "The hated checkpoints which cluttered the roadways of America were gone. They had never existed. . . . The president was still limited to two four-year terms, and it appeared that the constitution had not been suspended as before. There were no roaming mobs of 'Unity Activists' and their brand of vigilante terrorism to intimidate southerners."[60] The discovery of the successful *Hunley* in 1995 had filled southerners with a pride that enabled them to protect Confederate monuments and save the United States.

Clardy, who presented a musical tribute to the *Hunley* crew at the memorial service organized by the Friends for the burial of the crew in April 2004, distilled several of the main themes of the commemorative initiative in *TimeLight*. His cynical depiction of Gray typified increasingly extravagant claims about the number and loyalty of black Confederate soldiers.[61] Recognizing that the flag controversy of the 1990s was a watershed in white South Carolinians' integration of Civil War remembrance and civil rights remembrance, friends of the *Hunley* longed to prove that celebration of the Confederacy was not morally obsolete. The pursuit of this goal through the invention of a futuristic Civil War submarine yielded a postmodern commemoration that jettisoned all *Hunley* precedents and injected the conservation project squarely into the historical narrative, much as Clardy's fictional engineer used twenty-first-century expertise to help the fish-boat sink a Union ship. Concluding that Americans in 2003 lived not in a nation forged in the 1860s but in a thoroughly contingent culture shaped by time travelers in 2019, Clardy's novel challenged the basic concept of historical reality. Similar philosophical questions would surround the funerals for *Hunley* crew members and the making of a *Hunley* museum.

Clardy's *TimeLight* typified twenty-first-century *Hunley* remembrance in embracing science fiction rather than the historical romance tradition exemplified by Cyrus Townsend Brady's *A Little Traitor to the South* and Francis Van Wyck Mason's *Our Valiant Few*. The other *Hunley* novels written after the discovery of the submarine also followed fantasy genres. Dixon's crew became zombies in Derek Smith's *The Sentinels* (2001), murdering or imprisoning African Americans and northern tourists in Charleston until the salvage of the vessel. David Stallworth and Dianne Brady identified the *Hunley* and its excavation as crucial to a titanic collision between biblical fundamentalism and evolutionary science in the Christian apocalyptic novel *Why the Wind Blows* (2006). Promoters of the *Hunley* began to claim that its foremost literary remembrance was Jules Verne's *Twenty Thousand Leagues under the Sea*, despite the lack of evidence that the French novelist ever heard of the then-obscure Confederate torpedo boat.[62] Not coincidentally, Verne also stood at the head of the precedents claimed by the steampunk fad of the late twentieth and early twenty-first centuries. His fiction particularly suited that aesthetic because he expanded on familiar nineteenth-century machines when proposing futuristic technology. Steampunk historicized Verne's approach to invent pseudo-Victorian airships and submersibles, much as *Hunley* enthusiasts described the Civil War vessel as a long-lost artifact decades ahead of its time. Shaped by the historical romance and its modernist challengers during the days of William Gilmore Simms and Mary Boykin Chesnut, the Confederate imagination now turned toward the fantastic.

Hunley commemoration mirrored the steampunk pose of ambivalence toward current technology. Steampunk invited a fond look back at an era when ordinary citizens might singlehandedly make machines or at least understand their workings; *Hunley* enthusiasts reveled in its intricate but readily comprehensible workings. At the same time, technological innovation also rendered the steampunk nineteenth century a dystopia. The most spectacular social disorder of the age, the Civil War featured prominently in steampunk fiction, often in a modified form that permanently blurred lines between warfare and civilian life.[63] The commemorative depiction of Charleston in the age of the *Hunley* was a typically grim setting, as bombarded Confederates scrambled desperately for supplies denied by the Union blockade.

But steampunk was not tragedy; it was fantasy. Bleak as a hypothetical gaslit society dominated by analytical engines might have been, the steampunk fad thrived on Photoshop and the Internet with the same brio with which the *Hunley* conservation project celebrated current technology. Although the faux-retro look differed from styles promoted at the Apple Store, steampunk was characteristic of the millennial era in urging Americans to love innovative technology for more than mere functionality. *Hunley* remembrance, too, focused on aesthetic appreciation rather than operational performance. By far the feature most often identified by admirers as evidence for the sophisticated design of the submarine was its streamlined profile, though the hand-cranked vessel lumbered through the water at an absurdly slow pace. The conservation director speculated that it must have made "a very fine entrance" into Charleston Harbor; McConnell called it "a sleek technological marvel." Promoters invested in the belief that the salvage constituted a revelation quickly dismissed the problem that the boat looked much as Chapman had depicted it. Without citing any evidence, Hicks and Kropf reported that "for nearly a century Chapman would be ridiculed as fanciful and inaccurate. There was no way, most people would argue, that the *Hunley* could be that hydrodynamic." The elegant Confederate submarine was a nineteenth-century daydream come true.[64]

"Steampunk is to science what civil war re-enactions are to history," observed a leading pseudo-Victorian gadgeteer.[65] *Hunley* commemoration stood at the convergence of the analogous riffs on nineteenth-century technology. As breathless praise for the submarine injected a future into the Civil War, meticulous replication of period weaponry, uniforms, and other military gear proposed to present "living history." Reenactment was a performance that insisted on the power of outward appearances to constitute inward authenticity. Reenactors described the wearing of simulated uniforms as an earnest tribute to men who had worn identical dress. Participants also believed that scrupulous imitation of Civil War costumes and diet and military routine—without regard for nineteenth-century politics or religion or social patterns—might lead to a "period rush," an over-

Burial of final *Hunley* crew, April 17, 2004. Glenn McConnell stands at left.
Courtesy of Evening Post Publishing.

whelming sense of living in the past. Judged authentic by the community
of Civil War reenactors, these dreamlike experiences were private fantasies
made real.[66]

The April 2004 funeral for Dixon and his crew was the most extravagant claim for the authenticity of Civil War reenactment. In preparatory
publicity for the occasion, organizers emphasized that the event was not a
reenactment but a genuine funeral. Participants would bury the remains
of eight individuals, following standard Episcopal rites. From the outset,
however, the *Hunley* Commission was committed to interring Dixon and
his crew alongside Hunley and his crew after a grand costumed procession. The opportunity for a dress rehearsal developed when a construction project at the Citadel enabled state archaeologists to confirm the
long-standing suspicion that in the 1940s the school had built its football
stadium atop a Confederate cemetery that contained the graves of the five
men who died in the initial Charleston sinking of the *Hunley*. In March
2000, several hundred reenactors accompanied these exhumed skeletons
in a procession from the Battery to Magnolia Cemetery. The burial of Dixon
and his crew four years later was a much more elaborate affair that attracted three hundred journalists from seventy news organizations for the
eight-hour-long ceremony. Newspaper reporters estimated that the procession involved four thousand reenactors in Civil War military costumes

and several dozen women in pseudo-Victorian mourning regalia. About ten thousand onlookers lined the parade route; hundreds more crowded the Magnolia Cemetery grounds. McConnell, who participated in the raiment of a three-star Confederate general, billed the spectacle as "one of the biggest historical events of our lifetime if not the biggest funeral ever to be held in South Carolina."[67]

"We want to make it as authentic as we can," McConnell promised in July 1999 as he anticipated the funeral of the first crew. He envisioned "a processional true to the era, just like the one featured in tonight's TV movie." And indeed, the ceremonies in 2000 and 2004 were more faithful to the Turner Network Television (TNT) movie *The Hunley* than to any model from the Civil War. As scholars have observed, the war followed hard upon a transitional phase in American attitudes toward death. The proliferation of rural cemetery corporations like Magnolia reflected a privatization of death, a recognition that the end of most individuals' lives profoundly touched family members but could not have much wider direct emotional impact in large-scale communities. Increasing formalization of dress for nonfamily mourners acknowledged "that genuine grief might not be counted upon to carry the attendant through the ceremony with proper gravity." Amid widespread anxiety over this genteel hypocrisy, the hurried funeral ceremonies of the Civil War were emotionally powerful precisely because they broke through hollow conventions. William D. Washington's painting *Burial of Latané* (1864) was a Confederate icon that depicted an improvisational, heartfelt interment as the expression of a political community that connected strangers.[68]

The few wartime funerals comparable to the *Hunley* pomp centered exclusively on elite individuals. The elaborate Charleston rites in July 1861 for Confederate generals Barnard Bee and Francis Bartow and Hampton's Legion lieutenant colonel Beverly Jenkins Johnson, killed at Manassas in the first major battle of the war, made for a hefty civic occasion. The *Mercury* reported that not since the legendary funeral for Calhoun had "so universal a gush of sorrow welled up from the hearts of our people." The rank-and-file Charleston volunteers who died in the same battle, however, remained in unmarked graves where they fell. The most direct wartime precedent for the millennial *Hunley* funerals, the 1864 service for Horace Hunley, similarly reinforced military and social hierarchy. Beauregard ordered the captain's interment "with the military honors due to his rank," which turned out to be two companies of soldiers and a band of music. Only afterward was the rest of the crew extracted from the submarine and,

Mort Künstler, *The Final Mission.* © 2003 by Mort Künstler, Inc.
Courtesy of Künstler Enterprises, Ltd.

at the expense of Hunley's executor, buried without military escort.[69] To
the extent that formal Confederate funerals imagined community, it was a
community defined by stratification.

The climactic funeral for Dixon's crew shunned these commemorative
precedents. The scheduling of the ceremony for April 17 underscored that
Memorial Day was a dead institution. Unlike traditional Lost Cause orators,
McConnell carefully avoided public affairs in his eulogy. Focusing on the
crew's thoughts moments before the final departure, he structured his eulogy as a complement to Mort Künstler's newly unveiled painting *The Final
Mission*, which the *Hunley* Commission commissioned from the foremost
maker of the Civil War prints that McConnell had long sold at csa Galleries. As Künstler's work incorporated the faces that forensic speculation
offered for the crew members, McConnell emphasized their conjectural
personalities, most notably Dixon's supposed love for Queenie Bennett.
Commission member and leading Charleston reenactor Randall Burbage,
who delivered the eulogy in White Point Garden before the procession left
for the cemetery, similarly imagined the dead as personal acquaintances.
"It's hard to say goodbye," Burbage concluded tearfully. "We have come to
regard you as family."[70] Such sentiments disregarded Victorian anxieties
about ersatz grief for strangers as well as Lost Cause veneration for the
Confederate dead as representatives of an ideological and cultural com-

munity. The spectacle envisioned a more direct emotional connection to the crew, a collective "period rush." Reenactors did not don simulated Civil War uniforms and mourning garb to lend authenticity to the interment of human remains; they used the bones of Dixon and his crew to lend authenticity to the pretensions of Civil War reenactment.

The illusion of unmediated entry into the past was also central to the last *Hunley* commemorative initiative to follow from the salvage of the vessel, the preparations for its display in a museum. The *Hunley* Commission initially planned to place the rehabilitated submarine in the Charleston Museum. By the summer of 2001, however, McConnell decided to promote a separate *Hunley* museum and arranged for the state to buy a collection of Confederate ship models, maritime prints, and naval artifacts to begin outfitting such a facility. The purchase price was six times the amount that the South Carolina State Museum had spent on all acquisitions during the past ten years, which illustrated not only McConnell's political influence but also the scale of the museum he had in mind. "This will probably be the No. 1 tourist attraction in South Carolina if not one of the greatest tourist attractions in the world," he predicted.[71] The commission received proposals from the municipalities of Mount Pleasant, Charleston, and North Charleston for budgets running from 29 to 40 million dollars. The acceptance of the North Charleston bid reflected several factors, including the municipal commitment to large subsidies for the most lavishly scaled proposal, the lack of competing tourist attractions in the sparsely developed city, the proximity to the *Hunley* conservation laboratory and future site of the Clemson University Restoration Institute, and the opportunity to leverage real estate speculation in the former Charleston Naval Shipyard. Underlying these considerations was McConnell's clear vision that the museum "will not only house the *Hunley* but through modern technology bring the project to life as it creates virtual reality."[72] The antithesis of the Confederate reliquaries founded a century earlier, the *Hunley* museum would center on simulation.

Despite the huge expenditures for salvage and restoration of the *Hunley*, the commission showed little confidence in the artifact's unique power to stir the historical imagination. Copies took several forms. Tours of the conservation laboratory invited visitors to sit inside a replica built by the production team for the 1999 television movie. The commission licensed a Myrtle Beach developer to open an interactive exhibit, *The H. L. Hunley Experience*, in a family entertainment complex. The *Blue Light* promised that the full-sized model "will truly allow you to see and feel what it was like to be aboard this historical marvel." The commission also insisted that all bids for the *Hunley* museum offer waterfront property because McConnell aimed to offer visitors the Disney-like chance to ride through the water in a working *Hunley* reproduction, with anachronistic safety devices.[73]

The climax to these simulacra entailed more sophisticated technology. Museum visitors would encounter lifelike holographic representations of the crew members that would be able to speak. An advanced projection system would present a version of the crew's experience on the night of the attack on the *Housatonic*. "We have the capability for you to meet the crew of the *Hunley* and to go on the journey into history with the crew," McConnell claimed. "The technology exists to create virtual reality of the inside of the submarine, and we will do that." Manipulation of visitors' sensory perceptions would be essential to their inward response. McConnell promised that "this facility will embody the newest forms of computer technology including virtual reality so that the visitors will have an emotional experience when they come to the museum."[74] The fundamental concept of the *Hunley* museum was much the same as the premise of the *Hunley* funeral, although generated by highly complex apparatus rather than facsimiles of nineteenth-century military equipment. Virtual-reality exhibits and Civil War reenactment were twin expressions of Confederate commemoration as fantasy.

This approach contrasted sharply with the memorial imagination to which Charleston mayor Joseph P. Riley Jr. appealed unsuccessfully in presenting his city's bid for the museum. When the *Hunley* first arrived from Mobile in August 1863, he noted, Confederates removed it from the train and hauled it by carriage "amid great fanfare" to a wharf at the end of Calhoun Street. The city of Charleston proposed to situate the *Hunley* museum in the same place. From that location, a visitor could look out on Fort Sumter, the other fortifications that defended Charleston Harbor during the Civil War, the point at which Confederates pulled the sunken vessel from the water and removed the bodies of Horace Hunley and his crew, the site at which Dixon and his men sank the *Housatonic*, and the area in which divers found the submarine in 1995 and the salvage team raised it five years later. When the city withdrew its bid for a separate museum and returned to the proposal to install the *Hunley* in the Charleston Museum, complemented by a *Hunley* park on the waterfront, Riley went on to suggest that "this site without a building becomes a far more powerful and emotional place."[75] His observation returned to the perspective through which Theodore Jervey's protagonist Rupert Gordon had looked along the water and back at the fish-boat in *The Elder Brother*.

Riley's argument was that historical memory abided in place. Like spatial orientation, remembrance was a relational process. The presence of the past depended on the density of reference points. The climactic phase of *Hunley* tributes dispensed with such fidelity to locality and connections between events. *Hunley* admirers instead proposed to obliterate the distinction between past and present. Like Dr. Albert Gray's invention in *Time-Light*, the hyperreal *Hunley* funerals and museum sought to provide an unmediated experience of the Civil War. Critics of the Confederate battle flag may have protested that Confederate commemoration was obsolescent, but the *Hunley* project aimed for the Confederate image to outlast the fundamental concept of time.

During the relative lull in *Hunley* remembrance shortly before the controversy over the Confederate battle flag heated up and divers found the wreck, journalist James Kloeppel suggested a fresh view of the significance of the *Housatonic* sinking. Far from a triumph of stealth technology, the *Hunley* was spotted from a distance by Union lookout Robert Flemming as it traveled on the surface of the water. The nearest officer dismissed the prompt report because Flemming was an African American. Not until white sailors confirmed the sighting did the *Housatonic* respond, and by then it was too late to escape or deploy cannons.[76] The narrative encapsulated much of the Civil War and Reconstruction era by highlighting white northerners' slowness in attending to black Americans' alarm over slavery. That failure resulted in the destruction of the Union ship, but the Confederate boat had also sunk; another vessel had rescued the surviving Federals.

This interpretation gained little traction in the enthusiasm for the *Hunley* that followed a few years later. The suggestion that the *Housatonic* might well have stopped the *Hunley* by heeding Flemming does not appear in any of the books published after discovery of the wreck.[77] His warning reduced to supportive evidence for his postexplosion report that he saw a blue light on the water, Flemming became part of a story about supposed technological innovation rather than race. The Confederacy was not a product of outmoded values; it was a realm of extraordinary possibilities.

History would not easily surrender the *Hunley* to its new mission as the flagship of the steampunk Confederacy. The wreck began to disintegrate as soon as the excavation team removed it from the ocean. Conservators relied on prolonged immersion in cold water, sophisticated chemical treatment, and a steady flow of funds to prevent the iron hull from corroding. Publicists undertook similarly energetic measures to prevent the flag debate from tarnishing the submarine. They repudiated almost all professional scholarship on the meanings of the Civil War and discarded a long legacy of Confederate commemoration. The approaches that prevailed in the late nineteenth century, the early twentieth century, and the Cold War were not adequate for the millennium. Only by breaking free from academic and previous popular interpretations and floating new stories about the marvelous *Hunley*, its crew, and its conservators could Confederate remembrance hope to present the past as a transcendent model for the future.

The project was the most audacious Civil War commemorative initiative of the era. The race against historical oblivion was daunting. But the friends of the *Hunley* believed in the blue light, the orgiastic future that year by year receded before them. So they cranked on, fish-boat against the current, borne back ceaselessly into the past.

Modern Times

TED PHILLIPS DIED exactly nine months after the final *Hunley* burial. He had brought his teenaged daughters to the spectacle so that they could see what the past was coming to mean in the society that they were entering and he was departing. His own funeral evoked community precedent more poignantly. St. Philip's Church was as full for his service as it had been at Calhoun's death in 1850; the building could never have held any more people. Ted and his family had a remarkable number of friends, but it pleased me to think that some mourners knew him only as a public figure. Although his sense of office differed from Calhoun's positions in government, Ted had come to represent Charleston in his time. For years, knowledgeable visitors to the city had been contacting him to arrange for one of his tours of Magnolia Cemetery. He had almost completed his book, and he had helped to shape the institution as a trustee. He soon established a posthumous influence on the cemetery landscape. His widow brilliantly chose to mark his burial place with a large boulder reminiscent of the family retreat in the South Carolina mountains. As singular at Magnolia as Timrod's grave was in the Trinity Cathedral

churchyard, the monument signaled a correspondence between the antiquarian and the poet.[1]

Both stones probably rolled over in September 2006 when the Confederate poet laureate drew national attention for the first time since the Timrod Revival a century earlier. A listener had entered lyrics from Bob Dylan's
new album *Modern Times* into an Internet search engine and determined
that the record incorporated about a dozen snippets from Timrod's poetry
without attribution. Suzanne Vega, one of countless performers to flourish in the singer-songwriter role popularized by Dylan, suggested in the
New York Times that this practice violated the ethical standards of musical composition. Poet and critic Robert Polito retorted that accusations of
plagiarism confused "art with a term paper" and that the Timrod allusions
typified Dylan's tendency to make "Modernist collages," a category that
presumably encompassed postmodern pastiches. Ted would have reveled
in Dylan's interest in the South Carolinian whom Vega called "a forgotten
Civil War–era poet." Ted listened mostly to jazz, but he was a Dylan fan.
The memoir *Chronicles: Volume One* (2004) was one of the last books he
read before he entered the hospital for the final time. Dylan's recollections
of Manhattan in the early 1960s framed his later turn to Timrod by empha-
sizing the budding songwriter's fascination with the language of the Civil
War era. "It wasn't like it was another world, but the same one only with
more urgency," Dylan remarked as he recalled reading period newspapers
on microfilm in the New York Public Library. He concluded that "back
there, America was put on the cross, died and was resurrected. There was
nothing synthetic about it. The godawful truth of that would be the all-
encompassing template behind everything I would write."[2]

Like most autobiographies, *Chronicles* revealed more about the period
in which the author wrote it than the period about which he was writing,
but Dylan's early work did feature some of the timeliest reflections on the
Civil War in the era of the centennial anniversary. He sought to update folk
wisdom associated with Abraham Lincoln for an age of nuclear anxiety in
"Talkin' World War III Blues" (1963). He situated the Civil War in a tradition of American militarism in "With God on Our Side" (1963). One of
the "outlined epitaphs" he printed on the album cover for *The Times They
Are A-Changin'* (1964) reported that a German acquaintance regarded
Adolf Hitler "as we here in the states / regard / Robert E. Lee." The implication was that both countries needed to reassess their national pasts.
More oblique but most important was his contribution to the pivotal centennial invocation of the Civil War, the March on Washington in August
1963. Shortly before Martin Luther King Jr. renovated the emancipatory

legacy of the Lincoln Memorial, Dylan illuminated another side of the oration site, its connection across Memorial Bridge to the plantation home of Robert E. Lee and the Confederate monument in Arlington National Cemetery. Dylan described the murderous white supremacism of the 1960s in an image he might have applied equally to many members of Lee's army:

> When the shadowy sun sets on the one
> That fired the gun
> He'll see by his grave
> On the stone that remains
> Carved next to his name
> His epitaph plain:
> Only a pawn in their game.[3]

Forty years after the centennial anniversary, Dylan's turn to Timrod was part of a reengagement with the Civil War and more specifically the Confederacy. The fresh attention resulted in part from a commission to contribute to the soundtrack for the film *Gods and Generals* (2003). Produced by Ted Turner shortly after his television movie about the *Hunley*, the cinematic adaptation of Jeff Shaara's novel was a patently pro-Confederate prequel to Turner's profitable *Gettysburg* (1993). But the attempt to channel current evangelicalism into a deepened admiration for Stonewall Jackson sparked little enthusiasm. Dylan's "'Cross the Green Mountain" suggested the failure of the Confederate commemorative project. The song consisted largely of extracts from Civil War poetry, all of it northern except for one line from Timrod. The last verse reprised Whitman's "Come Up from the Fields, Father" and concluded with the Whitmanesque reflection that "we loved each other more than we ever dared to tell." Dylan quoted three different poems by the Civil War pastor of the First Church in Cambridge, Massachusetts, as well as several other poems by New England Unitarians, although the theological perspective of the song was more apocalyptic. Dylan followed Lincoln's Second Inaugural Address in attributing the war to "an avenging God," and he mentioned a famous image of divine judgment on the slaveholding South, the 1833 meteor shower in which stars fell on Alabama. The single quotation from Timrod reversed the Confederate poet's point of view. In "Charleston" (1863), Timrod anxiously watched the "dim Atlantic line" of battle ships in the harbor, wondering if the Union would attempt another invasion of the city. Dylan looked at the "dim Atlantic line" from the opposite direction and noted that "the ravaged land lies for miles behind," a passage lifted from Melville.[4]

This inversion foreshadowed Dylan's more extensive manipulation of

Timrod's work in *Modern Times*. About half of the quotations were disconnected snippets that merely established Timrod as a presence on the
album, but the other half dozen allusions dominated "When the Deal Goes
Down." Dylan borrowed the melody for this composition from "Where the
Blue of the Night (Meets the Gold of the Day)," once the theme for Bing
Crosby's radio show. Dylan half offered the adapted tune as his own possible theme song, and he performed "When the Deal Goes Down" regularly
in concert. He promoted the song with an elaborate video featuring youthful actress Scarlett Johansson in a simulated splicing of home movies from
Dylan's formative years. The motif of an angelic muse was the ground on
which Dylan joined with Timrod.

"When the Deal Goes Down" mirrored a series of late antebellum poems
in which Timrod described the poetic vocation as a sublimated love that
transported the speaker to a timeless realm of artistic inspiration. In "A
Rhapsody of a Southern Winter Night" (1857), the speaker "strove, with
logic frailer than the flowers, / To justify a life of sensuous rest." Kissed by a
sprite, he experienced a blissful dawning of creative power across "a round
of precious hours." Dylan spoke for the blue of the night against Timrod's
gold of the day. In "When the Deal Goes Down," it was instead the "precious hours" of emotional intimacy that were "more frailer than flowers."
Timrod similarly organized "Retirement" (1857) around a contrast between
the public realm where "there is a wisdom that grows up in strife" and a
vastly more pleasant domesticity. Dylan replied that it was "In the still of
the night, in the world's ancient light / Where wisdom grows up in strife."
Timrod systematically identified flowers with poetry; Dylan retorted, "I
picked up a rose, and it poked through my clothes / I followed the winding
stream / I heard the deafening noise, I felt transient joys / I know they're
not what they seem."[5] These inverted echoes did not merely set an obscure
young Victorian aesthete against a jaded, elderly rock star, a juxtaposition
unlikely to interest Dylan. Timrod's narrative was significant because his
major antebellum work, "A Vision of Poesy" (1859), emphasized that his
dream was a delusion. Sublimated striving for Parnassus distanced the poet
from life and from readers. The true bard would recognize "all the weird
wonders of the common day." Even before the Civil War, the poet laureate
of the Confederacy personified an experience of defeat and self-recognition
that would complement Dylan's conception of modernity in *Modern Times*.[6]

The title of the album encapsulated several meanings. It paid homage
to the classic 1936 film by Charlie Chaplin, whom Dylan had long admired. Chaplin's decision to make a predominantly silent film despite the

ascendancy of talkies resonated with Dylan's determination to use some old-fashioned recording techniques on *Modern Times*. At the same time, Dylan's extensive lyrical borrowings situated *Modern Times* in the contemporary age of the Internet, which enabled listeners to identify lines taken even from a little-read author like Timrod almost immediately after the release of an album. Modern technology in some ways made the past more readily available than ever before.[7] The foreseeable brouhaha over Dylan's method, expanding on similar reactions to his other recent albums, also opened a parallel with the debt of Chaplin's *Modern Times* to René Clair's *A Nous la Liberté* (1931), which the French director treated as an honor even as the company that produced his film pursued a lawsuit for copyright infringement.

In a different register, the title of *Modern Times* signaled the influence of Ovid, the ancient Roman poet who shared with Timrod the historical spotlight as a source of lyrics for the record. Dylan had previously expressed interest in the classical conception of the ages of humanity, which was originated by Hesiod and adapted in Ovid's *Metamorphoses*. The schematization envisioned a decline from an idyllic golden age through silver and bronze periods to the present iron age, ushered in by the theft of fire and the creation of Pandora. By this definition, any art that addressed the primordial Fall could be modern. Expounding in 2001 on the iron age—or the stone age, as the rock star alternatively labeled it—Dylan noted that "something doesn't have to just drop out of the air yesterday to be current." The concluding song on *Modern Times* approvingly paraphrased poetry written by Ovid while in exile on the Black Sea during the first years of the common era.[8]

Timrod's shattered dream of a poetic paradise mapped the sectional conflict onto this mythic plane of modernity. For Dylan, the antebellum white South suffered from a cultural sterility inflicted by failure to acknowledge the strictures of the iron age, specifically the sinfulness of slaveholding. *Modern Times* saluted the countervailing creative impulse of the late 1850s in "Nettie Moore," the most ambitious composition on the album. The title and the first lines of the refrain derived from a blackface minstrel ballad published in the same year as Timrod's "A Rhapsody of a Southern Winter Night." A lamentation for a South Carolina slave sold down the river, "Gentle Nettie Moore" became Dylan's starting point for a tour through highlights of twentieth-century music.[9] This approach to history built on Dylan's nod toward Eric Lott's academic study of antebellum minstrelsy in the title of his previous album, *"Love and Theft"* (2001). As Lott pointed out, the blackface entertainment industry centered in New York City on the eve of the Civil War responded in sophisticated ways to current social and economic change. Progenitors of the downtown bohemian culture that Dylan inherited a century later in Greenwich Village, the minstrels assailed the coalescing class stratification of the urban Northeast. Their bawdy humor flouted middle-class moralism and drew on appreciative interactions with the African American culture they purloined and parodied. They understood the banishment from Eden that the young Timrod ignored. "Gentle Nettie Moore" was a song of exile, which Dylan identified in *Modern Times* as the characteristic location of modernity, whether in ancient Roman poetry or antebellum blackface minstrelsy. "The place I love best is a sweet memory," Dylan mourned at one point on the album. Timrod's eventual recognition of this alienation in "A Vision of Poesy" prepared him to become a voice of lasting significance in the Civil War.

Dylan similarly imagined the Confederacy as a state of exile in another important moment of his reengagement with the Civil War, his performance of "Dixie" in the film *Masked and Anonymous* (2003). The movie featured Dylan in the role of a renegade singer pressed by an authoritarian government to sabotage a political benefit concert with popular but vacuous rock-and-roll songs of social protest. Dylan and his band instead work up the genuinely dissident "Dixie." Thoroughly versed in the American musical tradition of comic utopias, Dylan recognized that the rebellious force of the Confederate anthem began not with secession but with blackface minstrelsy and its African American antecedents. First called "Dixie's Land," the song introduced by minstrel Dan Emmett in the late 1850s took its title from a black idiomatic expression for an imaginary place of contentment. The most thorough researcher has suggested that the term originally referred to an eighteenth-century maroon colony, known by the name of the absentee landowner, on an undeveloped island in Charleston Harbor. Whatever the etymology may have been, Emmett turned the legendary refuge from slavery into a satire of plantation life. The minstrel punned on the name of the male figure Dixie by incorporating an allusion to a relatively new slang term for the penis. If he could return from exile, the singer of the walk-around fantasized, he would take his stand in Dixie's land exactly as stallions stood at stud on horse farms. There he would live and "die," a euphemism for the achievement of orgasm. This depiction of "the land of cotton" as a latter-day Land of Cockaigne, a world turned upside down for the sexual satisfaction of the black male Dixie, converged with the antislavery attack on southern slave breeding. Multiple layers of black and white alienation lurked beneath the orchestration of Confederate memory. *Masked and Anonymous* underscored the point by featuring a blackface minstrel as a soothsaying personification of political courage.[10]

Confederate enthusiasm for "Dixie" earned no mention in an 1864 newspaper editorial Timrod wrote about southern desire for a national anthem. The sensational wartime popularity of the song decidedly confirmed his observation that collective adoption of a musical standard "depends upon some fortunate conjunction of time, mood, association, and circumstance." Its nostalgic longing for home abundantly satisfied his requirement that a successful lyric "must contain somewhere, either in a stanza or a refrain, a sentiment, tersely and musically expressed, which appeals to some favorite pride, prejudice or passion of the people."[11] Perhaps the poet refused to recognize white southerners' embrace of the blackface walk-around for some of the same reasons he declined to acknowledge his own ancestry. The palimpsest of "Dixie" resembled the traces of slavery evident in the ode Timrod wrote for the inaugural observance of Memorial Day at Magnolia Cemetery. Dylan's rendition of the de facto anthem, like his juxtaposition of Timrod and Ovid in *Modern Times*, extracted usable nuggets from the Lost Cause. The protean musician found apt expression in a song remarkably adaptable to variation and appropriation.[12] "Dixie" invented a mythical identity for the slaveholding South by combining fixity of place with flexibility of signification, like other enduring sites of Confederate commemoration.

The party held at the Confederate Home in January 2010 to celebrate the publication of Ted Phillips's *City of the Silent: The Charlestonians of Magnolia Cemetery* on the fifth anniversary of his death affirmed that postmodern renewal of Confederate remembrance was not limited to the approach favored by friends of the *Hunley*. Facilitation of such festivity was now central to the institutional mission of the Home, conceived as a living memorial to the Confederate dead. Wedding receptions routinely filled the former federal courtroom where judicial officers had declared the Union dissolved. *City of the Silent* similarly replotted the epic southern tragedy in a more comedic vein.

The strongest parts of Ted's book realized his vision of Magnolia Cemetery as an antiquarian playground. The alphabetical organization of the biographical compendium undercut the privileging of Lost Cause heroes in the didactic landscape, signaled by the massing of the soldiers' ground and the decoration of graves with United Daughters of the Confederacy crosses or miniature battle flags. Ted's entry for the Confederate secretary of the treasury followed the entry for a pickle magnate known as the Duchess of Wadmalaw. He laughingly saluted Langdon Cheves Jr. as "father of the Confederate air force" for constructing a reconnaissance balloon and fondly recalled Charlestonians' support for hard-drinking commander Roswell S. Ripley, saluted as the "gay chieftain" in a Timrod poem quoted on his grave. Robert E. Lee's grandson figured prominently in the book as the celebrity husband of a serial spouse hunter ("Mary Middleton Pinckney Lee / On the prowl for number three"). Ted repeatedly called attention to Confederates who died in accidental friendly fire, which like the suicide mission of the *Hunley* encapsulated South Carolina's war as an absurd self-inflicted casualty.[13]

Remembrance of the Confederate past was also a potential source of local pride in *City of the Silent*. Ted pointed tourists to the unmarked grave of Nelson Mitchell, a prominent Charleston lawyer who successfully defended six captured soldiers of the 54th Massachusetts Regiment against capital criminal charges that their Union military service constituted participation in a slave insurrection. He noted that Mitchell lies near Confederate officer Robert Gilchrist, southern chronicler of the assault on Battery Wagner. A talented painter, Gilchrist provided instruction to his daughter Emma Susan Gilchrist, who in turn was an early influence on abstract artist William Halsey, one of the most creative figures in mid- and late-twentieth-century Charleston and the younger brother of Ashley Halsey Jr. The climax of these ironic redemptions was the sketch of J. Waties Waring, who was born into the heart of the Lost Cause tradition in 1880 but became an influential supporter of civil rights as a federal judge.[14]

For Ted, the lasting value of the Confederacy rested in its demonstration that shared remembrance might serve as a basis for everyday performance of community. He recognized that this collective memory was a form of fiction, and he addressed the quintessential fictionalization of the Confederate saga, *Gone with the Wind*, more thoroughly than he covered any military campaign. He took a Charlestonian satisfaction in the casting of Alicia Rhett in the role of Ashley Wilkes's sister. He noted the speculation that Rhett Butler was based on blockade-running entrepreneur George Alfred Trenholm and reported parallel claims that Scarlett O'Hara was based on Buck Preston. The Confederate bazaar at which Rhett buys a dance with Scarlett, he added, was said to have been based on the fund-raising fairs organized by Amarinthia Snowden.[15] He did not necessarily put stock in these theories; his purpose was to record urban legends. Like the adaptation of novel into movie, the unauthorized stories about the relationship of fact and fiction demonstrated the energy generated by a successful act of commemoration. The local glosses showed that even the most widely marketed versions of the past might become material for community memory.

The profile of John Mitchel Jr. epitomized Ted's response to the Confederate project of commemoration that Timrod had identified as an impending crisis for the founding ideals of Magnolia Cemetery. At the dedication of the long-delayed monument in November 1882, former Confederate general Benjamin Huger Rutledge concluded his oration by singling out Mitchel as the martyr who best personified the meaning of the memorial. According to Rutledge, the young Irish and southern nationalist had died while in command of Fort Sumter because his "heroic generosity" prompted him to take the place of a sentinel on duty on the parapet during an especially heavy bombardment. After ordering the lower-ranking soldier to take shelter, Mitchel was struck by a fragment of an exploding shell. He recognized that the wound was fatal and told a friend to write to Mitchel's mother that "the dearest wish of my heart was to die for Irish independence, but I have died in a just cause, and not to mourn for me, I am content."[16] His readiness to give his life for his comrade and the Confederacy made him an exemplar of southern sacrifice.

In place of this panegyric, *City of the Silent* turned to a memoir published five months before Rutledge's oration by a woman whom Mitchel reportedly courted during the war, Robert Barnwell Rhett's daughter Claudine. Evidently informed about the circumstances of Mitchel's death in minute detail, she did not pretend that he had simply substituted himself for the endangered sentinel. When the bombardment escalated, the man on the parapet sent down a request to take shelter, which Mitchel denied as "a bad precedent to establish." Upon receiving an urgent second request moments later, he went up to the parapet to investigate the situation and "give the men under his command an example of courage and coolness." He watched through a spyglass as a mortar shell arced across the sky and exploded outside the fort until a fragment ripped into him. His fellow captain and civil engineer John Johnson was the first to reach the parapet in response to the sentinel's call. Johnson later wrote wryly that the fallen commander's immediate response to the obviously fatal injury was an "unexpected but characteristic" exclamation: "They have killed me, captain, but I ought to have been a major." Only upon lingering for several hours did Mitchel adapt for his last words the famous valedictory of an Irishman who fell in the French army during the seventeenth century: "I willingly die for South Carolina, but would that I could have died for Ireland." The Ladies' Memorial Association inscribed this more heroic sentiment on a monument placed at his grave in 1878. A group of Irish Americans embellished the tribute in 1914 by enclosing it within a replica of the Fort Sumter parapet.[17]

Challenging Rutledge's tale with the testimony of Rhett and Johnson was only partly a matter of following the more reliable evidence. Ted's sketch transformed the representative Confederate from a paragon of self-lessness into a model of determined self-presentation. Artfully playing the part he developed for himself, Mitchel most regretted that his superiors had not sufficiently appreciated his performance. Claudine Rhett played her role as well, never marrying in the long years before she joined Mitchel at the cemetery in 1929. Her memoir indulged only a brief accusatory glimpse of the future forsaken by a possible suitor, including the unsentimental observation that the immigrant war hero would have enjoyed exceptional political advantages in Charleston. She ended her memoir with the bittersweet reflection that "of all the hallowed spots at Magnolia, none is so well known, or is ever heaped so high with roses, as the Irish officer's grave, which, for fourteen years, was utterly unmarked, save by this touching tribute of honor to his memory."[18] Rather than a didactic inspiration, the headstone misquoted by Rutledge dramatized the comical, poignant inventions of Confederate vanity.

The history of Mitchel's resting place at Magnolia Cemetery paralleled the trajectory of Timrod's grave at Trinity churchyard in Columbia: unmarked but reverently attended for years after the Civil War, triumphantly garlanded after the overthrow of Reconstruction, and more elaborately decorated in the early twentieth century. The similarity was ironic, for the replica of the Fort Sumter parapet was one of the most heavy-handed examples of the "cannon-moulded pile" that Timrod dreaded in his "Ode." Writing almost a century and a half later, Ted Phillips saw that the thoughtful remembrancer must embrace such weird wonders of the common day. He updated the romantic poet's countermemorial by sampling, remixing, and subverting the long line of Lost Cause commemorations. His humorous and humane biographical collage added to as it drew from a tangled genealogy of local remembrance. The struggle to develop a usable Confederate memory remained a fertile field of engagement with modern times.

Notes

ABBREVIATIONS

BL   *Blue Light*
CC   *Charleston Courier*
CDN   *Charleston Daily News*
CDP   *Columbia Daily Phoenix*
CEP   *Charleston Evening Post*
CM   *Charleston Mercury*
CNC   *Charleston News and Courier*
CPC   *Charleston Post and Courier*
CR   *Columbia Register*
CS   *Columbia State*
CV   *Confederate Veteran*
MAYSP   Mary Amarinthia Yates Snowden Papers, South Caroliniana Library,
         University of South Carolina, Columbia
MCCW   Mary Chesnut, *Mary Chesnut's Civil War*. Ed. C. Vann Woodward.
         New Haven: Yale University Press, 1981.
NYT   *New York Times*
SCDAH   South Carolina Department of Archives and History, Columbia
SCL   South Caroliniana Library, University of South Carolina, Columbia
SCMA   *The South Carolina Monument Association: Origin, History, and Work,*
         with an Account of the Proceedings at the Unveiling of the Monument
         to the Confederate Dead, and the Oration of Gen. John S. Preston.
         Charleston, S.C.: News and Courier Book Presses, 1879.

MAP

    1. Casey, *Earth-Mapping*, 216 n. 18. Anderson, *Imagined Communities*, 170–78,
    offers a classic introduction to maps and nationhood.

    2. Marshall, *Creating Confederate Kentucky*, provides a local study that is excep-

tionally typical of the Lost Cause in the opposite sense, focusing on a state that joined the Confederacy after the war ended.

3. O'Brien, *Conjectures*, is the climax of a generation of scholarship that has emphasized the importance of South Carolina in American intellectual history and resurrected many forgotten figures.

4. Lewis Pinckney Jones, *Stormy Petrel*, 319 n. 15.

5. Blight, *Race and Reunion*. Roberts and Kytle, "Looking the Thing in the Face," and Yuhl, "Hidden," are recent applications of this analytic framework to South Carolina.

6. Blight, *Race and Reunion*, 274; Blight, "'What Will Peace among the Whites Bring?,'" 400. In treating reconciliation as a field of discourse, my approach differs from that of Janney, *Remembering*, 7, which purports to measure "the degree to which former Confederates and advocates of the Union had agreed to forgive and forget—to embrace true, heartfelt reconciliation."

7. Foster, *Ghosts*, is a powerful statement of this argument. For an examination of its influence, see Brown, "Civil War Remembrance," 212–18.

8. In addition to the works discussed in Brown, "Civil War Remembrance," see especially Janney, *Burying*.

9. Robert Pogue Harrison, *Dominion*. Brown, "Civil War Remembrance," 208–12, 232–33, surveys scholarship on religion and death in Civil War memory. See also Faust, *This Republic of Suffering*.

CHAPTER 1

1. *MCCW*, 452, 665; Andrew, *Wade Hampton*, 243–50.

2. *MCCW*, 153, 285–86, 328, 401–3, 452–53.

3. This moral tale combined two separate stories. Emily Timrod Goodwin to Paul Hamilton Hayne, November 23, 1867, Henry Timrod Papers, SCL, reports that her brother was born in 1829 but had taken to claiming 1830. But both siblings were wrong about the poet's birthdate, which was in 1828. Caldwell, "Date." My thanks to Ward Briggs for the account of Lowell at Timrod's grave. Cisco, *Henry Timrod*, 81, reports that Timrod began to be called the poet laureate of the Confederacy during the war, which may have been a commentary on his emulation of Tennyson as well as the national importance of Timrod's work.

4. Bruns, "Henry Timrod," 267.

5. Simms, "Late Henry Timrod," 157–58, 165; Simms, *War Poetry*, v; Emily Goodwin to Edith, November 23, 18[67], Timrod Papers; "Dr. Bruns' Lecture," *CDP*, May 7, 1868; "The Poet Timrod," *CDN*, October 28, 1870.

6. Timrod, *Poems*, 53, 65; Paul Hamilton Hayne to Oliver Wendell Holmes, October 13, 1868, in *Man of Letters*, 74–75; Rayburn S. Moore, *Paul Hamilton Hayne*, 134–35.

7. Timrod, *Poems*, 55; "The Opinion of the Literary Oracle of 'The Hub,'" *CDN*, February 4, 1873; "Timrod's Last Days," *CDP*, February 20, 1873; untitled article, *CDP*, March 14, 1873; "The Last Days of Timrod," *CDN*, March 19, 1873. See also "Literature in the South," *Boston Daily Advertiser*, February 12, 1873.

8. McKinley, *Selections*, 34–36.

9. Rivers, *Little Book*; Seigler, *Guide*, 319–21; "The Grave of Timrod," unidentified clipping, "Timrod: In Memoriam," scrapbook [microform], SCL; *Keowee Courier*, May 6, 1880.

10. Paul Hamilton Hayne to Mary Middleton Michel Hayne, February 28, [1862], in *Man of Letters*, 55–56; W. A. Courtenay to Henry Timrod Goodwin, November 21, 1898, Timrod Papers; unidentified newspaper clipping, "The Timrod Memorial Association," April 10, 1899, in "Timrod: In Memoriam."

11. Circular, "Henry Timrod, Poet, 1829–1867," n.d., in "Timrod: In Memoriam"; William Ashmead Courtenay, memo, October 7, 1902, in "Memories of the Timrod Revival," scrapbook [microform], SCL; *Timrod Memorial Association*, 40. The final Timrod Memorial Association surplus of $126 did not fully cover the new work on Timrod's grave; doubtless Courtenay covered the remaining costs. See William Ashmead Courtenay to J. C. Hemphill, October 1, 1901, in "Memories of the Timrod Revival."

12. William Ashmead Courtenay to Houghton Mifflin (draft), August 7, [1897], "Timrod: In Memoriam"; Tooker, "Timrod the Poet"; Colcock, *Her American Daughter*, 190–91. The publication of "A Theory of Poetry" in *The Independent* in three installments with slight abridgment in 1901 underscores Courtenay's eagerness to place the full essay in *The Atlantic* in 1905. Timrod, *Essays*, 165 n. 1.

13. "Boulder Monuments," *Monumental News* 13 (August 1901): 458; "Timrod Memorial Association," *Charleston Yearbook—1901*, 76, 78–79.

14. Timrod, *Poems*, 21.

15. Gurganus, "Man Who Loved Cemeteries," 98; Phillips, *City*, 149.

16. Wauchope, *Henry Timrod*, 9; Clare, *Harp*, 12.

17. J. H. Easterby, ed., *The Journal of the Commons House of Assembly, March 28, 1749–March 19, 1750* (Columbia: South Carolina Archives Department, 1962), 293, 302–4, 326, 478–80; R. Nicholas Olsberg, ed., *The Journal of the Commons House of Assembly, April 23, 1750–August 31, 1751* (Columbia: University of South Carolina Press, 1974), 150, 211, 375; "Bite of a Rattlesnake," *Southern Cultivator* 13 (July 1855): 228.

18. The wills of Doctor Caesar, John Norman, Hannah Caesar, and Sarah Norman Caesar Faesch are in the Works Progress Administration transcription of Charleston County Wills, SCDAH. See Doctor Ceser [*sic*] (proved May 17, 1754) in Charleston Wills 7:186–87; John Norman (proved November 11, 1757) in Charleston Wills 13:855–57; Hannah Ceazer [*sic*] (proved May 26, 1791) in Charleston Wills 24:888–89; Sarah Faesch (proved February 28, 1816), in Charleston Wills 33:1030–35. On the postemancipation career of Hannah Caesar, see also the will of Elizabeth Metheringham (proved February 24, 1758), Charleston Wills 13:909–10, and the proceedings in *Hannah Caesar v. Moses Mitchel* (filed May 13, 1760), SCDAH. John Faesch announced his recent immigration to Charleston in an advertisement in the *South Carolina and American General Gazette*, December 12, 1768. He is one of the 137 men on the original May 1775 roll of the German Fusiliers of Charleston, a list headed by Henry Timrod.

19. 1790 Federal Manuscript Population Census for Charleston County, South Carolina, p. 36, available at www.ancestry.com; Hagy, *People and Professions*, 53, 57, 78, 84. Rupert Taylor, "Henry Timrod's Ancestress" reprints newspaper coverage of the court proceedings (quotation at 423). Hannah Caesar noted that "her granddaughter, in particular, was married in Europe to a person of noble blood." She was referring to Sarah Norman Caesar Faesch's daughter Rebecca Faesch, who was in a relationship in Jamaica with Edward Sainthill that caused her to be known as Rebecca Sainthill. See John Gabriel Stedman, *The Journal of John Gabriel Stedman, 1744-1797, Soldier and Author*, ed. Stanbury Thompson (London: Mitre, 1962), 321, in which the diarist refers to her as "the most original character in the world." The history of this family certainly invites further research.

Rupert Taylor, "Henry Timrod's Ancestress," claimed that the enslaved Hannah Caesar who was the daughter of Doctor Caesar was not the same person as the Hannah Caesar who was robbed in 1786. According to Taylor, the robbed Hannah Caesar did not have mixed-race ancestry. For these assertions he relied entirely on two pieces of evidence. Most important to him were the affidavits presented by Hannah Caesar after the exclusion of her testimony in the criminal proceeding. As I indicate in the text, however, the criminal proceeding presented no occasion to determine the exact meaning and reliability of the affidavits. Second, Taylor cited a clause in Doctor Caesar's will that provided that if Hannah obtained her freedom, she should receive any remaining portion in her share of the estate upon reaching the age of eighteen. Reporting that a Hannah Caesar was old enough to deed two slaves to her daughter Sarah and granddaughter Rebecca in 1767, Taylor reasoned that the testator (unquestionably Timrod's great-great-grandmother) could not have been an enslaved eighteen-year-old in 1754.

Taylor's evidence crumbles on close inspection. The 1767 deed he purports to quote does not in fact mention Hannah Caesar's granddaughter Rebecca. See Charleston Miscellaneous Record Book NN (1765–69), SCDAH. In any case, the reference to Hannah's age in Doctor Caesar's will is weak evidence that the slave was not already beyond the age of eighteen when Doctor Caesar dictated the document. The boilerplate provision did not necessarily reflect the situation of this testator's family. Moreover, Doctor Caesar might not have known his daughter's exact age, which may well have been around eighteen at the time of the will. The date of the instrument could have been as early as Doctor Caesar's serious illness during the 1750 legislative proceedings to arrange his emancipation, not necessarily—as Taylor suggests—the 1754 date of probate proceedings. If Hannah was in her teens at the birth of Sarah around 1745, Hannah might have been close enough to eighteen in 1750 and her father uncertain enough about her true age to account more fully for the reference to her age in his will, if the inclusion of such a routine provision had any basis in the specific circumstances of these individuals. See Mrs. William Barnhart, "Inscriptions from the Independent or Congregational (Circular) Church Yard, Charleston, S.C.," *South Carolina Historical Magazine* 69 (October 1968): 258.

Taylor offered no alternative account for the origins of the Hannah Caesar robbed in 1786. He did not consider the possibility that Pinckney might have investigated the victim of his clients' crime or known previously about Hannah Caesar. Taylor's article is also inconsistent with the 1790 federal manuscript census identification of "Free Sarah Fash" as a person of color. Racial bias may have influenced Taylor's conclusion that "the material here presented, and the interpretation put on the ascertainable facts, should be enough to settle the matter for all but that type of mind which, unfortunately, seems born to believe evil or which, obsessed with the idea of miscegenation, leaps eagerly to seize upon any hint of tainted blood in any one who has achieved prominence" (430).

20. Hagy, *Charleston City Directories*, 22, 27; Cisco, *Henry Timrod*, 38; *South Carolina Death Records, 1821–1955*, online database, available at www.ancestry .com. State death records identify Sarah Faesch Prince as a ninety-year-old white woman. She was interred at Trinity Methodist Church, Charleston.

21. Emily Timrod Goodwin to Paul Hamilton Hayne, May 18, 1870, Timrod Papers.

22. Timrod, *Poems*, 18; Bruns, "Life and Genius," in "Memories of the Timrod Revival"; "The Late Congressman Mackey," *Washington Evening Star*, February 11, 1884; Lewisohn, "South Carolina," 36.

23. George W. Cable, "After-Thoughts of a Story-Teller," *North American Review* 158 (January 1894): 18. Cable refers here to Henry Laurens Pinckney (1794–1863), an editor of the *Charleston Mercury* and participant in city literary circles as well as a longtime political leader.

24. Bruns, "Life and Genius." Benfey, *Degas in New Orleans*, 197–213, discusses Bruns's influence on Cable.

25. "Henry Timrod," in *Papers of Daniel Murray* (microfilm), ed. Jane Wolff and Eleanor McKay (Madison: State Historical Society of Wisconsin, 1977), reel 21.

26. Henry Timrod, "Ethnogenesis," in *Collected Poems*, 92–95. Hutchison, *Apples and Ashes*, 4–14, analyzes "Ethnogenesis" as a template for Confederate literature. The deeds and census records cited earlier show that Hannah Caesar, Sarah Norman Caesar Faesch, and Charles and Sarah (Faesch) Prince were all slaveholders.

27. "A New Yankee Doctrine," April 6, 1864; "The Message," November 13, 1864; "Emancipation," January 16, 1865; "Negroes for the Army," January 17, 1865, reprinted in West, "Southern Editor," 1:254–56, 2:793–96, 918–20, 920–25. All editorials in the *Daily South Carolinian* were unsigned, but the quoted articles appeared during periods when Timrod reported in his correspondence that he was supplying almost all of the editorial content. The editorials are consistent with his writing style. No editorials published in the *Daily South Carolinian* express disagreement with the positions summarized in the quotations.

28. "The Opinion of the Literary Oracle of 'The Hub,'" *CDN*, February 4, 1873; Rubin, *Edge*, 221.

29. Rubin, *Edge*, 38; Timrod, "Literature in the South," in *Essays*, 100.

30. Sachs, *Arcadian America*, chap. 1, cites much of the scholarship on the rural cemetery movement.

31. Rusk, *Life of Ralph Waldo Emerson*, 471–72; Simpson, *Mind and the American*

Civil War, 91; Emerson, *Parnassus*, 258; Rubin, *Gallery*, x; Wauchope, *Henry Timrod*, 30; Parks, *Henry Timrod*, 116; Barrett, *To Fight Aloud*, 189–97.

32. Henry Timrod, "Ode: Sung on the Occasion of Decorating the Graves of the Confederate Dead, at Magnolia Cemetery, Charleston, S.C., 1866," in *Collected Poems*, 129–30. I follow the version sung on June 16 and published in the *Courier* on June 18 rather than the amended version published in the *Courier* on July 23. Timrod, *Collected Poems*, 198 n. 74, details the differences. See also Strange, "Henry Timrod's Final Revisions," on the version published in the *Daily South Carolinian* on June 19. Strange observes that "the popular version was actually the first" because Hayne followed it, with a few variations, in his edition of Timrod's poetry. Scarry, *Body in Pain*, 60–157, discusses the relationship between war as a process of unmaking and art as a process of making.

33. "Celebration of the Sixteenth of June in Memory of the Confederate Dead," *CDN*, June 18, 1866.

34. Timrod, *Collected Poems*, 22–23; Timrod, *Essays*, 98–99, 124.

35. Allen Tate, "Ode to the Confederate Dead," in *Collected Poems*, 20–23; Allen Tate, "Narcissus as Narcissus," in *Essays*, 598; Underwood, *Allen Tate*, 123, 260; Robert Pogue Harrison, *Dominion*, 125–33. Barrett, *To Fight Aloud*, 283, notes that Timrod's poem was a point of reference for Tate, from whom she moves to Lowell, Young, and Trethewey, but she does not discuss specific resonances of the "Ode."

36. Cisco, *Henry Timrod*, 90; Burial Register, Magnolia Cemetery, July 1863, Magnolia Cemetery Archives, Charleston.

37. Robert Lowell, "For the Union Dead," in *For the Union Dead*, 70–72. In the large literature on this poem, see especially Axelrod, "Colonel Shaw"; Helen Vendler, "Art, Heroism, and Poetry," in *Hope and Glory*, ed. Blatt, Brown, and Yacovone, 202–14.

38. Kevin Young, "For the Confederate Dead," in *For the Confederate Dead*, 97–99.

39. Natasha Trethewey, "Pastoral," "Miscegenation," and "Blond," in *Native Guard*, 35–36, 39.

40. Natasha Trethewey, "Native Guard," "Elegy for the Native Guards," and "South," in *Native Guard*, 25–30, 44–46. Trethewey first published "Native Guard" in *Callaloo* 24 (Fall 2001): 1194–97, and "Elegy for the Native Guards" in *Atlanta Review* 9 (Fall 2002): 15.

41. Henry Timrod, "Ethnogenesis," "The Cotton Boll," and "Ode," in *Collected Poems*, 93, 95–99, 129–30. The mixed metaphor in the original version of the "Ode," combining laurel seeds and cotton blossoms, doubtless influenced Timrod's decision to change this line to "the garlands of your fame are sown." The poet sighed to his sister in a February 25, 1862, letter that "we have over-rated the power of King Cotton. When King Wheat gets upon his throne, he is just as strong" (Parks, *Henry Timrod*, 137 n. 3).

42. Magnolia Cemetery developed from a larger landholding known as Magnolia Umbra plantation, established in 1705 and modestly augmented during a succession of ten different owners over the next seventy-five years. In the eighteenth century the property was a rice plantation that became most closely as-

sociated with Revolutionary War veteran William Cunnington (ca. 1736–1804), a Charleston factor who acquired it in 1781. He and his heirs divided the property. Attorney and Baptist temperance advocate Benjamin Chaplin Pressley bought the parcel that became the nucleus of Magnolia from the family of his wife, the former Louisa M. Wheeler, in 1842. He remained there for seven years while he built a law practice, served as a magistrate, and ran unsuccessfully for sheriff. Pressley was a political protégé of Ker Boyce, Charleston's leading cotton factor until he concentrated his energies on banking; in 1851 they would found the *Southern Standard* newspaper with shipping magnate Moses Cohen Mordecai. Boyce's son, James Petigru Boyce, praised Pressley's sponsorship of religious meetings for neighborhood masters and slaves in "Mission among the Southern Slaves," *Southern Baptist*, March 28, 1849. With the guidance of Ker Boyce, it is likely that the ambitious Pressley applied his land and slaves at least partly to growing cotton. Six weeks after his wife's death in April 1849, Pressley sold his tract to William S. Walker, one of the founders of Magnolia Cemetery, who transferred it to the cemetery corporation. For the owners of Magnolia Umbra through William Cunnington's tenure, see Henry A. M. Smith, *Historical Writings*, 3:44–45. For abstracts of subsequent transfers, see "Magnolia Umbra," Magnolia Cemetery File, Charleston Vertical Files, Charleston County Public Library, Charleston, S.C.

43. Blight, *Race and Reunion*, 64–71. The newspaper published by Timrod's former partner at the *Daily South Carolinian* responded indirectly to the reverberating jubilation over the destruction of slavery by reporting that one participant in the Magnolia ceremony was an African American who had lost a limb in fighting for the Confederacy at Secessionville. "The Ceremonies of 16th June," *CDP*, June 19, 1866.

44. Beagle and Giemza, *Poet of the Lost Cause*, 67–68.

45. Chaps. 2 and 3 of this book are thorough revisions of Brown, "Monumental Legacy" and Brown, "Confederate Retreat."

46. Nora, "Between Memory and History," 7, 13, 19, 23, 24.

47. James, *American Scene*, 419.

48. Gurganus, "Man Who Loved Cemeteries," 98.

CHAPTER 2

1. Humphreys, *Rich in Love*, 46–47.

2. Important accounts of South Carolina secessionism include Channing, *Crisis of Fear*; Ford, *Origins*; Freehling, *Road to Disunion*; McCurry, *Masters*; Sinha, *Counterrevolution*. Rogers, *Charleston*, is a classic argument that "by the 1830s, Charlestonians had turned away from cosmopolitanism to a conservative sectional patriotism" (159). Rogers uses the Calhoun funeral and monument as the epilogue to this transition (167–68). But conservative sectional patriotism could be cosmopolitan and modern, as Michael O'Brien has shown in *Conjectures*.

3. Peterson, *Lincoln*, 234–35; Sandweiss, *Passing Strange*.

4. "Hon. N. P. Tallmadge on Spiritual Manifestations," *CC*, May 31, 1853; "Ghostology," *CC*, June 1, 1853; Osterweis, *Romanticism and Nationalism*, 144; Derry, "John C. Calhoun and South Carolina"; Dillenbeck, "Decade after Moses."

5. J. P. Thomas, *Carolina Tribute*, 201. See also Schantz, *Awaiting*, 31–34.

6. Martha Cornelia Calhoun to Anna Maria Calhoun Clemson, April 12, 1850, in Calhoun, *Papers*, 27:259. For full details, see J. P. Thomas, *Carolina Tribute*, 65–82.

7. J. P. Thomas, *Carolina Tribute*, 65; "The Calhoun Procession," *CM*, February 17, 1851; McInnis, *Politics of Taste*, 154–55. See also Selby, *Memorabilia*, 18, for remembrance of the Calhoun funeral with a "dionamic-cosmorama."

8. Wunder, *Hiram Powers*, 1:194–206, 2:26–28, 115–16.

9. Ibid., 1:204; "Proceedings of Council," *CC*, September 2, 1850; "Calhoun Temple and Statue," *CM*, September 13, 1850; "Calhoun's Statue," *CM*, November 21, 1850.

10. Whitemarsh B. Seabrook, "Message of the Governor of South Carolina to the Legislature," in J. P. Thomas, *Carolina Tribute*, 330; William Gilmore Simms, "The City of the Silent," in *Magnolia Cemetery*, 53, 81; Bryan, *Creating*, 55.

11. "The Statue of Calhoun," *CM*, May 8, 1850.

12. Porcher, "Modern Art," 106–7, 109, 113, 114.

13. Wunder, *Hiram Powers*, 1:205; "The Fair," *CM*, May 13, 1851; "The Carolina Tribute," *CC*, September 24, 1857; *International Magazine of Literature, Art, and Science* 3 (April 1, 1851): 8.

14. Dillenbeck, "Decade after Moses," 111–28; "The Fair," *CM*, May 13, 1851. See also Louisa S. McCord, "Separate Secession," in *Louisa S. McCord: Selected Writings*, 42–45.

15. "Calhoun Monument," *CM*, June 18, 1852; "Calhoun Monumental Association," *CM*, June 23, 1852; "The Calhoun Monument," *CM*, July 1, 1852.

16. "Monument to Calhoun," *CM*, November 4, 1852; "Meeting of the Calhoun Association of St. John's Colleton, at Rockville, January 3d, 1853," *CM*, January 13, 1853.

17. "Calhoun Monument Association," *CM*, March 4, 1853; "Constitution of the Calhoun Monument Association," *CM*, March 22, 1853; "Calhoun Monument Association," *CM*, June 1, 1853.

18. Freehling, *Road to Disunion*, 2:168–84.

19. "The Calhoun Monument," *CM*, June 24, 1852; *Constitution of the South-Carolina Institute*; Severens, *Charleston Antebellum Architecture*, 153–56, 162–64, 187–91, 217–20.

20. "The Calhoun Monument," *CC*, July 27, 1854.

21. "South-Carolina Historical Society," *CC*, June 4, 1855; Bryan, *Creating*, 40–42; Chambers, *Memories of War*, 166–70.

22. The *Mercury* blamed the legislative defeat on the Rhetts' upcountry antagonist Benjamin Perry, who firmly maintained that alliance with the national Democratic Party could protect slavery. In the same week that he spoke against state funding of a Calhoun monument, Perry's criticisms of a recent speech by William Taber prompted the publisher to challenge him to a duel. *CM*, December 10, 1853; "A Card," *CM*, December 14, 1853.

23. "The Calhoun Monument," *CC*, August 10, 1854.

24. "The Calhoun Monument," *CM*, July 15, 1854; "The Calhoun Monument," *CC*, August 10, 1854.

25. "The Monumental Plans," *CC*, July 17, 1854; "The Calhoun Monument Plans," *CC*, July 20, 1854; "The Calhoun Monument," *CC*, July 22, 1854 (emphasis in original); "The Calhoun Monument," *CC*, August 9, 1854; "The Calhoun Monument," *CC*, August 10, 1854.

26. "The Calhoun Monument," *CC*, August 10, 1854.

27. Jane H. Pease and Pease, *Ladies, Women, and Wenches*, 122.

28. Clarence Cunningham, "A Sketch of the Foundation, Progress and Work of the Ladies' Calhoun Monument Association, as Prepared from the Minute Books," in *History of the Calhoun Monument*, 3–4, identifies the founders and officers of the LCMA. Margaret Simons Middleton, "A Sketch of the Ladies Benevolent Society, Founded 1813," in *City of Charleston Yearbook—1941* (Charleston: Walker, Evans, and Cogswell, 1942), 247–55, lists members of that organization. See also Bellows, *Benevolence among Slaveholders*, 166–67.

29. A Southern Matron, "To the Ladies of the South," *CM*, December 2, 1853; E.C., "To the Women of Carolina," *CC*, February 1, 1854; Yates Snowden to Mrs. W. M. Burney, September 28, 1928, enclosing Louisa Cunningham to Mary Amarinthia Yates, January 3, 1854, MAYSP; Sutherland, "Rise and Fall"; Grace Brown Elmore, "Reminiscences," 38, typescript, Grace Brown Elmore Papers, SCL. Elmore phrased her description of Amarinthia Snowden slightly differently in the version of the journal published as Weiner, *Heritage of Woe*, 95. Varon, *We Mean to Be Counted*, discusses the sectional and gender politics of the Mount Vernon campaign and an earlier effort to erect a Henry Clay monument in Richmond.

30. "Calhoun Monument," *CM*, February 2, 1854; "Calhoun Celebration," *CC*, March 20, 1854.

31. "Calhoun Monument Association," *CM*, April 25, 1856; Cunningham, "Sketch," 7–9.

32. "The Affair of Honor between Edward Magrath, Esq., and William R. Taber, Jr., Esq.," *CM*, October 2, 1856.

33. "Ladies' Calhoun Monument Association and the Children," *CM*, July 1, 1854; "The Calhoun Monument," *CC*, July 8, 1857; James Petigru Carson, *Life, Letters, and Speeches*, 294.

34. "The Theatre and the Monument," *CC*, March 26, 1855; "Ladies' Calhoun Monument Association," *CC*, March 29, 1855; "Ole Bull's Concert," *CC*, May 3, 1856; "The Calhoun Concert," *CC*, May 15, 1856; Simms, "Charleston," 22; Bailey, *Music*; Lyons, *Brigadier-General Thomas Francis Meagher*, 105–6. Cunningham, "Sketch," 16, itemizes the revenue sources; here, I set aside income from dividends and interest.

35. "The Ladies Floral Fair," *CC*, May 18, 1855; "The Ladies and the Calhoun Monument," *CM*, June 4, 1855; "The Calhoun Fair," *CC*, May 10, 1859; "The Calhoun Monument Fair," *CC*, May 11, 1859; "The Floral Offering to Calhoun," *CC*, May 12, 1859; "The Floral Fair," *CC*, May 13, 1859; Gordon, *Bazaars and Fair Ladies*.

36. "Woman's Tribute," unidentified newspaper clipping, March 18, [?], LCMA

Scrapbook, MAYSP; E.C., "The Calhoun Monument," *CC*, February 1, 1854; "Calhoun Monument Association," *CM*, April 25, 1856; Esther Cheesborough, "The Calhoun Monument," *CNC*, April 29, 1882.

37. J. P. Thomas, *Carolina Tribute*, 411, quoting John Milton's "On Shakespeare" (1630); "The Carolina Tribute to Calhoun," *CC*, November 16, 1857. On the republican critique of public monuments, see Savage, *Monument Wars*, 35–44.

38. "Magnificent Donation of the Hon. James Gadsden," *CC*, March 24, 1857; "To the Ladies of the Calhoun Monument Association," *CC*, March 11, 1858; "The Calhoun Monument," *CC*, April 10, 1858; Simms, "Charleston," 6, 20.

39. "The Calhoun Monument," *CC*, May 4, 1858.

40. Esther Cheesborough, "The Calhoun Monument," *CNC*, April 29, 1882; Simms, "Charleston," 12. Severens, *Charleston Antebellum Architecture*, 252–55, sees a contraction of civic ambition in the shift away from White Point Garden and the frustration of the plans of Edward Brickell White and Jones and Lee, but this brief discussion does not analyze the ideology of the LCMA. Severens's excellent book also mistakenly identifies the present monument as the work erected in 1887.

41. Jane H. Pease and Pease, "Blood-Thirsty Tiger"; Ford, *Origins*, 308; Poston, *Buildings of Charleston*, 363–84.

42. Esther Cheesborough, "The Calhoun Monument," *CNC*, April 29, 1882; McInnis, *Politics of Taste*, 73–82; Severens, *Charleston Antebellum Architecture*, 164–66, 221–33, 246.

43. Freehling, *Road to Disunion*, 2:259–60; "The Calhoun Monument," *CC*, June 28, 1858.

44. "The Calhoun Monument," *CC*, May 29, 1858; Rivers, *Eunice*, ix–xii; Durrill, "Power," 495–97.

45. McInnis, *Politics of Taste*, 154; Bremer, *Homes*, 1:304–5; Radford, "Race, Residence, and Ideology"; John C. Calhoun, "Remarks on Receiving Abolitionist Petitions (Revised Report), February 6, 1837," and "Further Remarks in Debate on His Fifth Resolution," in Calhoun, *Papers*, 13:395, 14:84.

46. Freehling, *Road to Disunion*, 2:346–47; Hollis, *University of South Carolina*, 1:209; Bonner, *Mastering America*, 158–61; Travers, "Paradox."

47. Cunningham, "Sketch," 10–12; Esther Cheesborough, "The Calhoun Monument," *CNC*, April 29, 1882; "Calhoun Monument," *CC*, June 8, 1858; "The Monumental Celebration," *CC*, June 29, 1858; "Promenade Concert," *CC*, July 2, 1858; Jacob Schirmer, Diary, June 28, 1858, Schirmer Family Papers, South Carolina Historical Society, Charleston.

48. "Oration by Hon. Laurence M. Keitt, Delivered at the Laying of the Cornerstone of the Calhoun Monument on Citadel Green, Charleston, S.C.," *CM*, June 29, 1858; Walther, *Fire-Eaters*, 181–84.

49. Cunningham, "Sketch," 20–21; "Calhoun Monument," *CC*, August 16, 1859; Henry Kirke Brown to Lydia Brown, June 2, 1858, Henry Kirke Bush-Brown Papers, Library of Congress, Washington, D.C.; Committee on Ways and Means, *Report on a Resolution to Appropriate $50,000 for Erecting a Monument to John C. Calhoun*, December 12, 1859, SCDAH. On Brown's work at the statehouse, see Bryan, *Creating*, 47–51; Savage, *Standing Soldiers*, 31–51.

50. Edward G. Mason, "A Visit to South Carolina in 1860," *Atlantic Monthly*, February 1884, 244; May and Faunt, *South Carolina Secedes*, 80; "The Calhoun Monument," *CC*, November 12, 1860; "Procession to the Tomb of Calhoun," *CM*, December 20, 1860.

51. Cunningham, "Sketch," 16.

52. John C. Calhoun, "Speech on the Slavery Question," in *Papers*, 27:259.

53. Wunder, *Hiram Powers*, 2:116; Coulter, *Confederate States of America*, 100–101; Criswell and Criswell, *Criswell's Currency Series*, 1:1, 37, 2:3, 4; "John Drinkwater's Poem"; U.S. War Records Office, *Local Designations*, 22–23; Seigler, *South Carolina's Military Organizations*, 1:325–48. Binnington, *Confederate Visions*, 80–81, reproduces an earlier Confederate treasury note that also featured the Brady portrait of Calhoun.

54. United Daughters of the Confederacy, *South Carolina Women*, 1:11–14, 70–75, 97, 113, 115.

55. Ibid., 109–14; "Calhoun," *CC*, March 18, 1862.

56. *Harper's Weekly*, November 24, 1860, 737; Anna Ella Carroll, "John C. Calhoun a Secessionist," *NYT*, July 23, 1861; Carroll, *Reply*; Coryell, *Neither Heroine nor Fool*, 57.

57. William Mumford Baker, *Inside*, 56. *Harper's Weekly* serialized the novel.

58. Robert Newman Gourdin to Andrew P. Calhoun, April 6, 1863, in *Gentlemen Merchants*, ed. Racine, 580. The narrative of sexton John N. Gregg, recorded in 1901, is a similar account but understandably misdates the precipitating event to the fall of Morris Island ("Exhumation of the Body"). See also Ringold, "John C. Calhoun."

59. Whitman, *Specimen Days*, 106; "Calhoun's Grave," *NYT*, May 7, 1865; Jacob Schirmer, August 1865 note to diary, Schirmer Papers.

60. "The Dark Iconoclast," *Harper's Weekly*, March 25, 1865, 178; Mayer, *All on Fire*, 582; Reid, *Southern Tour*, 65. Sidney Andrews, *South since the War*, 10–11, reported in September 1865 that "every stranger is curious to see . . . the grave of the father of the Rebellion."

61. Grace Brown Elmore, "Reminiscences," 34, typescript, Grace Brown Elmore Papers, SCL; Gordon, *Bazaars and Fair Ladies*, 97–99.

62. Bryan, *Creating*, 69; Royster, *Destructive War*, 19–25.

63. Cunningham, "Sketch," 14–15; "Calhoun Statue in Heart of City," *CNC*, July 15, 1957; *Historical Sketch*, 6.

64. James G. Holmes, *Memorials*, 10; Simms, *Sack and Destruction*, 54, 67. See also Simkins and Patton, *Women*, 238 ("Perhaps the most bitterly resented act of violence that was committed against the women of the Confederacy was the sack and burning of Columbia."); Lisa Tendrich Frank, "'Between Death and Dishonor.'"

65. Wunder, *Hiram Powers*, 1:205; "Letter from Charleston," April 17, 1866, unidentified newspaper clipping, LCMA Scrapbook, MAYSP.

66. "The Calhoun Monument Fund," *CNC*, December 17, 1873.

67. Mary Amarinthia Snowden to Thomas Green Clemson, December 1873 (copy), MAYSP.

68. F. A. Porcher, *A Brief History of the Ladies' Memorial Association of Charles-

ton, S.C., ed. Mary A. Sparkman, in *City of Charleston, South Carolina, Yearbook—1944* (Charleston: Walker, Evans, and Cogswell, 1947), 203–15.

69. Poston, *Buildings of Charleston*, 162–63.

70. *Historical Sketch*, 8–12; "The Widow's Home," *CDN*, November 11, 1869; *Semi-Annual Report of the Home for the Mothers, Widows, and Daughters of Confederate Soldiers, for the Half-Year ending 15th April, 1868* (Charleston: Walker, 1868).

71. *Anniversary and Fifth Annual Report of the Home for Mothers, Widows, and Daughters of Confederate Soldiers, Wednesday, January 15, 1873, Charleston, S.C.* (Charleston: Courier Book and Job, 1873), 2. The first available list of students is in *Home for the Mothers, Widows, and Daughters of Confederate Soldiers, Charleston, S.C., Seventh Annual Report* (Charleston: News and Courier Job, 1875), 9–10. Ralph, *Dixie*, 259, reported that the students "are the offspring of the families of the upper grade, as a rule, though the only requirement is that they shall be white. The women are not all of the same social standing."

72. Anna C. Clemson to Mary Amarinthia Snowden, October 28, 1873, MAYSP.

73. "The Calhoun Monumental Home," *CNC*, October 20, 1873; "The Calhoun Memorial Fund," *CNC*, October 23, 1873; "The Calhoun Memorial Fund," *CNC*, November 15, 1873; "The Calhoun Memorial Fund," *CNC*, November 18, 1873; "The Calhoun Monument Fund," *CNC*, December 9, 1873; "The Calhoun Monument Fund," *CNC*, December 17, 1873; "The Calhoun Monument Home," *Edgefield Advertiser*, October 30, 1873.

74. Thomas Green Clemson to Mary Amarinthia Snowden, November 23, 1873, MAYSP.

75. Thomas Green Clemson to Mary Amarinthia Snowden, November 23, December 13, 1873, Mary Amarinthia Snowden to Thomas Green Clemson, December 1873, all in MAYSP; "The Calhoun Monument," *CNC*, January 13, 1874; "The Calhoun Monument," *CNC*, February 11, 1874; "The Calhoun Monument," *Anderson Intelligencer*, April 16, 1874.

76. Undated newspaper clipping [Cheesborough letter, December 22, 1873], LCMA Scrapbook, MAYSP; *Home for the Mothers . . . Seventh Annual Report*, 6.

77. Cunningham, "Sketch," 18–20; "The Calhoun Monument," *CNC*, January 21, 1874.

78. United Daughters of the Confederacy, *South Carolina Women*, 1:114–15; Jane H. Pease and Pease, *Family of Women*, 218.

79. Cunningham, "Sketch," 21–23; Margaret J. Preston to Mary Amarinthia Snowden, June 10, [?], MAYSP; *Appendix to History of the Calhoun Monument*, 2; Caroline Carson, *Roman Years*, 30–31, 34–35, 111.

80. Savage, *Standing Soldiers*, 102–3; Sarah Shields, Wilson, and Winthrop, *Monument Avenue*, 41.

81. "The Calhoun Monument," *CNC*, February 11, 1886; Williams and Hoffius, *Upheaval in Charleston*, 14, 107, 158, 285 n. 30, 305 n. 12.

82. "Calhoun Day for Carolina," *CNC*, March 17, 1887; "Calhoun Day," *CNC*, March 18, 1887; "Worthy of Calhoun," *CNC*, March 30, 1887; "Calhoun Day," *CNC*, April 6, 1887.

83. *History of the Calhoun Monument*, 112–47; M. M. Hayne to Mary Amarinthia Snowden, November 20, 1885, MAYSP.

84. Cate, *Lucius Q. C. Lamar*, 464–67.

85. "Oration of the Hon. L. Q. C. Lamar," in *History of the Calhoun Monument*, 65, 68, 70–72, 75–78, 94.

86. "Calhoun Day," *CNC*, March 18, 1887; "John C. Calhoun," *CNC*, April 26, 1887.

87. "Oration of the Hon. L. Q. C. Lamar," 85; Certification of Election, March 29, 1888, MAYSP.

88. Ringold, "John C. Calhoun"; "The Grave of Calhoun," *CNC*, March 25, 1880; *Acts and Joint Resolutions of the General Assembly of the State of South Carolina Passed at the Regular Session of 1883* (Columbia: Calvo, 1884), 661–62; "The Calhoun Sarcophagus," *NYT*, March 14, 1884; "The Grave of Calhoun," *CNC*, November 15, 1884; "Carolina to Calhoun," *CNC*, November 15, 1884.

89. Crawford, "Classical Orator," 65.

90. M. G. van Rensselaer, "Saint Gaudens's Lincoln," *The Century* 35 (November 1887): 38.

91. Cunningham, "Sketch," 24–26; "The Statue of Calhoun," *CNC*, December 22, 1883; Cash, *Mind of the South*, 110.

92. *Appendix to History of the Calhoun Monument*, 2; *American Architect and Building News* 46 (December 22, 1894): 122.

93. Cunningham, "Sketch," 27; "The Calhoun Memorial," *CNC*, March 13, 1882; "The Calhoun Memorial," *CR*, March 30, 1882.

94. Cunningham, "Sketch," 28–33; Caroline Carson, *Roman Years*, 130, 147; "The Calhoun Monument," *CNC*, April 14, 1882; "The Calhoun Monument," *CNC*, April 17, 1882; "The Statue of Calhoun," *CNC*, December 22, 1883; A. Hunter to Mrs. Fitch, April 11, [1882], A. P. Aldrich to Mary Amarinthia Snowden, April 26, 1882, both in MAYSP; O'Brien, *Character*, 251.

95. "John C. Calhoun," *CNC*, April 26, 1887; "After Many Years," *CR*, April 27, 1887; *NYT*, April 27, 1887.

96. Mamie Garvin Fields with Fields, *Lemon Swamp*, 57; "Concerning Chalk Marks," *CNC*, December 2, 1894; Karen Fields, "What One Cannot Remember," 156–58; Roberts and Kytle, "Looking the Thing in the Face," 22.

97. *Appendix to History of the Calhoun Monument*, 2; "The Calhoun Monument," *CNC*, October 31, 1895; "A Picture in Bronze," *CNC*, June 10, 1896; "The Calhoun Monuments," *Harper's Weekly*, April 3, 1897, 343.

98. *Appendix to History of the Calhoun Monument*, 3; "A Picture in Bronze," *CNC*, June 10, 1896; "Work on the Monument," *CNC*, June 12, 1896; "John C. Calhoun's Statue," *NYT*, June 3, 1896.

99. "The Calhoun Monuments," *Harper's Weekly*, April 3, 1897, 343.

100. See "In the World of Art," *NYT*, January 12, 1896, for the LCMA's debate over a previous version that described Snowden hiding the securities in her "petticoat."

101. *Historical Sketch*, 20.

102. Ibid., 15; Bellows, *Talent for Living*, 27; "Historic Charleston Institution Provides Assistance for Many," *CNC*, April 26, 1948; "History of City's Confeder-

ate Home Pays Tribute to Gallant Women of the South," *CNC*, July 3, 1956; Marion Gerard Draine, "Confederate Home . . . A Serene Haven," *CNC*, August 21, 1960; Ellen Bryan, "The Return of the Native," *CNC*, November 15, 1971; Bob Summer, "Josephine Humphreys," *Publishers Weekly* 232 (September 4, 1987): 49.

103. Arlie Porter, "Sans a Cap: Calhoun Won't Get New Headwear This Year," *CPC*, December 25, 2002.

104. Humphreys, *Rich in Love*, 97; Drago, *Initiative, Paternalism, and Race Relations*, 6, 291 n. 9; Green, "Ex-Slave," 196. Shortly after the installation of the new monument, the Marion Square commissioners issued an ordinance prohibiting "the digging up of pebbles on the drill ground, the throwing of the same, or of rocks, brickbats, or other missiles; the marking, cutting, or otherwise defacing the trees, tree boxes or fencing, or the Calhoun Monument" (*City of Charleston Yearbook for 1896* [Charleston: Lucas and Richardson, 1897], 257–58). Later accounts of vandalism were more explicit. See "Annual Report of the Historical Commission, 1939," in *Year Book of the City of Charleston—1939* (Charleston: Walker, Evans, and Cogswell, 1941), 148; "Annual Report of the Historical Commission, 1945," in *Year Book of the City of Charleston, 1945* (Charleston: Walker, Evans, and Cogswell, 1947), 167.

105. Roberts and Kytle, "Looking the Thing in the Face," 39, 44–45; Jamaica Kincaid, "Sowers and Reapers," *New Yorker*, January 22, 2001, 41–42.

CHAPTER 3

1. Williamson, *After Slavery*; Zuczek, *State of Rebellion*, 72–74.

2. "The Confederate Dead," *CDP*, November 5, 1869; "Survivors' Association for Richland," *CDP*, November 7, 1869; "State Monumental Association," *CDP*, November 9, 1869; "The South Carolina Club," *CDP*, November 18, 1869; "The State Survivors' Association," *CDP*, November 20, 1869; "Young Men's Christian Association," *CDP*, November 25, 1869; "Memorial Address," 225.

3. McCord, "Enfranchisement of Woman," 325, 335; Louisa S. McCord to the Board of Managers of the South Carolina Monument Association, June 17, 1870, in *Louisa S. McCord: Poems, Drama, Letters*, 386–87. Faust, *Mothers of Invention*, 92–113, discusses Confederate ambivalence toward women nurses.

4. "South Carolina Monument Association," *CDP*, November 26, 1869; "South Carolina Monument Association's Appeal," *CR*, May 14, 1879. In the later stages of the campaign, fund-raising involved a wider variety of sources, including "penny readings" that featured singing as well as other spectacles. "Tableau[x] Vivants, for the Benefit of the Confederate Monument," *CDP*, April 25, 1875; "The Penny Reading," *CR*, May 12, 1876; "The Penny Reading," *CR*, May 13, 1877; "Choral Union Hall Last Night," *CR*, May 23, 1877; Brenda Kathryn Wentworth, "The First City Hall Opera House in Columbia, South Carolina: 1875–1899" (master's thesis, University of South Carolina, 1978), 68. The SCMA affirmed its original aspirations by indicating in its final report that all $10,119.76 raised by the group came from donations and interest except for a

$650 appropriation from the state legislature and the $97.11 surplus from Governor Wade Hampton's inaugural ball (*SCMA*, 69–70).

5. The text alludes to the *Aeneid*, 2.799, at which the Trojans assemble on the beach after the destruction of their city, "prepared with heart and fortune" to follow Aeneas to restored power.

6. *SCMA*, 13, 48.

7. Ibid., 48; Harwell, *Confederate Music*, 82–83; Fahs, *Imagined Civil War*, 118–19.

8. *In Memoriam*, 7–8, 14, 21; John P. Thomas, "Gen. Stephen Elliott, C.S.A.," *CS*, May 7, 1903; Bryan, *Creating*, 91. Comparison of photographs of Elliott and the original statue indicates that the Italian sculptor with whom Muldoon contracted may not have acted on the suggestion. An observer familiar with Elliott reported that "we recognize not the remotest resemblance," though the newspaper article shows that the SCMA's intent was widely known ("The Sentinel at His Post," *CR*, May 11, 1879).

9. "Confederate Monument at Columbia, S.C.," *CV* 15 (March 1907): 127; Wauchope, *Writers*, 398–400; Hungerpiller, *South Carolina Literature*, 222; Naipaul, *Turn in the South*, 99, 107; Mindy Lucas, "The Two Worlds of Larry McMurtry," *CS*, April 17, 2011. Confederate monuments that borrow from Trescot's inscription include works in Newnan, Georgia (1885); Staunton, Virginia (1888); Fairfax, Virginia (1890); Fayetteville, Arkansas (1897); Elberton, Georgia (1898); Eufaula, Alabama (1904); Gadsden, Alabama (1907); Cartersville, Georgia (1908); Cross Hill, South Carolina (1908); Millen, Georgia (1909); Burgaw, North Carolina (1914); and Oklahoma City, Oklahoma (1923).

10. W. H. Trescot to Isabella D. Martin, February 14, 1879, Isabella D. Martin Papers, SCL. For the full inscription, see Brown, *Public Art*, 40–41.

11. W. W. Ball, "Columbia in Reminiscence," undated newspaper column, W. W. Ball Collection, SCL; "Unveiling the Monument to the Confederate Dead," *CR*, May 14, 1879; "Carolina to Her Slain," *CNC*, May 14, 1879; "The Citizen Military of South Carolina," *CR*, May 15, 1879; *SCMA*, 46.

12. "The Sentinel at His Post," *CR*, May 11, 1879; Poole, *Never Surrender*, 94.

13. *SCMA*, 49–51, 60.

14. Ibid., 42–43; "The Monument Unveiled," *Chester Reporter*, May 15, 1879; "Communication," *CR*, May 20, 1879; "General Preston's Oration," *CNC*, May 22, 1879; "General Preston's Oration," *CNC*, May 27, 1879.

15. *SCMA*, 40, 44.

16. "South Carolina's Monument to the Confederate Dead," *CR*, May 13, 1879; "The Monument," *CR*, June 24, 1882. Poole, *Never Surrender*, 156–57, asserts that the new statue "resembled the cherubic guardians that flourished around the borders of Victorian-era greeting cards more than a battle-hardened warrior of Carolina" and argues that the replacement symbolized the decline of an aggressively confrontational culture of honor. Whatever a twenty-first-century observer might think of the two faces, both sculpted in Italy with limited guidance from South Carolina, Poole's evidence indicates that Carolinians understood the "manly strength" of the original statue largely in terms of its "poise"

and "*latent* vigor" (emphasis added). A contemporary described its visage as an "open, sweet young Southern face." See "Our Confederate Soldier Fallen," *CR*, June 23, 1882.

17. "Our Gallant Dead," *CDP*, July 6, 1866; A. C. Haskell, "Memorial Day," *CR*, May 10, 1876; "In Memoriam," *CR*, May 11, 1876; Carlyle McKinley, "Memorial Day in Columbia," *CNC*, May 12, 1876. Scholarship focused on Virginia has traced similar trajectories. See Blair, *Cities*; Janney, *Burying*; Kinney, "'If Vanquished'"; Litwicki, *America's Public Holidays*, 9-49; Van Zelm, "Virginia Women."

18. "A Solemn Scene," *CDP*, May 11, 1867; "A Pleasing but Mournful Scene," *CDP*, May 13, 1868; "Memorial Day," *CR*, May 11, 1886; John Hammond Moore, *Columbia and Richland County*, 277.

19. "The Heavens Wept," *CR*, May 11, 1888; "High Honor to Heroes," *CS*, May 11, 1894; "A Magnificent Address," *CR*, May 11, 1894. Foster, *Ghosts*, chaps. 6-10, remains the essential overview of "the Confederate celebration."

20. "Honoring the Dead," *CR*, May 11, 1897; "Memorial Day," *CR*, May 11, 1898; "Hampton Rode at Head of War Worn and Aged Heroes," *CS*, May 11, 1901; "Graves of the Dead of Lee's Great Army," *CS*, May 10, 1905; "South Carolina Division United Daughters of the Confederacy," *The Keystone* 12 (May 1911): 11.

21. "Observing Memorial Day in Late October," *CS*, October 15, 1899; "This Is Memorial Day in Columbia," *CS*, October 20, 1899; "Unveiling of the Shaft to Unknown," *CS*, October 21, 1899. Newspaper articles report a particular intention to honor the unknown dead of the Confederacy, but the monument expresses no such limitation. The verse is a quotation from Abram J. Ryan, "Lines," in *Poems*, 388-89.

22. "Though Dead He Speaketh," *CR*, May 11, 1888.

23. "R.V.R.C.," *CR*, August 7, 1875, mentioned Rose's participation in a rifle club parade during Reconstruction, but he received much more attention during the decade before his death in 1899. See "Our Honored Dead," *CR*, May 10, 1890; "Dead, But Not Forgot," *CR*, May 11, 1892; C. M. Douglas, "A Notable Colored Veteran," *CV* 2 (August 1894): 233; "Billy Rose's Unique Life," *NYT*, August 8, 1897. For later developments in the imagery of faithful servants, see McElya, *Clinging to Mammy*.

24. "Hampton Rode at Head of War Worn and Aged Heroes," *CS*, May 11, 1901; "Observing Memorial Day in Late October," *CS*, October 15, 1899.

25. "Sponsors Greeted by a Great Crowd," *CS*, May 10, 1901; "Ball to Sponsors the Great Function," *CS*, May 12, 1903; "Annual Opening Exercises," *CS*, May 13, 1903; Foster, *Ghosts*, 136-37.

26. Lumpkin, *Making*, 126, 147; Hall, "'You Must Remember This,'" 458.

27. Overton, "Girls," 4-5; Adams, "History"; Sally Elmore Taylor, "The Unparliamentary Woman an Impediment," *The Keystone* 1 (November 1899): 5; Hollis, *University of South Carolina*, 2:172. Cox, *Dixie's Daughters*, offers an overview of the early UDC.

28. Carolina, "The Problem of the Feminine," *The Keystone* 2 (April 1901): 9. The pseudonymous essay tracks the understanding of gender, work, and evolution

explored in Bederman, *Manliness and Civilization*, 121–69; Newman, *White Women's Rights*, 132–51. Joan Marie Johnson, *Southern Ladies*, situates *The Keystone* and the UDC in the club movement of the era. *The Keystone* only became the official organ of the UDC in November 1903 but served informally in that capacity from the outset of the journal.

29. Sally F. Elmore Taylor to Marie Taylor Elliott, April 3, 1895, Marie Taylor Elliott Papers, SCL; "South Carolina Daughters," *CV* 5 (January 1897): 14–15; "Daughters of Confederacy," *CNC*, December 7, 1900; Sally Elmore Taylor, "Report of the South Carolina Division U.D.C. at the Wilmington, N.C., Convention, November 13, 1901," *The Keystone* 3 (January 1902): 7.

30. Overton, "Girls," 9; "Collecting the Relics," *CS*, May 14, 1896. My reading of the Relic Room founding contrasts with Hillyer, "Relics of Reconciliation."

31. "Collecting the Relics," *CS*, May 14, 1896.

32. "History of the Wade Hampton Chapter"; "Mrs. Clark Waring, President, Wade Hampton Chapter, U.D.C., Columbia, S.C.," *CV* 10 (July 1902): 303; Harwell, *Confederate Music*, 13. The catalog did note ownership of "Mother, Is the Battle Over?"

33. "Collecting the Relics," *CS*, May 14, 1896; Sally Elmore Taylor, "Report of the South Carolina Division U.D.C. at the Wilmington, N.C., Convention, November 13, 1901," *The Keystone* 3 (January 1902): 7; Overton, "Girls," 21.

34. "South Carolina Daughters," *CV* 10 (January 1902): 56–58; Sally Elmore Taylor, "Deeds of Southern Women Should Live," in United Daughters of the Confederacy, *South Carolina Women*, 2:218; "Leaders in South Carolina," *The Keystone* 5 (April 1904): 10.

35. United Daughters of the Confederacy, *South Carolina Women*, 1:3–4; Censer, *Reconstruction*, 78–82, 153–83.

36. "South Carolina Daughters," *CV* 5 (January 1897): 14–15; Seigler, *Guide*, 238–39. Theodore Roosevelt, "The Flag-Bearer," in Lodge and Roosevelt, *Hero Tales*, 203–4, singled out this incident as one of the most memorable instances of Civil War valor.

37. "History of the Wade Hampton Chapter."

38. *Minutes of the Fourth Annual Meeting of the United Daughters of the Confederacy, Held in Baltimore, Maryland, November 10–12, 1897* (Nashville, Tenn.: Foster and Webb, 1898), 36–37; *Minutes of the Sixth Annual Meeting of the United Daughters of the Confederacy Held in Richmond, Virginia, November 8–11, 1899* (Nashville, Tenn.: Foster and Webb, 1900), 63–64; *Lost Cause* 3 (February 1900): 114; "Plea for Confederate Home," *CS*, February 22, 1909; "Increased Interest in Women's Monument," *CS*, March 18, 1909. For overviews of the debates, see Foster, *Ghosts*, 175–78; Mills, "Gratitude"; Elise L. Smith, "Belle Kinney."

39. "Judge Keiley Contributes," *Lost Cause* 4 (August 1900): 10; "An Appeal for the Memorial to the Women of the Confederacy," *Lost Cause* 6 (March 1902): 122–23; *Minutes of the Thirteenth Annual Convention of the United Daughters of the Confederacy, Held in Gulfport, Mississippi, November 14–17, 1906* (Opelika, Ala.: Post, 1907), 12, 27.

40. Margaret Drane Tichenor to Margaret L. Watson, March 1910, Margaret Drane Tichenor Scrapbook, Museum of the Confederacy, Richmond, Va.; "Concerning Southern Woman's Monument," *CV* 17 (August 1909): 371–72.

41. Carlton, *Mill and Town*, 133–35.

42. Savage, *Standing Soldiers*, 155–61; Seigler, *Guide*, 331–41; "Citizens of Lowndesville," *CS*, May 1, 1909.

43. John C. Roper, "Are Mills a Curse to this Sunny Land?," *CS*, January 12, 1898; "The Misleading Leaders," *CS*, January 21, 1905; Carlton, *Mill and Town*, 129, 157, 168. Otis, *Organic Memory*, 93–112, surveys influential theories of heredity and culture.

44. "York County Active in Monument Fund," *CS*, May 15, 1909; "Maj. Richards Tells of Monument Idea" and "How the Fund Grew in *The State*'s Care," both in *CS*, April 12, 1912; invitation to unveiling ceremony, n.d., Yates Snowden Papers, SCL.

45. "Women Taking a Hand in Care for Aged," *CS*, March 19, 1909; "A Misunderstanding," *CS*, April 6, 1909; "Soldiers' Home Opens Next Week," *CS*, May 29, 1909; "Soldiers' Home Is Now Opened," *CS*, June 4, 1909; "Nineteen Thousand Dollars," *CS*, August 22, 1909.

46. "How the Fund Grew in *The State*'s Care," *CS*, April 12, 1912; "Ruckstuhl Says We Are Growing," *CS*, May 15, 1909; F. Wellington Ruckstuhl, "Sculptor Interprets the Memorial," *CS*, April 12, 1912. Ruckstuhl changed his surname during World War I to a spelling he considered less Germanic. My discussion, focused on the prewar period, adopts the version he used at the time.

47. "Noted Sculptor Spoke Last Night," *CS*, January 6, 1912; Ruckstull, *Great Works*, 26; Boime, *Unveiling*, 348.

48. F. Wellington Ruckstuhl, "Sculptor Interprets the Memorial," *CS*, April 12, 1912; F. W. Ruckstuhl to Yates Snowden, March 5, 21, 1909, January 7, 1910, all in Yates Snowden Papers.

49. F. Wellington Ruckstuhl, "Sculptor Interprets the Memorial," *CS*, April 12, 1912; "Concerning Southern Woman's Monument," *CV* 17 (August 1909): 372.

50. F. Wellington Ruckstuhl, "Sculptor Interprets the Memorial," *CS*, April 12, 1912; "Concerning Southern Woman's Monument," *CV* 17 (August 1909): 372; Bederman, *Manliness and Civilization*, 129–34.

51. "Monument Fund Is Increasing," *CS*, April 16, 1909; Elise L. Smith, "Belle Kinney," 24–26; Kathleen W. Jones, "Mother's Day." Fahs, *Imagined Civil War*, 121–28, emphasizes that maternal figures were important during the war, but her book also provides abundant evidence that soldiers' wives and sweethearts enjoyed a wartime significance that would later decline.

52. "The Sentinel at His Post," *CR*, May 11, 1879; Russett, *Sexual Science*, 92–100.

53. "A Northern Tribute," *CS*, February 3, 1909.

54. F. Wellington Ruckstuhl, "Sculptor Interprets the Memorial," *CS*, April 12, 1912.

55. Ibid.; Seigler, *Guide*, 225–26.

56. "Addresses at Monument Unveiling Yesterday," *CS*, April 12, 1912.

57. Timrod, *Collected Poems*, 125–26.

58. Rosenburg, *Living Monuments*, 140, 148.

CHAPTER 4

1. See Blight, *Race and Reunion*; Blum, *Reforging*; Novick, *That Noble Dream*, 72–80; Silber, *Romance of Reunion*, 44–45, 116–17.

2. Light, *John William De Forest*, 84–163. Other late-nineteenth-century novels set in postwar South Carolina by northern writers include Goff, *Other Fools*; Robinson, *Shadow*; Roe, *Earth Trembled*.

3. Richardson, *Death of Reconstruction*, 89–121.

4. Trent, *William Gilmore Simms*, 247 n. 2.

5. Muhlenfeld, *Mary Boykin Chesnut*, 239 n. 47.

6. See Bonner, *Mastering America*, 150–61.

7. Those novels are Ashleigh, "Cavalier and the Puritan"; Chapin, *Fitz-Hugh St. Clair*; Means, *Thirty-Four Years*; Meynardie, *Amy Oakly*; and Rivers, *Eunice*. Capers, *Belleview*, shares features with the group but is less squarely focused on Reconstruction in South Carolina.

8. Diffley, *Where My Heart Is Turning Ever*.

9. McCurry, *Masters*.

10. Chapin, *Fitz-Hugh St. Clair*, 131. On the southern male work ethic in postwar fiction, see Censer, "Reimagining." For other readings of *Fitz-Hugh St. Clair*, see Gardner, *Blood and Irony*, 55–57; Poole, *Never Surrender*, 166–67; Kantrowitz, *Ben Tillman*, 181–82. Joan Marie Johnson, "Sallie Chapin," provides a biographical sketch of Chapin.

11. William J. Rivers to Yates Snowden, September 17, 1906, Yates Snowden Papers, SCL, reports that Rivers wrote the novel in 1874–75. He revised the manuscript, apparently in the early 1890s, but did not change the story substantially.

12. Rivers, *Eunice*, 75, 202.

13. Censer, *Reconstruction*, 32–41.

14. Diffley, *Where My Heart Is Turning Ever*; Fahs, *Imagined Civil War*, 225–55.

15. Means, *Thirty-Four Years*, 199.

16. Ibid., 131.

17. Ibid., 273.

18. Means, *Palmetto Stories*.

19. Ashleigh, "Cavalier and the Puritan," chap. 48, *CNC*, February 25, 1883; Dekker, *American Historical Romance*; Wimsatt, *Major Fiction*, 35–46.

20. Edmund Wilson, *Patriotic Gore*, 279; Aaron, *Unwritten War*, 253; O'Brien, "Flight"; Stern, *Mary Chesnut's Civil War Epic*; William L. Andrews et al., *Literature*, 220–34. Chopin, Tate, and Welty receive ten, eleven, and twelve pages, respectively, in this anthology.

21. *MCCW*, 37.

22. Ibid., 649.

23. Woodward took this approach even as he informed scholars about Chesnut's revision of her wartime diary (ibid., xxiv–xxvii). Many historians have followed the same emphasis, although some have disagreed with Woodward's reading of Chesnut. See, e.g., Faust, "In Search"; Fox-Genovese, *Within the Plantation*

Household, 339–71; Freehling, *Road to Disunion*, 1:245–49; Michael P. Johnson, "Mary Boykin Chesnut's Autobiography"; Stowe, "City, Country."

24. O'Brien, *Conjectures*, 2:1191. For another interpretation that stresses the postwar context of Chesnut's writing, see Glymph, "African-American Women."

25. The revised chronicle refers thirty-six times to Shakespeare, twenty-five times to Scott, and twenty-one times to Thackeray.

26. *MCCW*, 41, 191 n. 7, 698; Twain, *Life*, chap. 46. Wachtell, *War No More*, 36–40, includes Chesnut among the southern writers who emulated Scott.

27. Last Will and Testament of James Chesnut of Mulberry, Estate of James Chesnut, Kershaw County Estate Papers (microfilm), SCDAH.

28. The 1850 census records that Harriet Grant's older sister, Mary, was also in residence at Mulberry. Mary later married planter James J. Frierson.

29. Chesnut, *Private Mary Chesnut*, 174, 185, 187, 188, 253, 263; Muhlenfeld, *Mary Boykin Chesnut*, 132, 210–11. The will provided an annuity for Grant and made her one of the beneficiaries of a bond through which James Chesnut Jr. had purchased the Hermitage plantation from his father.

30. *MCCW*, 326.

31. Emma Holmes, *Diary*, 184.

32. *MCCW*, 190, 195, 203, 673, 818, 829.

33. Chesnut, *Private Mary Chesnut*, 244; *Camden Journal*, March 20, 27, 1844, May 18, 1852.

34. Chesnut, *Private Mary Chesnut*, 164, 212; *MCCW*, 130, 145, 278, 816.

35. *MCCW*, 139, 140, 411, 718, 724, 814, 835, 836.

36. Muhlenfeld, *Mary Boykin Chesnut*, 163–66.

37. Woodward, *Origins*, 76. John Hammond Moore, *Carnival of Blood*, chap. 1, provides an overview of the Cash-Shannon duel and Cash's political career. See also Kantrowitz, *Ben Tillman*, 93–95, 104–7; Poole, *Never Surrender*, 143–44; Clark, *Francis Warrington Dawson*, 105–8.

38. John Hammond Moore, *Carnival of Blood*, 25.

39. Kurant, "Mary Chesnut's Civil War," 133–67. In fact, Preston married in 1868 and died twelve years later.

40. *MCCW*, 365, 566, 816.

41. Ibid., 89.

42. Ibid., 707, 803, 811, 826, 832.

43. Freehling, *Road to Disunion*, 1:246.

44. *MCCW*, 789, 801, 828 (quotation); Rivers, *Eunice*, 44, 177, 223, 227.

45. *MCCW*, 44, 794, 833; Stern, *Mary Chesnut's Civil War Epic*, 230; Farnham, *Education*, 168–70.

46. Silber, *Romance of Reunion*, 185–95; Kantrowitz, *Ben Tillman*, 284–86; John Hammond Moore, "South Carolina's Reaction."

47. Bruce E. Baker, *What Reconstruction Meant*, 47–48; Holden, *In the Great Maelstrom*, 67–86; "Funeral Services Last Wednesday," *Beaufort Gazette*, March 3, 1927.

48. Daniel, *Maid*, 7–8; J. W. Daniel, "Dixon and the Ku Klux," *CS*, October 10, 1905.

49. Daniel, *Maid*, 212; Bruce E. Baker, *What Reconstruction Meant*, 48–49.

50. Jervey, *Elder Brother*, 296, 411.

51. Seabrook, *Daughter*, 7, 11.

52. Ibid., 168, 209, 237.

53. *MCCW*, 65.

54. Myrta Lockett Avary, undated reminiscence, Myrta Lockett Avary Papers, Atlanta History Center, Atlanta.

55. Myrta Lockett Avary, memorandum, [ca. October 1, 1904], Myrta Lockett Avary to Isabella D. Martin, October 12, 1904, Francis W. Halsey to Isabella D. Martin, December 13, 1904, Isabella D. Martin to Francis W. Halsey, November 24, December 1, 12, 15, 1904, W. W. Appleton to Isabella Martin, December 5, 1904, Isabella D. Martin and Myrta Lockett Avary to Francis W. Halsey, January 9, 190[5], Isabella D. Martin to D. Appleton and Co., January 23, 1905, all in Avary Papers. Appleton later adopted the title devised by the *Saturday Evening Post* for the serial preview of the book.

56. Isabella D. Martin to Myrta Lockett Avary, August 9, 1904, October 13, [1904], Myrta Lockett Avary to Francis W. Halsey, October 19, December 12, 1904, Isabella D. Martin to Francis W. Halsey, December 12, 1904, all in Avary Papers; "Isabella Martin Has Passed Away," *CS*, March 5, 1913.

57. Draft, [ca. October 19, 1904], Isabella D. Martin and Myrta Lockett Avary to Francis W. Halsey, January 9, 190[5], both in Avary Papers.

58. Chesnut, *Diary from Dixie*, 404.

59. Chesnut, *Private Mary Chesnut*, 262; *MCCW*, 805.

60. The letter reads, "General Hampton has returned from Cashier Valley with his arm broken—badly dislocated, I ought to say—and he does look so crushed. This has not been a summer disappointment to him. How the return of this season must bring back the tragedy of last year which closed forever the blue eyes of that glorious boy Preston. Now! There strikes up a serenade to Gen. Ames—a military Band. It recalls last summer so vividly" (Mary Boykin Chesnut Notebooks, Williams-Chesnut-Manning Family Papers, SCL).

61. Chesnut, *Diary from Dixie*, 350; Isabella D. Martin to Yates Snowden, October 7, [?], Yates Snowden Papers; *Journal of the Senate of the General Assembly of the State of South Carolina, Regular Session Beginning Tuesday, January 14, 1908* (Columbia: Gonzales and Bryan, 1908), 88. The four daughters of Wade Hampton II inherited Millwood at his death in 1858. Wade Hampton III built a Columbia home called Diamond Hill, also burned in the Civil War. Hampton replaced it with a Columbia residence called Southern Cross. This home burned in 1899.

62. John Preston Arthur, "Through Southern Eyes," chaps. 24–25, John Preston Arthur Papers, SCL.

63. Isabella D. Martin to Francis W. Halsey, November 24, 1904, Avary Papers.

64. Ravenel, *Charleston*, 486.

65. Wister, *Lady Baltimore*, 52, 85.

66. McCants, *White Oak Farm*, 259, 316. The South Carolinian contributions to a regional anthology of Reconstruction literature further illustrated the shift in interest. See Ambrose E. Gonzales, "Old Pickett," and John Bennett, "In Pompion Swamp," in *In Dixie Land*, ed. Palmer, 111–21, 133–43. South Carolina re-

mained conspicuous in novels about Reconstruction politics written by authors from other states, including Griswold, *Sea Island Lady*; Fast, *Freedom Road*.

67. "Wade Hampton," *CS*, November 20, 1906; Bruce E. Baker, *What Reconstruction Meant*, 40–43.

68. Bruce E. Baker, *What Reconstruction Meant*, 102; Simon, *Fabric*, 188–218; Holden, "'Is Our Love?,'" 60–62, 77–81.

69. David Duncan Wallace, "The Life of Martin Witherspoon Gary," 153–54, David Duncan Wallace Papers, SCL; Oakley Park Collection, SCL; Sheppard, *Red Shirts Remembered*, 48, 149–56; Collett, *Oakley Park*; Cornelia G. Walker, *Red Shirt*; *Presentation of Oakley Park*.

CHAPTER 5

1. Greene, *Why We Never Danced*, 4.

2. Yuhl, *Golden Haze*, 13, 171; Brundage, *Southern Past*, 201.

3. Greene, *Why We Never Danced*, 136; Greene, *Mr. Skylark*; Hutchisson, *DuBose Heyward*, 249.

4. Yablon, *Untimely Ruins*, 297 n. 18.

5. Yuhl, *Golden Haze*, 145, 146, 153–54; "Tribute Is Paid to Confederate Dead," *CNC*, May 11, 1918; "Memorial Day Is Observed Here," *CNC*, May 11, 1921; "South's Heroes Warmly Praised," *CNC*, May 11, 1923; "To Honor Memory of Confederates," *CNC*, May 10, 1927; "Charleston Pays Honor to Men of Confederacy," *CNC*, May 11, 1928; "Annual Exercises Honor War Dead," *CNC*, May 11, 1930; "Honor Veterans of Confederacy," *CNC*, May 11, 1931; Simons, *Stories*; Leiding, *Charleston*.

6. "Honor Veterans of Confederacy," *CNC*, May 11, 1931.

7. Yuhl, *Golden Haze*, 12; Dorman, *Revolt*.

8. Janney, "War," shows that intersectional commemoration foundered during this period at Appomattox, which centered on Confederate surrender, in part for the same reason that it flourished at Fort Sumter, which denied Confederate surrender.

9. Yuhl, *Golden Haze*, 173; "*Gone with the Wind* Period Costume in Museum Display," *CNC*, January 21, 1940; "1870 and 1860 Period Gowns in Museum Collections," *CNC*, January 24, 1940; "'Selling a City' Lengthy Process," *CNC*, February 1, 1940; Howard, *GWTW*, 412. The script compresses and in some ways modifies the parallel passage in Mitchell, *Gone with the Wind*, 1034.

10. *MCCW*, 51.

11. Reid, *Southern Tour*, 61–62; Trowbridge, *Picture*, 517–20; Carter, *Magnolia Journey*, 78–79; Rosenheim, *Photography*, 35–41.

12. Prentiss, *Charleston City Guide*, 81; "To Meet on the Ramparts of Fort Sumter," *NYT*, February 14, 1891; "South Carolina Comrades Reunion," *CV* 4 (May 1896): 139–40; C. Irvine Walker, "Notes about the Reunion City," *CV* 7 (March 1899): 103; McClure, *The South*, 54; Howells, "In Charleston," 747. *New Guide*, 45, reported that Fort Sumter was not "open to visitors except under restrictions."

13. James, *American Scene*, viii, 404.

14. Ibid., 412–21.

15. "Tourist Bureau Is Recommended," *CNC*, May 5, 1924; "Welcome the Fort Sumter," *CNC*, May 6, 1924; "The Fort Sumter Hotel," *CEP*, May 6, 1924. McIntyre, *Souvenirs*, discusses Charleston tourism from 1840 to 1920.

16. *Haesloop v. City Council of Charleston*, 123 S.C. 272, 115 S.E. 596 (1923); "Formal Opening of Fort Sumter Hotel Facing the Battery," *CNC*, May 6, 1924; "Hotel on Battery Ready for Guests," *CEP*, May 6, 1924, tourist ed.; "Harbor Forts of Charleston Have Notable Records," *CEP*, May 6, 1924, tourist ed.

17. "W. R. Greer Rites This Afternoon," *CNC*, December 30, 1932; Comstock, "Short History," 9–11.

18. "Name Sumter Hero in Lawton Will," *NYT*, October 9, 1919; "Lawton Bequests Puzzle Officials," *NYT*, November 11, 1919; "Exercises Today at Fort Sumter," *CNC*, April 11, 1931; "Exercises at Fort Sumter," *CEP*, April 11, 1931; "Confederate and Federal Memorials Are Dedicated," *CNC*, April 12, 1931; *Report of the Commission of Fine Arts*, 96–97; *Fort Sumter, South Carolina, April 12, 1861–April 11, 1931* (n.p., n.d.), program of exercises, SCL. The Anderson flagpole was supplemented a year later with a plaque listing the names of the soldiers in the Union garrison.

19. Stevens, *Charleston*, 284–93.

20. "Another Gun for Battery," *CEP*, May 16, 1928.

21. "Andrew Murray, Philanthropist, Has Passed Away," *CNC*, December 21, 1928; "MacNeil Designs Sumter Memorial," *CNC*, April 17, 1930; *Account of the Fort Sumter Memorial*, 3–8; Seigler, *Guide*, 110, 112.

22. Hobson, *Serpent in Eden*; Wingate, "Doughboys."

23. "Memorial to Be Unveiled," *CEP*, October 19, 1932; "Designer of Monument Interprets Its Motive," *CEP*, October 20, 1932.

24. "The Right Word—by Gerald Johnson," *CNC*, December 25, 1929.

25. *Account of the Fort Sumter Memorial*, 21, 27, 28.

26. "Writers See Fort Sumter," *CEP*, October 22, 1932. It is indicative of the development of Fort Sumter tourism that Charleston Museum director Laura Bragg had been unable to arrange a similar outing in 1923 when hosting the annual meeting of the American Association of Museums (Allen, *Bluestocking*, 81, 83).

27. O'Brien, "'South Considers Her Most Peculiar,'" similarly emphasizes local faith in the continuity of tradition as a crucial point of contrast with the southern intellectual movements based in Chapel Hill and Nashville. Greene, *Mr. Skylark*, 230, notes that Heyward and Sass were part of the same writing group during part of the drafting of the two novels.

28. Hutchisson, *DuBose Heyward*, 16; Rubin, *Edge*. Greene, "'Little Shining Word,'" traces additional connotations in Heyward's selection of a name for his protagonist.

29. Hutchisson, *DuBose Heyward*, 23; William Gilmore Simms to Paul Hamilton Hayne, July 4, 1863, in Simms, *Letters*, 4:431; Heyward, "Charleston," 280. John Bennett, "Story of Forgotten Bells, Sacrificed to Confederate Guns, Is Told," *CNC*, December 12, 1937, testifies to the popularity of the Saint Michael's story as context for his research on other churches that sacrificed bells.

30. Heyward, *Peter Ashley*, 100.

31. Ibid., 40, 62, 172, 234, 241–42.

32. Ibid., 80, 165, 206; Pressly, *Americans Interpret*, 279–80.

33. Heyward, *Peter Ashley*, 313–16.

34. Bland, *Preserving Charleston's Past*, 88; Heyward, *Peter Ashley*, 213; Lesesne, *Landmarks*, 38; William H. Pease and Pease, *James Louis Petigru*, 7–9; Stevens, *Charleston*, 96–98. Lesesne, grand-nephew of Petigru, was a longtime member of the *News and Courier* editorial staff, and his guidebook was the most influential of the 1930s.

35. Ball, "Back to Calhoun," 8; Stark, *Damned Upcountryman*, 84–85, 89, 152; Sass, *Outspoken*, 59; Sass, "Look Back." Sass followed the influential portrait of Calhoun as a realist presented in Parrington, *Main Currents*, 2:69–82.

36. Sass, *Look Back*, 66. The character's surname saluted Lord Acton, the aristocratic hero of political realism who maintained that the Civil War illustrated the dangers of unchecked democracy.

37. Sass, "Look Back," 7.

38. Sass, *Look Back*, 272, 274–75; Sass, "Look Back," 7.

39. Sass, *Look Back*, 274, 351.

40. Ibid., 348; Sass, "Look Back," 3.

41. Greene, *Mr. Skylark*, 243.

42. Heyward and Sass, *Fort Sumter*, vii, 108; Hutchisson, *DuBose Heyward*, 178.

43. Stevens, *Charleston*, 300–301; Daniels, *Southerner*, 331–33. See also Branston, *Let the Band Play*, 216–17.

44. Comstock, "Short History," 13, 18; "Report of Historical Commission, 1933–1936," in *Yearbook of the City of Charleston—1932–1935* (Charleston: Walker, Evans, and Cogswell, n.d.), 242.

45. Comstock, "Short History," 21; "Annual Report of Historical Commission, 1947," in *Year Book of the City of Charleston—1947* (Charleston: Nelsons' Southern Printing, 1949), 161.

46. Johnson Hagood, "Defense of Fort Sumter," *CNC*, April 23, 1948; Carman, "Fort Sumter."

47. Heyward, *Peter Ashley*, 61, 107–8, 268. Charles Ramsdell, "Lincoln and Fort Sumter," *Journal of Southern History* 3 (August 1937): 259–88, and John S. Tilley, *Lincoln Takes Command* (Chapel Hill: University of North Carolina Press, 1941) amplified this line of interpretation.

48. Heyward and Sass, *Fort Sumter*, 104; Johnson Hagood, "Defense of Fort Sumter," *CNC*, April 23, 1948; *Fort Sumter, South Carolina, April 12, 1861–April 11, 1931* (n.p., n.d.), program of exercises, SCL; *South Carolina: A Guide*, 391. The first sentence of Burton, *Siege*, 1, insists that "it was a siege even though the back door was open."

49. Frank Barnes, *Fort Sumter*, 1.

50. Ibid., 6, 12. Barnes's account was closer to Potter, *Lincoln and His Party*, and Randall, *Lincoln the President*, than to Stampp.

51. Frank Barnes, *Fort Sumter*, 1, 33, 38.

52. Ibid., 39–40; Blight, *Race and Reunion*, 67–68.

53. Comstock, "Short History," 26, 42, 60; "Civil War's Last Shells Are Exploded," *Life*, September 5, 1949, 61–64.

54. Rugh, *Are We There Yet?*, 19; Weeks, *Gettysburg*, chaps. 5–6; Weiss, *To Have and to Hold*, 115–23; Frank, "Economic Impact."

55. Comstock, "Short History," 25, 39–40.

56. Jensen, "Fort Sumter Flags."

57. "Fort Sumter Museum Dedication Set," *CNC*, April 11, 1961; Mike Ryan, "The Guns of Forts Sumter and Moultrie," 73; Ferguson, "Overview," 53–54; Comstock, "Short History," 91; "NPS Stats"; Bell I. Wiley to J. H. Easterby, May 26, 1958, and CWCC Press Release No. 141, September 27, 1960, both in South Carolina Confederate War Centennial Commission Files, SCDAH Director's Records, Agencies, Commissions and Organizations File, 1955–65, SCDAH.

58. Joint Resolution S. 17, South Carolina General Assembly, January 14, 1959, South Carolina Confederate War Centennial Commission Files; "City Ready for Fort Sumter Week," *CNC*, April 9, 1961.

59. Cook, *Troubled Commemoration*, 94; "Charleston, New Jersey Are Refighting 'the War,'" *CNC*, March 11, 1961.

60. Cook, *Troubled Commemoration*, 105; *South Carolina Speaks*, 41; "A Worse War," *CS*, April 13, 1961.

61. *South Carolina Speaks*, 5.

62. Bennett, *Doctor*, 44, 56. In the same volume, see also "Tales from the Trapman Street Hospital," 123–25.

63. Yarbrough, *Passion for Justice*, 64; Schmidt, "J. Waties Waring," 178; Axelrod, *Robert Lowell*, 156–59.

64. Cook, *Troubled Commemoration*, 149; Bruce E. Baker, *What Reconstruction Meant*, 135.

65. Cook, *Troubled Commemoration*, 151; Nevins, *War*, 1:74; Current, *Lincoln*, 182–208. Pressly, *Americans Interpret*, and Stampp, "Irrepressible Conflict," survey the debates.

66. Cook, *Troubled Commemoration*, 112; CWCC Press Release No. 138, June 28, 1960, South Carolina Confederate War Centennial Commission Files; "Citadel to Begin War Observance," *CNC*, January 7, 1961; Connelly, *Will Success Spoil?*, 31. See also *Confederate War Centennial*, 29.

67. Cook, *Troubled Commemoration*, 115–18; CWCC Press Release No. 151, March 1, 1961, South Carolina Confederate War Centennial Commission Files; Halsey, "Untold Stories."

68. "NPS Stats" (figures after April 1, 1963, include visitation at Fort Moultrie); Stewart R. King, "Rebel Flag Flies Again," *CNC*, April 13, 1970; Robert Behre, "Confederate Flags Still Fly at Fort Sumter," *CPC*, June 4, 2007; Halsey, *Who Fired?*; "Washington, Lincoln, and Firearms," *American Rifleman* 115 (February 1967): 14.

69. On remembrance of the 54th Massachusetts Regiment and the impact of *Glory*, see Blatt, Brown, and Yacovone, *Hope and Glory*. Comstock, "Short History," 36, and Frank Barnes, *Fort Sumter*, 44, date the 1950 marker depicted at www .hmdb.org/marker.asp?marker=19498, accessed May 29, 2012; my thanks to

National Park Service ranger Nathan Johnson for information about the date of the marker depicted at www.hmdb.org/marker.asp?marker=30811, accessed May 29, 2012. Ferguson, "Overview," 55, presents the conclusions of the Historic American Buildings Survey report. Five years before the release of *Glory*, an update of the Fort Sumter National Monument handbook expanded briefly on Barnes's passing reference to the 54th Massachusetts (*Fort Sumter: Anvil of War*, 40–41). Charleston Renaissance histories and guidebooks that describe the combat at Morris Island without acknowledging African American soldiers include Simons, *Stories*; Leiding, *Charleston*; Lesesne, *Landmarks*; C. Irvine Walker, *Historic Charleston*. Von Kolnitz, *Panorama*, 29, briefly mentions the 54th Massachusetts.

70. Andrew Curry, "The Better Angels," *U.S. News and World Report*, September 30, 2002, 63; "Fountain Named for Septima Clark," *CPC*, June 26, 2003; Sutton, *Rally*, v; *Slavery: Cause and Catalyst*.

71. Fort Sumter National Monument Visitor Education Center, Exhibit Text; Minutes of the Charleston Confederate Centennial Commission, August 2, 1960, South Carolina Confederate War Centennial Commission Files.

72. Bruce Smith, "War Site Sees Record Visitors," *CS*, April 7, 2012.

CHAPTER 6

1. Olwell, *Masters, Slaves*, 271–74; D. E. Huger Smith, "Wilton's Statue," 34–35. The statue now decorates the entrance hall of the Charleston County Courthouse, near its original position, embellished by a different quotation from Pitt about law as the guarantor of liberty.

2. Bill Swindell, "Hodges' Flag Plan Leads Pack," *CPC*, February 16, 2000. See Thomas J. Brown, "The Confederate Battle Flag and the Desertion of the Lost Cause Tradition," in *Remixing the Civil War*, ed. Brown, 37–72, for additional citations to newspaper material illustrating patterns described in this chapter.

3. "Letters," *CS*, April 10, 1997 (William Higgins); Martinez, Richardson, and McNinch-Su, *Confederate Symbols*, 4; Prince, *Rally 'Round the Flag*, 53, 57; Coski, *Confederate Battle Flag*, 271. See also Martinez, "Georgia Confederate Flag Dispute."

4. See Webster and Leib, "Whose South?"; Woliver, Ledford, and Dolan, "South Carolina Confederate Flag."

5. "Letters," *CS*, June 10, 2000 (Gary Bunker); Rachel Graves, "Flag Could Obscure Other Legislative Issues," *CPC*, December 12, 1999 (quoting Joseph Darby); "Colleton Request Illustrates Difference between Symbols," *CS*, February 3, 1997; Lisa Hofbauer, "Civil War Monument Issue Dies," *CPC*, February 4, 1997. This pattern, which should be distinguished from disputes over attempts to commission new government tributes to the Confederacy, has a few exceptions across the South. In 2000, for example, Richmond changed the names of two bridges that honored Stonewall Jackson and J. E. B. Stuart, substituting the names of local civil rights leaders. More common have been broader retreats from remembrance of slavery that related to or overlapped

with Confederate commemoration, such as the renaming of New Orleans public schools that honored slaveholders. The most widespread retractions of public tributes to the Confederacy have occurred in high school and college athletics, the realm of recreation and consumption in which this essay situates the battle flag.

6. "Letters," *CS*, June 12, 1996 (J. R. Owen Jr.).

7. Samuel W. Howell IV, "Flying Rebel Banner Does Honor to S.C.'s Confederate Veterans," *CS*, March 19, 1997; Bryan Collier, "Tribute Paid to Confederate Dead at Exercises," *CNC*, May 11, 1952.

8. Coski, *Confederate Battle Flag*, chaps. 4–8. On the flapper origins of *Gone with the Wind*, see Elizabeth Young, *Disarming*, 238–73.

9. Coski, *Confederate Battle Flag*, 86–87; Prince, *Rally 'Round the Flag*, 28–32; Frederickson, *Dixiecrat Revolt*, 100–102.

10. Coski, *Confederate Battle Flag*, 130, 166–67; "Confederate War Group Wins Yanks with Kindness," *CNC*, April 11, 1961. On commercialism in the Civil War centennial, see Cook, *Troubled Commemoration*, 45–47.

11. Coski, *Confederate Battle Flag*, 106; "Traditions and Code for Correct Use of the Confederate Flags—How to Display and Respect Our Flags," *United Daughters of the Confederacy Magazine* 24 (September 1961): 19. See also *United Daughters of the Confederacy Magazine* 24 (July 1961): 3, (October 1961): 3, (November 1961): 15.

12. John Hammond Moore, "Running Up the Flag, or How John Amasa May Thumbed His Nose at JFK," research file, South Carolina Political Collections, Ernest F. Hollings Special Collections Library, University of South Carolina, Columbia.

13. Beirich, "Struggle," 284–85.

14. "Governor Hollings Gets Official Bid to Centennial Ceremonies," *CS*, April 7, 1961, includes a photograph of May in the vest.

15. Cook, *Troubled Commemoration*, 88–119; "The 'Stars and Bars' Fly Again," *CS*, April 8, 1961; Joe Barnett, "No Confederate Flag Graced Capitol Dome," *CS*, April 12, 1961; John R. Moye, "Rebel Landing Party Invades Fort Sumter," *CNC*, April 13, 1961.

16. Cook, *Troubled Commemoration*, 151; Joseph P. Barnett, "State House Flags Wave Once More," *CS*, January 10, 1962; "Three Flags Flying," *Columbia Record*, March 28, 1962; *Journal of the House of Representatives of the Second Session of the 94th General Assembly of the State of South Carolina, Being the Regular Session Beginning Tuesday, January 9, 1962* (Columbia, S.C.: State Budget and Control Board, n.d.), 458–59; *Journal of the Senate of the Second Session of the 94th General Assembly of the State of South Carolina, Being the Regular Session Beginning Tuesday, January 9, 1962* (Columbia, S.C.: State Budget and Control Board, n.d.), 316–17.

17. Boime, *Unveiling*, 46; Bellah, "Religion."

18. William E. Mahoney, "Pickens County's Sen. Morris Deplores 'Cheapening' Abuse of Confederate Flag," *Columbia Record*, December 2, 1965; "Morris: Dixie Flag Proposal Supported," unidentified clipping, Confederate Flag Verti-

cal File, SCL. On Confederate flags during and immediately after the Civil War, see Bonner, *Colors and Blood.*

19. "Flag-Burning Arrest Made," *CS,* February 18, 1969. The Supreme Court decision in *United States v. O'Brien* (391 U.S. 367 [1968]) clearly indicated that prosecution would be untenable. A narrow majority later ruled in *Texas v. Johnson* (491 U.S. 397 [1989]) that the First Amendment protects burning of the American flag, but the dissent in that case rested squarely on the uniqueness of the national flag.

20. Brian Hicks, "CSA Galleries Closing Its Doors," *CPC,* February 24, 2009. Gallagher, *Causes Won,* 135–207, analyzes and provides illustrations of prints in the vein sold by CSA Galleries. This description draws on my visit to the store.

21. Cindi Ross Scoppe, "House Unravels on Flag," *CS,* April 4, 1997; "Be It Resolved . . . ," *CS,* March 29, 2000; "Letters," *CS,* April 30, 2000 (Joseph K. Taylor Jr.). Notable interventions by professional historians include Tom Terrill, "In Search of a Suitable Past," *CS,* January 7, 1997; Eric Foner, "Rebel Yell," *The Nation* 270 (February 14, 2000): 4–5; Charles W. Joyner, "The Flag Controversy and the Causes of the Civil War: A Statement by Historians," *Callaloo* 24 (Winter 2001): 196–98. This issue of *Callaloo,* devoted to the Confederate flag, is a stimulating collection of southern intellectuals' reflections on the theme.

   Not all disagreements over the flag were historical in nature. The most common objection to the display on the capitol dome was that the site should be reserved for flags of governments with authority in South Carolina. This argument centered on the meaning of the dome rather than the meaning of the flag, as nobody supposed that the battle flag was the emblem of a current government.

22. Margaret O'Shea, "Flag Tug of War Focus," *CS,* July 19, 1972; Neville Patterson, "Groups Request Flag's Removal," *Columbia Record,* July 18, 1972.

23. "Letters," *CS,* December 25, 1999 (Bob Brown), May 3, 1989 (Fred Boyd).

24. Coski, *Confederate Battle Flag,* 238, 252–55.

25. Ibid., 255–56; Clark Surratt, "Flag Flap," *CS,* February 22, 1987; "Patterson Suggests Flying Stars and Bars over Capitol," *Columbia Record,* June 17, 1987; *CS,* November 20, 1999 (image of Klansman).

26. Prince, *Rally 'Round the Flag,* 180; Brian Hicks, "Dixie Divided: Trip Ends in Fla. City as Divided as S.C. over Flag," *CPC,* March 16, 2000.

27. The narrative of the civil rights movement suggested by the flag campaign was in these respects much like commemorative initiatives discussed in Romano and Raiford, *Civil Rights Movement.*

28. Kenneth A. Harris, "Civil Rights Veterans Greet New Generation," *CS,* January 18, 2000; Kathryn Winiarski, "Columbia Marcher Remembers Segregation," *CS,* April 5, 2000.

29. Nina Brook, "Flag Compromise Support Grows," *CS,* October 16, 1993; "Letters," *CS,* May 28, 1989 (Glenn McConnell), June 11, 1991 (Keith A. Edwards), February 17, 1996 (J. Dale Weaver). See also Wayne Wall, "With Common Heritage, We Face Common Enemy," *CS,* March 13, 2000, which asserted that "the kind of genocide inflicted on the ancestors of our black citizens by the Yankee

slave traders and ship owners is not that much different from the cultural genocide still being waged against the South."

30. "Letters," *CS*, July 15, 1992 (Catherine D. McDonald), May 21, 1994 (Felicia For-
man Dryden).

31. Warren Bolton, "Shhh! No Debating the Flag while the Legislature Is in Session!" *CS*, May 12, 1999; April Simun, "Why a Mom Fights the Flag," *CS*,
December 17, 1999.

32. Anna Griffin, "Southerners Line Up to Defend Heritage," *CS*, April 20, 1997;
Joseph S. Stroud, "Flag Losing Favor with S.C. Voters," *CS*, September 27, 1999;
June Murray Wells, "Talk at South Carolina State House, January 8, 2000" and
"Update, January 29, 2000," www.electricscotland.com/, accessed August 4,
2009; Susan Hill Smith, "June Wells: Preserving History of Confederacy Is
Her Life's Work," *CPC*, February 26, 2000. Of the 931 individuals who contributed more than eleven hundred letters and guest editorials on the flag issue to
the *State* from January 1991 through July 2000, contributors' names provide a
strong basis for identification of the gender of 815 contributors. Women constituted 204 individuals in this group. Women contributed twenty-six of the
forty-three letters or guest editorials from contributors identifiable by gender
that explicitly called for relocation of the flag to a museum or elsewhere entirely
removed from the capitol grounds.

33. Lee Bandy, "Beasley Seeks Truce on Flag," *CS*, November 12, 1996; Bill Swindell and Rachel Graves, "McConnell Offers Flag Plan with 'Healing Pool,'" *CPC*,
March 30, 2000.

34. "Letters," *CS*, June 11, 1989 (Teddy Spencer).

35. See, e.g., "Letters," *CS*, April 8, 1993 (Herbert O. Chambers III), December 9,
1993 (Jason B. Owen), January 8, 1997 (William Rush), March 27, 2000 (Gene
Graj).

36. Joseph S. Stroud, "Flag Supporter Rallies His Forces," *CS*, January 6, 2000;
Kenneth A. Harris and Chuck Carroll, "Flag's Battle Lines Redrawn," *CS*, January 21, 2000; "S.C. House Votes to Move Flag," *CS*, May 11, 2000. Watts, *Contemporary Southern Identity*, 110–11, offers more examples.

37. "Confederate Battle Flag Should Be Moved in '93," *CS*, June 17, 1992; "Debating
the Flag: Three Views," *CS*, December 1, 1996.

38. "Letters," *CS*, December 14, 1999 (J. Wesley Peace); David Broder, "Confederate Banner Controversy Tests GOP Unity in SC," *CS*, January 15, 1997; Lewis F.
Galloway, "Living Together in Peace Must Be Our Goal," *CS*, January 16, 1997;
"A Statement from South Carolina Religious Leaders Concerning the Confederate Battle Flag," *CS*, January 19, 1997.

39. "Voices of the Flag," *CS*, December 22, 1996; Brad Warthen, "It Seems the
Romans Had this Dispute over 'Heritage' . . . ," *CS*, January 14, 1997; "Letters,"
CS, September 25, 1997 (Bobby Eubanks), January 28, 2000 (Ronald E. Lee),
May 17, 2000 (L. Carroll Pope Jr.), and the guest editorials of Wayne Wall: "The
Flag Flap: A More Excellent Way," *CS*, August 6, 1999; "Our Flag and Our Cul-
ture: Compromise or Capitulation," *CS*, January 5, 2000; "With Common Heri-
tage, We Face Common Enemy," *CS*, March 13, 2000.

40. "The Sun Rises on the Evil and the Good," *CS*, January 26, 1997 (quoting Ravenel); "Letters," *CS*, April 25, 1989 (W. Randolph Bass), November 18, 1996 (Richard Towell Hines).

41. "Debating the Flag: Three Views," *CS*, December 1, 1996.

42. Nina Brook and Cindi Ross Scoppe, "Campbell Could Call for Flag Session Soon," *CS*, June 25, 1994. The legislature thwarted the lawsuit by enacting clear authorization for the display.

43. Sonny DuBose, "Confederate Flag Issue Is Turning into Three-Ring Circus," *CS*, March 21, 1994; David G. Ellison Jr., "Confederate Leaders Themselves Signaled Furling Wartime Banner," *CS*, January 30, 1997; "Letters," *CS*, July 2, 1994 (William A. Byrd), November 22, 1996 (Mary Pinckney Powell), December 23, 1996 (Gail Richards Dunn), January 4, 1997 (Virginia Baker), April 2, 1997 (Elizabeth Beard), February 10, 2000 (Ann H. Brown). The only partial exception is "Letters," *CS*, February 7, 1994 (R. B. Dunovant Jr.).

44. David G. Ellison Jr., "Confederate Leaders Themselves Signaled Furling Wartime Banner," *CS*, January 30, 1997; Robert N. Rosen, "Lower the Flag in Honor of Southern Icon, Robert E. Lee," *CS*, December 12, 1999; Mary Foster Dillard, "South Represents Gentility, Grace, Not Hatred," *CS*, February 27, 2000; "Letters," *CS*, October 23, 1995 (Kenneth Emory Bell), March 27, 1997 (Kevin Lewis), January 25, 2000 (John Jay Jones), May 6, 2000 (Bill Rogers).

45. "Letters," *CS*, July 27, 1972 (Clif Judy Jr.), April 22, 1994 (William Carter).

46. Rachel Graves, "Flag Could Obscure Other Legislative Issues," *CPC*, December 12, 1999; Steve Piacente, "Ravenel Stepped Outside 'Civility,' Clyburn Says," *CPC*, January 15, 2000; "Debating the Flag: Three Views," *CS*, December 1, 1996. See also Poole, "Lincoln in Hell."

47. "Debating the Flag: Three Views," *CS*, December 1, 1996 (Condon, McConnell); "Letters," *CPC*, April 24, 2007 (Bill Norris). For the standard estimate that 45.8 percent of free South Carolina families owned slaves in 1860, see Schaper, *Sectionalism and Representation*, 155.

48. Clyde Wilson, "Southern Commitment to Self-Government Was Main Cause of War between the States," *CS*, January 11, 1997; Hobson, *But Now I See*; "Letters," *CS*, June 18, 1993 (Eugene E. Downs).

49. Schuyler Kropf, "Two Lawmakers Push Full Acceptance of Confederate Holiday," *CPC*, May 11, 2006.

50. "Confederate Memorial Day," *NYT*, April 27, 1878; Seigler, *Guide*, 23, 57, 358, 408.

51. Fredrickson, *Inner Civil War*, 220; *Address by Sen. John D. Long*, 5.

52. "Letters," *CS*, August 31, 1991 (C. W. Otto); "Debating the Flag: Three Views," *CS*, December 1, 1996; Rachel Graves, "Flag Deal Offered, Rejected," *CPC*, January 19, 2000.

53. Hagopian, *Vietnam War*; Savage, *Monument Wars*, 265–84.

54. Unidentified newspaper clipping, Confederate Flag Vertical File, Richland County Public Library, Columbia, S.C.

55. "Letters," *CS*, June 13, 1994 (Linda L. McCall), March 22, 1996 (Jane D. Floyd), August 30, 1999 (J. Stuart Torrey); "Letters," *CPC*, August 19, 2006 (Barry Barrineau).

56. "Letters," *CPC*, November 8, 2003 (Sandy Priester); *Address by Sen. John D. Long*, 3; Bill Swindell and Rachel Graves, "McConnell Offers Flag Plan with 'Healing Pool,'" *CPC*, March 30, 2000. See Foster, "Coming to Terms" for comparisons of Confederate memory and responses to the Vietnam War.
57. Seigler, *Guide*, 216–17; W. H. Trescot to Isabella D. Martin, February 14, 1879, Isabella Martin Papers, SCL.
58. "Letters," *CPC*, April 9, 2003 (Kenneth S. Anderson Jr.); Abraham Lincoln, "First Inaugural Address," in *This Fiery Trial*, 93. Steele, *Hiding from History*, 1–4, similarly treats the flag debate as an example of the privatization of values in contemporary political dialogue.
59. Clauda Smith Brinson, "Flag Furor Dialogue Was Unique in S.C. History," *CS*, July 1, 2001.
60. Valerie Bauerlein, "Change Waves Red Flag," *CS*, December 7, 2001.
61. Brian Hicks, "Politics Spices Barbecue Brothers' Conflicts," *CPC*, January 14, 2001. The chain began substituting the Stars and Bars for the Southern Cross after six years and took down the last of its Confederate flags after twelve years. "Maurice's Owner Flies New Confederate Flag," *CS*, October 27, 2007; "Moving On," *CS*, October 26, 2013.
62. "Spurrier: Take Down That Flag," *CS*, April 14, 2007.
63. Kenneth A. Harris, "Flag on Capitol Grounds Torched," *CS*, April 18, 2002; Roddie A. Burris, "Methodist Ministers Lead Protest against Flag," *CS*, May 2, 2007; Wiley B. Cooper, "Called to Stand against the Flag," *CS*, May 25, 2007.
64. See Boime, *Unveiling*, 52–81; Lonn Taylor, Kendrick, and Brodie, *Star-Spangled Banner*.
65. Bonner, *Colors and Blood*, 96–103.
66. Wates, *Flag*; Susan Hill Smith, "The Other Flag: Retailers and Buyers Just Can't Get Enough of the Simple and Striking Design of the South Carolina Flag," *CPC*, March 11, 2001.
67. Ernest Renan, "What Is a Nation?," in *Becoming National*, ed. Eley and Suny, 52.

CHAPTER 7

1. Beauregard, "Torpedo Service," 153; *CM*, November 9, 1863; H. W. Feilden to Augustine T. Smythe, June 25, 1914, Henry Wemyss Feilden Papers, South Carolina Historical Society, Charleston.
2. Ragan, *The Hunley*, 68, 116, 212; Conrad Wise Chapman, Notes on Painting of *H. L. Hunley*, photocopy, E. Milby Burton research files on the *Hunley*, Charleston Museum, Charleston.
3. "Scientists Discover New Stealth Feature on the H. L. Hunley," *BL* 16 (July 2005): 6; Vandermeer with Chambers, *Steampunk Bible*, 33–34.
4. Carol E. Harrison and Johnson, "Introduction."
5. Davis, *Rise and Fall*, 2:207. See also John Sanford Barnes, *Submarine Warfare*; Beauregard, "Torpedo Service"; Butler, "Southern Genius," 284–85; Newton, "Has the Day?"; Parker, *Confederate States Navy*, 75–76; Porter, "Torpedo Warfare"; Scharf, *History*, 753–68; James Russell Soley, "The Union and Confederate Navies," in *Battles and Leaders*, 1:612; von Scheliha, *Treatise*, 219–316.

6. Davis, *Rise and Fall*, 2:210; Maury, "Defence."

7. John Sanford Barnes, *Submarine Warfare*, 62; Porter, "Torpedo Warfare," 213–14. See Leonard, *Above the Battle*, 75–110.

8. Roland, *Underwater Warfare*, 162.

9. Glassell, "Torpedo Service"; Sass, "Story," is the most extreme tribute to the *David* as an achievement of the Charleston elite. See also Bellows, *Talent for Living*, 171.

10. Davis, *Rise and Fall*, 2:209; Beauregard, "Torpedo Service"; Roman, *Military Operations*, 2:21–23, 78–80, 181; John Johnson, *Defense*, cxliv.

11. Alexander, "Thrilling Chapter," 170; von Scheliha, *Treatise*, 315; Newton, "Has the Day?," 303; James H. Tomb, "Submarines and Torpedo Boats, C.S.N.," *CV* 22 (April 1914): 168.

12. Barber, *Lecture*, 17; John Sanford Barnes, *Submarine Warfare*, 152; Roland, *Underwater Warfare*, 130; von Scheliha, *Treatise*, 300. Beauregard, "Torpedo Service," 154, reported that he consented to use of the vessel after Hunley's death "not as a submarine machine, but in the same manner as the David."

13. Beauregard, "Torpedo Service," 151; John Johnson, *Defense*, xxxiv–xxxv.

14. Chaffin, *H. L. Hunley*, 127; Wise, *Lifeline*, 121–24.

15. "Charleston's Public Buildings," *CV* 7 (April 1899): 199.

16. "Long Neglected Heroes," *CNC*, May 9, 1899; Shirley Carter Hughson, "Torpedo Boat Heroes," *CNC*, May 10, 1899; "The Confederate Navy," *CNC*, May 10, 1899.

17. Alexander, "Thrilling Chapter," appeared in the *New Orleans Picayune*, June 19, 1902, *Mobile Daily Herald*, July 6, 1902, *Richmond Dispatch*, July 21, 1902, and *Gulf States Historical Magazine* 1 (September 1902): 81–91; Alexander, "Heroes," 746; "The Confederate Submarine 'Hunley,'" *Harper's Weekly*, December 24, 1910, 22; C. L. Stanton, "Submarines and Torpedo Boats," *CV* 22 (September 1914): 398.

18. Holland, "Submarine Navigation," 550; Lake, *Submarine in War and Peace*, chap. 2.

19. Lake, *Submarine in War and Peace*, 14; Butcher, *Jules Verne*, 187. For period histories of the submarine, see Bishop, *Story*; Burgoyne, *Submarine Navigation*; Lake, *Submarine*; Delpeuch, *Navigation*; Fyfe, *Submarine Warfare*; Pesce, *Navigation*; Sueter, *Evolution*.

20. Beauregard, "Torpedo Service," 152–54; Glassell, "Torpedo Service," 226; Olmstead, "Reminiscences," 66; Alexander, "Heroes"; Barber, *Lecture*, 17n; Scharf, *History*, 760–61. John Sanford Barnes, *Submarine Warfare*, 131, reported five sinkings.

21. C. L. Stanton, "Submarines and Torpedo Boats," *CV* 22 (September 1914): 398; Augustine T. Smythe Jr., "Torpedo and Submarine Attacks on the Federal Blockading Fleet off Charleston during the War of Secession," in *City of Charleston Year Book—1907* (Charleston: Walker, Evans, and Cogswell, 1908), 53–64; "C of C Program for January, 1919: A Confederate Submarine," *CV* 27 (January 1919): 34–35. For a representative sample of other accounts by white southerners, see Gadsden C. Zimmerman, "Anchors Aweigh," *CS*, June 14, 1936

(six sinkings); "Confederate Submarine Was First to Sink Battleship at Charleston 79 Years Ago," *CS*, January 31, 1943 (six sinkings); Harry von Kolnitz, "The Confederate Submarine," *United States Naval Institute Proceedings* 63 (October 1937): 1453–57 (five sinkings); "The Submarine of the Confederacy," *UDC Magazine* 10 (April 1946): 18, 21 (six sinkings); James Spotswood, "Memorial Shaft to Honor Crew of First Submarine," *CNC*, April 21, 1948 (four sinkings).

22. "C of C Program for January, 1919: A Confederate Submarine," *CV* 27 (January 1919): 34–35; Gadsden C. Zimmerman, "Anchors Aweigh," *CS*, June 14, 1936; Mrs. Edwin J. Palmer, "The Submarine in the War between the States," *UDC Magazine* 23 (March 1960): 24.

23. The source of the Barnum story was Confederate veteran James Gadsden Holmes of Charleston, who claimed in 1915 that a local diver had told him about the offer. See Ragan, *The Hunley: Submarines, Sacrifice, and Success*, 161–63; "The Sinking of the Housatonic," *CV* 24 (June 1916): 281. Chaffin, *H. L. Hunley*, 287 n. 20, debunks the tale. DuBose Heyward, "The Last Crew," in Heyward and Allen, *Carolina Chansons*, 54–64, 127–28; Heyward, "Charleston," 297; E. Milby Burton to Newman Bustead, May 10, 1939, E. Milby Burton Papers, Charleston Museum, Charleston.

24. "C of C Program for January, 1919: A Confederate Submarine," *CV* 27 (January 1919): 35; Heyward, "Charleston," 297; Klaxon [John Graham Bower], "Sailor's View," *Literary Digest*, December 28, 1918, 38, quoted in "Contribution of the Confederacy to Naval Architecture and Naval Warfare," *CV* 31 (August 1923): 336. See also "Long Neglected Heroes," *CNC*, May 9, 1899; Smythe, "Torpedo and Submarine Attacks," 53, 60.

25. Jervey, *Elder Brother*, 264–65.

26. Dabney H. Maury, "How the Confederacy Changed Naval Warfare," *Southern Historical Society Papers* 22 (1894): 80; Smythe, "Torpedo and Submarine Attacks," 53.

27. Brady, *Little Traitor*, 61, 57, 138–39.

28. Mrs. W. J. Behan, "The Confederated Southern Memorial Association," *CV* 24 (February 1916): 63.

29. Robert S. Henry, "The Sub That Sank Six Times," *Collier's*, July 10, 1943, 64; "The Submarine of the Confederacy," *UDC Magazine* 10 (April 1946): 18, 21; James Spotswood, "Memorial Shaft to Honor Crew of First Submarine," *CNC*, April 21, 1948.

30. *Life in America*, xxi, 104, 127–28, 156–60.

31. Ibid., xxiv, 140–42.

32. "Art Traps," *Time*, May 8, 1939, 63–64.

33. Parrish, *Submarine*, 432, 457–59.

34. Langer, "Why the Atom."

35. Parrish, *Submarine*, 479.

36. Mason, *Our Valiant Few*, vii, 370; "Navy May Name Ship for Hundley," *CNC*, August 25, 1958; "Nautilus Gets Papers on Confederate Hunley," *CNC*, January 28, 1958; "Plaque Presentation," *UDC Magazine* 23 (November 1960): 10; "Sub Tender Hunley Joins Polaris Fleet," *CNC*, September 29, 1961; "Message of

the President General," *UDC Magazine* 24 (November 1961): 3–4; Amma Nell Hall, "USS Dixon Commissioned at Norfolk Naval Shipyard," *UDC Magazine* 34 (October 1971): 14–15. On the spelling of Hunley, see "Now It's Official! It's 'The Hunley,'" *CNC*, March 10, 1961.

37. Foote, *Civil War*, 896–98.

38. Francis Cockrell, *The Great Adventure: The Hunley*, revised script, May 31, 1963, George S. Lindsey Collection, Collier Library Archives, University of North Alabama, Florence.

39. Frederickson, "Confronting."

40. Hopkins, "From Naval Pauper to Naval Power," 23; Huntley, "Mendel Rivers."

41. "Museum to Accept Model of Hundley," *CNC*, February 17, 1961; "Imposing New Stone Honors Crewmen of First Submarine," *CNC*, October 14, 1963; Everett Laitala to R. Bentham Simons, March 11, 1961, Robert C. Edwards to F. J. Jervey, March 23, 1961, both in *Hunley* Papers, Charleston Museum, Charleston; Phillips, *City*, 149.

42. "Fact Sheet: *Hunley* Museum" [1967?], Fred C. Craft to Charleston Hunley Museum, October 24, 1975, both in *Hunley* Papers, Charleston Museum, Charleston; Les Dane, "Small Museums Big in Value, *CNC*, March 31, 1970.

43. Donald G. Herold to Julius E. Burges, March 10, 1977, February 6, 1978, January 31, 1980, all in *Hunley* Papers, Charleston Museum, Charleston; *The Hunley Museum: A Branch of the Charleston Museum*, brochure (1980), Vertical Files, SCL; Ron Chepesiuk, "The Birth of the Submarine," *The State Magazine*, June 14, 1987.

44. Tom Perry, "Salvage of Sub Hunley Has 50–50 Chance for Success," *CNC*, June 18, 1957; Stewart R. King, "Skin Diver Thinks He's Found the Hunley," *CNC*, February 18, 1964; Hicks and Kropf, *Raising the Hunley*, 107, 143–44.

45. S. 844 (1995–96), South Carolina Legislature Online, www.scstatehouse.gov, accessed May 6, 2011; Glenn McConnell, "Hunley Crew Deserving of Respect," *CS*, October 14, 2003.

46. Mark K. Ragan, "Hunting for a Lost Confederate Submarine," *Washington Times*, September 4, 1993; "S.C. to Dive Alone for Sunken Artifact," *CS*, September 20, 1993; Dave Moniz, "Discovery of Confederate Sub Could Solve Mysteries of Sinking," *CS*, May 17, 1995; Oeland, "H. L. Hunley"; John Monk, "Day Belonged to Lost Confederacy," *CS*, April 18, 2004; Hicks and Kropf, *Raising the Hunley*, 34.

47. Parrish, *Submarine*, 20; Oeland, "H. L. Hunley," 84; John Monk, "McConnell's Hunley Claims Questionable," *CS*, May 14, 2006.

48. Bruce Smith, "New Hunley Details Revealed," *CS*, June 16, 2005; Tony Bartelme, "Preservation Work Leads to Discoveries," *CS*, December 28, 2009.

49. "A Letter from the Senator," *BL* 3 (Winter 2002): 1.

50. Hicks and Kropf, *Raising the Hunley*, 160; *Raising the Hunley: The Resurrection of the Civil War Submarine* (National Geographic Television, 2007).

51. John Monk, "Next Week's Hunley Crew Burial Is Golden Opportunity to Raise Funds," *CS*, April 9, 2004; Wayne Washington, "Hunley Group Has $1.3 Million That Deal Says Belongs to State," *CS*, October 6, 2004; "'Hunley' Money,

Like 'Hunley' Itself, Belongs to State," *CS*, October 8, 2004; Ed McMullen, "Let's Not Sink the 'Hunley' Again," *CS*, October 22, 2004; Wayne Washington, "McMaster Rules State Not Entitled to Hunley Funds," *CS*, October 29, 2004; John Monk, "How Senator Steers Sub under Radar," *CS*, May 14, 2006; John Monk, "Hunley Audit Unlikely," *CS*, July 6, 2006; John O'Connor, "Audit Council Won't Examine Hunley Finances," *CS*, July 26, 2006; "The State Wins Award for Its Hunley Series," *CS*, July 30, 2006; *Sloan v. Friends of the Hunley*, 369 S.C. 20, 630 S.E. 2d 474 (2006); "The Price of Stonewalling," FITSNews, March 18, 2009, www.fitsnews.com/2009/03/18/the-price-of-stonewalling/, accessed March 6, 2011.

52. Chaffin, *H. L. Hunley*; Oeland, "H. L. Hunley"; Hicks and Kropf, *Raising the Hunley*, 3, 38, 56, 175; Ragan, *The Hunley: Submarines, Sacrifice, and Success*, 40–42, 52–54; Sally M. Walker, *Secrets*; Leland, "Middleton Correspondence," 167; Bruce Smith, "First Tour Group Gets Up-Close Look at Hunley Submarine," *CS*, October 15, 2000.

53. Chaffin, *H. L. Hunley*, 226; Bruce Smith, "C.S.I. *Hunley*: Fate of Historic Sub a Cold-Case File," www.foxnews.com/story/0,2933,475811,00.html (Associated Press), accessed July 19, 2012; "Cornwell Pledges to Give $500,000 to Hunley Probe," *CS*, February 16, 2006; "A Letter from the *Hunley* Staff," *BL* 20 (Summer 2006): 3.

54. "Hunley Coin Pulled after Protest," *CS*, October 10, 2001; "Hunley Coin to Be Displayed," *CS*, February 23, 2002; "Replicas Available of Legendary Gold Coin," *BL* 4 (May 2002): 3. See also Ragan, *The Hunley: Submarines, Sacrifice and Success*, 79–81; Hicks and Kropf, *Raising the Hunley*, 62–63, 85–86, 236, 242; Chaffin, *H. L. Hunley*, 234–37; Hawk, *Story*. Bennett's age is reported in the 1860 manuscript census, available at www.ancestry.com.

55. Chaffin, *H. L. Hunley*, 205; "Expert Studies Jewelry," *BL* 9 (August 2003): 3; "Timeless Artifact Recovered from H. L. Hunley," press release, Friends of the *Hunley*, June 7, 2002, www.hunley.org, accessed May 3, 2011.

56. Ragan, *The Hunley*, 231–32.

57. Eric Velasco, "After Tense Recovery, Team Basks in Glow of Hunley's Successful Return," *CS*, August 10, 2000; "A Letter from the Senator," *BL* 5 (September 2002): 2; "The Teeth Are Telling," *BL* 7 (February 2003): 6; "The Hunley Crew Rests at Last," *BL* 12 (June 2004): 3. For a more thoughtful and less confident assessment of the accuracy of facial reconstruction, see Wilkinson, *Forensic Facial Reconstruction*, 200–219.

58. Kloeppel, *Danger*, 94–95; Cardozo, *Reminiscences*, 124–25. Kloeppel did not include the last sentence in his quotation from Cardozo's memoir.

59. "Door to *Hunley* Found Open," *BL* 19 (April 2006): 4, 6–7. Chaffin, *H. L. Hunley*, 240–47, features a good discussion. Most other *Hunley* books report the signaling without question. See, e.g., Hoyt, *Voyage*, 63. The story of the blue light became even less plausible when conservators concluded that the torpedo spar still connected the *Hunley* directly to the *Housatonic* at the time of explosion. Brian Hicks, "Hunley Research 'Changes Some Things,'" *CS*, January 29, 2013.

60. Clardy, *TimeLight*, 237.

61. Madsen-Brooks, "'I Nevertheless Am a Historian.'"

62. Hicks and Kropf, *Raising the Hunley*, 3; Butcher, *Jules Verne*, 185–95; Eric Velasco, "Hunley Made Waves in Military Strategy," *CS*, July 23, 2000. Verne's short story "The Blockade Runners," originally published in 1865, shows the extent of his familiarity with operations in Charleston Harbor during the latter stages of the Civil War.

63. See, e.g., Chabon, "Martian Agent"; Gibson and Sterling, *Difference Engine*; Priest, *Boneshaker*; Priest, *Dreadnought*; Priest, *Clementine*.

64. Hicks and Kropf, *Raising the Hunley*, 56–57; Chaffin, *H. L. Hunley*, 231; Eric Velasco, "Hunley Made Waves in Military Strategy," *CS*, July 23, 2000; "Divers Say Hunley's Rudder Missing," *CS*, May 24, 2000; Glenn McConnell, "A Letter from the Senator," *BL* 3 (Winter 2002): 2.

65. Krista Zala, "Crafters Tinker with Technology," *Nature*, March 6, 2008, 32.

66. Gordon L. Jones, "'Gut History.'"

67. Wendy C. Burbage, "Where Are the Missing Confederate Seamen?," *UDC Magazine* 55 (June–July 1992): 23; Dan Lewerenz, "Dig to Give Soldiers Proper Burial," *CS*, June 30, 1999; Bruce Smith, "Officials Finish Dig for Hunley Crew," *CS*, July 21, 1999; Bruce Smith, "First Crew of Historic Submarine Reburied," *CS*, March 26, 2000; "The Last Confederate Burial: Hunley Crew Interment Date Announced," *BL* 8 (May 2003): 6; Jeff Wilkinson, "Thousands Step to Beat of Hunley Parade," *CS*, April 18, 2004.

68. "Hunley Military Funeral Planned for Fall," *CS*, July 11, 1999; Halttunen, *Confidence Men*, 148.

69. Ragan, *The Hunley: Submarines, Sacrifice and Success*, 73–74; "Last Honors to the Heroes of Manassas," *CM*, July 27, 1861; Emma Holmes, *Diary*, 69–70.

70. John Monk, "U.S. Flag Focus of Hunley Flap," *CS*, September 14, 2003; John Monk, "Day Belonged to Lost Confederacy," *CS*, April 18, 2004.

71. Valerie Bauerlein, "McConnell Defends Purchase of Artifacts," *CS*, June 29, 2001; Valerie Bauerlein, "Plan to Buy War Relics Criticized," *CS*, July 22, 2001; Schuyler Kropf, "Decision on Hunley Museum Site Delayed," *CPC*, August 14, 2001; Brian Hicks and James Scott, "Panel Tours Sites Wooing the Hunley," *CPC*, April 2, 2002.

72. "A Letter from the Senator," *BL* 11 (March 2004): 2.

73. Bruce Smith, "Hunley Replica May Roam Coast," *CS*, May 12, 2001; "Virtual Hunley Experience Awaits Visitors," *CS*, August 14, 2004; John Monk, "With No Market Study, Sub Museum Risks Sinking," *CS*, May 16, 2006; "*Hunley* Exhibit Sails into Myrtle Beach," *BL* 12 (June 2004): 6; "Experience the *H. L. Hunley* in Myrtle Beach," *BL* 17 (October 2005): 3.

74. Bruce Smith, "Groups Vie to Build Hunley Museum," *CS*, February 22, 2002; John Monk, "Hunley Price Tag Rising for S.C. Taxpayers," *CS*, October 27, 2002; "A Letter from the Senator," *BL* 12 (June 2004): 2; *The Big Picture Explores the H. L. Hunley*, www.scetv.org, originally aired August 7, 2008, accessed March 21, 2011.

75. Joseph P. Riley Jr., "A Museum on the Harbor at City's Liberty Square," *CPC*, April 7, 2002; "Riley Suggests New Hunley Plan," *CS*, December 31, 2002.

76. Kloeppel, *Danger*, 73–80. Bak, *CSS Hunley*, 157–78, reprints the proceedings of the U.S. Navy court of inquiry on which Kloeppel's analysis relied.

77. See Bak, *CSS Hunley*; Chaffin, *H. L. Hunley*; Hicks and Kropf, *Raising the Hunley*; Hoyt, *Voyage*; Ragan, *The Hunley: Submarines, Sacrifice and Success*; Ragan, *The Hunley*; Campbell, *CSS H. L. Hunley*.

CHAPTER 8

1. Warren Wise, "Ted Ashton Philips Jr., Attorney, Collector, Local Historian Dies at 45," *CPC*, January 18, 2005; "Ted Ashton Phillips Jr.," *CPC*, January 22, 2005. The trustees of Magnolia Cemetery dedicated a memorial garden in honor of Ted Phillips on April 3, 2008.

2. Suzanne Vega, "The Ballad of Henry Timrod," *NYT*, September 17, 2006; Robert Polito, "Bob Dylan: Henry Timrod Revisited," www.poetryfoundation .org/article/178703, accessed September 8, 2011; Dylan, *Chronicles*, 84, 86.

3. All Dylan lyrics from www.expectingrain.com, accessed September 12, 2011.

4. For details on the borrowings from Timrod, Whitman, Melville, Nathaniel Graham Shepherd, and Unitarian poets William Channing Gannett, Louisa Jane Hall, Robert C. Waterston, and Cambridge minister William Newell, see "'Cross the Green Mountain' Quotes a William Newell Poem," http://expectingrain .com/discussions/, accessed September 12, 2011.

5. Timrod coquettishly worried in a sonnet if he misread into a gift "things which you never meant nor wished to say." Dylan sighed that "I laugh and I cry and I'm haunted by / Things I never meant nor wished to say."

6. David S. Shields, "Henry Timrod," describes this mythic narrative of poetic vocation. Quotations from "Retirement," "A Rhapsody of a Southern Winter Night," and "A Vision of Poesy," in *Collected Poems*, 44, 47, 78. For Timrod verses in Dylan's lyrics, see http://dylanchords.info/45_modern/timrod.html. To the list for "When the Deal Goes Down" should be added Dylan's adaptation ("we all wear the same thorny crown") of Timrod's report that "In all its realms I saw no mortal crown / Which did not wound or crush some restless head." The paraphrase underscores that Dylan's engagement with Timrod was not merely a lifting of well-worded passages.

7. Wilentz, *Bob Dylan*, 305–8.

8. Richard F. Thomas, "Streets of Rome," 39.

9. Wilentz, *Bob Dylan*, 314–19.

10. Thurber, "'Dixie,'" 58–69, 71–77, 87 n. 27; Rammel, *Nowhere in America*. Green, *Green's Dictionary of Slang*, 1:1578, first documents "dick" as a term for penis in 1836, although several seventeenth-century examples demonstrate its much earlier usage as an expression for a male sexual partner. Emmett's puns on "stand" and "die" followed several centuries of precedents. Lott, *Love and Theft*, 25, emphasizes that antebellum minstrelsy reflected "white men's obsession with a rampageous black penis." On the cross-racial origins of "Dixie," see also Sacks and Sacks, *Way Up North*.

11. Timrod, *Essays*, 163.

12. Hutchison, *Apples and Ashes*, 143–72.

13. Phillips, *City*, 26–27, 66, 73–76, 80–81, 85–86, 133–34, 169–71.

14. Ibid., 47–48, 111, 177–79.

15. Ibid., 92, 127, 161, 171.

16. *Confederate Monument at Charleston*, 26–27.

17. Phillips, *City*, 108–10; Rhett, "Sketch"; John Johnson, *Defense*, 227–28; Seigler, *Guide*, 124–27; Quinlan, *Strange Kin*, 78; Keneally, *Great Shame*, 390.

18. Rhett, "Sketch," 272.

Bibliography

PRIMARY SOURCES

An Account of the Fort Sumter Memorial. Charleston, S.C.: Furlong, 1933.

Adams, Margaret Crawford. "History of Wade Hampton Chapter, Daughters of the Confederacy, of Columbia, S. C., from Its Organization, December 20th, 1895, to May 26th, 1904." United Daughters of the Confederacy, Wade Hampton Chapter Papers, South Caroliniana Library, University of South Carolina, Columbia.

An Address by Sen. John D. Long of Union County on the Confederate Battle Flag to the Senate of South Carolina, Tuesday, January 22, 1957. N.p., n.d.

Alexander, W. A. "The Heroes of the *Hunley*." *Munsey's Magazine* 29 (August 1903): 746–49.

———. "Thrilling Chapter in the History of the Confederate States Navy: Work of Submarine Boats." *Southern Historical Society Papers* 30 (January–December 1902): 164–74.

Andrews, Sidney. *The South since the War: As Seen by Fourteen Weeks of Travel and Observation in Georgia and the Carolinas*. Boston: Ticknor and Fields, 1866.

Andrews, William L., Minrose C. Gwin, Trudier Harris, and Fred Hobson, eds. *The Literature of the American South: A Norton Anthology*. New York: Norton, 1997.

Appendix to History of the Calhoun Monument, Published in 1888. N.p., 1898.

Ashleigh, Rose. "The Cavalier and the Puritan; or, Love and Loyalty: A Tale of the Reconstruction Era." *Charleston News and Courier*, November 1882–February 1883.

Bak, Richard. *The CSS Hunley: The Greatest Undersea Adventure of the Civil War*. Rev. ed. New York: Cooper Square, 2003.

Baker, William Mumford [pseud. George F. Harrington]. *Inside: A Chronicle of Secession*. New York: Harper, 1866.

Ball, W. W. "Back to Calhoun." In *Essays in Reaction*, 5–31. Columbia, S.C.: n.p., 1925.

Barber, F. M. *Lecture on Submarine Boats and Their Application to Torpedo Operations.* Newport, R.I.: U.S. Torpedo Station, 1875.

Barnes, Frank. *Fort Sumter National Monument, South Carolina.* Historical Handbook Series No. 12. Washington, D.C.: National Park Service, 1952.

Barnes, John Sanford. *Submarine Warfare, Offensive and Defensive.* New York: Nostrand, 1869.

Battles and Leaders of the Civil War. 4 vol. New York: Yoseloff, 1956.

Beauregard, P. G. T. "Torpedo Service in the Harbor and Water Defences of Charleston." *Southern Historical Society Papers* 5 (April 1878): 145–61.

Bennett, John. *The Doctor to the Dead: Grotesque Legends and Folk Tales of Old Charleston.* New York: Rinehart, 1946.

Bishop, Farnham. *The Story of the Submarine.* New York: Century, 1916.

Brady, Cyrus Townsend. *A Little Traitor to the South: A War-Time Comedy with a Tragic Interlude.* New York: Grosset and Dunlap, 1903.

Branston, Ursula. *Let the Band Play 'Dixie.'* London: Harrap, 1940.

Bremer, Fredrika. *The Homes of the New World: Impressions of America.* Trans. Mary Howitt. 2 vols. New York: Harper, 1853.

Brown, Thomas J., ed. *The Public Art of Civil War Commemoration: A Brief History with Documents.* Boston: Bedford/St. Martin's, 2004.

Bruns, Peirce. "Henry Timrod." *Conservative Review* 1 (May 1899): 263–77.

Burgoyne, Alan H. *Submarine Navigation: Past and Present.* 2 vols. London: Richards, 1903.

Burton, E. Milby. *The Siege of Charleston.* Columbia: University of South Carolina Press, 1970.

Butcher, William. *Jules Verne: The Definitive Biography.* New York: Thunder's Mouth, 2006.

Butler, Matthew C. "Southern Genius: How War Developed It in an Industrial and Military Way." *Southern Historical Society Papers* 16 (January–December 1888): 281–95.

Calhoun, John C. *The Papers of John C. Calhoun.* 28 vols. Columbia: University of South Carolina Press, 1959–2003.

Campbell, R. Thomas. *The CSS H. L. Hunley: Confederate Submarine.* Shippensburg, Penn.: Burd Street, 2000.

Capers, Henry D. *Belleview: A Story of the Past and of the Present.* New York: Hale, 1880.

Cardozo, J. N. *Reminiscences of Charleston.* Charleston, S.C.: Walker, 1866.

Carman, E. A. "Fort Sumter." *Encyclopedia Americana.* 30 vols. New York: Encyclopedia Americana Corporation, 1918–20. 11:509–10.

Carroll, Anna Ella. *Reply to the Speech of the Hon. J. C. Breckinridge.* Washington, D.C.: Polkinhorn, 1861.

Carson, Caroline. *The Roman Years of a South Carolina Artist: Caroline Carson's Letters Home, 1872–1892.* Ed. William H. Pease and Jane H. Pease. Columbia: University of South Carolina Press, 2003.

Carson, James Petigru. *Life, Letters, and Speeches of James Louis Petigru: The Union Man of South Carolina.* Washington, D.C.: McQueen, 1920.

Carter, Joseph C., ed. *Magnolia Journey: A Union Veteran Revisits the Former Confederate States*. University: University of Alabama Press, 1974.

Chabon, Michael. "The Martian Agent, an Interplanetary Romance." *McSweeney's Mammoth Treasury of Thrilling Tales*, ed. Michael Chabon. New York: Vintage, 2003. 447–76.

Chaffin, Tom. *The H. L. Hunley: The Secret Hope of the Confederacy*. New York: Hill and Wang, 2008.

Chapin, Sallie F. *Fitz-Hugh St. Clair, the South Carolina Rebel Boy; or, It Is No Crime to Be Born a Gentleman*. 2nd ed. Philadelphia: Claxton, Remsen, and Haffelfinger, 1873.

Chesnut, Mary Boykin. *A Diary from Dixie, as Written by Mary Boykin Chesnut, Wife of James Chesnut, Jr., United States Senator from South Carolina, 1859– 1861, and Afterward an Aide to Jefferson Davis and a Brigadier-General in the Confederate Army*. Ed. Isabella D. Martin and Myrta Lockett Avary. New York: Appleton, 1906.

———. *Mary Chesnut's Civil War*. Ed. C. Vann Woodward. New Haven: Yale University Press, 1981.

———. *The Private Mary Chesnut: The Unpublished Civil War Diaries*. Ed. C. Vann Woodward and Elisabeth Muhlenfeld. New York: Oxford University Press, 1984.

Clardy, Stan. *TimeLight: A Journey into the Past*. Statesville, N.C.: Gray Note, 2003.

Clare, Virginia Pettigrew. *Harp of the South*. Oglethorpe University, Ga.: Oglethorpe University Press, 1936.

Colcock, Annie T. *Her American Daughter*. New York: Neale, 1905.

Collett, Sarah Rainsford. *Oakley Park, Edgefield, South Carolina: Home of Brig. Gen. Martin Witherspoon Gary*. Edgefield, S.C.: Edgefield Advertiser, [1942].

Confederate Memorial Day at Charleston, S.C. Charleston, S.C.: Mazyck, 1871.

The Confederate War Centennial: An Opportunity for All South Carolinians. Columbia: South Carolina Confederate War Centennial Commission, n.d.

Connelly, T. Lawrence. *Will Success Spoil Jeff Davis?: The Last Book about the Civil War*. New York: McGraw-Hill, 1963.

Constitution of the South-Carolina Institute for the Promotion of Art, Mechanical Ingenuity, and Industry. Charleston, S.C.: Walker and James, 1849.

Dalberg-Acton, John Emerich Edward. "The Civil War in America." In *Historical Essays and Studies*, ed. John Neville Figgis and Reginald Vere Laurence, 123– 42. London: Macmillan, 1907.

Daniel, J. W. *A Maid of the Foot-Hills; or, Missing Links in the Story of Reconstruction*. New York: Neale, 1905.

Daniels, Jonathan. *A Southerner Discovers the South*. New York: Macmillan, 1938.

Davis, Jefferson. *The Rise and Fall of the Confederate Government*. 2 vols. New York: Appleton, 1881.

Delpeuch, Maurice. *La Navigation Sous-Marine à travers les Siècles*. Paris: Juven, 1903.

Dylan, Bob. *Chronicles: Volume One*. New York: Simon and Schuster, 2004.

Eley, Geoff, and Ronald Grigor Suny, eds. *Becoming National: A Reader*. New York: Oxford University Press, 1996.

Elmore, Grace Brown. *A Heritage of Woe: The Civil War Diary of Grace Brown Elmore, 1861–1868*. Ed. Marli F. Weiner. Athens: University of Georgia Press, 1997.

Emerson, Ralph Waldo, ed. *Parnassus*. Boston: Osgood, 1875.

"Exhumation of the Body of John C. Calhoun, 1863." *South Carolina Historical Magazine* 57 (January 1956): 57–58.

Fast, Howard. *Freedom Road*. New York: Duell, Sloan, and Pearce, 1944.

Fields, Mamie Garvin, with Karen Fields. *Lemon Swamp and Other Places: A Carolina Memoir*. New York: Free Press, 1983.

Foote, Shelby. *The Civil War: A Narrative*. Vol. 2, *Fredericksburg to Meridian*. New York: Vintage, 1986.

Fort Sumter: Anvil of War. Washington, D.C.: Division of Publications, National Park Service, 1984.

Fort Sumter National Monument Visitor Education Center, Liberty Square, Charleston, S.C. Exhibit Text. February 2002. www.nps.gov/fosu/history culture/lisqexhibit.htm. Accessed May 30, 2012.

Fyfe, Herbert C. *Submarine Warfare, Past and Present*. Rev. John Leyland. London: Richards, 1907.

Gibson, William, and Bruce Sterling. *The Difference Engine*. New York: Bantam, 1991.

Glassel[l], W. T. "Torpedo Service in Charleston Harbor." *Southern Historical Society Papers* 4 (November 1877): 225–35.

Goff, Harriet Newell. *Other Fools and Their Doings; or, Life among the Freedmen*. New York: Ogilvie, 1880.

Green, Elijah. "Ex-Slave Born December 25, 1843." In *The American Slave: A Composite Autobiography*, ed. George P. Rawick, vol. 2, part 2, 195–99. Westport, Conn.: Greenwood, 1972.

Greene, Harlan. *Why We Never Danced the Charleston*. New York: St. Martin's/ Marek, 1984.

Griswold, Francis. *A Sea Island Lady*. New York: Morrow, 1939.

Hagy, James W., ed. *Charleston City Directories for the Years 1816, 1819, 1822, 1825, and 1829*. Baltimore: Genealogical Publishing, 1996.

———, ed. *People and Professions of Charleston, 1782–1802*. Baltimore: Genealogical Publishing, 1992.

Halsey, Ashley, Jr. "The Untold Stories of the Civil War, I: Who Fired the First Shot?" *Saturday Evening Post*, December 17, 1960, 22–23, 82–83.

———. *Who Fired the First Shot? And Other Untold Stories of the War*. New York: Hawthorn, 1963.

Hawk, Fran. *The Story of the H. L. Hunley and Queenie's Coin*. Chelsea, Mich.: Sleeping Bear, 2004.

Hayne, Paul Hamilton. *A Man of Letters in the Nineteenth-Century South: Selected Letters of Paul Hamilton Hayne*. Ed. Rayburn S. Moore. Baton Rouge: Louisiana State University Press, 1982.

Heyward, DuBose. "Charleston: Where Mellow Past and Present Meet." *National Geographic* 75 (March 1939): 273–312.

————. *Peter Ashley*. New York: Farrar and Rinehart, 1932.

Heyward, DuBose, and Hervey Allen. *Carolina Chansons: Legends of the Low Country*. New York: Macmillan, 1922.

Heyward, DuBose, and Herbert Ravenel Sass. *Fort Sumter*. New York: Farrar and Rinehart, 1938.

Hicks, Brian, and Schuyler Kropf. *Raising the Hunley: The Remarkable History and Recovery of the Lost Confederate Submarine*. New York: Random House, 2002.

Historical Sketch of the Confederate Home and College, Charleston, South Carolina, 1867–1921. Charleston, S.C.: Walker, Evans, and Cogswell, n.d.

A History of the Calhoun Monument at Charleston, S.C. Charleston, S.C.: Lucas, Richardson, 1888.

"History of Wade Hampton Chapter, Daughters of the Confederacy, and of the Record and Relic Room." South Carolina Confederate Relic Room and Military Museum, Columbia.

Holland, John P. "Submarine Navigation." *Cassier's Magazine* 12 (1897): 541–60.

Holmes, Emma. *The Diary of Miss Emma Holmes, 1861–1866*. Ed. John F. Marszalek. Baton Rouge: Louisiana State University Press, 1979.

Holmes, James G., ed. *Memorials. To the Memory of Mrs. Mary Amarinthia Snowden Offered by Societies, Associations and Confederate Camps*. Charleston, S.C.: Walker, Evans, and Cogswell, 1898.

Howard, Sidney. *GWTW: The Screenplay*. Ed. Andrew Sinclair. London: Lorrimer, 1980.

Howells, William Dean. "In Charleston." *Harper's Magazine*, October 1915, 747–57.

Hoyt, Edwin P. *The Voyage of the Hunley*. Short Hills, N.J.: Burford, 2002.

Humphreys, Josephine. *Rich in Love*. New York: Viking, 1987.

Hungerpiller, J. C., ed. *South Carolina Literature*. Columbia, S.C.: Bryan, 1931.

In Memoriam. Gen. Stephen Elliott. Columbia, S.C.: Selby, 1866.

James, Henry. *The American Scene*. Bloomington: Indiana University Press, 1968.

Jervey, Theodore D. *The Elder Brother: A Novel in Which Are Presented the Vital Questions Confronting the South Growing Out of Reconstruction, and in Which the Author Defines the True Relations between the Races Now Existing in the South*. New York: Neale, 1905.

Johnson, John. *The Defense of Charleston Harbor, Including Fort Sumter and the Adjacent Islands, 1863–1865*. 2nd ed. Charleston, S.C.: Walker, Evans, and Cogswell, 1890.

Kloeppel, James E. *Danger beneath the Waves: A History of the Confederate Submarine H. L. Hunley*. College Park, Ga.: Adele, 1987.

Lake, Simon. *Submarine: The Autobiography of Simon Lake as told to Herbert Corey*. New York: Appleton-Century, 1938.

————. *The Submarine in War and Peace: Its Developments and Possibilities*. Philadelphia: Lippincott, 1918.

Leiding, Harriette Kershaw. *Charleston: Historic and Romantic*. Philadelphia: Lippincott, 1931.

Leland, Isabella Middleton, ed. "Middleton Correspondence, 1861–1865." *South Carolina Historical Magazine* 64 (July 1963): 158–68.

Lesesne, Thomas Petigru. *Landmarks of Charleston, Including Description of an Incomparable Stroll*. Richmond: Garrett and Massie, 1932.

Lewisohn, Ludwig. "South Carolina: A Lingering Fragrance." *Nation*, July 12, 1922, 36–38.

Life in America: A Special Loan Exhibition of Paintings Held during the Period of the New York World's Fair, April 24 to October 29. New York: Metropolitan Museum of Art, 1939.

Lincoln, Abraham. *This Fiery Trial: The Speeches and Writings of Abraham Lincoln*. Ed. William E. Gienapp. New York: Oxford University Press, 2002.

Lodge, Henry Cabot, and Theodore Roosevelt. *Hero Tales from American History*. New York: Century, 1911.

Lowell, Robert. *For the Union Dead*. London: Faber and Faber, 1964.

Lumpkin, Katharine Du Pre. *The Making of a Southerner*. New York: Knopf, 1946.

Magnolia Cemetery: The Proceedings at the Dedication of the Grounds. Charleston, S.C.: Walker and James, 1851.

Mason, F. Van Wyck. *Our Valiant Few*. Boston: Little, Brown, 1956.

Maury, Dabney H. "The Defence of Mobile in 1865." *Southern Historical Society Papers* 3 (January 1877): 1–13.

McCants, Elliott Crayton. *White Oak Farm*. New York: Longmans, Green, 1928.

McClure, Alexander Kelly. *The South: Its Industrial, Financial, and Political Condition*. Philadelphia: Lippincott, 1886.

McCord, Louisa S. "Enfranchisement of Woman." *Southern Quarterly Review* 21 (April 1853): 322–41.

McCord, Louisa S. *Louisa S. McCord: Poems, Drama, Biography, Letters*. Ed. Richard C. Lounsbury. Charlottesville: University Press of Virginia, 1996.

———. *Louisa S. McCord: Selected Writings*. Ed. Richard C. Lounsbury. Charlottesville: University Press of Virginia, 1997.

McKinley, Carlyle. *Selections from the Poems of Carlyle McKinley*. n.p., 1904.

Means, Celina E. *Palmetto Stories: A Reader for Fifth Grades*. New York: Macmillan, 1903.

——— [pseud. John Marchmont]. *Thirty-Four Years: An American Story of Southern Life*. Philadelphia: Claxton, Remsen, and Haffelfinger, 1878.

"Memorial Address of General Wade Hampton." *Southern Magazine* 13 (August 1873): 225–32.

Meynardie, Florella. *Amy Oakly; or, The Reign of the Carpet-Bagger*. Charleston, S.C.: Walker, Evans, and Cogswell, 1879.

Mitchell, Margaret. *Gone with the Wind*. New York: Macmillan, 1936.

Naipaul, V. S. *A Turn in the South*. New York: Knopf, 1989.

Nevins, Allan. *The War for the Union*. 4 vols. New York: Scribner's, 1959–71.

A New Guide to Modern Charleston. Charleston, S.C.: Walker, Evans, and Cogswell, 1911.

Newton, Isaac. "Has the Day of Great Navies Passed?" *Galaxy* 24 (September 1877): 293–304.

"NPS Stats: Fort Sumter National Monument, Recreational Visitors." https://irma.nps.gov/stats/reports/park/. Accessed August 13, 2014.

Oeland, Glenn. "The H. L. Hunley: Secret Weapon of the Confederacy." *National Geographic* 202 (July 2002): 82–101.

Olmstead, Charles H. "Reminiscences of Service in Charleston Harbor in 1863." *Southern Historical Society Papers* 11 (April–May 1883): 158–71.

Palmer, Henrietta Raymer, ed. *In Dixie Land: Stories of the Reconstruction Era.* New York: Purdy, 1926.

Parker, William Harwar. *The Confederate States Navy.* Vol. 17 of *Confederate Military History*, ed. Clement A. Evans. Extended ed. Wilmington, N.C.: Broadfoot, 1989.

Parrington, Vernon Louis. *Main Currents in American Thought.* 3 vols. New York: Harcourt Brace, 1927–30.

Pesce, G. L. *La Navigation Sous-Marine.* Saint-Laurent-le-Minier, France: Decoopman, 2010.

Phillips, Ted Ashton, Jr. *City of the Silent: The Charlestonians of Magnolia Cemetery.* Ed. Thomas J. Brown. Columbia: University of South Carolina Press, 2010.

Porcher, Frederick A. "Modern Art—Powers' Statue of Calhoun." *Southern Quarterly Review* 5 (January 1852): 86–114.

Porter, David Dixon. "Torpedo Warfare." *North American Review* 127 (September–October 1878): 213–36.

Prentiss, James Clayton. *The Charleston City Guide.* Charleston, S.C.: DeLano, 1872.

Presentation of Oakley Park, Historic Home of Gen. Martin Witherspoon Gary, C.S.A., to the Town of Edgefield by the Honorable John Gary Evans and Mrs. Evans, March 12, 1941, Edgefield, S.C. N.p., n.d.

Priest, Cherie. *Boneshaker.* New York: Tor, 2009.

———. *Clementine.* New York: Subterranean, 2010.

———. *Dreadnought.* New York: Tor, 2010.

Racine, Philip N., ed. *Gentlemen Merchants: A Charleston Family's Odyssey, 1828–1870.* Knoxville: University of Tennessee Press, 2008.

Ragan, Mark K. *The Hunley.* Orangeburg, S.C.: Sandlapper, 2005.

———. *The Hunley: Submarines, Sacrifice, and Success in the Civil War.* Miami, Fla.: Narwhal, 1995.

Ralph, Julian. *Dixie; or, Southern Scenes and Sketches.* New York: Harper, 1896.

Ravenel, Harriott Horry Rutledge. *Charleston: The Place and the People.* New York: Macmillan, 1906.

Reid, Whitelaw. *A Southern Tour: May 1, 1865, to May 1, 1866.* New York: Moore, Wilstach, and Baldwin, 1866.

Report of the Commission of Fine Arts: Message from the President of the United States Transmitting the Twelfth Report of the Commission of Fine Arts, July 1, 1929, to December 31, 1934, 74th Cong., 2nd sess. Washington, D.C.: U.S. Government Printing Office, 1936.

Rhett, Claudine. "Sketch of John C. Mitchel, of Ireland, Killed Whilst in Command of Fort Sumter." *Southern Historical Society Papers* 10 (June 1882): 268–72.

Rivers, William J. *Eunice: A Tale of Reconstruction Times in South Carolina.* Ed. Tara Courtney McKinney. Columbia: University of South Carolina Press, 2006.

————. *A Little Book: To Obtain Means for Placing a Memorial Stone upon the Grave of the Poet Henry Timrod*. Charleston, S.C.: Walker, Evans, and Cogswell, n.d.

Robinson, Stephen T. *The Shadow of the War: A Story of the South in Reconstruction Times*. Chicago: Jansen, McClurg, 1884.

Roe, Edward P. *The Earth Trembled*. New York: Dodd, Mead, 1887.

Roman, Alfred. *The Military Operations of General Beauregard in the War between the States, 1861–1865*. 2 vols. New York: Harper, 1884.

Ruckstull, F. W. *Great Works of Art and What Makes Them Great*. Rev. ed. New York: Putnam's, 1925.

Ryan, Abram J. *Poems: Patriotic, Religious, Miscellaneous*. 25th ed. New York: Kennedy, 1880.

Sass, Herbert Ravenel. *Look Back to Glory*. Indianapolis: Bobbs-Merrill, 1933.

————. "Look Back to Glory: The Old South and the New America." Text of address, WBT radio, Charlotte, N.C., December 8, 1933. South Caroliniana Library, University of South Carolina, Columbia.

————. *Outspoken: 150 Years of the News and Courier*. Columbia: University of South Carolina Press, 1953.

————. "The Story of *Little David*." *Harper's Magazine*, May 1943, 620–25.

Scharf, J. Thomas. *History of the Confederate States Navy: From Its Organization to the Surrender of the Last Vessel*. New York: Rogers and Sherwood, 1887.

Seabrook, Phoebe Hamilton. *A Daughter of the Confederacy: A Story of the Old South and the New*. New York: Neale, 1906.

Selby, Julian A. *Memorabilia and Anecdotal Reminiscences of Columbia, S.C., and Incidents Connected Therewith*. Columbia, S.C.: Bryan, 1905.

Sheppard, William Arthur. *Red Shirts Remembered: Southern Brigadiers of the Reconstruction Period*. Atlanta: Ruralist, 1940.

Simkins, Francis Butler, and James Welch Patton. *The Women of the Confederacy*. Richmond: Garrett and Massie, 1936.

Simms, William Gilmore. "Charleston: The Palmetto City." *Harper's New Monthly Magazine*, June 1857, 1–22.

————. "The Late Henry Timrod." In *The Last Years of Henry Timrod, 1864–1867*, ed. Jay B. Hubbell, 152–65. Durham: Duke University Press, 1941.

————. *The Letters of William Gilmore Simms*. Ed. Mary C. Simms Oliphant, Alfred Taylor Odell, and T. C. Duncan Eaves. 6 vols. Columbia: University of South Carolina Press, 1952–82.

————. *Sack and Destruction of the City of Columbia, S.C.* Ed. A. S. Salley. N.p.: Oglethorpe University Press, 1937.

————, ed. *War Poetry of the South*. New York: Richardson, 1867.

Simons, Katherine Drayton. *Stories of Charleston Harbor*. Columbia, S.C.: State, 1930.

Slavery: Cause and Catalyst of the Civil War. Atlanta: National Park Service, Southeast Region, 2011.

South Carolina: A Guide to the Palmetto State. New York: Oxford University Press, 1941.

The South Carolina Monument Association: Origin, History, and Work, with an Account of the Proceedings at the Unveiling of the Monument to the Confederate Dead, and the Oration of Gen. John S. Preston, at Columbia, S.C., May 13, 1879. Charleston, S.C.: News and Courier Book Presses, 1879.

South Carolina Speaks. Columbia: South Carolina Confederate War Centennial Commission, 1961.

Stevens, William Oliver. *Charleston: Historic City of Gardens.* New York: Dodd, Mead, 1940.

Sueter, Murray F. *The Evolution of the Submarine Boat, Mine, and Torpedo, from the Nineteenth Century to the Present Time.* 2nd ed. Portsmouth, England: Gieve's, 1907.

Sutton, Robert K., ed. *Rally on the High Ground: The National Park Service Symposium on the Civil War.* Fort Washington, Penn.: Eastern National, 2001.

Tate, Allen. *Collected Poems, 1919–1976.* New York: Farrar, Straus, Giroux, 1977.

————. *Essays of Four Decades.* Chicago: Swallow, 1968.

Thomas, J. P., ed. *The Carolina Tribute to Calhoun.* Columbia, S.C.: Bryan, 1857.

Timrod, Henry. *The Collected Poems of Henry Timrod: A Variorum Edition.* Ed. Edd Winfield Parks and Aileen Wells Parks. Athens: University of Georgia Press, 1965.

————. *The Essays of Henry Timrod.* Ed. and intro. Edd Winfield Parks. Athens: University of Georgia Press, 1942.

————. *The Poems of Henry Timrod.* Ed. Paul Hamilton Hayne. New York: Hale, 1872.

The Timrod Memorial Association. Charleston, S.C.: Lucas and Richardson, n.d.

"The Timrod Memorial Association." In *City of Charleston Yearbook—1901,* app. 59–80. Charleston, S.C.: Walker, Evans, and Cogswell, 1901.

Tooker, L. Frank. "Timrod the Poet." *Century* 33 (April 1898): 932–34.

Trethewey, Natasha. *Native Guard: Poems.* Boston: Houghton Mifflin, 2006.

Trowbridge, John Townsend. *A Picture of the Desolated States, and the Work of Restoration.* Hartford, Conn.: Stebbins, 1868.

Twain, Mark. *Life on the Mississippi.* Boston: Osgood, 1883.

United Daughters of the Confederacy, South Carolina Division. *South Carolina Women in the Confederacy.* 2 vols. Columbia, S.C.: State, 1903–7.

von Kolnitz, Alfred H. *A Panorama of Three Centuries of History Viewed from Charleston's Famous Battery.* Charleston, S.C.: Historical Commission of the City of Charleston, 1937.

von Scheliha, Viktor Ernst Karl Rudolf. *A Treatise on Coast-Defence: Based on the Experience Gained by Officers of the Corps of Engineers of the Army of the Confederate States, and Compiled from Official Reports of Officers of the Navy of the United States, Made during the Late North American War from 1861 to 1865.* London: Spon, 1868.

Walker, C. Irvine. *Historic Charleston: Colonial, Revolutionary, and Confederate.* Charleston, S.C.: Southern, 1927.

Walker, Cornelia G. *The Red Shirt: Oakley Park, "Red Shirt Shrine," Edgefield, S.C.* N.p., n.d.

Walker, Sally M. *Secrets of a Civil War Submarine: Solving the Mysteries of the H. L. Hunley*. Minneapolis: Carolrhoda, 2005.

Wauchope, George Armstrong. *Henry Timrod: Man and Poet*. Columbia, S.C.: University Press, 1915.

——. *The Writers of South Carolina*. Columbia, S.C.: State, 1910.

Wells, Edward [pseud. Quentin Saxon]. "The Voodoo Doctor: A Story of Reconstruction in South Carolina." 1901. Edward Laight Wells Papers, South Carolina Historical Society.

West, William Franciscus, Jr. "A Southern Editor Views the Civil War: A Collection of Editorials by Henry Timrod and Other Editorial Materials Published in the *Daily South Carolinian*, January 14, 1864, to February 17, 1865." Ph.D. diss., Florida State University, 1983.

Whitman, Walt. *Specimen Days*. New York: New American Library, 1961.

Wister, Owen. *Lady Baltimore*. Nashville, Tenn.: Sanders, 1992.

Young, Kevin. *For the Confederate Dead*. New York: Knopf, 2007.

SECONDARY SOURCES

Aaron, Daniel. *The Unwritten War: American Writers and the Civil War*. New York: Knopf, 1973.

Allen, Louise Anderson. *A Bluestocking in Charleston: The Life and Career of Laura Bragg*. Columbia: University of South Carolina Press, 2001.

Anderson, Benedict. *Imagined Communities: Reflections on the Origin and Spread of Nationalism*. Rev. ed. London: Verso, 1991.

Andrew, Rod, Jr. *Wade Hampton: Confederate Warrior to Southern Redeemer*. Chapel Hill: University of North Carolina Press, 2008.

Axelrod, Steven. "Colonel Shaw in American Poetry: 'For the Union Dead' and Its Precursors." *American Quarterly* 24 (October 1972): 523–37.

——. *Robert Lowell: Life and Art*. Princeton: Princeton University Press, 1978.

Bailey, Candace. *Music and the Southern Belle: From Accomplished Lady to Confederate Composer*. Carbondale: Southern Illinois University Press, 2010.

Baker, Bruce E. *What Reconstruction Meant: Historical Memory in the American South*. Charlottesville: University of Virginia Press, 2007.

Barnwell, John. *Love of Order: South Carolina's First Secession Crisis*. Chapel Hill: University of North Carolina Press, 1982.

Barrett, Faith. *To Fight Aloud Is Very Brave: American Poetry and the Civil War*. Amherst: University of Massachusetts Press, 2012.

Beagle, Donald Robert, and Bryan Albin Giemza. *Poet of the Lost Cause: A Life of Father Ryan*. Knoxville: University of Tennessee Press, 2008.

Bederman, Gail. *Manliness and Civilization: A Cultural History of Gender and Race in the United States, 1880–1917*. Chicago: University of Chicago Press, 1995.

Beirich, Heidi. "The Struggle for the Sons of Confederate Veterans: A Return to White Supremacy in the Early Twenty-First Century?" In *Neo-Confederacy: A Critical Introduction*, ed. Euan Hague, Heidi Beirich, and Edward H. Sebesta, 280–308. Austin: University of Texas Press, 2008.

Bellah, Robert N. "Religion in America." *Daedalus* 96 (Winter 1967): 1–21.

Bellows, Barbara L. *Benevolence among Slaveholders: Assisting the Poor in Charleston, 1670–1860.* Baton Rouge: Louisiana State University Press, 1993.

———. *A Talent for Living: Josephine Pinckney and the Charleston Literary Tradition.* Baton Rouge: Louisiana State University Press, 2006.

Benfey, Christopher. *Degas in New Orleans: Encounters in the Creole World of Kate Chopin and George Washington Cable.* Berkeley: University of California Press, 1997.

Binnington, Ian. *Confederate Visions: Nationalism, Symbolism, and the Imagined South in the Civil War.* Charlottesville: University of Virginia Press, 2013.

Blair, William A. *Cities of the Dead: Contesting the Memory of the Civil War in the South, 1865–1914.* Chapel Hill: University of North Carolina Press, 2004.

Bland, Sidney R. *Preserving Charleston's Past, Shaping Its Future: The Life and Times of Susan Pringle Frost.* Westport, Conn.: Greenwood, 1994.

Blatt, Martin H., Thomas J. Brown, and Donald Yacovone, eds. *Hope and Glory: Essays on the Legacy of the 54th Massachusetts Regiment.* Amherst: University of Massachusetts Press, 2001.

Blight, David W. *Race and Reunion: The Civil War in American Memory.* Cambridge: Belknap Press of Harvard University Press, 2001.

———. "'What Will Peace among the Whites Bring?': Reunion and Race in the Struggle over the Memory of the Civil War in American Culture." *Massachusetts Review* 34 (Autumn 1993): 393–410.

Blum, Edward J. *Reforging the White Republic: Race, Religion, and American Nationalism, 1865–1898.* Baton Rouge: Louisiana State University Press, 2005.

Boime, Albert. *The Unveiling of the National Icons: A Plea for Patriotic Iconoclasm in a Nationalist Era.* Cambridge: Cambridge University Press, 1998.

Bonner, Robert E. *Colors and Blood: Flag Passions of the Confederate South.* Princeton: Princeton University Press, 2002.

———. *Mastering America: Southern Slaveholders and the Crisis of American Nationhood.* Cambridge: Cambridge University Press, 2009.

Brown, Thomas J. "Civil War Remembrance as Reconstruction." In *Reconstructions: New Perspectives on the Postbellum United States,* ed. Thomas J. Brown, 206–36. New York: Oxford University Press, 2006.

———. "Confederate Retreat to Mars and Venus." In *Battle Scars: Gender and Sexuality in the American Civil War,* ed. Catherine Clinton and Nina Silber, 189–213. New York: Oxford University Press, 2006.

———. "The Monumental Legacy of Calhoun." In *The Memory of the Civil War in American Culture,* ed. Alice Fahs and Joan Waugh, 130–56. Chapel Hill: University of North Carolina Press, 2004.

———, ed. *The Public Art of Civil War Commemoration: A Brief History with Documents.* Boston: Bedford/St. Martin's, 2004.

———, ed. *Remixing the Civil War: Meditations on the Sesquicentennial.* Baltimore: Johns Hopkins University Press, 2011.

Brundage, W. Fitzhugh. *The Southern Past: A Clash of Race and Memory.* Cambridge: Belknap Press of Harvard University Press, 2005.

Bryan, John M. *Creating the South Carolina State House*. Columbia: University of South Carolina Press, 1999.

Caldwell, Guy A., Jr. "The Date of Henry Timrod's Birth." *American Literature* 7 (May 1935): 207–8.

Carlton, David L. *Mill and Town in South Carolina, 1880–1920*. Baton Rouge: Louisiana State University Press, 1982.

Casey, Edward S. *Earth-Mapping: Artists Reshaping the Landscape*. Minneapolis: University of Minnesota Press, 2005.

Cash, W. J. *The Mind of the South*. New York: Vintage, 1969.

Cate, Wirt Armistead. *Lucius Q. C. Lamar, Secession and Reunion*. Chapel Hill: University of North Carolina Press, 1935.

Censer, Jane Turner. *The Reconstruction of White Southern Womanhood, 1865–1895*. Baton Rouge: Louisiana State University Press, 2003.

———. "Reimagining the North-South Reunion: Southern Women Novelists and the Intersectional Romance, 1876–1900." *Southern Cultures* 5 (Summer 1999): 64–91.

Chambers, Thomas A. *Memories of War: Visiting Battlegrounds and Bonefields in the Early American Republic*. Ithaca: Cornell University Press, 2012.

Channing, Steven A. *Crisis of Fear: Secession in South Carolina*. New York: Norton, 1974.

Cisco, Walter Brian. *Henry Timrod: A Biography*. Madison, N.J.: Fairleigh Dickinson University Press, 2004.

Clark, E. Culpepper. *Francis Warrington Dawson and the Politics of Restoration: South Carolina, 1874–1889*. University: University of Alabama Press, 1980.

Comstock, Rock L., Jr. "Short History, Fort Sumter." National Park Service Report. June 1956. www.nps.gov/fosu/historyculture/fosu_docs.htm. Accessed May 29, 2012.

The Confederate Monument at Charleston, South Carolina: Orations of Gen. M. C. Butler and Gen. B. H. Rutledge at the Unveiling of the Monument in Magnolia Cemetery, November 30th, 1882. Charleston, S.C.: News and Courier Book Presses, 1884.

Connelly, Thomas, and Barbara L. Bellows. *God and General Longstreet: The Lost Cause and the Southern Mind*. Baton Rouge: Louisiana State University Press, 1982.

Cook, Robert J. *Troubled Commemoration: The American Civil War Centennial, 1961–1965*. Baton Rouge: Louisiana State University Press, 2007.

Coryell, Janet L. *Neither Heroine nor Fool: Anna Ella Carroll of Maryland*. Kent, Ohio: Kent State University Press, 1990.

Coski, John M. *The Confederate Battle Flag: America's Most Embattled Emblem*. Cambridge: Harvard University Press, 2005.

Coski, John M., and Amy R. Feely. "A Monument to Southern Womanhood: The Founding Generation of the Confederate Museum." In *A Woman's War*, ed. Edward D. C. Campbell Jr. and Kym S. Rice, 131–63. Richmond, Va.: Museum of the Confederacy, 1996.

Coulter, E. Merton. *The Confederate States of America, 1861–1865*. Baton Rouge: Louisiana State University Press, 1950.

Cox, Karen. *Dixie's Daughters: The United Daughters of the Confederacy and the Preservation of Confederate Culture.* Gainesville: University Press of Florida, 2003.

Crawford, John Stephens. "The Classical Orator in Nineteenth Century American Sculpture." *American Art Journal* 6 (November 1974): 56–72.

Criswell, Grover C., Jr., and Clarence L. Criswell. *Criswell's Currency Series.* Vol. 1, *Confederate and Southern State Currency.* Pass-a-Grille Beach, Fla.: Criswell's, 1957.

———. *Criswell's Currency Series.* Vol. 2, *Confederate and Southern State Bonds.* St. Petersburg Beach, Fla.: Criswell's, 1961.

Current, Richard N. *Lincoln and the First Shot.* Philadelphia: Lippincott, 1963.

Dekker, George. *The American Historical Romance.* Cambridge: Cambridge University Press, 1987.

Derry, Margaret Elsinor. "John C. Calhoun and South Carolina, 1850–1860." Master's thesis, University of Toronto, 1970.

Diffley, Kathleen. *Where My Heart Is Turning Ever: Civil War Stories and Constitutional Reform, 1861–1876.* Athens: University of Georgia Press, 1992.

Dillenbeck, Bruce L. "The Decade after Moses: The Political Legacy of John C. Calhoun." Ph.D. diss., Florida State University, 1990.

Dorman, Robert L. *Revolt of the Provinces: The Regionalist Movement in America, 1920–1945.* Chapel Hill: University of North Carolina Press, 1993.

Drago, Edmund L. *Initiative, Paternalism, and Race Relations: Charleston's Avery Normal Institute.* Athens: University of Georgia Press, 1990.

Durrill, Wayne K. "The Power of Ancient Words: Classical Teaching and Social Change at South Carolina College, 1804–1860." *Journal of Southern History* 65 (August 1999): 469–98.

Fahs, Alice. *The Imagined Civil War: Popular Literature of the North and South, 1861–1865.* Chapel Hill: University of North Carolina Press, 2001.

Farnham, Christie Anne. *The Education of the Southern Belle: Higher Education and Student Socialization in the Antebellum South.* New York: New York University Press, 1994.

Faust, Drew Gilpin. "In Search of the Real Mary Chesnut." *Reviews in American History* 10 (March 1982): 54–59.

———. *Mothers of Invention: Women of the Slaveholding South in the American Civil War.* Chapel Hill: University of North Carolina Press, 1996.

———. *This Republic of Suffering: Death and the American Civil War.* New York: Knopf, 2008.

Ferguson, James N. "An Overview of the Events at Fort Sumter, 1829–1991." Historic American Buildings Survey Recording Team. November 8, 1991. www.nps.gov/fosu/historyculture/fosu_docs.htm. Accessed May 29, 2012.

Fields, Karen. "What One Cannot Remember Mistakenly." In *History and Memory in African-American Culture,* ed. Geneviève Fabre and Robert O'Meally, 150–63. New York: Oxford University Press, 1994.

Ford, Lacy K., Jr. *Origins of Southern Radicalism: The South Carolina Upcountry, 1800–1860.* New York: Oxford University Press, 1988.

Foster, Gaines M. "Coming to Terms with Defeat: Post-Vietnam America and the Post–Civil War South." *Virginia Quarterly Review* 66 (Winter 1990): 17–35.

———. *Ghosts of the Confederacy: Defeat, the Lost Cause, and the Emergence of the New South, 1865–1913*. New York: Oxford University Press, 1987.

Fox-Genovese, Elizabeth. *Within the Plantation Household: Black and White Women of the Old South*. Chapel Hill: University of North Carolina Press, 1988.

Frank, Lisa Tendrich. "'Between Death and Dishonor': Defending Confederate Womanhood during Sherman's March." In *Southern Character: Essays in Honor of Bertram Wyatt-Brown*, ed. Lisa Tendrich Frank and Daniel Kilbride, 116–27. Gainesville: University Press of Florida, 2011.

Frank, Robert Lee. "The Economic Impact of Tourism in Charleston, South Carolina, 1970." Master's thesis, University of South Carolina, 1972.

Frederickson, Kari. "Confronting the Garrison State: South Carolina in the Early Cold War Era." *Journal of Southern History* 72 (May 2006): 349–78.

———. *The Dixiecrat Revolt and the End of the Solid South, 1932–1968*. Chapel Hill: University of North Carolina Press, 2001.

Fredrickson, George M. *The Inner Civil War: Northern Intellectuals and the Crisis of the Union*. Urbana: University of Illinois Press, 1993.

Freehling, William W. *The Road to Disunion*. 2 vols. New York: Oxford University Press, 1990, 2007.

Gallagher, Gary W. *Causes Won, Lost, and Forgotten: How Hollywood and Popular Art Shape What We Know about the Civil War*. Chapel Hill: University of North Carolina Press, 2008.

Gardner, Sarah E. *Blood and Irony: Southern White Women's Narratives of the Civil War, 1861–1937*. Chapel Hill: University of North Carolina Press, 2004.

Gillespie, Michele K., and Randal L. Hall. *Thomas Dixon Jr. and the Birth of Modern America*. Baton Rouge: Louisiana State University Press, 2006.

Glymph, Thavolia. "African-American Women in the Literary Imagination of Mary Boykin Chesnut." In *Slavery, Secession, and Southern History*, ed. Robert Louis Paquette and Louis A. Ferleger, 140–59. Charlottesville: University Press of Virginia, 2000.

Gordon, Beverly. *Bazaars and Fair Ladies: The History of the American Fundraising Fair*. Knoxville: University of Tennessee Press, 1998.

Green, Jonathan. *Green's Dictionary of Slang*. 3 vols. London: Chambers, 2010.

Greene, Harlan. "'The Little Shining Word': From Porgo to Porgy." *South Carolina Historical Magazine* 87 (January 1986): 75–81.

———. *Mr. Skylark: John Bennett and the Charleston Renaissance*. Athens: University of Georgia Press, 2001.

Gurganus, Allan. "The Man Who Loved Cemeteries: Ted Ashton Phillips Jr., 1959–2005." *American Scholar* 74 (Summer 2005): 98–104.

Hagopian, Patrick. *The Vietnam War in American Memory: Veterans, Memorials, and the Politics of Healing*. Amherst: University of Massachusetts Press, 2009.

Hale, Grace Elizabeth. *Making Whiteness: The Culture of Segregation in the South, 1890–1940*. New York: Pantheon, 1998.

Hall, Jacquelyn Dowd. "'You Must Remember This': Autobiography as Social Critique." *Journal of American History* 85 (September 1998): 439–65.

Halttunen, Karen. *Confidence Men and Painted Women: A Study of Middle-Class Culture in America, 1830–1870*. New Haven: Yale University Press, 1982.

Harrison, Carol E., and Ann M. Johnson. "Introduction: Science and National Identity." *Osiris* 24 (2009): 1–14.

Harrison, Robert Pogue. *The Dominion of the Dead*. Chicago: University of Chicago Press, 2003.

Harwell, Richard B. *Confederate Music*. Chapel Hill: University of North Carolina Press, 1950.

Hillyer, Reiko. "Relics of Reconciliation: The Confederate Museum and Civil War Memory in the New South." *Public Historian* 33 (November 2011): 35–62.

Hobson, Fred C., Jr. *But Now I See: The White Southern Racial Conversion Narrative*. Baton Rouge: Louisiana State University Press, 1999.

———. *Serpent in Eden: H. L. Mencken and the South*. Chapel Hill: University of North Carolina Press, 1974.

Holden, Charles J. *In the Great Maelstrom: Conservatives in Post–Civil War South Carolina*. Columbia: University of South Carolina Press, 2002.

———. "'Is Our Love for Wade Hampton Foolishness?': South Carolina and the Lost Cause." In *The Myth of the Lost Cause and Civil War History*, ed. Gary W. Gallagher and Alan T. Nolan, 60–88. Bloomington: Indiana University Press, 2000.

Hollis, Daniel Walker. *University of South Carolina*. 2 vols. Columbia: University of South Carolina Press, 1951–56.

Hopkins, George W. "From Naval Pauper to Naval Power: The Development of Charleston's Metropolitan-Military Complex." In *The Martial Metropolis: U.S. Cities in War and Peace*, ed. Roger W. Lotchin, 1–34. New York: Praeger, 1984.

Huntley, William. "Mendel Rivers and the Expansion of the Charleston Naval Station." *Proceedings of the South Carolina Historical Association* (1995): 31–39.

Hutchison, Coleman. *Apples and Ashes: Literature, Nationalism, and the Confederate States of America*. Athens: University of Georgia Press, 2012.

Hutchisson, James M. *DuBose Heyward: A Charleston Gentleman in the World of Porgy and Bess*. Jackson: University Press of Mississippi, 2000.

Janney, Caroline E. *Burying the Dead but Not the Past: Ladies' Memorial Associations and the Lost Cause*. Chapel Hill: University of North Carolina Press, 2008.

———. *Remembering the Civil War: Reunion and the Limits of Reconciliation*. Chapel Hill: University of North Carolina Press, 2013.

———. "War over the Shrine of Peace: The Appomattox Peace Monument and Retreat from Reconciliation." *Journal of Southern History* 77 (February 2011): 91–120.

Jensen, Leslie D. "The Fort Sumter Flags: A Study in Documentation and Authentication." U.S. Department of the Interior, National Park Service, Harpers Ferry Center. March 1982. www.nps.gov/fosu/historyculture/fosu_docs.htm. Accessed May 29, 2012.

"John Drinkwater's Poem about a Confederate Stamp." *Manuscripts* 6 (Spring 1954): 176–78.

Johnson, Joan Marie. "Sallie Chapin: The Woman's Christian Temperance Union and Reconciliation after the Civil War." In *South Carolina Women: Their Lives and Times*, ed. Marjorie Julian Spruill, Valinda W. Littlefield, and Joan Marie Johnson, 2:87–104. Athens: University of Georgia Press, 2009–12.

———. *Southern Ladies, New Women: Race, Region, and Clubwomen in South Carolina, 1890–1930*. Gainesville: University Press of Florida, 2004.

Johnson, Michael P. "Mary Boykin Chesnut's Autobiography and Biography: A Review Essay." *Journal of Southern History* 47 (November 1981): 585–92.

Jones, Gordon L. "'Gut History': Civil War Reenacting and the Making of an American Past." Ph.D. diss., Emory University, 2007.

Jones, Kathleen W. "Mother's Day: The Creation, Promotion, and Meaning of a New Holiday in the Progressive Era." *Texas Studies in Literature and Language* 22 (Summer 1980): 175–96.

Jones, Lewis Pinckney. *Stormy Petrel: N. G. Gonzales and His State*. Columbia: University of South Carolina Press, 1973.

Kantrowitz, Stephen. *Ben Tillman and the Reconstruction of White Supremacy*. Chapel Hill: University of North Carolina Press, 2000.

Keneally, Thomas. *The Great Shame and the Triumph of the Irish in the English-Speaking World*. New York: Talese, 1998.

Kinney, Martha E. "'If Vanquished I Am Still Victorious': Religious and Cultural Symbolism in Virginia's Confederate Memorial Day Celebrations, 1866–1930." *Virginia Magazine of History and Biography* 106 (Summer 1998): 237–66.

Kurant, Wendy Ann. "Mary Chesnut's Civil War: Formulations of Femininity in the Novels and Diary." Ph.D. diss., University of Georgia, 2001.

Laderman, Gary. *The Sacred Remains: American Attitudes toward Death, 1799–1883*. New Haven: Yale University Press, 1996.

Lanchner, Carolyn. *Jasper Johns*. New York: Museum of Modern Art, 2010.

Langer, Mark. "Why the Atom Is Our Friend: Disney, General Dynamics, and the USS *Nautilus*." *Art History* 18 (March 1995): 63–96.

Leonard, Thomas. *Above the Battle: War-Making in America from Appomattox to Versailles*. New York: Oxford University Press, 1978.

Light, James F. *John William De Forest*. New York: Twayne, 1965.

Link, William A. *Atlanta, Cradle of the New South: Race and Remembering in the Civil War's Aftermath*. Chapel Hill: University of North Carolina Press, 2013.

Litwicki, Ellen M. *America's Public Holidays, 1865–1920*. Washington, D.C.: Smithsonian Institution Press, 2000.

Long, Lisa A. *Rehabilitating Bodies: Health, History, and the American Civil War*. Philadelphia: University of Pennsylvania Press, 2004.

Lott, Eric. *Love and Theft: Blackface Minstrelsy and the American Working Class*. New York: Oxford University Press, 1993.

Lyons, W. F. *Brigadier-General Thomas Francis Meagher: His Political and Military Career*. New York: Sadlier, 1870.

Madsen-Brooks, Leslie. "'I Nevertheless Am a Historian': Digital Historical Practice and Malpractice around Black Confederate Soldiers (Spring 2012 Version)." In *Writing History in the Digital Age*, ed. Jack Dougherty and Kristen Nawrotzki. http://writinghistory.trincoll.edu/crowdsourcing/madsen-brooks-2012-spring. Accessed July 27, 2012.

Marshall, Anne. *Creating Confederate Kentucky: The Lost Cause and Civil War Memory in a Border State*. Chapel Hill: University of North Carolina Press, 2010.

Martinez, J. Michael. "The Georgia Confederate Flag Dispute." *Georgia Historical Quarterly* 92 (September 2008): 200–228.

Martinez, J. Michael, William D. Richardson, and Ron McNinch-Su, eds. *Confederate Symbols in the Contemporary South*. Gainesville: University Press of Florida, 2000.

May, John Amasa, and Joan Reynolds Faunt. *South Carolina Secedes*. Columbia: University of South Carolina Press, 1960.

Mayer, Henry. *All on Fire: William Lloyd Garrison and the Abolition of Slavery*. New York: St. Martin's, 1998.

McCurry, Stephanie. *Masters of Small Worlds: Yeomen Households, Gender Relations, and the Political Culture of the Antebellum South Carolina Low Country*. New York: Oxford University Press, 1995.

McElya, Micki. *Clinging to Mammy: The Faithful Slave in Twentieth-Century America*. Cambridge: Harvard University Press, 2007.

McInnis, Maurie D. *The Politics of Taste in Antebellum Charleston*. Chapel Hill: University of North Carolina Press, 2005.

McIntyre, Rebecca Cawood. *Souvenirs of the Old South: Northern Tourism and Southern Mythology*. Gainesville: University of Florida Press, 2011.

Mills, Cynthia. "Gratitude and Gender Wars: Monuments to the Women of the Sixties." In *Monuments to the Lost Cause: Women, Art, and the Landscapes of Southern Memory*, ed. Cynthia Mills and Pamela H. Simpson, 183–200. Knoxville: University of Tennessee Press, 2003.

Moore, John Hammond. *Carnival of Blood: Dueling, Lynching, and Murder in South Carolina, 1880–1920*. Columbia: University of South Carolina Press, 2006.

———. *Columbia and Richland County: A South Carolina Community, 1740–1990*. Columbia: University of South Carolina Press, 1993.

———. "South Carolina's Reaction to the Photoplay, *The Birth of a Nation*." *Proceedings of the South Carolina Historical Association* (1963): 30–40.

Moore, Rayburn S. *Paul Hamilton Hayne*. New York: Twayne, 1972.

Muhlenfeld, Elisabeth. *Mary Boykin Chesnut: A Biography*. Baton Rouge: Louisiana State University Press, 1981.

Neff, John R. *Honoring the Civil War Dead: Commemoration and the Problem of Reconciliation*. Lawrence: University Press of Kansas, 2005.

Newman, Louise Michele. *White Women's Rights: The Racial Origins of Feminism in the United States*. New York: Oxford University Press, 1999.

Nora, Pierre. "Between Memory and History: *Les Lieux de Mémoire*." Trans. Marc Roudebush. *Representations* 26 (Spring 1989): 7–24.

Novick, Peter. *That Noble Dream: The "Objectivity Question" and the American Historical Profession*. Cambridge: Cambridge University Press, 1988.

Nudelman, Franny. *John Brown's Body: Slavery, Violence, and the Culture of War*. Chapel Hill: University of North Carolina Press, 2004.

O'Brien, Michael. *A Character of Hugh Légaré*. Knoxville: University of Tennessee Press, 1985.

———. *Conjectures of Order: Intellectual Life and the American South, 1810–1860.* 2 vols. Chapel Hill: University of North Carolina Press, 2004.

———. "The Flight Down the Middle Walk: Mary Chesnut and the Forms of Observance." In *Haunted Bodies: Gender and Southern Texts,* ed. Anne Goodwyn Jones and Susan V. Donaldson, 109–31. Charlottesville: University Press of Virginia, 1997.

———. "'The South Considers Her Most Peculiar': Charleston and Modern Southern Thought." *South Carolina Historical Magazine* 94 (April 1993): 119–33.

Olwell, Robert. *Masters, Slaves, and Subjects: The Culture of Power in the South Carolina Low Country, 1740–1790.* Ithaca: Cornell University Press, 1998.

Osterweis, Rollin G. *Romanticism and Nationalism in the Old South.* New Haven: Yale University Press, 1949.

Otis, Laura. *Organic Memory: History and the Body in the Late Nineteenth and Early Twentieth Centuries.* Lincoln: University of Nebraska Press, 1994.

Overton, Rachel Wynne. "Girls of the Sixties: The Wade Hampton Chapter, United Daughters of the Confederacy and the Founding of the South Carolina Confederate Relic Room and Museum." Master's thesis, University of South Carolina, 2003.

Parks, Edd Winfield. *Henry Timrod.* New York: Twayne, 1964.

Parrish, Thomas. *The Submarine: A History.* New York: Viking, 2004.

Pease, Jane H., and William H. Pease. "The Blood-Thirsty Tiger: Charleston and the Psychology of Fire." *South Carolina Historical Magazine* 79 (October 1978): 281–95.

———. *A Family of Women: The Carolina Petigrus in Peace and War.* Chapel Hill: University of North Carolina Press, 1999.

———. *Ladies, Women, and Wenches: Choice and Constraint in Antebellum Charleston and Boston.* Chapel Hill: University of North Carolina Press, 1990.

Pease, William H., and Jane H. Pease. *James Louis Petigru: Southern Conservative, Southern Dissenter.* Athens: University of Georgia Press, 1995.

Peterson, Merrill D. *Lincoln in American Memory.* New York: Oxford University Press, 1994.

Poole, W. Scott. "Lincoln in Hell: Class and Confederate Symbols in the American South." In *National Symbols, Fractured Identities: Contesting the National Narrative,* ed. Michael E. Geisler, 121–48. Middlebury College: University Press of New England, 2005.

———. *Never Surrender: Confederate Memory and Conservatism in the South Carolina Upcountry.* Athens: University of Georgia Press, 2004.

Poston, Jonathan H. *The Buildings of Charleston: A Guide to the City's Architecture.* Columbia: University of South Carolina Press, 1997.

Potter, David. *Lincoln and His Party in the Secession Crisis.* New Haven: Yale University Press, 1942.

Pressly, Thomas J. *Americans Interpret Their Civil War.* New York: Free Press, 1962.

Prince, K. Michael. *Rally 'Round the Flag, Boys!: South Carolina and the Confederate Flag.* Columbia: University of South Carolina Press, 2004.

Quinlan, Kiernan. *Strange Kin: Ireland and the American South*. Baton Rouge: Louisiana State University Press, 2005.

Radford, John P. "Race, Residence, and Ideology: Charleston, South Carolina in the Mid-Nineteenth Century." *Journal of Historical Geography* 2 (1976): 333–41.

Rammel, Hal. *Nowhere in America: The Big Rock Candy Mountain and Other Comic Utopias*. Urbana: University of Illinois Press, 1990.

Randall, James G. *Lincoln the President: Springfield to Gettysburg*. 2 vols. New York: Dodd, Mead, 1945.

Richardson, Heather Cox. *The Death of Reconstruction*. Cambridge: Harvard University Press, 2001.

Ringold, May Spencer. "John C. Calhoun: Post Mortem." *Emory University Quarterly* 11 (June 1955): 98–102.

Roberts, Blain, and Ethan J. Kytle. "Looking the Thing in the Face: Slavery, Race, and the Commemorative Landscape in Charleston, South Carolina, 1865–1920." *Journal of Southern History* 78 (August 2012): 639–84.

Rogers, George C., Jr. *Charleston in the Age of the Pinckneys*. Norman: University of Oklahoma Press, 1969.

Roland, Alex. *Underwater Warfare in the Age of Sail*. Bloomington: Indiana University Press, 1978.

Romano, Renee C., and Leigh Raiford, eds. *The Civil Rights Movement in American Memory*. Athens: University of Georgia Press, 2006.

Rosenburg, R. B. *Living Monuments: Confederate Soldiers' Homes in the New South*. Chapel Hill: University of North Carolina Press, 1993.

Rosenheim, Jeff L. *Photography and the American Civil War*. New York: Metropolitan Museum of Art, 2013.

Royster, Charles. *The Destructive War: William Tecumseh Sherman, Stonewall Jackson, and the Americans*. New York: Knopf, 1991.

Rubin, Louis D., Jr. *The Edge of the Swamp: A Study of the Literature and Society of the Old South*. Baton Rouge: Louisiana State University Press, 1989.

———. *A Gallery of Southerners*. Baton Rouge: Louisiana State University Press, 1982.

Rugh, Susan Sessions. *Are We There Yet?: The Golden Age of American Family Vacations*. Lawrence: University Press of Kansas, 2008.

Rusk, Ralph L. *The Life of Ralph Waldo Emerson*. New York: Columbia University Press, 1957.

Russett, Cynthia Eagle. *Sexual Science: The Victorian Construction of Womanhood*. Cambridge: Harvard University Press, 1989.

Ryan, Mike. "The Guns of Forts Sumter and Moultrie." May 1997. www.nps.gov /fosu/historyculture/fosu_docs.htm. Accessed May 29, 2012.

Sachs, Aaron. *Arcadian America: The Death and Life of an Environmental Tradition*. New Haven: Yale University Press, 2013.

Sacks, Howard L., and Judith Rose Sacks. *Way Up North in Dixie: A Black Family's Claim to the Confederate Anthem*. Washington, D.C.: Smithsonian Institution Press, 1993.

Sandweiss, Martha A. *Passing Strange: A Gilded Age Tale of Love and Deception across the Color Line*. New York: Penguin, 2009.

Savage, Kirk. *Monument Wars: Washington, D.C., the National Mall, and the Transformation of the Memorial Landscape*. Berkeley: University of California Press, 2009.

——. *Standing Soldiers, Kneeling Slaves: Race, War, and Monument in Nineteenth-Century America*. Princeton: Princeton University Press, 1997.

Scarry, Elaine. *The Body in Pain: The Making and Unmaking of the World*. New York: Oxford University Press, 1985.

Schantz, Mark S. *Awaiting the Heavenly Country: The Civil War and America's Culture of Death*. Ithaca: Cornell University Press, 2008.

Schaper, William A. *Sectionalism and Representation in South Carolina*. New York: Da Capo, 1968.

Schmidt, Christopher W. "J. Waties Waring and the Making of Liberal Jurisprudence in Postwar America." In *From the Grassroots to the Supreme Court: Brown v. Board of Education and American Democracy*, ed. Peter F. Lau, 173–97. Durham: Duke University Press, 2004.

Seigler, Robert S. *A Guide to Confederate Monuments in South Carolina: "Passing the Silent Cup"*. Columbia: South Carolina Department of Archives and History, 1997.

——. *South Carolina's Military Organizations during the War between the States*. 4 vols. Charleston, S.C.: History Press, 2008.

Severens, Kenneth. *Charleston Antebellum Architecture and Civic Destiny*. Knoxville: University of Tennessee Press, 1988.

Shields, David S. "Henry Timrod." In *Encyclopedia of American Poetry: The Nineteenth Century*, 428–33. Chicago: Fitzroy Dearborn, 1998.

Shields, Sarah, Richard Guy Wilson, and Robert P. Winthrop. *Richmond's Monument Avenue*. Chapel Hill: University of North Carolina Press, 2001.

Silber, Nina. *The Romance of Reunion: Northerners and the South, 1865–1900*. Chapel Hill: University of North Carolina Press, 1993.

Simon, Bryant. *A Fabric of Defeat: The Politics of South Carolina Millhands, 1910–1948*. Chapel Hill: University of North Carolina Press, 1998.

Simpson, Lewis P. *Mind and the American Civil War: A Meditation on Lost Causes*. Baton Rouge: Louisiana State University Press, 1989.

Sinha, Manisha. *The Counterrevolution of Slavery: Politics and Ideology in Antebellum South Carolina*. Chapel Hill: University of North Carolina Press, 2000.

Smith, D. E. Huger. "Wilton's Statue of Pitt." *South Carolina Historical Magazine* 15 (January 1914): 18–38.

Smith, Elise L. "Belle Kinney and the Confederate Women's Monument." *Southern Quarterly* 32 (Summer 1994): 7–31.

Smith, Henry A. M. *Historical Writings*. 3 vols. Spartanburg, S.C.: Reprint, 1988.

Stampp, Kenneth M. "The Irrepressible Conflict." In *The Imperiled Union: Essays on the Background of the Civil War*, 191–245. New York: Oxford University Press, 1980.

Stark, John D. *Damned Upcountryman: William Watts Ball, a Study in American Conservatism*. Durham: Duke University Press, 1968.

Steele, Meili. *Hiding from History: Politics and Public Imagination*. Ithaca: Cornell University Press, 2005.

Stern, Julia A. *Mary Chesnut's Civil War Epic*. Chicago: University of Chicago Press, 2010.

Stowe, Steven M. "City, Country, and the Feminine Voice." In *Intellectual Life in Antebellum Charleston*, ed. Michael O'Brien and David Moltke-Hansen, 295–324. Knoxville: University of Tennessee Press, 1986.

Strange, Carl B., Jr. "Henry Timrod's Final Revisions to 'Ode on the Confederate Dead.'" *Caroliniana Columns* 23 (Spring 2008): 15–17.

Sutherland, Daniel E. "The Rise and Fall of Esther B. Cheesborough: The Battles of a Literary Lady." *South Carolina Historical Magazine* 84 (January 1983): 22–34.

Taylor, Lonn, Kathleen M. Kendrick, and Jeffrey L. Brodie. *The Star-Spangled Banner: The Making of an American Icon*. New York: Smithsonian, 2008.

Taylor, Rupert. "Henry Timrod's Ancestress, Hannah Caesar." *American Literature* 9 (January 1938): 419–30.

Thomas, Richard F. "The Streets of Rome: The Classical Dylan." *Oral Tradition* 22 (March 2007): 30–56.

Thurber, Cheryl. "'Dixie': The Cultural History of a Song and Place." Ph.D. diss., University of Mississippi, 1993.

Travers, Len. "The Paradox of 'Nationalist' Festivals: The Case of Palmetto Day in Antebellum Charleston." In *Riot and Revelry in Early America*, ed. William Pencak, Matthew Dennis, and Simon P. Newman, 273–95. University Park: Pennsylvania State University Press, 2002.

Trent, William P. *William Gilmore Simms*. Boston: Houghton Mifflin, 1892.

Underwood, Thomas A. *Allen Tate: Orphan of the South*. Princeton: Princeton University Press, 2000.

U.S. War Records Office. *Local Designations of Confederate Troops*. Ithaca: Cornell University Library, 2009.

Vandermeer Jeff, with S. J. Chambers. *The Steampunk Bible*. New York: Abrams Image, 2011.

Van Zelm, Antoinette G. "Virginia Women as Public Citizens: Emancipation Day Celebrations and Lost Cause Commemorations, 1863–1890." In *Negotiating the Boundaries of Southern Womanhood: Dealing with the Powers That Be*, ed. Janet L. Coryell, Thomas H. Appleton Jr., Anastatia Sims, and Sandra Gioia Treadway, 71–88. Columbia: University of Missouri Press, 2000.

Varon, Elizabeth R. *We Mean to Be Counted: White Women and Politics in Antebellum Virginia*. Chapel Hill: University of North Carolina Press, 1998.

Wachtell, Cynthia. *War No More: The Antiwar Impulse in American Literature, 1861–1914*. Baton Rouge: Louisiana State University Press, 2010.

Walther, Eric H. *The Fire-Eaters*. Baton Rouge: Louisiana State University Press, 1992.

Wates, Wylma. *A Flag Worthy of Your State and People*. 2nd ed. Columbia: South Carolina Department of Archives and History, 1990.

Watts, Rebecca Bridges. *Contemporary Southern Identity: Community through Controversy*. Jackson: University Press of Mississippi, 2008.

Webster, Gerald R., and Jonathan I. Leib. "Whose South Is It Anyway?: Race and the Confederate Battle Flag in South Carolina." *Political Geography* 20 (March 2001): 271–99.

Weeks, Jim. *Gettysburg: Memory, Market, and an American Shrine*. Princeton: Princeton University Press, 2003.

Weiss, Jessica. *To Have and to Hold: Marriage, the Baby Boom, and Social Change*. Chicago: University of Chicago Press, 2000.

Wilentz, Sean. *Bob Dylan in America*. New York: Doubleday, 2010.

Wilkinson, Caroline. *Forensic Facial Reconstruction*. Cambridge: Cambridge University Press, 2004.

Williams, Susan Millar, and Stephen G. Hoffius. *Upheaval in Charleston: Earthquake and Murder on the Eve of Jim Crow*. Athens: University of Georgia Press, 2011.

Williamson, Joel. *After Slavery: The Negro in South Carolina during Reconstruction, 1861–1877*. Chapel Hill: University of North Carolina Press, 1965.

Wilson, Charles Reagan. *Baptized in Blood: The Religion of the Lost Cause, 1865–1920*. Athens: University of Georgia Press, 1980.

Wilson, Edmund. *Patriotic Gore: Studies in the Literature of the American Civil War*. New York: Oxford University Press, 1962.

Wimsatt, Mary Ann. *The Major Fiction of William Gilmore Simms: Cultural Traditions and Literary Form*. Baton Rouge: Louisiana State University Press, 1989.

Wingate, Jennifer. "Doughboys, Art Worlds, and Identities: Sculpted Memories of World War I in the United States." Ph.D. diss., Stony Brook University, 2002.

Wise, Stephen R. *Lifeline of the Confederacy: Blockade Running during the Civil War*. Columbia: University of South Carolina Press, 1988.

Woliver, Laura R., Angela D. Ledford, and Chris J. Dolan. "The South Carolina Confederate Flag: The Politics of Race and Citizenship." *Politics and Policy* 29 (December 2001): 708–30.

Woodward, C. Vann. *Origins of the New South, 1877–1913*. Baton Rouge: Louisiana State University Press, 1951.

Wunder, Richard P. *Hiram Powers: Vermont Sculptor, 1805–1873*. 2 vols. Newark: University of Delaware Press, 1991.

Yablon, Nick. *Untimely Ruins: An Archaeology of American Urban Modernity, 1819–1919*. Chicago: University of Chicago Press, 2009.

Yarbrough, Tinsley E. *A Passion for Justice: J. Waties Waring and Civil Rights*. New York: Oxford University Press, 1987.

Young, Elizabeth. *Disarming the Nation: Women's Writing and the American Civil War*. Chicago: University of Chicago Press, 1999.

Yuhl, Stephanie E. *A Golden Haze of Memory: The Making of Historic Charleston*. Chapel Hill: University of North Carolina Press, 2005.

———. "Hidden in Plain Sight: Centering the Domestic Slave Trade in American Public History." *Journal of Southern History* 79 (August 2013): 593–624.

Zuczek, Richard. *State of Rebellion: Reconstruction in South Carolina*. Columbia: University of South Carolina Press, 1996.

Acknowledgments

THIS BOOK SEEKS to record debts that I could never fully satisfy, owed for many years to the two southerners who figure in the opening paragraphs. When I turned the key to unlock my assigned dormitory room on the day that I arrived at college, it was Ted Phillips who opened the door from the inside and welcomed me to a new phase of life. Three semesters later I enrolled in my first seminar with David Donald, who pointed the way to my professional career. I benefited from the intellectual guidance of my dear friend and the warm generosity of my distinguished teacher. I regret that I am too late to tender this token of my gratitude to both bibliophiles.

The book cannot begin to hint at the scale of my debts to a third southerner. Carol Harrison cheerfully engaged in discussion of virtually every factual tidbit and interpretation as I was writing. She read the entire manuscript twice and some parts of it more often, contributing her expert historical and authorial judgment. She visited the sites featured in the book and incorporated them into our marital *lieux de mémoire*. She also took several of the photographs. Beyond her direct participation in the making of this book, Carol is the center of the world in which everything I do takes place. I am delighted to present to her this souvenir of my love.

Many friends refreshed the memories underlying this book and complimented me by their interest in my work. Rowan Wilson was at the Charleston visit mentioned in the first paragraph and the Charleston party described in the last paragraphs, and he has been an essential participant in many other important events of my life. Charles Kimball has also shared in common interests and formative experiences since our days in Holworthy 23. I am thankful to Dick and Athena Kimball for their gracious tutelage.

Jim Duane joined the roommate group later but made up for it with his fast mind and good heart. Betsy Barrett, a friend for all seasons, gave a timely lift to a scared and lonely writer. Karen Albrecht, Ward Briggs, Glen and Mary Fossella, Jo Humphreys, Brad Moody, Caroline O'Brien, and Mike and Denise Reiss strengthened remembrance and hope.

Several families have nurtured this book. Helen and Lou Brown, Mary Beth Brown, BJ Brown Devlin, Chris Borgman, Gerard Brown, Margie Kuzminski, and Mary Smith helped me to enjoy nostalgia and also to try something new. Doug and Kay Harrison and Steve and Hannah Harrison inspired me with confidence. LaVonne N. Phillips, Mark Phillips, Al Phillips, and Sarah Phillips Marshall accepted Ted's friend as their friend. Janet Hopkins demonstrated transcendent love for her husband. Sally Parker Phillips and Alice M. Phillips made me a proud godfather and goduncle.

Most of my research for this book took place in the South Caroliniana Library at the University of South Carolina. Allen Stokes started the progress on the project by showing me the Mary Amarinthia Yates Snowden scrapbooks in the Yates Snowden papers shortly after I arrived in Columbia, and he continued to champion my work as it slowly advanced. Beth Bilderback, Robin Copp, Brian Cuthrell, Graham Duncan, Henry Fulmer, Fritz Hamer, Craig Keeney, Nick Meriwether, Harold Newfield, Lorrey Stewart, Ann Troyer, and Elizabeth West upheld the high standards of the institution. Their generosity typified the welcome of the community interested in South Carolina history, particularly Chuck Lesser and Alex Moore. Lacy Ford, Larry Glickman, Dean Kinzley, Tom Lekan, Tara Powell, Dave Snyder, Saskia Coenen-Snyder, and Rebecca Stern were especially supportive colleagues. Leon Jackson and Elizabeth Young kindly and thoughtfully read early drafts of my chapter on South Carolina fictions of Reconstruction.

My research received valuable aid from the National Endowment for the Humanities, the Center for Advanced Study in the Visual Arts at the National Gallery of Art, the American Antiquarian Society, the Gilder Lehrman Institute of American History, and the Virginia Historical Society. University of South Carolina programs to further faculty scholarship have also been vital.

I am pleased that this book bears the imprint of the University of North Carolina Press. Mark Simpson-Vos's support for the project was crucial. Civil War America series editor Caroline Janney spurred me to sharpen my arguments, and an anonymous reader provided insightful comments. Caitlin Bell-Butterfield, Lucas Church, Ellen Goldlust, and Ron Maner ably guided the manuscript through the copyediting process and into production. Lynne Parker prepared the maps of Columbia and Charleston. Bob Ellis provided administrative assistance as well as the encouragement of a friend interested in his native South.

Every student of the Civil War knows that Walt Whitman observed that "the real war will never get in the books." Fewer recall that he went on to argue that "its interior history will not only never be written" but "perhaps must not and should not be." So it is with the shipwreck of the family with which I came to South Carolina. I look forward with love and pride to the stories that Veronica Brown will create for her life. I stand in silence with Josie Brown as we look back on our beloved son, Lucian. I submitted this manuscript for publication two weeks before his death. I have learned much about memory that the book does not reflect.

Index

Darwinism, 8. *See also* Social Darwinism

David, 241–44, 254

Davis, Jefferson, 25, 78, 137, 226–27, 231, 240, 242

Dawson, Francis Warrington, 72, 79–80, 83

Deas, Alston, 165

De Fontaine, Felix G., 15

De Forest, John W., 128

Delany, Martin, 188

DeSaussure, Henry Alexander, 53

DeSaussure, John McPherson, 142

DeSaussure, Wilmot Gibbes, 47

Dickey, James, 11

Disney, 218, 252–53, 274

"Dixie" (song), 6, 211, 282–83

Dixiecrats, 206–7

Dixon, George, 238–39, 248–49, 253–55, 263–68, 270, 272–74

Dixon, Thomas, 128, 147, 149, 152

Domesticity, 2, 58, 93–95, 134–35, 152, 167

Donald, David, 9

Douglass, Frederick, 199

Downs, Eugene, 225

Du Bois, W. E. B., 27, 170

Dueling, 53–54, 143–44, 158, 177, 294 (n. 22)

Dukes of Hazzard (television series), 211

DuPont, Samuel F., 65–66, 174, 182–83, 185–86

DuPont Corporation, 255

Dylan, Bob, 32, 35, 278–83

Eakins, Thomas, 252

Education, 6, 58, 106, 109–10, 115, 180, 189, 196, 219–20. *See also specific institutions*

Eisenhower, Dwight D., 209, 252–53

Elliott, Stephen, 97

Elliott, William, 114

Elmore, Franklin, 40

Elmwood Cemetery, 95, 101–4, 106, 113, 205

Emancipation, 6, 32–33, 66, 188, 195. *See also* Reconstruction

Emancipation Proclamation, 195, 210

Emerson, Ralph Waldo, 17, 28, 35

Emmett, Dan, 282

Evans, John Gary, 160

Factory labor, 3, 6, 115–16, 119, 180, 245, 251, 258

Faesch, John, 21

Faesch, Rebecca, 290 (n. 19)

Faesch, Sarah Norman Caesar, 21–23, 25, 290 (n. 19), 291 (n. 26)

Fantasy, 7, 235, 239, 268–70, 274

Farragut, David Glasgow, 240

Fast, Howard, 195

Faulkner, William, 24, 35, 137, 164, 176

Fiction, 5, 127–30, 161–62, 284–85. *See also specific authors*

Fields, Mamie Garvin, 84, 88

Fish, Hamilton, 78

Flags: Confederate, 5, 34, 95, 102, 113, 125, 141, 185, 197; United States, 66, 78, 169, 172–73, 197–98, 210, 234; regimental, 99, 141; South Carolina, 234–35. *See also* Anderson, Robert; Confederate battle flag; Standard-bearers

Flemming, Robert, 275

Foote, Shelby, 254

Forensic reconstruction, 265

Fort Mill Confederate Park, 114–15

Fort Sumter: and outbreak of war, 2; tourism at, 3, 6–7, 167–77; Confederate defense of, 65–66, 97, 166, 228, 243, 285–86; in literature, 163–64, 177–79, 182–84; and National Park Service, 184–92, 197–200; and Civil War centennial, 193–98, 207, 209, 255; and *Hunley* museum, 274

Fort Sumter Memorial, 174

Fort Sumter National Monument. *See* National Park Service

Frank, Waldo, 166

Friends of the *Hunley*, 262–67

Frost, Susan Pringle, 180, 184

Fuller, Margaret, 41

Fulton, Robert, 238, 246, 251, 259–60

Gadsden, James, 56

Gaillard, Peter C., 70–71

Garrison, William Lloyd, 66, 181, 188

Gary, Martin Witherspoon, 94, 130, 143, 160–61

Gender, 7, 24; and Calhoun Monument, 55–56, 68; and Confederate Home, 73; and South Carolina Monument to

Charleston, 192; and Confederate battle flag, 207–8, 219–20, 224; and *Hunley*, 245, 247, 250, 253, 256

U.S. Civil War Centennial Commission (CWCC), 191–97, 207–10

University of South Carolina: through World War II, 5, 20, 110, 118, 180; after World War II, 9–11, 18, 196, 211, 225, 233; during Reconstruction, 72, 101, 132, 158. *See also* South Carolina College

Urban life, 3, 7, 112, 132, 164, 181, 258, 282, 284; and Calhoun Monument, 38, 47–49, 51, 54–62, 88; and industrialization, 112, 114, 116. *See also* Monuments; Rural cemetery movement

Valentine, Edward, 16
Vanderbilt, Cornelius, 251
Vedder, Charles, 70
Vega, Suzanne, 278
Verne, Jules, 245–46, 252, 268
Vesey, Denmark, 58–59, 89–90, 188
Veterans, Confederate, 7, 71, 96, 98–99, 101–6, 108, 112–14, 220; and Charleston Renaissance, 2, 172, 176; reunions of, 17, 93, 101, 104–5, 168, 222, 244–45; and Calhoun Monument dedication, 77–79. *See also* Soldiers' Home
Vietnam Veterans Memorial, 228–29
Vietnam War, 7, 19, 204, 226–31, 259
Villepigue, James Irwin, 142
Virtual reality, 7, 239, 273–75

Wagener, John A., 46
Walker, C. Irvine, 105, 112–14, 116–17, 125, 172
Walker, William Aiken, 250–51
Walker, William S., 293 (n. 42)
Wallace, George, 213–14
Waring, J. Waties, 195, 284
Waring, Malvina, 108–9
Warner, Susan, 135
Warren, Robert Penn, 164
Washington, George, 43, 52, 63, 135, 144–45
Washington, William D., 271

Washington Light Infantry Monument: Cowpens, 48; Charleston, 84
Wauchope, George Armstrong, 20–21, 28
Wayside Hospital, 100, 122
Webster, Daniel, 14, 49, 78, 86
Weinman, Adolph, 174
Wells, Edward L., 148, 150
Wells, June Murray, 219
Welsman, Amelia, 66
Welty, Eudora, 137
Weston, Francis, 117
Wheeler, Louisa, 293 (n. 43)
Whipple, Edwin, 13
White, Edward Brickell, 62
White, Samuel E., 114–15
Whitman, Walt, 32, 66, 251, 279
Whittier, John Greenleaf, 13, 14
Wigfall, Louis, 138
Wiley, Bell I., 195
Wilkins, David, 221
Williams, George Walton, 70
Williams, Madaline A., 192–93, 209
Wilson, Clyde, 225
Wilson, Edmund, 137, 139
Winkler, Edwin, 29
Winthrop, Robert, 78
Wister, Owen, 147, 158–59, 161–62, 169, 172, 177, 183
Witte, Beatrice, 75
Women, 7, 28, 90, 102, 124–26, 131, 217–21. *See also* Gender; *and specific institutions*
Woodward, C. Vann, 10, 137
World War I, 178–79, 186, 227, 232, 246, 250
World War II, 185, 206, 227, 250
Wright brothers, 260

Yates, Mary Amarinthia. *See* Snowden, Mary Amarinthia Yates
Yeadon, Mary, 52
Yeadon, Richard, 48, 52–53
Yellow Submarine (film), 253
Young, Henry E., 70, 75, 78
Young, Kevin, 32–34
Young Men's Christian Association, 94